PRINCE
BORGHESE'S
TRAIL

PRINCE
BORGHESE'S
TRAIL

10,000 MILES OVER TWO
CONTINENTS, FOUR DESERTS
AND THE ROOF OF THE WORLD
IN THE PEKING TO PARIS
MOTOR CHALLENGE

GENEVIEVE OBERT

WOMEN'S CUP WINNER

COUNCIL OAK BOOKS   SAN FRANCISCO/TULSA

THE QUOTATIONS AT THE BEGINNING OF EACH CHAPTER ARE
FROM *PEKING TO PARIS: PRINCE BORGHESE'S JOURNEY ACROSS TWO
CONTINENTS IN 1907* BY LUIGI BARZINI, TRANSLATION BY L. P. DE
CASTELVECCHIO, PUBLISHED BY THE LIBRARY PRESS, 1973.
ADDITIONAL INFORMATION WAS PROVIDED BY *THE MAD MOTORISTS:
THE GREAT PEKING-PARIS RACE OF '07* BY ALLEN ANDREWS,
PUBLISHED BY J. B. LIPPINCOTT COMPANY, 1965.

COUNCIL OAK BOOKS, LLC
1290 CHESTNUT STREET, SAN FRANCISCO, CA 94109
1350 E. 15TH STREET, TULSA, OK 74120

PRINCE BORGHESE'S TRAIL: *10,000 MILES OVER TWO CONTINENTS,
FOUR DESERTS AND THE ROOF OF THE WORLD IN THE PEKING
TO PARIS MOTOR CHALLENGE.*

LIBRARY OF CONGRESS CATALOGING–IN–PUBLICATION DATA

Obert, Genevieve, 1959–
  Prince Borghese's trail : 10,000 miles over two continents, four
deserts, and the roof of the world in the Peking to Paris Motor
Challenge / Genevieve Obert, -- 1st ed.
    p.   cm.
  ISBN 1-57178-085-8 (hard)
  1. Peking to Paris Motor Challenge (2nd : 1997) 2. Obert,
Genevieve, 1959– . 3. Automobile racing drivers--United States
Biography.   4. Women automobile racing drivers--United States
Biography   I. Title.
GV1029.2.O34 1999
796.72'092–dc21
(B)   99-34574
                                                       CIP

FIRST EDITION / FIRST PRINTING.
PRINTED IN
99 00 01 02 03 04 05   5 4 3 2 1

COVER ILLUSTRATION/BOOK DESIGN: SHANNON WILLIS

CONTENTS

START

The old tales of adventure, whose characters, from beginning to end, travelled over all the continents and sailed over all the seas, are now written no longer, because even children nowadays think them too unlike life; and yet one man still lives them through and through—the journalist.

—Peking to Paris: Prince Borghese's Journey Across Two Continents in 1907

SAN FRANCISCO
[SATURDAY, MARCH 22]

The Golden Gate Bridge glowed in the crisp spring sunshine and white sails dotted the blue bay beyond the large window in Linda Dodwell's posh living room. I had never met Linda before, and had only recently met the woman who was to be her co-driver on one of the greatest classic car rallies of all time.

I first spoke to the woman I'll call Karen the week before, at the annual potluck of the Arcane Auto Society, a loose-knit bunch of car devotees with a preference for odd automobiles. My husband Chris, our two children and I had been coming to these meetings for years. We had several arcane automobiles to choose from, but we usually drove either our baby-blue 1959 Fiat 500, or our 1955 Messerschmitt. Though the 'Schmitt, a three-wheeler that looks like an airplane cockpit without wings, attracts more attention, our little bubble-shaped Fiat is closer to our hearts, since we consider ourselves Fiat fanatics; we own and Chris runs a Fiat parts importing business and auto repair shop.

We pulled into the Arcane Auto Society's clubhouse and parked between two other micro-cars. On one side was a 600cc red-and-black Citroën 2CV, on the other a 300cc blue-and-white BMW Isetta, an egg-shaped car noted for its front-opening door. The Isetta belonged to Karen, who was talking to the 2CV owner about a new acquisition.

"I just bought a Zundapp Janus," she said.

"What's that?" the fellow said. "I've never heard of it."

She described it, and listening in, I remembered seeing one in a micro-car museum in Germany: it's a two-passenger four-wheeler, but the driver and passenger sit back-to-back. Its triangular shape makes it look like a miniature push-me-pull-you-mobile.

"I didn't think there were any of those in the States," I said, introducing myself. "I'm a freelance automotive journalist, and that car sounds like it would make a great story."

"Well, you're right, there aren't any in the States," Karen said. "Mine's still in England. But if you want to write a story, I've got a better one for you. Linda Dodwell and I are going to be driving from Beijing to Paris in the Second Peking to Paris Motor Challenge."

By some trick of synchronicity, I'd just read an article about the 1907 Peking to Paris race the week before. I'd been researching early auto races, sorting through reprints of old articles looking for women's names among the competitors. It was slow going, not because there weren't any women—in fact, there were many—but because I'd get so caught up in reading about those early races I'd lose track of time. In 1903, for example, Camille du Gast, reportedly the first woman racer, entered the Paris-Madrid. Halfway through, two drivers, three riding mechanics, and several spectators were killed in a series of accidents; Camille had been in eighth place until she stopped to assist a bleeding competitor. The 1907 Peking to Paris remarkably had no casualties, but it was the longest and toughest race of its day, and that reputation wasn't topped until the 1968 London to Syndey Marathon.

I couldn't pass up the chance to interview two women who would be participating in a re-creation of this great event. Karen and I set the interview date for the following Saturday.

After the potluck, I asked my librarian to dig a very old book out of storage: the tenth edition of Luigi Barzini's *Peking to Paris: Prince Borghese's Journey Across Two Continents in 1907*. When she produced the worn volume, I took it home and finished reading it in two days.

By the time I met up with Linda and Karen in San Francisco, I was hooked. Somehow, some way, I had to be a part of their adventure.

In 1907, the automobile had only been around for twenty-one years. Those years were filled with a kind of mania that's difficult to imagine today—no contemporary innovation comes close to replicating the effect the automobile had on the world. Our current enthusiasm over the Internet, for example, is profound, but it's sedentary, intellectual. Not until someone invents Star-Trek-style "transporters" will anything come close to creating the kind of excitement the early automobile engendered.

Though the actual date is still argued along nationalist lines, it's generally agreed that Karl Benz's "vehicle with gasengine drive" qualifies as the first automobile, patented on January 29, 1886. The oft-quoted phrase says "The Germans invented the car, the French developed it, and the English opposed it," and Americans fell head-over-heels in love with it. In 1900, eight thousand passenger automobiles had been registered in the United States; by 1905, the number of registrations had increased nearly tenfold, to 77,000—nobody knows how many more were unregistered. In 1904, American author Edith Wharton wrote, "The motor-car has restored the romance of travel. Freeing us from all the compulsions and contacts of the railway, the bondage to fixed hours and the beaten track, the approach to each town through the area of ugliness created by the railway itself, it has given us back the wonder, the adventure, and the novelty which enlivened the way of our posting grandparents." Thanks to Henry Ford's egalitarian ideal of a motor-car for everyman, the automobile literally transformed America's way of life. The "Tin Lizzy" Model T, for example, put over fifteen million Americans on four wheels between its introduction in 1908 and the end of its run in 1927. In Europe, on the other hand, cars remained playthings for the rich until well past the First World War.

All nationalities, including the tradition-bound Brits, started racing motor-cars as soon as they got hold of them. The first formal race, called a "reliability trial" since race winners were always the cars that held together longest, was organized by a French magazine in 1894, and ran 127 kilometers (79 miles) from Paris to Rouen. The Tour de France began in 1899, and was won that year by a car averaging 35 mph over 1,350 miles. Hill-climbs pitted the early machines against gravity, and grim "dust trials" required a jury to stand by the road as cars roared by, then judge which car made them the dirtiest. Circular tracks sprung up all over, and city-to-city contests began between London-Brighton, Paris-Madrid, Paris-Berlin; then came the most audacious trek, the 1907 Peking-Paris.

In the article that appeared in *Le Matin* in January of 1907, the editors wrote:

> *The whole* raison d'être *of cars is that they make possible the most ambitious and unpremeditated trips to far horizons. For this reason the general public fails to see the logic of making motor-cars chase their tails in tight circles. We believe that the motor industry, the finest industry in France, has the right to claim a wider field in which to demonstrate its potential. Progress does not emerge from backing mediocrity or routine. What needs to be proved today is that as long as a man has a car, he can do anything and go anywhere....We ask this question of car manufacturers in France and abroad: Is there anyone who will undertake to travel this summer from Paris to Peking by automobile? Whoever he is, this tough and daring man, whose gallant car will have a dozen nations watching its progress, he will certainly deserve to have his name spoken as a byword in the four quarters of the earth.*

Some thirty entrants clamored to be that "tough and daring man." The start was set for mid-May, and based on the editors' estimated travel time of eighty-five days, the contestants would drive into Peking in the middle of August—monsoon season. So the direction was reversed, and Paris-Peking became Peking-Paris. The route was projected to traverse China's forbidding Western Mountains (between Peking and Mongolia), the Gobi Desert, and Siberia by way of a cart-track that had largely been abandoned, thanks to the recently completed Trans-Siberian

Railway. By the end of March, when reports had come in from St. Petersburg and various outposts in China about the deplorable state of the roads, all but five entrants withdrew.

Among the five crews was a French con man named Charles Godard. Godard considered himself a professional driver, which in those days meant he drove motorcycles up a "Wall of Death" at circuses and traveling shows. He preferred to drive automobiles, but he hadn't yet found anyone who would loan him a car. The Peking to Paris, he decided, offered the perfect opportunity to prove himself to the world. He convinced a French manufacturer to list him as its driver, but that company soon pulled out of the event. Godard would not be thwarted so easily. He set to work on Josef Spijker, the Dutch manufacturer of Spyker Motor Cars. Godard convinced young Spijker that the cost of the 15HP model, and all the ancillary expenses, would be paid in full out of the proceeds of the ten-thousand-franc prize money Godard would collect when he won the race. Spijker agreed, and Godard then conned the merchant marine into shipping the car carriage-forward (cash-on-delivery). He ordered as many spare parts as the car could carry, then sold them all just before loading it onto the boat—he needed the proceeds to purchase his first-class ticket. His co-driver, *Le Matin*'s special correspondent Jean du Taillis, protested: "You can't set out on a journey like this without a *sou*. You can't do it!"

"Why not?" Godard answered. "Either I shall never see Paris again, or I shall come back to it in my Spyker, hot from Peking."

Joining Godard and du Taillis and their 15HP Spyker were nine other men in four other cars. Two teams of aristocratic French auto dealers would drive matching 10HP De Dion Boutons. A young Frenchman named Auguste Pons entered a 6HP Contal, a tiny one-cylinder "tri-car." The last and biggest car, a 40HP Itala, would be crewed by three Italians. The pilot was Scipione Luigi Marcantonio Francesco Rodolfo, Prince Borghese, Prince Sulmona, Prince Bassano, Prince Aldobrandini, the holder of four ancillary Italian dukedoms and four marquisates, a duke in the peerage of France, a grandee of Spain of the first class, a noble Roman and conscript, a patrician of Naples, Genoa, and Venice, and the grandson of the brother of Prince Camillo Borghese, who became Pope Paul V. Restrained, formal and clean-shaven in an era of luxurious moustaches, this man went by the less cumbersome name of Prince Scipio Borghese. His family had lost the bulk of their considerable fortune in the market crash of 1889, when Scipio was eighteen, so he enlisted in the army, which offered a "gentlemanly" income. There he developed a love of planning and organizing, and became somewhat of a socialist, unusual for a man with so many titles.

After he completed artillery school, Borghese's parents shipped him to France for diplomatic training, and also to find a wealthy and titled wife. He succeeded on both counts, but foreswore the foreign service in favor of breaking horses, climbing mountains, and planning long expeditions. In 1900, he traveled to Syria, Mesopotamia, Turkestan and Persia by horse, camel and foot, then followed the great rivers of Siberia—with occasional jaunts on the Trans-Siberian Railway—

all the way to the Pacific. He wrote about this excursion, but his book wasn't like the popular travelogues of the day: it was a technical explorer's handbook. He considered himself a man of science, and he had a knack for reading a map in a single glance. He responded to *Le Matin*'s challenge as soon as he heard of it, ordered the Itala made to his specifications in February, and spent his thirty-sixth birthday examining detailed military maps of every inch of the presumed route. His brother, conveniently, was Italy's *chargé d'affaires* in Peking, and his wife had highly-placed relatives in Russia. While he knew *Le Matin* would arrange for basic supplies along the route, Borghese nevertheless contacted his wide network of relatives and friends to make sure additional stocks of petrol, food, and spares would meet him at frequent intervals.

Beside Borghese would be his riding mechanic Ettore Guizzardi, and behind him, perched on an extra fuel tank, would be Luigi Barzini, a journalist who had made his reputation as a foreign correspondent for Italy's *Corriere della Serra* and London's *Daily Telegraph* covering the 1904–05 Russo-Japanese War, and San Francisco's 1906 earthquake. When Barzini first met the mechanic, Guizzardi "was flat on his back under the Itala, lying quite still, with his arms folded. My first thought was that he was busy working. But he was relaxing. I discovered later that he was in his favourite place of off-duty pleasure. When there is nothing else to do he simply lies on his back under his motor-car and observes it, contemplates it item by item, every bolt and screw, in mystic communion with his machine."

Cars in those days were defined by their horsepower and their weight, using French terms, since the French (Peugeot and Panhard-Levassor) had been the first to build commercial motorcars: *voitures* were heavy cars, *voiturettes* were lighter cars, and *mototris* or motor-cyclettes were three-wheeled "tri-cars" or "cycle-cars." Steam and electric models abounded, but the gasoline-powered internal combustion engine was already proving its superiority. The most popular cars at the time were the mid-sized *voiturettes*, generally between eight and twenty horsepower and 3000 to 5000 cc's (though engine sizes sound similar today—for example, a Chevy Corvette displaces 5700 cc's or 5.7 liters—horsepower-per-cubic-inch has skyrocketed: that Chevy puts out 345 horsepower). The tri-cars or cycle-cars (precursors of our modern micro-cars) were much lighter and therefore needed much less power. Pons, in fact, boasted to his competitors that if the Chinese roads were truly as bad as everyone claimed, "the first to get through, perhaps the only one to get through, will be the Contal. Whenever you are stranded you can pick it up in your arms like a toy."

The *voitures*, on the other hand, needed much more power to propel their heavy frames. Borghese's Itala weighed 2700 pounds unladen, and two tons fully loaded. It was powered by a 7433cc four-cylinder engine that was expected to reach a top speed of 40 mph, very fast for the day. None of the cars had any kind of windshield. Their tops were cloth that dissolved soon after exposure to sun, wind or rain, and the shock absorbers were the passengers. There was no starter or electrical system of any kind; the brass headlight buckets would normally have been filled with candles, but some of the Peking-Paris raiders obtained newfangled carbide headlamps with built-in generators. Starting the cars each morning required manual cranking.

Godard's car was the closest in power to Borghese's—and the Spyker was lighter by 1200 pounds loaded—but those twenty-five extra horses made an immediate difference. Borghese took the lead right out of Peking.

All along the route, which followed the recently-installed telegraph wires, Luigi Barzini sent off dispatches to his two newspapers. These were reprinted in *The New York Times,* and his translated book was as big a hit in America as it was in Europe. The copy my librarian found for me ninety years later included a foreword by Luigi Barzini's son explaining the book's longevity. It had become something of a bible for young Italian men, proof of Italy's natural gift for world travel as direct descendants of Marco Polo, and their prowess as racers, from Borghese to Nuvolari to Ferrari and on. For the rest of the world, Barzini's book found a place on the shelf near Jules Verne, Edmund Hillary's tales of Everest and other stories of exotic places conquered by extraordinary men with (or without) fantastic machines.

In England, as in Italy, the Peking-Paris had remarkable staying power. One Briton, Allen Andrews, wrote what many consider a more rounded account than Barzini's (which, by virtue of Borghese's huge lead—he drove into Paris a full three weeks ahead of the rest—had given scant attention to the other teams). *The Mad Motorists,* published in 1965, featured the entertaining Godard as its main protagonist.

Just as Barzini's book had captured my imagination, Andrews' book changed the life of one Philip Young, a British motoring-journalist who had driven a Morris Minor in the first rally to traverse India, from Bombay up into India's Himalayas. Young later co-founded the Classic Rally Association, which organizes classic car rallies like the Monte Carlo Challenge. The first Monte Carlo Rally in 1911 created the term: competing cars started from points all over Europe and "rallied" at the finish line in Monte Carlo, Monaco. The CRA's Monte Carlo Challenge duplicates the earlier event for "classics," i.e., cars over twenty-five years old, every winter.

After reading *The Mad Motorists,* Young vowed to make the Peking-Paris happen again. Many had tried, including Luigi Barzini, Jr., but the Chinese, or the Russians, or myriad organizational problems, always prevented it. But not this time. Not if Young could help it.

I turned away from the radiant Golden Gate Bridge to focus on my two interview subjects, Karen and her co-driver, Linda Dodwell. Linda wore a soft black sweater and black jeans over a compact, powerful frame; she had blond, blunt-cut hair and striking blue eyes. A quick glance around the living room made it obvious that Linda's passion is motorcycling. Two detailed models of BMW motorcycles held pride of place directly in front of a framed photograph of her grown daughter, and the marque's blue, white and black emblem was stenciled on the side of her coffee mug and patched onto her black backpack. Cycling magazines were piled atop the coffee table where most women of Linda's social strata would display *Town and Country* and *Vanity Fair*. Phosphorescent issues of *WIRED* suggested computer literacy, and large black-and-white pastels on the walls revealed a taste for modern art.

She was evidently and proudly single, and unashamed to state her age: fifty-two. I soon learned that she was an artist (the pastels were her own), that this would be her first rally, classic or otherwise, and that she had very little knowledge of automobiles beyond what several good men-friends had shared with her. She had traversed Australia twice—she winters every year in Melbourne—once on a solo motorcycle journey and the second time with her daughter in a Toyota Land Cruiser. She figured that her trips around the world on BMW motorcycles—through Russia, India, South Africa and, of course, Europe—had provided adequate training for an event like the Second Peking to Paris.

While I talked with Linda, Karen sat quietly on the couch, saying little and seeming oddly uninterested in the conversation. At the potluck, Karen had been bubbly and talkative; now, she appeared distracted and uncomfortable. Beyond giving short answers to my questions, Karen acted as if she really didn't want to talk about this Peking to Paris thing. She looked away often, flipping through Linda's magazines and avoiding eye contact.

I was stunned at both women's ignorance of classic car racing and rallying. I had assumed that anyone entering something like the Second Peking to Paris Motor Challenge would be an experienced rallier, or at minimum a rally fan; he or she would want to campaign a long-owned, beloved automobile; that any two co-drivers would be very, very good friends—the kind who had traveled extensively together and knew each other's idiosyncrasies—and that one or the other would be an excellent mechanic.

I was wrong on all counts. Linda and Karen had only met a few months before, brought together by mutual friends (two men) who had already signed up for the event. Karen did have a beloved marque, oddly enough the same as Linda's: BMW. But Karen's beloved Bavarians were Isettas. We joked about an Isetta making this long, difficult journey; though the Isetta's a four-wheeler, the rear wheels are placed only inches apart, so the car tracks like a tri-car. Auguste Pons had proved back in 1907 that the three-wheeled configuration put the vehicle at the mercy of every bump and pothole—even minor road-surface elevation changes stranded the Contal when the rear drive-wheel lost contact with the ground. Neither of them was seriously considering using one of Karen's Isettas for this journey.

Linda, remarkably, owned no car at all. She did have a car in mind, though. She had called the Classic Rally Association in England to ask if she could compete in a 1968 Toyota Land Cruiser. Philip Young told her that the four-wheel-drive Toyota "was not in keeping with the spirit of the event." He had recommended, instead, a Hillman Hunter. Neither woman had ever heard of it; I had heard of the

British marque Hillman, but never the model name Hunter. They searched the Internet and discovered that the sedan, though not much to look at, was popular in England and Australia, and had made a name for itself back in 1968 when it beat out Porsches to win the London–Sydney. According to Young, the car had two additional advantages: it would be teamed with an identical car piloted by a British lord, and parts and mechanical expertise would be readily available in Iran, where the car is still being built as a "Peykan."

The two women hadn't yet decided if the Hillman would be right for them. I found it incredible that, with only six months until the starting line, they had yet to choose a car.

Both women professed some mechanical abilities, Linda with motorcycles and Karen with micro-cars, and they were both well-traveled. But the real reason they had decided to sign up was the route: it passed through China, Tibet, Nepal, India, Pakistan, Iran, Turkey, Greece, Italy, Austria, Germany and finally France. The road through Tibet is the highest in the world; Mount Everest's base camp would host an overnight. Seven days in the Islamic Republic of Iran would require that any women involved cover themselves from head to toe. I asked Linda and Karen if they were worried about this country's politics, and neither seemed concerned. "Iran's one of those places I wouldn't be able to see any other way," Linda said. Her main worries focused on health—everything from bacteria-laden food to the possibility of altitude sickness.

By the end of the interview, I realized that I was doing most of the talking, telling the women the history I knew of the original event, describing the vintage races I'd covered in California and Europe. I even admitted to the epic drive my now-husband and I took as teenage hippies—from central California to Alaska and back by way of western Canada, a four-month odyssey living in a 1959 Fiat Multipla. As I left, I promised to try and figure out a way to meet them en route, maybe in Kathmandu or Istanbul.

As I drove home in my ratty but reliable 1968 Fiat sedan—a car that, with some major suspension work, would be perfectly suited to the Peking to Paris Motor Challenge—I thought about the odd discomfort of the interview. Something about those two women bothered me, though I couldn't quite put my finger on what. It just didn't make sense: two women who hardly knew each other, spending ten thousand miles and forty-three days cooped up together in a thirty-year-old box they'd never seen before. Chris and I, for instance, would make a much more logical team. We're both certified car nuts; he's an excellent mechanic and driver, I'm a good navigator and decent driver, and we actually argue less on the road than we do at home. As I rounded the curves of the Santa Cruz Mountains highway, I kept thinking, if only we had forty thousand dollars for the fees and another twenty thousand to prep our Fiat. If only....

By the time I got home, I knew what it was that had been bothering me. "Those two women," I told Chris, "are going to kill each other long before they get to Beijing."

PRINCE BORGHESE'S TRAIL

Two days later, my e-mail box held two messages. "Please call me!" was the subject of the first, and "Sad news" headed the other, originating from an e-mail address I didn't recognize. "Call me" said simply "Can you give me a call sometime soon? It's about the rally . . . I can't find your card, Thx Karen."

"Sad news" was longer.

Dear Gennie, Jenny, Genny? (sp)

This is to inform you that after much consideration I have decided to move on with the Rally project without Karen. You don't need to know the particulars . . . just say I have decided to go with my intuition. It is not my style to renege on a commitment, but in this case I have reason to believe we were not a good match. She is very angry with me and is hoping I will change my mind. This will not happen. I have decided I will take my chances with losing out myself knowing I have made the right decision at this time.

I don't know how this affects you since I'm not clear how you are connected with Karen. I did get the impression that if you could figure out a way to participate you would be very interested. If you feel comfortable talking about that with me I will be glad to hear from you. If you decide not to get involved I will certainly understand.

All the best,

Linda

I printed this one out and showed it to Chris. "Do you think she's actually inviting me to go with her?" I asked him.

"You can't afford it."

"I know, but can't I dream a little?" I clicked *Reply* and wrote a response, half-heartedly suggesting some women I knew as possible replacements, mentioning how much I'd love to myself, if only. A phone call came the next day.

"I have a feeling about you," she said. "I think it might work out."

I parroted Chris. "I can't afford it."

"If that's your only problem," she said, "I think we can work something out."

I held the phone out and stared at the receiver. "Really?" I finally asked, squeaking like a pre-teen girl who's just been offered a pony. We talked and talked, brainstorming ideas on how to find sponsors. By the end of the conversation it seemed as if we were old friends. "Give me a couple of days to talk to my family," I told her. "I'll come up Thursday. We can talk in person."

I was shaking when I hung up. I walked barefoot over the jagged gravel in our long driveway—too excited to put on my sandals—to our garage barn, where Chris labored over the engine of a Fiat Spider he hoped to sell.

"You can't afford it." He didn't even look up from the head he was re-torquing.

"Maybe if I can get a sponsor . . ."

"It's a long time to be away. Who's supposed to take care of the kids?" His bushy eyebrows shot up and his head lifted just enough to see me.

I tried to stand still, but I felt like I was vibrating, shivering in the full sun. "I know. I don't know. You, maybe, with some help from Mom . . ."

"Your *mother?*" He stepped out of the barn, and began walking toward the house. I followed. "You want me to take care of the kids and deal with your mother while you drive halfway around the world?"

"It's a long shot that I'll even get sponsorship. But I'd like to try." He kept walking. "Look at it this way," I pleaded. "What would you say if a guy asked you?" He stopped, looked down at the ground, then at his grease-blackened fingernails, then at the sky. He heaved a big sigh: air rushed out of him, as if he'd flicked the switch on his air compressor.

"You're right," he said, and walked silently into the house.

I spent the next few days poring over the brochures Linda had given me. I lingered long over the day-to-day route descriptions. For September 7 it read, "Zhang Jiakou to West Baotou, 507 kms. A longer day, into Inner Mongolia, along the southern edge of the Daqing mountain range, towards the great Yellow River. Northern China is fairly industrious, we do our best to choose the quietest roads." Six days later would be "Golmud to Tuotuoheyan, 439 kms. Golmud marks the start of the 'Roof of the World' section. Although mainly tarmac, the road across the plateau is constantly being repaired because of the severe weather conditions and diversions and delays are to be expected. Ground clearance is important on this section. First there is the long steep climb up to the Kunlun Pass (16,000 ft). The scenery is awe-inspiring with expanses of snow and moorland pierced by numerous peaks. Tuotuoheyan is an army garrison on the Tuotuo River, one of the major tributaries of the Yangtze."

The more I read, the more convinced I became that there are two kinds of people: those who read something like this and think "Oh my God! How arduous! I'd never want to deal with all that"; and those who, like me, like Linda, simply say, "Sign me up."

CHAPTER

2

The usual inconveniences of automobilism are due rather to carelessness or want of skill in chauffeurs than to any congenital weakness of the car itself.

SAN FRANCISCO TO ITALY
[MARCH AND APRIL]

I arrived in San Francisco on March 27 with my notebook and my mother, Ann. The notebook was full of ideas for sponsors, and an IOU plan in case no one bit. Ann was there as head cheerleader and future web-mistress, and to see if she might hitch a ride. She had offered to mortgage her just-paid-for home to cover her third of the fees. Ann is even more passionate about travel than I, and after many trips together we'd grown to be each other's best travel companions. Ann being only six years older than Linda, I thought the two would get along fine.

Linda was taken aback when two of us showed up at her door, but warmed to Ann as quickly as she had to me. We sat around her sun-filled living room very much at ease with each other; the anxiety that had permeated our earlier interview had disappeared with Karen. The only irritant was my own fixation on the money issue. "I can't get past all these zeros," I told Linda. "I've been firmly lower-middle-class for too long." Linda laughed, and confessed that she'd already paid the bulk of the fees. Her twenty-three-year marriage had been to the president of one of the nation's leading corporations, and their amicable divorce had left Linda more than comfortable. Since the divorce, her own intelligent investments had continued to pay off. Money was the least of her concerns.

Still, I assured her I would do what I could to raise my share of the fees before the start, and if those funds were insufficient, whatever I earned after the fact—from my writing—would be hers. She accepted, and we moved on to the issue of the car.

Since our last meeting, Linda had put her money down on the Hillman Hunter. It sounded like a complex purchase arrangement: though Philip Young had

11

recommended the car to her, she actually purchased it from a man named Tom Coulthard, and the mechanic in charge of its preparation was a fellow named Paul Jackson who ran an auto shop in Oxfordshire, England. Philip assured Linda that Paul had an excellent track record with rally cars, and stressed again that Linda's Hillman would be prepared exactly like the one Paul was prepping for the British lord.

Linda called Philip back to ask him about a crew of three.

"Philip's a strange one," she said, shaking her head after the call. "He doesn't want to talk about the car; all he can talk about is the competition, and how we've got to stay competitive. He really wants us to win. He says a third person would be too much weight, and besides, there's no back seat."

"No back seat?" I said. "I thought it was a four-door!"

"It is, but the back seat's been taken out to make room for the spare tires."

I tried to picture it and couldn't. Fear and frustration hit me with physical force. It wasn't disappointment that Ann couldn't come; I'd expected her to realize that a new mortgage wasn't a sound idea. It was the mystery of this Hillman. I'd heard of a Hillman Minx, and a Hillman Imp, but I'd never seen any of them. I'd been writing about cars for four years and had lived with a car nut for more than half my life. There weren't many cars I couldn't picture.

Didn't Linda realize how much extra risk we invited by driving a car neither one of us had ever heard of before, much less driven? It was bad enough that we weren't allowed any support crew—no mechanics, no husbands or mothers or hand-holders of any stripe.

And the competition? Linda had never rallied before. "It can't be that difficult," she said dismissively. "You read maps and keep track of the time, right?"

"It's a little more complicated than that," I told her. Unlike speed races, the goal in a rally is to beat the clock. The route is mapped into sections or stages, and timed to the hundredth of a second in advance by the organizers' "recce" (reconnaissance) crew. Sometimes the required average speed is really fast; these are called "speed stages." The speed stages are separated by more generously timed "transport" stages or timed gravel, dirt, or other "off-road" stages. Since the route directions are often confusing, rallies test the navigators as well as the drivers. Professional rallies, like the famous Paris-Dakar, require big-dollar vehicles and large support crews; teams are often backed by the manufacturers hoping to prove their vehicles' reliability and endurance. Most classic car rallies allow slower average speeds, but depending on the terrain and the degree of competition the organizers desire, they can still be very challenging.

"I'll see if we can do some trial runs in one of the local rallies," I said.

Over the next few weeks we both got very busy. Linda prowled the Internet for information on Hillman Hunters and forwarded me the reams of entry paperwork that were already late. The original deadline to register with the Classic Rally Association had been three months before. They'd stretched as many of the deadlines for us as they could, but there was one absolute that we could not miss: Iranian visa applications had to be in London by April 6. There was no domestic source for these, as diplomatic relations between the US and the Islamic Republic remained non-existent, as they had been since the 1979 hostage crisis. Further complicating things, Linda took off for a two-week Baja dirt-bike ride on April first, and I had to leave for Europe on April fifteenth. Every year in the spring, I go to Europe with a photographer to cover a year's worth of automotive stories (races, collections, museums, etc.). The trip usually took at least a month, and this one had been arranged long before I'd even heard of the Second Peking to Paris.

Linda's trip to Baja was with a couple of old biking buddies, including Burt Richmond. Burt and Linda had motorcycled through northern India in February, on a trip arranged by Burt's company, Lotus Tours. Burt's friend Rich Newman—another motorcyclist, but also a collector of classic Citroëns and Isettas—had been along on that trip. Burt and Rich had already signed up for the Peking to Paris, which they intended to conquer in a 1953 Citroën 2CV, the "people's car" of France, often called a *deux-chevaux* or two-horses (CV is the French abbreviation for horsepower, but 2CVs actually have between twelve and twenty-two horse-power). Somewhere on that earlier bike trip around Rajasthan, the two men told Linda all about the Peking to Paris and urged her to enter. Rich recommended Karen as a co-driver; he had met her in England, where both micro-car fans were attending a Christie's auction liquidating one of the world's largest micro-car collections (which was where Karen bought her Zundapp).

On her return from Baja, Linda called me up to say that Burt thought I'd make a better co-driver than Karen could have. He'd seen my article on Messerschmitts for *AutoWeek*'s Christmas issue ("Have a Merry Messer"), and for him, that was enough.

At the beginning of April, with less than a week before I had to leave on my European trip, I arranged for family members to follow up on the hundreds of things that needed to be done. Ann took charge of contacting my long list of potential sponsors; Chris began a long search for a spare Hillman Hunter, contacting everyone he knew in the classic car world in hopes of finding a wreck we could tear apart and put back together again as a quick-study course in Hillman mechanics.

My father, three-thousand miles away, wanted to play a role, too. He and I had a good but difficult relationship. He and Ann had split up when I was seven; he stayed in Maryland and Ann drove me and my three brothers back to her native California. Dad flew all four of us kids back east every summer and during the school year exerted his own brand of long-distance influence. His field was computers, and he'd been using e-mail professionally long before I even knew what it was. By the time I got on-line, it was only natural for e-mail to become the principal mode by which my father and I kept in touch.

His immediate reaction to the news that his daughter had signed up for a major classic car rally was to mine the Internet for every possible piece of information on the event. He'd always loved research, and here was a new topic for him to delve into. He sent me an aged copy of a book titled *Sports Car Rallies, Trials, Gymkhanas,* by D. Hebb and A. Peck, a thorough guide to the sport. Though the book had been published in 1960, the Peking to Paris was a "classic" rally, so the old rules would still apply. Despite its heavy sexism, the book turned out to be helpful reading, so I lent it to Linda as an easy way of answering her many questions. Next, Dad sent a copy of an Australian-made video of the 1991 London to Sydney Classic Marathon, an event closer in distance and organization to the Peking to Paris than any other. I slid the video into my VCR, popcorn ready, thinking, "Cool, a rally movie!" By the time it was over I was a nervous wreck. There were several deaths from accidents and heat exhaustion (there'd been record heat when the rally went through India). A Hillman Hunter just like the one we'd be driving was the star of the video, but it had an incredible number of mechanical problems, mostly electrical. I kept Chris up late that night, quizzing him about quick fixes for everything that I had just seen go wrong. I wrote up detailed notes in my trip notebook.

I sent the video to Linda with a note carefully revealing nothing of my distress: "Call me after you've watched this."

Before leaving for Europe, I faxed over to Tom Coulthard, the man from whom Linda was purchasing the Hillman, to ask if he could arrange for the car to meet me in Paris. I could then test-drive it the two-thousand kilometer length of the fifty-sixth Tour de France Auto, France's premiere classic car event, as my press car. It would be a fine way to "sort out" the Hillman and make sure it was up to the much longer journey. Tom refused, claiming there were "still some electrics to fettle."

When I relayed this comment to Chris, he laughed. "Of course," he said. "It's a British car. It's Lucas."

Lucas was the name of the British auto electrics manufacturer. "So?" I asked.

"You know why the British drink warm beer?"

"No."

"Their refrigerators are made by Lucas. How do you tell if a Lucas electrical system is bad?"

"How?"

"Smoke comes out of the wires. Lucas is the Prince of Darkness. Remember that video?"

London–Syndey . . . all those electrical problems. "Of course."

"You'll be lucky if you're not 'fettling' electrics all forty-three days," he said.

After I left for Europe, Tom Coulthard faxed back saying that even though the Hillman wouldn't be in Paris, he and Philip Young would, and they wanted to meet me. Using Chris's fax as our intermediary, we arranged to meet in the Trocadéro during the Tour de France's scrutineering (the organizers' inspection of the race cars to make sure they meet regulations). I was to recognize Philip and Tom by the large yellow Peking to Paris stickers they'd have on their briefcases. Chris faxed them back and told them to look for an unusually tall woman (I'm six-foot-three) in a long brown raincoat.

The Trocadéro metro stop released me into a hectic tourist-filled traffic circle before the grand marble Musée Nationale, directly across the Seine from the Eiffel Tower. Huge neon numbers mounted on the tower counted down the remaining days of the millennium. A few of the Tour de France Auto cars had gathered far below, in the plaza at the base of the many long stairs behind the Palais de Chaillot. I wasn't certain if Young would be up in the Trocadéro proper or down below with the cars. I prowled the touristy top for awhile, then gave up and headed down to the cars; after all, I had work to do.

My assignment was to cover the Tour for the Ferrari magazine *Forza,* so I immediately made my way to the group of bright red machines already surrounded by people. I recognized former World Champion Grand Prix driver Phil Hill, who would be my quarry as he piloted a rare Ferrari 250 GTO through the four-day race. Nearby, standing beside a gorgeous blue Alfa Romeo TZ1, was Stirling Moss. I'd met Stirling, England's equal to Phil Hill, the year before at the Mille Miglia, Italy's one-thousand-mile classic car race, but I didn't expect him to remember me. I had just decided to snap a candid shot of these two racing greats, when a large man in a grey overcoat stepped between us, ruining my photo. As I put my camera down he turned and stared in my direction, squinting and frowning, then walked over to me.

"You must be Genny."

He didn't smile and made no effort to disguise his up-and-down full-body examination. I returned the favor: he was tall, with thin brown hair, and he had the look of someone who'd been thin once, but now had to suck air to keep his middle in. He didn't have a briefcase and there were no yellow stickers, but I stuck out my hand.

"You must be Philip."

Over five-dollar cafés-au-lait back up on the Place du Trocadéro, where Tom Coulthard joined us, we discussed the Hillman, the race, and my efforts to find sponsorship. "Don't bloody count on it," Philip commented on the latter. I'd expected Coulthard to look like a car-guy: rough and athletic, or aging-athletic like Philip. Instead he looked like the stage actor I soon learned he was: his short-cropped hair showed dark roots under a blond dye-job (left over from his last role) over a round Anthony-Hopkins-like face. When he wasn't acting, he wrote books about Austin Healeys and sold cars. Philip had been trying to help him sell the Hillman that Linda eventually bought (he had offered it to at least one other rally participant). Tom had been unemployed so long, and he'd sunk so much money into the Hillman, he had nearly gone bankrupt. Philip hired him on to the rally staff to help him regain his solvency.

Both of them refused to give more than vague reassurances regarding the mechanical status of our Hillman, so I asked instead about the other half of our "Hillman Team," the driver of the identical Hunter.

"None other than the famous David Steel," Philip answered, assuming I would know the name.

"Who?" I asked.

"A Scottish MP and experienced rally driver." He paused for effect. "He's about to be made a lord."

I was glad; it's always good to have a lord in your corner. Would Lord Steel mind if we augmented the name "Hillman Team" with our own name, "California Gals"? I asked. Ann had designed a logo based on the California license plate that we wanted to put on the car. Philip hemmed and hawed and acted terribly put out, but finally gave his consent.

While Philip grimaced, drank his coffee, and ate the sandwich I'd ordered for him (if he spoke any French he apparently preferred not to use it), he kept repeating a few phrases, like "You can win this thing," and "If you persevere, you can win it," and "If you jog three miles a day you can win it." I wondered if these were stock lines he fed all the contestants. But then the conversation turned to the other all-female team, and I realized that, more than anything else, Philip wanted us to beat them.

These two British women would be driving an old Volvo. The Honorable Francesca Sternberg was the daughter of a lord who split her time between Kent, England, and Kansas, where she and her American husband raised thoroughbreds. Her co-driver, Jennifer Gillies, had made her name in "the British fashion industry" (whether that meant in design, retailing or modeling, I hadn't a clue). The two women had earned Philip's ire by stringing him along for many months—over a year, apparently—on the entrance fee. "We'll pay as soon as we get sponsorship," they'd said, but had only just gotten the money a few weeks ago. According to Philip, they got far more than they actually needed, so they could donate the excess to charity and claim to be driving for a good cause. Philip seemed to think the whole thing somehow distasteful; he clearly didn't like these two women.

"Are you going to the Chicago drivers' meeting?" he snapped.

"No, I have to be in Italy for the Mille Miglia."

He grunted in disapproval. "Well," he warned again, "don't expect to get anybody else's money."

His nasty comments only steeled my determination to hit up all the wealthy Americans I met—men who annually shipped cars to Europe to race in the Tour de France Auto and Italy's Mille Miglia. Unfortunately, it wasn't as easy as all that. Following the TdFA, I grew pretty friendly with a group of Ferrari-owning American competitors that included an auto dealer, a couple of lawyers and a dentist. One chatty afternoon I finally got up the nerve to broach the subject.

"Have any of you guys heard of the Peking to Paris Motor Challenge?" I started.

"Is that the one where they're driving ten thousand miles next year?" the dentist said.

"Yeah. This September."

"That's pure insanity!" one of the lawyers exclaimed. All the men nodded and smiled. "Why would anyone want to ruin a perfectly good classic car by flogging it halfway round the world? Talk about masochists! Plus I've heard it costs a fortune."

"Yeah, twenty-thousand pound sterling entry fee," I offered, eyes appropriately wide.

"Jeez. That's outrageous. You'd never catch me doin' something like that," the other lawyer said.

I decided not to say anything about my intended participation. *Maybe I'm not. Am I really? Did I say I would?*

A week later, in Italy at a pre-Mille-Miglia dinner arranged specially for American participants, I couldn't deny my masochistic ambitions. Martin Swig was there.

Swig is a big name in San Francisco and an even bigger name in the classic car world. I'd first met him in Italy at the 1996 Mille Miglia, and he'd muttered a pleasant hello and that was that. I would never have expected him to remember me. But the day after Linda and I first met, as she was leaving the city on her BMW for her regular Sunday ride, she stopped for gas at a station in the Marina. Filling up nearby was a beautiful red classic car, bedecked with emblems from some kind of rally. Three men stood talking by the car. Linda watched as one of the men left, and the other two climbed into their roadster and prepared to leave.

Linda had made her decision about Karen that morning, but she didn't have a replacement candidate. "It took all my courage to introduce myself," she later told me, "but I went ahead and walked over and when I told these two guys that I was driving the Peking to Paris, they practically fell out of their car!"

She told them she was looking for a woman co-driver, and asked if they knew anyone. They both admitted they were new to rallying themselves, but suggested she call Martin Swig. "Who?" Linda asked. "The man who just left," they answered. She got Swig's phone number and gave him a call.

Two days later, Martin Swig sat sipping mineral water in Linda's flat. "I met this woman named Genny Obert," Linda said. "Have you heard of her?"

Martin Swig laughed, a wicked grin lighting his face. "Genny would be perfect!" he exclaimed. Martin has a sly sense of humor, and when I first heard this I wondered if his response had been more joking than genuine, but Linda took the statement at face value. (In fact, Martin had read some of my articles and thought better of me than I would ever have imagined.) She e-mailed me the same day.

After Linda had told me this little story, I'd come to see Martin as a cosmic manifestation of the power of connections and coincidence. Now, two months later, in this fabulous Italian castle restaurant, Martin waved me over.

"Genny, I want you to meet Carl Schneider." I shook hands with a handsome silver-haired gentleman. "He's doing that Peking-Paris thing too!"

"What're you driving?" Carl asked. "Who're you going with?" His excitement and genuine pleasure at seeing a compatriot was instantly contagious. We traded details—he knew what a Hillman Hunter was, and I learned about his '54 Packard convertible—and he confided in a conspiratorial voice, "these people and their Ferraris and Maseratis, they just don't understand an event like ours. All they'd think about would be the price of repairing the dents they'd get along the way." Carl almost convinced me that it wasn't a purely insane, thoroughly masochistic undertaking, but rather a noble, once-in-a-lifetime adventure. I began to realize that indeed it was me, not one of my interview victims, who had promised to co-drive from Beijing to Paris.

But then, there in Italy on my fourth week away from home, I had a painful realization: it would take forty-three days just to drive, plus a week in Beijing before and several days in Paris after. All that time *away from my family*: my smart, beautiful, ballet-dancing five-year-old Molly, just getting ready to start kinder-garten; and my bright, dragon-drawing son Jesse, who at seven already towered over half the kids in the elementary school. Not to mention my husband, whose absence these last few days in frigid Italian hotel beds came to represent my pun-ishment for thinking that the traveling life could ever be anything other than heavy luggage, delayed airplanes, and abject loneliness.

Only discuss a plan long enough, and you will end by thinking it absurd; objections are the necessary food for discussions. Enthusiasm grows stronger by action, but weaker through words. Speech is too reasoning a thing; it foresees all obstacles and mishaps— it is pessimistic. If every hero were made to discuss for a moment the brave act he is about to perform, heroism would perish.

SANTA CRUZ—OXFORDSHIRE—SANTA CRUZ
[MAY TO AUGUST]

My father's e-mails hadn't slowed while I was gone. My e-mail box had almost filled to capacity. He had forwarded reprints from government advisories on every country on our route and dissected the Classic Rally Association's website. Here's a sample of just two of the e-mails that came in on one day, April 24, three weeks before I got back from Italy.

On February 24, 1997, the American Embassy in Islamabad, Pakistan issued the following warden message:

Pakistan is suffering from a marked increase in sectarian violence. Subsequent to the burning down of the Iranian Cultural Center in Lahore last month, and the massacre at the Iranian Cultural Center in Multan this past week, radical elements in Pakistan pointed the finger directly at the U.S. Government as the orchestrator in the abovementioned acts of violence.

U.S. DEPARTMENT OF STATE - Office of the Spokesman - NEPAL January 27, 1997

For the past year, Nepal has experienced a rural Maoist insurgency which has resulted in the deaths of at least 67 people. To date, attacks have not occurred in traditional tourist destinations, nor have American citizens specifically been targeted. Because of the potential for violence, the U.S. Embassy restricts the official travel of government employees to affected areas, and has evacuated U.S. Peace Corps volunteers from several districts.

He followed these two official warnings with his own two days later:

Genevieve -

I looked at the Peking to Paris "Draft Route and Schedule" and have the following observations:

1) I strongly oppose you (or female you're with) driving in Iran, and recommend you hire a male driver for that segment. It could also be worth your life if females drive in parts of Afghanistan and Pakistan, through which your route may take you: I can't tell from the detail available. I don't consider this any less sporting than hiring the ferry boat captain to take your car from Greece to Italy, as you are scheduled to do (for a day and a night in the Adriatic!). Cars don't go at sea. Females don't drive in sharia areas. Simple. . . . From an Islamic fundamentalist's point of view (much less an Iranian conned to think of the US as the "Great Satan"), you are idle rich from hostile foreign countries, doing something (racing old cars in strange places) completely unnecessary, wasteful, and culpably provocative, exploiting him and his country, and shaming him and his people before Allah;

2) There are many apparent discrepancies in leg lengths vs. map measurements, enough to go beyond mere typos;

3) I find several checkpoint/destination misspellings, as opposed to variant spellings, both raising some question about the thoroughness of the planning thus far. I hope somebody has actually driven the route described, within the last two months, and that rally officials will continue to do so right up to the race.

The letter continued with a detailed analysis of every stage of the route—he'd taken out his Atlas and calculated kilometers, coming up with different figures than the rally office. He was worried about the Taliban in nearby Afghanistan, and when he got to the Iran section he wrote:

I had many friends who lived and worked in Iran under the Shah, and one's eighteen-year-old son was abducted from a street corner in Teheran, raped many times, and dumped in an alley. Such brutality was common, and is just under the surface in many of these countries. Islam has provided a civilizing code of great merit, but it does imply that any deed is permissible to an infidel. When extremists, urban or rural, are inflamed by the sight of an infraction of sharia (such as women driving), and an infidel is the perpetrator (as you will obviously be) there is no religious restraint: the ancient savagery too often reemerges.

Four days later, he retracted his earlier advice:

DON'T PLAN TO HIRE A MALE DRIVER to get through Iran, as I advised in an earlier message. Although the Wahhabi sect in power in Saudi Arabia and the Shia sect in Iran differ religiously, and are political enemies as well, the details of the sharia, Islamic Law, that they enforce are likely to be very similar WITH RESPECT TO FOREIGNERS LIKE YOU. Here's an important USDOS excerpt on Saudi Arabia, with odd/important notes from me set off by >> <<:

Dress. Although Westerners have some leeway in dress and social contacts within *company residential compounds, both men and women should dress conservatively in public. Women's clothing should be loose fitting and concealing, with high necks, skirts worn well below the knee, and sleeves below the elbow. >>It is recommended that women not wear pants [e.g. jeans] <<.*

Social Behavior in Public. >>Females are prohibited from driving vehicles or riding bicycles on public roads, or in places where they might be observed.<< Males and females beyond childhood are not free to congregate together in most public places, and >>a man may be arrested for<< being seen with, walking with, traveling with, or >>driving a woman other than his wife or immediate relative<<. In Saudi Arabia, playing of music or dancing in public, mixed bathing, public showing of movies, and consumption of alcoholic beverages are forbidden. Saudi religious police, known as Mutawwa, have been empowered to enforce the conservative interpretation of Islamic codes of dress and behavior for women, and may rebuke or harass women who do not cover their heads or whose clothing is insufficiently concealing. In addition, in more conservative areas, there have been incidents of >>private Saudi citizens stoning, accosting, or pursuing foreigners, including U.S. citizens, for perceived dress code or other infractions<<. While most such incidents have resulted in little more than inconvenience or embarrassment for the individual targeted, there have been incidents where >>Westerners were physically harmed<<.

Note that this is a strong ally of America, among the most modernized in technology and education including English as a second language, that has over 30,000 Americans living there, and yet there is still this hostility and danger. It is sure to be much worse in Iran, where the Government encourages fanatical hatred of the Great Satan, and in parts of Pakistan, Afghanistan and even Muslim Western China.

This stuff was bad enough in small doses, but now, I was reading a month's worth at once. He'd also sent me two books—Tom Clancy's *Op Center: Acts of War* about Kurdish terrorists, and *The World's Most Dangerous Places.* I didn't read Clancy until I got back, but I did read *Dangerous Places,* and concluded that if you walk into a Pakistan-Afghan border town and ask where you can buy an Uzi, you're likely to have trouble with the locals. I was torn—it's better to be forewarned, but did I need to get an ulcer worrying about it? I already felt like I was getting an ulcer worrying about the car—our mysterious Hillman Hunter.

As soon as I'd cranked out the stories I'd promised my editors from the trip, I fired off a string of faxes asking Tom Coulthard for details about the car's preparation. All of them went unanswered. To torment myself I'd pull out a twenty-five-page memo sent to all the American participants by a Maine man named Ned Thompson. He and his co-driver would be in a 1928 Bentley 4¹/² liter (that's another way of saying 4500cc), a car like the powerful roadsters that had conquered Le Mans from 1927 through 1929. Ned's list was anal in its thoroughness, listing everything from analgesics and Band-Aids to hose clamps and shock absorbers. Even parts specific only to the Bentley appeared—I wondered how many of them might be needed on a Hillman, too, even if it was forty-two years newer. Chris's search for a Hillman had failed; it turned out they'd never been imported onto American soil. He even tried to find the next best thing, a Plymouth Cricket. Chrysler had purchased the struggling Rootes Group, the Hillman's manufacturer, and brought a modified Hunter under the name Cricket to the US. Apparently, the car was such a failure it convinced Chrysler to close up the Rootes Group altogether (which might explain why Chrysler never answered my requests for sponsorship). No Crickets had survived, at least not anywhere Chris could find. All we had to go by was a photo Linda had received in the mail from Tom. It showed the body of a blue car, jammed in among other cars as if in a storage or wrecking yard. Tom's note called it our "Chrysler blue" Hillman.

With no car to examine, and Ned's tome implying that unending mechanical failures were to be expected, I began to feel desperate. Maybe my father was right; maybe Linda and I really had *no clue* what we were getting into. People every-where reacted negatively: "How can you leave your children for so long?" "Aren't you afraid of the Iranians?" "Have you ever tried to breathe over ten thousand feet? You could die!"

Our main antidote was each other. We got together often now, on the phone or in San Francisco. Linda admitted her own fear after she'd watched the London-Sydney videotape. "If I'd seen that a year ago," she said, "I probably wouldn't have signed up. But I'm glad I didn't see it—all this negative stuff, all this discourage-ment, it's always from people who don't have the courage to do this kind of thing themselves. They spend all their energy trying to convince us not to do it, so they can feel better about their own cowardice."

Thanks to the Internet, my fears about the Hillman were alleviated somewhat. Through the Australian Hillman Club's webpage, we purchased two books on the car: the actual workshop manual, which would be invaluable if we had to under-go some serious mechanical work en route, and *Hillman Hunter and Minx: Roadtests, Articles and Adverts* compiled from the "leading UK motoring journals" by Trevor Alder. The articles from 1966 through 1975 covered everything from technical specifications to special reports on the car that won the London-Sydney Marathon. I read the article titled "Hillman's Marathon Hunter: How to Win a 10,000 mile Road Race," from the 2 January 1969 *Autocar,* and wondered if nearly as much work was going into our Hunter as had gone into the one that had driven down the length of Europe through India and all the way across Australia to win that 1968 race.

At least now I knew that a stock 1968 Hillman Hunter had a 1725cc engine and was rated for 72 hp at 5000 rpm, with torque of 96 lb-ft at 3000 rpm. Torque is the power to pull at low speeds; if horsepower is the "go," torque is the "get-up." These numbers were comforting; they're similar to the ratings on the 1974-78 Fiat Spider, a car I was very familiar with and very comfortable dri-ving. That car's torque rating is only 89 lb-ft at 2800 rpm, so the Hillman would pull better up a hill; the Fiat's horsepower was better (83 at 5800 rpm), but horsepower really only makes a difference at speed—if the required average speeds were reasonable, we shouldn't need a more powerful car. The rev-ranges (those revolutions-per-minute) were comforting, too: the Fiat's a bit higher revving, but it was nice to know I wouldn't have to get used to a much higher or much lower revving engine.

Other troublesome questions arose from this study of the Marathon Hillman, though. That car had had its compression ratio lowered to accommodate lower octane fuels, and the CRA's bulletins had warned that gas in China could be as low as seventy octane (lower octane fuel is common in Third World Countries because it is cheaper to produce). A stock Hillman's 9.2:1 ratio is high; the car would need high octane gas to run properly. Would our Hillman have its combustion chambers enlarged to accept this poor quality Chinese gas? The three-man team that won the London-Sydney had carried three spare wheels (not just tires; and I wondered about Philip's claim that three women were too heavy). Would we have as many? And how many spare tires would we have? Reading the rest—about special rear-axle and transmission gear ratios, pressed steel sumps and alloy stone guards—made my head hurt.

Linda had gone to the Chicago drivers' meeting while I was in Europe. It was the only gathering the CRA arranged for the nineteen American and three Canadian teams that had signed up. Most of the North Americans, including Linda, met Philip Young there for the first time. He announced that record monsoons in Nepal had swollen the country's rivers to the point where thirteen of the twenty-two rivers we would have to cross now had no bridges. He recommended everyone carry a one-hundred-foot tow rope and plenty of one-dollar-bills, to pay the locals to tow our cars across the water.

Linda also got to meet some of the other competitors. One older couple from Ohio surprised her. The husband, Charles "Chic" Kleptz seemed worried about his pristinely-restored 1919 Marmon. Linda asked me if I'd ever seen a Marmon and I said no—all I knew was that the cars were built somewhere in the American Midwest, and that one had sold at auction a few years ago for over two-hundred thousand dollars. I had no idea if Chic's car was worth that much; if it was, it would be a little crazy to flog it so many hard miles. And Chic's wife, Arlene, admitted to Linda that she'd never camped a day in her life. "You mean you've never peed in the woods?" Linda asked incredulously. We both feared Arlene would have a difficult adjustment period.

In mid-June we had one bit of bad news that turned out to be a blessing: Lord David Steel, the other Hillman driver, dropped out. At first we were petrified, knowing that now we would really be on our own. Who would carry the extra spares? Who would we ask to help us out with repairs? But the blessing was the fact that we got David Steel's almost completed Hillman. Instead of the "Chrysler blue" shell that still needed an immense amount of work, we would get Steel's almost-ready racing-red car. Red wasn't Linda's color—she had already planned a thoroughly blue and black team wardrobe. Me, I never wear red, but I like it on automobiles for its Italian racing heritage. I wondered how Tom and Linda and Philip would compensate Lord David for his car—maybe the lord had never paid up and Tom still owned it? I was out of the financial loop and happy to stay that way, so I took it as a good sign.

But Ned's list still worried me. If I couldn't get my hands on the real car, I at least wanted to be sure we had lots of tools and spares on board. So I distilled Ned's twenty-five-page list down to a three-page fax and sent it off to Tom at the Rally Office. Philip Young intercepted it, scribbled "Stop worrying. Everything's fine" across the top and faxed it right back.

I took this dismissal as "Don't worry, you silly female. We know what we're doing and your female brain couldn't possibly comprehend it." I'm of a generation less accustomed to this kind of belittling sex discrimination. I wasn't about to suffer it now, especially as I spent the better part of every day playing up the feminist angle to potential sponsors on the phone ("Only all female American team!"). Linda heard about Philip's scribble pronto.

Next thing I knew, Linda, Chris, and I were on a plane. My growing anxiety—and her own—had convinced Linda that it was time to see the Hillman, and since the car would be leaving for China in three weeks, we had to see it now. A series of mishaps delayed our plane by more than twenty-four hours—I had asked United for sponsorship; I figured this was their reply—so by the time we were airborne Chris and I had become fast friends with an Ulsterman and a Lebanese expatriate who challenged us to a drinking contest. Chris, smartly, abstained, but I was swept up into the multicultural camaraderie of it all and arrived in England, forty-eight hours after we'd first boarded the plane, severely hung over.

I recognized Tom Coulthard at Heathrow (though his hair was now brown), and he drove us the hour or so north into Oxfordshire. In the quaint village of Didcot, we alighted in Paul Jackson's Brightwell Garage, where the shiny red sedan with a black vinyl roof awaited. The car never won any design awards; it was a typical four-door 1960s box, with slightly tapered headlights that hinted at the wedge-shapes that would be standard in the 1970s. But it was beautiful to us, already decked out with huge white digits reading *51,* our entry number, on either side.

In my compromised state, I neglected to pull out my list (Ned's entire opus was in my bag somewhere), but Chris immediately bent down deep into the open engine compartment, reached his thick hands down between every critical nook and cranny, and examined the car's insides, outsides, and undersides more thoroughly than either Linda or I could have. He and Paul got into a detailed discussion of suspension preparation—I could see that every joint had been re-welded for strength—and it turned out that Paul was in dire need of a suspension bushing that could no longer be found in England. Chris offered to order one through the same Australian club we'd contacted for the workshop manual (we gave a copy of that to Paul as well) and ship it to England as soon as we received it at our shop.

Paul and Chris hit it off immediately, which I considered a more important factor than the appearance of all the mechanical bits. They seemed to be about the same age, Paul had a daughter a little older than our son, and they spoke exactly the same language: auto mechanics. Chris said "I'm entrusting my wife to your work here," and Paul said "Believe me, I know it."

Linda and I examined the brake pads, learned how to adjust the struts, and asked to see the spares. Paul pointed to a couple of hoses in a nearly empty shoe box.

"That's it?" I asked, incredulous. "It can't be," Linda added. We were assured that more were to come.

Then Paul pulled the car down off the rack and let Philip take it out into the drizzling June rain. Linda and I took pictures of each other and our Hillman in front of a set of classic thatched-roof cottages, and then it was time for our test-drives. Linda went first, but before long Philip Young, ex-rally driver and impresario extraordinaire, plunked his ample bulk beside me on what I, thickly, still thought of as the driver's side. Only then, with jet-lag augmenting my alcohol-enhanced exhaustion, did I realize what a big mistake it had been to drink on the plane. How could I possibly drive in this condition? How could I not, after all the fuss I made insisting to see the car? I settled into the form-fitting competition seat, and tried to slide it back to accommodate my long legs. It wouldn't budge. "Paul will make it right," Philip promised, so I buckled my four-point harness and started the car.

It sounded marvelous; the familiar raspy, revving song of serious sports cars everywhere. Okay, I thought, I can do this. Then I bashed my hand against the door, seeking the gear shifter. Take a deep breath; there it is, on the left. First gear, step on it. The narrow one-lane road curved immediately, a warning sign said *30*—kilometers, not miles; that's only 20 mph—and then we were out on a straightaway, gaining speed. "Is that redline for real?" I asked Philip, watching the tachometer. He grunted a *yes*. Six-thousand rpm, I thought. Then I realized I was blind—rain washed the windshield; somehow I found the wiper switch.

"After the roundabout you can really pick up speed," Philip said. Was he encouraging me? Did he approve? I got onto the roundabout okay, but getting off, headed toward the right. "Oops, wrong lane," I said, correcting my error. I heard Philip say "She'll go all the way to eighty." Eighty what, I thought, kilometers or miles? But I didn't say it. We were back in those tight village turns, so I was too busy concentrating.

Then it was Chris's turn. I like to think he wowed Philip—he broke the rear tires loose, letting the car skid around corners: a classic rally technique, but hazardous in the rain. Philip would appreciate that.

Later, over dinner at a Tandoori restaurant, Philip fairly harped on driving technique and competition. He seemed to pick on Linda's driving more than mine—could it be I actually did all right? He urged Linda to sign up for a professional rally driving course, there in England, on all kinds of wet, dusty, gravelly surfaces. She sounded interested as she called the Indian waiter back to the table.

"I said Martini. That means gin, with just a touch of vermouth. This is all vermouth."

This was the first of many of Linda's bar-tending lessons I was to witness.

Philip had graciously arranged for us to stay in Sarah and Bruce Balmers' Bed and Breakfast, the same Tudor manor house that he'd adopted as his home. The grounds were gorgeous and had recently been featured in the glossy British *Country Living* magazine. Giant topiary sculptures of Gog and Magog bracketed the front door, and the grounds featured a life-size chessboard, a tree house, and a beautiful rose garden. Inside, the small, low-ceilinged rooms were warm, comfortable and utterly British.

After dinner we sat in the reading room and I fingered Philip's beloved copy of *The Mad Motorists,* the book that started it all. Philip was elsewhere, and Linda and Chris and I relaxed and talked. We'd had many conversations over the last few months, but always about rally business. Now, we talked about ourselves.

Like many women of the early1960s, Linda married young into what looked to be a perfect marriage. The middle-class daughter of Princeton's Director of Security, she eloped with a charming Princeton undergraduate who was on his way to Yale Law School. After he graduated, he decided law was not for him, and instead found a job on Wall Street. The family moved to suburban Connecticut.

Linda had studied to be a nurse and worked in a cancer ward for a time, but put away her uniform when her daughter Maida was born in 1971. The new baby did little to persuade Linda's husband to take time off. As Linda joined all the women and children of Westport waiting for the train from New York, her husband poured more and more of himself into his career, soon joining the exclusive Young President's Organization, a group for millionaire chief executives too young for the stodgy old-boys clubs.

Linda began taking art classes in 1973, and when business called the family to San Francisco in 1978, she hoped the move would rekindle the marriage. Instead, her husband worked as hard as ever, and Linda distracted herself from her loneliness by attending the San Francisco Art Institute. She painted daily in a small studio in an old warehouse in one of San Francisco's blighted, semi-industrial neighborhoods—a big change from her normal, comfortable surroundings. When she graduated from SFAI in May 1983, she became the first woman in her family to earn a college degree.

That same year, Linda and her husband separated for a time. They held on as their daughter grew, but ended the marriage the month Maida entered college, in September 1989.

Motorcycling came suddenly, while Linda was still married. She took a class to learn the basics, then tested her knowledge almost immediately on a trip to Baja, California, with a girlfriend. Right after she and her husband separated, Linda left California for an organized motorcycle tour of Australia. Nine days into the ten-day tour, Linda realized she was attracted to the tour's operator, an Aussie named Geoff. He was interested as well, and romance blossomed. Linda transplanted herself to Australia for half-year stints, and even joined up in Geoff's tour company leading packs of motorcyclists around that fascinating continent. But then Geoff had a serious solo accident in March 1991.

"We were on the fifth day of an eleven-day tour," Linda began, "and we'd just left the outback and were heading for South Australia's Flinders Ranges. After lunch the quick-to-suit-up ones and I headed for the next coffee break, and Geoff followed some minutes later with the pokey ones. Just forty-k shy of the break, the second group stopped for photos. Geoff left them there, telling them we'd all wait for them at the cafe. Twenty kilometers into the trip he went down like a ton of bricks. Moments later a fellow in a ute [sports utility vehicle] noticed all this debris scattered across the road and stopped to investigate. He discovered Geoff and the bike in a ditch about twenty feet off the road. The clients came up to this scene and sent the guy in the ute to get me. By the time I got to the site there were a half dozen bystanders."

"What happened?" I asked. "Why did he go down?"

"One of the clients and I looked at the bike later—it was a twisted, gnarled-up piece of metal that barely resembled a motorcycle—and we checked out the roadway. Marks and scrapes stretched for nearly half a football field, but there wasn't a skid mark to be found. No evidence of any animals, or other vehicles, and there were no witnesses. One of the bystanders was an off-duty cop, and his best guess was a willywilly—a dust devil. They're common there and have been known to take down eighteen-wheelers. I even had BMW and an independent mechanic check the bike out later—there was no sign of any mechanical failure."

"Was he all right?"

"Well," she took a deep breath. "As I drove that frantic twenty-k ride, all along I was convinced that I'd find him sitting up laughing with embarrassment with nothing but a cut on his tongue—the guy in the ute had said there was blood coming out of his mouth so that's the mind game I played. Instead, what I found was a body, completely covered by a sheet, and these people standing there guarding it. I thought he was dead. I expected someone to come rushing up to me as I settled the bike, but instead, these people just stood in place—the ones with their backs to me turned their faces toward me, ever so slowly—it was surreal! Finally one of them asked me if I knew how to take his helmet off. At that moment I knew he was alive. They had figured out how to open the strap, but it was a BMW helmet with a flip open jawlike piece. I rushed to his side and showed them, but luckily they couldn't get it off—it's one of the worst things you can do to a motorcyclist after an accident."

Geoff's physical recovery was quick—he was back on a motorcycle in three months. During that time Linda ran his tour business.

"It took a year," she continued, "for both of us to realize that he'd lost his sense of smell and was having memory, cognitive, and logic problems." He battled serious depression, and Linda struggled to help him; sadly enough, she'd had some experience, as her sister had suffered a head injury in 1989. But after holding Geoff's hand through six years and four different Australian psychologists, Linda had had enough. His depressions were dragging her down; he was fixating on side-issues like his financial dependence on her; he was still in denial about his health. She asked him to move out in October 1996.

He moved to Adelaide, close enough for Linda to continue helping with his health care. But two months later, Linda's father died. She was devastated; she'd been very close to him. She came back to the States in January and spent most of the month in tears.

That had been six months ago, but as she spoke it was clear that she still ached for Geoff, for her father, even for her sister. There in that dark Oxfordshire drawing room, I realized that my co-driver was a woman in mourning.

Back home in Santa Cruz, with two months to go before the race, I had six months' worth of stories to write and send off before leaving for China. In freelance auto writing, most of the checks don't come until publication—long after the stuff's been written. I needed that money to come in while I was gone to help pay the bills and keep Chris happy. So I typed away, jogged every other day (with Philip Young's harping about three miles—I was lucky to make two—always in my head), pestered potential sponsors on the phone, and clicked through a steady stream of e-mails. These last were usually from my father, and his distress had grown to a fever pitch. I awoke and logged on the morning of July 12 to open this one:

> On 6/29, we had dinner with a Hill denizen: used to be a staffer to then-Speaker of the House O'Neill, on the House Intelligence and other committees, etc. He has traveled in many of the "World's Most Dangerous Places," some of them recently. He was very concerned when he learned of your PTP itinerary. He observed that over most of the PTP's Asian course "$50k" kidnappings are becoming routine. He said warlords, chieftains and simple crooks have taken to kidnapping the Western middleclass traveler for ransoms of $50k, which they have learned most can raise and smuggle quickly by mortgaging their houses, etc. Of course, since you're traveling with a (website advertised) Duke, MP, etc. you may travel in more expensive circles.
>
> His most important warning was on Iran. He observed that we were not only effectively at war with Iran (through our embargo, seizure of their assets in the US, etc.), but that we would be bombing Iran just before you got there. He said the Administration (it's his party in power) is planning to retaliate for the Dhahran/Khobar Towers (Saudi Arabia) truck bomb that killed 19 Air Force, injured many others, and made us flee with our tail between our legs into the Saudi desert. You may remember that Bush retaliated for the Berlin disco bombing of our soldiers by flying F111s into Libya seeking Khaddhafi. You may also remember that Clinton retaliated against an Iraqi attempt to assassinate Bush in Kuwait (after he lost the election), by a nightlaunching of 24 Tomahawk missiles against an empty Intelligence office building in Baghdad, bagging a janitor or two. According to our source, the White House debate is only whether we can get away with the cruise missile sneak attack again, or must, to save Middle East face, use major armed forces. The time he says is already chosen: the late August doldrums, when the trial of the captured Saudi

Hezbollah lookout reveals publicly the evidence of Iranian responsibility.

Whether he was improperly revealing classified information I don't know, but today's paper had the following:

> *As the pieces of the Dhahran puzzle come together, a debate is still raging in Washington about what punishment should be meted out to Iran. The Pentagon has drawn up a target list for punitive US air strikes. The list includes up to a dozen terrorist training camps in Iran [some perhaps on the desolate Salt Desert PTP route?], {"The Man Behind the Saudi Bombing," Jamie Dettmer, Washington Times oped pg. A15, 7/10/97.}*

In this report, "The White House is extremely reluctant to launch raids" now, but will if the evidence seems, politically, strong enough. Like my friend said, this is only July, wait till late August. This article, at least, is a calculated saberrattling leak, to threaten Iran. From your point of view, it hardly matters if we bomb them in July, August, September or ever: it only matters that they THINK we did, or will, while you're there.

Your increasingly desperate,
Dad

I immediately clicked on *Reply* and said something flippant like "Clinton won't do it, he's too much of a wimp." But the e-mail stayed with me.

I don't know why this one sent me over the edge. He'd already sent me e-mails describing in intimate detail the way the Afghans punished women who violated Muslim strictures (I told him I wasn't going through Afghanistan); other e-mails described typical torture methods, or the sickening details of travel-related illnesses. But this e-mail was too much. Five days later, I wrote him back.

I got the e-mail about the kidnappings and bombings on a very bad day, and I was very upset by a number of other things—thus my immediate response about Clinton being a wimp. I have since had time to mull over how upset your letter really did make me, and I've talked to Ann and Linda about it, and it's time to just tell you flat out that I no longer want to receive any more e-mails on the subject of Iran, Pakistan or anywhere on the PTP route, in fact, unless it's something POSITIVE and UPLIFTING.

I have enough stress in my life—more than you can possibly understand, even though intellectually you may think you know what it's like to have too much work, too little time, too many emotional and physical obligations, and a deadline of less than six-weeks to get it all well and done and ready to die (at least if I believe the stuff you send me). So no more, please. From now on, THINK POSITIVE—YOUR DAUGHTER WILL BE ONE OF THE FIRST WOMEN TO CROSS THE EURASIAN CONTINENT ON FOUR WHEELS AND WIN A TROPHY WHILE SHE'S AT IT! (Say that to yourself several times a day. Maybe it will make you feel better.)

All my love, Genny

It may not have worked for him, but I felt immensely better. I'd never admitted to anyone, not even to Linda, that I wanted to win a trophy. It felt good to put it in black and white. And the scary e-mails stopped coming.

Meanwhile, Linda was miffed at a fax that came through from Rich Newman near the end of August, just before we left for China. It was a story titled "To Paris, By Rolls: The rich drive differently from you and me," in *Gentleman's Quarterly,* written by a man named Ted Allen, who had attended the Chicago drivers' meeting. It began like this:

> *Once, in the days before ecotourism and the Big Red Boat, man was a real explorer. A conqueror. Impolite and murderous, to be sure, but possessed of an unshakable sense of quest. Whither has gone that man today, he of the thirst for the exotic, of the purse fattened by tycoonery and graft, of the stable of the sort of motorcars to which one refers, rightly, as 'motorcars'?*

Then, near the end:

> *Who are the men (and women) among men to brave such a voyage? The Right Honorable David Steel, member of Parliament, will ply the sands in a 1965 Rover. Linda Dodwell of San Francisco and Australia, who faintly resembles Hillary Clinton but who is very sexy (wears black jeans, drinks gin), will pilot her 1968 Hillman Hunter, a small sedan that looks like a fedora with wheels.*

The article was wrong about Steel on three counts: He was now a Lord, not an MP; he'd dropped from the event; and if he were still in, he wouldn't have been in a Rover. But that wasn't the reason Linda was upset. She was insulted by the fact that yet again, the woman is dismissed by her looks; whether or not "sexy" is considered complimentary, it has nothing to do with one's ability to rally across two continents. Secondly, it echoed the same tiresome attitude my father had expressed in his e-mails; that this was an adventure for the idle rich. True, this kind of thing is *easier* for the rich, but the *impulse* is universal. I was going, wasn't I?

It was all too clear that I wouldn't be joining the ranks of the idle rich anytime soon. Philip Young had been right about sponsorship. Michelin offered a set of rally tires, but wouldn't deliver to the UK (which seemed odd, from a French company). The man at Castrol was excited—our route exactly paralleled their primary market—but he could never get anybody interested at the British headquarters. Every other company I tried came back with a flat-out *no.* I was back where I started, with nothing more than my pen and an IOU. Fortunately, Linda didn't mind.

My joy and my sorrow over the last few weeks were my two kids. The joy any conscious parent knows, but usually forgets to appreciate. The sorrow lay in knowing I'd be leaving them for seven weeks. I alternated between feeling guilty in the traditional "mothers should stay at home" way and feeling feminist pride that I could do what men had done for centuries—sail off into the unknown, leaving the family behind. I took comfort in the fact that my kids really did have an incredible, loving father, and a fabulous grandmother who lived only ten minutes away. Even more extended family (paternal grandparents, five uncles and an aunt) offered to relieve Chris and Ann if the need arose. That knowledge didn't make getting on the plane any easier. Seven-year-old Jesse was stoic, but five-year-old Molly wouldn't let go. Chris had to pry her off of me. It was the hardest goodbye I've ever said.

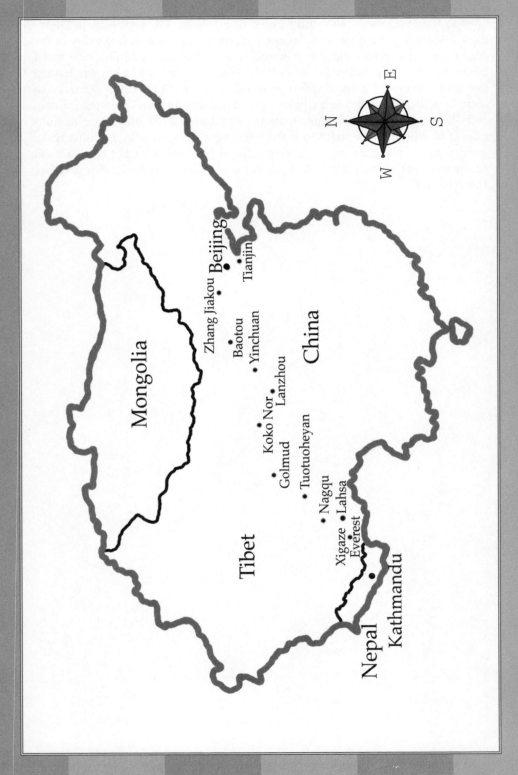

BEIJING
TO
KATHMANDU

~ 4 ~

These were capable men of some reputation as drivers, and picked by their respective
friends from among hundreds of other chauffeurs and mechanics who had eagerly sought
to join in the race.

BEIJING, CHINA
[SATURDAY AND SUNDAY, AUGUST 30 AND 31]

66 **W**hat was that?" I asked Ann. She'd decided to come to Beijing with me, to help with preparations and cheer me and Linda off at the start line. Now, on Air China, the heavily accented English offered by the attendants over the staticky P.A. system was impossible to decipher.

"I think she said ten hours," Ann guessed. Ten hours flight time? Shrug.

After twelve hours passed, we gave up guessing. After thirteen, we arrived in Shanghai, took all our bags and marched out to Customs down narrow white hallways. Then we all took a U-turn and came back to a room filled with hard white plastic seats, reminiscent of the futuristic George Lucas movie filmed in the unfinished BART tubes, *THX1138*. Dueling video monitors played the same perpetual loop: first a ping pong match, then a Chinese woman singing a slow torch song in English, with the words written out on the screen. "I have been to paradise but I've never been to me." All that was missing was a bouncing white ball. The next part of the loop was footage from the "555 Subaru China Rally." The rally had just finished in June—a real pro-rally around the mountain roads of southern China. Watching the cars skid through water, mud, and snow at top speed made my stomach hurt. Linda and I never had been able to do a trial-run rally. I'd gotten plenty of flyers from the local rally club, but the dates or places were always wrong. And Linda never took that British rally-driving course Philip had recommended. We were going into this almost as innocent as we'd started, six months before.

Some thirty-six hours later, when we finally landed in Beijing, the taxi men were ready for us. It was some time after three A.M. China time. I watched through the windshield intently. Though the city was still asleep, a little of everything was already on the wide, four-lane street: bicycles, walkers, bicycle-rickshaws, trucks.

Gray modern buildings rose out of the gloom, growing ever higher as we went downtown, until glass-fronted skyscrapers lined both sides of the four-lane street. We passed several recognizable hotel signs—Sheraton, Hilton—and buildings that might be embassies or conference halls with banners and flags and signs. Some of them, I realized, said "Welcome Beijing Paris Motor Challenge." The taxi driver swerved from side to side, choosing whichever of the four lanes tickled his fancy at any given moment.

That pre-dawn ride through China's swarming capital city gave me several important driving tips that would be useful on the rally: (1) No need to worry about which side of the road to drive on, just pick the clearest lane. (2) Always honk, loudly and repeatedly, at any object on the road, moving or immobile. (3) Lights are optional. (4) Speed limit? Nah.

As it turned out, that pretty much summed up our driving strategy for the rally's full forty-three days.

The Beijing Hotel had a huge empty lobby. The feeling it gave was not one of luxury but of interminable waiting, the anxious boredom of airports and train stations. Perhaps I judged it more harshly than most. This was my first-ever five-star hotel. In all my travels in Europe, I'd never ventured higher than three stars, and even those I tried to avoid, as on my budget, an extra fifty bucks just for a swankier lobby (too often the only difference) was too much to pay. I'd become expert at locating clean, pleasant one-stars that cost less than fifty dollars a night.

For the Peking to Paris Motor Challenge, I'd paid my own £2,500 accommodation fee. Since this included almost a week in Beijing and the last two nights in Paris, I figured it wasn't such a bad deal: only about fifty pounds a night, or eighty bucks, for first-class, five-star hotels. Plus it included some food (all breakfasts, all camping dinners, and a few other special meals).

I imagined that among the people competing, all of us converging on this cavernous hotel within the next few days, I was the only one bothering to compute the cost-effectiveness of my accommodation fee. For the rest of the competitors, £2,500 just wasn't worth worrying about.

Still, I noticed some touches that you'd never find in a one-star, like a separate concierge for every floor. This extra bit of courtesy or security or paranoia embarrassed me, as I felt obliged to explain to the fellow on my floor what I was doing riding up and down the elevator at three-thirty in the morning. I was looking for Linda's room, and when I found it, I slipped a note under her door so she'd know we'd arrived. Luckily, her concierge/guard was sound asleep, so I didn't have to explain myself to him. Only later did it occur to me that the fellow I'd jabbered at that morning probably didn't speak English.

I woke up sure it was September 2. At check-in I'd been handed a two-page memo from the Rally Organization. It stated that the first group would go pick up cars at 8:30 A.M. on that day. I knew we'd lost a day somewhere in the air, and I was petrified that I'd slept too late and Linda had already left to pick up the car without me.

Ann quickly set me straight. I was a jangle of nerves, but decided coffee would be the best antidote, so we headed down to breakfast. The hotel looked better in daylight. Once past an ugly expanse of plywood hiding construction work, we found a narrow passage that led to a series of boutiques, then to the old part of the hotel. Thick red carpets, plush red draperies, and ornate green gilded dragons crawled along all the wood trim that framed the restaurant and ballroom entrances. While we ate steam buns and drank good American-style coffee, I thought I heard someone say this Hotel Beijing was the same one that hosted the 1907 Peking-Paris raiders. I wondered.

Back then, China was still recovering from the Boxer Rebellion of 1900. Militia units called *yíhé quán* or "righteous harmony fists"—translated by the Western press as Boxers—rose up to rid their country of foreigners and foreign influences. This sentiment was widespread and in some ways justified. The First (1840-42) and Second (1858-60) Opium Wars—British and French efforts to prevent the Chinese from outlawing opium—had been humiliating defeats for the imperial government, and the foreign troops repeatedly ransacked Peking, leaving temples and parts of the emperor's Summer Palace in ruins.

The Chinese imperial government had been stagnating anyway, and by 1900, it was in an advanced state of decay. Dowager Empress Cixi supported the Boxers, but that, too, ended in defeat. Troops from England, France, Germany, Japan, and Russia ganged up on the Chinese, and when fighting ended in 1901, China was forced to pay a punitive indemnity, to allow foreigners to live and travel throughout the country, and to allow foreign troops to establish bases in Peking.

Troops and diplomats from these foreign legations greeted the 1907 Peking to Paris raiders with great fanfare. The Hôtel de Pékin, right across from the French Legation, hosted the French drivers, Borghese stayed within the Italian Legation, and Barzini stayed at the new Hôtel des Wagons-lits. The hotels and legations building were crowded into the Imperial City, where the high ranking Manchu bureaucrats lived and worked in relative luxury, just outside the Forbidden City's outer wall. The Imperial City was itself surrounded by a wall forty feet high, sixty-two feet thick at the base, and half that width at the top. This wall separated the bureaucrats from the Tartar and Chinese Cities, the ten square miles (also walled) holding most of Peking's residents. The Western legations were separately walled since the Boxer Rebellion. All those walled alleys must have been claustrophobically close.

Though we were only a few blocks from the Forbidden City's walls, I found out later it couldn't have been the same Hôtel Pékin; our Hotel Beijing dated back only to 1917. Today, Beijing ranges more than fifty square miles, and the wall that protected those bureaucrats has been demolished. Only two monumental arches, the northern Deshengmen gate and the southern Qianmen gate, survive. Instead of a vast expanse of Tartar and Chinese in crowded hovels, glass and concrete skyscrapers now march outward in all directions.

We had a free day since we couldn't fetch the cars, so the three of us took off on foot for Tiananmen Square and the Forbidden City. We walked along Chang An Dji, the grand boulevard that slices Beijing neatly in half east-to-west. Bicycle traffic was as thick and intense as I'd expected, and the wide street was arranged to accommodate it: the outer bicycle lanes were separated from the inner motor-vehicle lanes by barriers. The inner ones were crowded as well, with taxis, trucks and a few personal cars. Rickshaws and motor scooters seemed to go where they liked, barrier or no. The people atop these assorted vehicles looked as cosmopolitan as urban people anywhere do: very few Mao suits, most formally dressed in brightly colored Western clothing, even the ones pulling the rickshaws.

Tiananmen Square opened before us, the suddenly uncrowded airspace almost a shock after the long line of grand highrises. Its 123 acres of open space forms the largest public square in the world, and at the northern edge, where we stood, the Gate of Heavenly Peace that gave the square its name opens northward into the Forbidden City. Everything important in China opens on the south side, I learned. The north is *yang*: night, danger, evil, cold, and barbarians. To the south is the sun, warmth, safety, and *yin*. The sun and heaven are round, the earth is square, thus every building and open space must be defined by even edges.

It's pleasant to think of geometry and cosmic opposites, but Tiananmen Square immediately brought to mind two less pleasing things: modern fascism—the architecture of the grand government buildings and monuments (including Mao's tomb) reminded me of Mussolini's contributions to Italy—and the 1989 Democracy Movement massacre. Three million people had gathered here to hear Mao proclaim the People's Republic in 1949, and nearly one million gathered to protest the legacy of his governing forty years later. When army troops attacked those protesters in June 1989, many thousands were killed—exactly how many remains a mystery. It is impossible now to walk the edges of that neat square without thinking about them.

So we turned our backs to it and entered the Forbidden City, walking right under Mao's big nose. Behind the 125-foot-high gate upon which the Chairman's portrait hung, were fifty pavilions and palaces with names like Hall of Supreme Harmony and Palace of Heavenly Purity. Five marble bridges cross the Golden Water river, and dragons, dogs, and phoenixes stand at attention or lunge from high-up cornices. I gladly paid an extra five yuan for the "Memorial Card for Visiting Palace Museum of Beijing," a shiny yellow and red plastic card with a bright yellow ribbon so you can wear it around your neck. Indecipherable maps, one a line drawing, the other an aerial photograph, are supposed to help you find your way through the city-size park. Beside the maps were a few paragraphs of earnest English. "The Memorial Card presents the magnificent and resplendent complete picture of the Palace from macroscopic view, thus becoming a Precious Remember for visitors from all over the world." Tiny print at the bottom credits the text to "The Forbidden City Society Center for Remote Sensing." I wondered if that was a translation near miss, or if there were remote electronic sensing devices somehow embedded in my plastic Precious Remember.

Clearly, my father's paranoid e-mails had had some impact.

We were back at the hotel by cocktail hour, where tables in the bar had filled with casually-dressed Westerners speaking a cacophony of languages. British English rose audibly above the Dutch, German, and Italian. The British all seemed to know each other already—perhaps they'd met at their more numerous drivers' meetings, or more likely, they'd been drawn together by the breaking news of Princess Diana's sudden and tragic death.

It had happened on August 31, the day Ann and I lost when we crossed the international dateline. While the rest of the world was riveted to their televisions watching the tragedy unfold, we had been sitting comatose before that infinite loop of ping pong and pop music in Shanghai. I have never been a royal-watcher, so though I was saddened, I didn't think about it much. Actually, I didn't *want* to think about it: only later did I realize how this automobile accident, the death of a young mother of two children, had increased my family's worries.

Despite the tragedy, the air in the bar was charged with excitement and anticipation. Our fellow Americans began to appear; we ran into Linda's old biking buddies first, Burt Richmond and his co-driver Rich Newman, as they emerged from the bar. Both were short, fiftyish Chicagoans who spoke with broad vowels and shared an infectious sense of humor and a buzzing boyish excitement at the adventure of it all. Burt turned out to be the voluble one; he liked to talk or, more accurately, liked to hear himself talk. Rich was always ready with a one-liner, a pun, or a funny story, but sometimes couldn't get a word in edgewise when Burt was holding forth.

A college-aged American named Mark Fortune was there with an oil company executive named Bud Risser. They'd be driving Mark's parents' 1955 Chevy Bel Air. The Fortunes had prepared the car and even packed it for themselves, but then Mrs. Fortune found a lump in her breast; it proved to be a malignant, but operable, tumor. She bravely told her husband to go anyway, but he declined, calling his old friend Bud instead, and offering him the driver's seat. Bud, an experienced racer in the Sports Car Club of America, would pilot the Chevy all the way through; Mark could only stay the three weeks it would take to get to Kathmandu. For the Kathmandu-Istanbul leg, Bud's old college roommate would join him, then his wife Fran would take the passenger seat from Istanbul to the finish line. Bud had had little more than a month to arrange all his visas. The changing crew meant the Bel Air had to drive in the "Touring" category. Only ten of the ninety-four cars entered had opted for this non-competitive class, either because they couldn't keep the same crew the full forty-three days, or because they didn't want to bother with average speeds and time-distance calculations.

Linda first met a fellow Bay Area resident at the reception desk. Michael Veys had had even less time to prepare than Bud Risser. Though Michael was British, he had left his homeland fifteen years before and settled in Marin County, right across the bridge from his job at San Francisco's British Motor Cars. It was already mid-August when a Rolls Royce owned by a Bahamian millionaire arrived in the shop. Michael was handed a list of mechanical work to complete on the car. The owner's son had brought the Rolls up from Texas after his father summarily fired his Dallas mechanic, who was also supposed to be his Peking-Paris navigator. The son was impressed with Michael's work, and when the father called his son in search of a new co-driver, Michael was offered the job. He took it, even though it meant unemployment upon his return—seven weeks was too long for a leave-of-absence. Michael had to spend every minute of his week in Beijing chasing embassies for all the required visas. Despite his years in the States, Michael still had a thick British accent and a voice and face that reminded me of a young Michael York.

His new boss turned out to be Danish, not Bahamian. Eric Christiansen, a retired CEO of Louis Dreyfus, actually had domiciles in the Bahamas, Texas, Brussels, and Paris. The same *GQ* article that had annoyed Linda said of Eric:

He is a Hemingway look-alike (there is always at least one in these circles), a ruddy-faced Dane in khakis, an ascot and a 1965 Rolls Royce Silver Cloud. His partner is a certified Rolls Royce mechanic (that's stacking the deck a bit, but billionaires can do that). 'You have to separate the major and minor issues,' Christiansen proclaims. 'And one of the most important things I'm going to bring along is two cases of good white wine.'

When a table finally cleared, Linda, Ann and I settled down and ordered drinks. Our two gin-and-tonics arrived quickly, but it was quite awhile before a very young woman, dressed in the uniform of a tight black floor-length skirt and white blouse cinched by a red cummerbund, set a tall glass full of clear liquid before Linda.

She sipped. "This is straight vermouth," Linda told the girl, who looked embarrassed. "Let me tell you how to make a martini." Linda spoke slowly and clearly, and the girl listened intently, but then instead of returning with a drink, she came back to the table with three other young women and her boss, a man not much older than she, dressed in a black-tie suit. Linda launched into her recipe once more, and the young man seemed genuinely thrilled to learn how to make a proper martini.

We listened to the pianist perched high above us in an alcove playing "It Don't Mean a Thing (If It Ain't Got That Swing)," with such a rushed, choppy beat it sounded more like "Flight of the Bumblebee." I sipped my drink slowly, trying to make it last. Finally the young man returned with the fluttering young women still in his wake, and presented Linda with her drink with great ceremony. All eyes watched anxiously as she took a sip.

"Better," she declared, smiling. "Thank you all very much."

Once all the servers had gone, she made a face and mumbled, "but not quite." That phrase had suddenly become popular with the Americans. We laughed about it with the crew of Team Retromobile, three boisterous Alabamans—Vic Zannis, Ted Thomas, and Andy Vann—and a Texan named John Jung, driving two identical 1950 Ford Club Coupes. The Chinese efforts to produce common Western products, like faucets, telephones, and even Coca Cola, always seemed somehow slightly off. "Seems like the designer went to the West," Vic said, "then came home and tried to remember, as best he could, what he had seen. But he couldn't remember all of it, so no matter how hard he tries, it's just not quite right."

That first night's dinner we played it safe in the hotel's restaurant. We ordered two kinds of duck, pea sprouts, and spare ribs, and the food immediately reminded me of San Francisco's Chinatown. After dinner we attended our first rally meeting, and Philip Young told us that we wouldn't be able to bus down to the docks in Tianjin, where most of our cars were (some had come by air, and would be fetched separately from the airport) until Wednesday, the third. That memo we'd received at check-in turned out to be only the first of many peppered with erroneous information.

Ann and I decided to take a walk. We started up a side street lined with high-rise office buildings. Hanging banners and swinging strings of colorful Christmas-type lights criss-crossed over our heads—they seemed to be signs of celebration, but the street was oddly empty of people. In less than ten minutes, all the lights began to blink sequentially out; it was barely past 9:00 P.M. and our part of Beijing was going to bed. So we turned back and found Linda in the lobby, talking excitedly with Burt and Rich.

"You'll never believe what just happened!" she exclaimed when she saw us. "I was getting ready to go up to my room, so I was standing right there in front of the elevator. The door opened, and there were these six guys. I looked at them and said, 'Are you the Iranians?' One of them put both his hands out on my shoulders, shook me and said right in my face 'Why, do I look like a terrorist?'"

It was Amirali Javid, whose excellent English and open smile made Linda laugh at this unusual introduction. I met them all a moment later. Amirali introduced his mates and handed us his business card. He sold tires in Tehran, but more importantly, he was the Iranian National Rally Champion; all five of his mates were experienced rally drivers and navigators. They had that charm Persian men some-how exude, with their dark eyes, well-trimmed mustaches and serious smiles. We told them about our Hillman Hunter, supposedly identical to their three Iranian Peykans, and Philip Young's comment that we could all be one big "defacto" Hillman team. They all smiled and agreed to help us out if the need ever arose.

On the elevator up to our room we met another contestant: a fast-talking, heavily-accented man from Malaysia. Mr. Wong was difficult to converse with because of the large mole topped with several black and gray hairs perched on the side of his nose; it was hard not to stare at it. In our first conversation he jokingly asked us for money, then explained that he and his family (he planned to ride each leg with a different son or daughter) were using their 1954 MGA to raise money for an orphanage in Malaysia's capital city, Kuala Lumpur.

I had heard that Mr. Wong's sovereign, the crown prince of Malaysia, was among the contestants. Other royal ralliers included Lord Montagu of England and sev-eral Dutch and German barons. With my ignorance of royals, I wondered if I'd be likely to recognize any of them.

The spectacle of an automobile race left the good inhabitants of Peking in utter indifference. They looked at us without curiosity or aversion . . . The fact is, that nothing which a European can do has now the power to surprise a Son of Heaven.

BEIJING
[TUESDAY, SEPTEMBER 2]

Neither Linda, Ann, nor I had been to Beijing before, and since our Hillman was still inaccessible, we had a free day to explore further. We decided to start with Wang Fu Jing Durjie, Beijing's biggest shopping street; we had a short list of oddments we still needed for the trip.

The street was conveniently located right next to our hotel, and our first stop only a few paces away: the Baihuo Dalou, Beijing's biggest department store. As soon as we stepped through the doors, the chaotic clatter of competing demos assaulted our ears, eyes, and noses—blenders crushed and pureed odd concoctions on every counter, buckets with the multi-colored dregs of earlier demos overflowed on the floor. It seemed as if every electrical gadget ever made was on, making noise, shaving, massaging, slicing and dicing, with stacks of sliced and diced vegetables piling up on the counter and falling to the floor. The odor of fresh fruit and vegetables and perfumes competed with the electrical smell of hot irons and overheated appliances. Sales girls and guys, three or more at every counter, were always moving, pushing their appliance buttons, whirling their spoons, talking and yelling at customers and each other across the aisles. We soon retreated to the relative quiet of the street.

But that wasn't quiet either. I hadn't been conscious of it before, but along with normal city noises and the incessant honking of traffic, speakers blasted some variety of music or talk from every store, both Chinese and Western pop, all mixing in a hectic non-stop soundtrack. Even the man walking in front of us held an empty mineral water bottle in his hands and cracked the plastic rhythmically as he walked, a sound like fire crackers on Chinese New Year. I looked up at what I thought might be a bird in a tree, but the repetitive *ack ack* was coming from a mechanical device: a tin box with wings, propped on a tree branch for our passing auditory enjoyment.

Coming upon a toy store, we had to look inside. The place seemed as big as a Macy's, though the staffing level had to be three times that of any US store. The noise here made the other department store seem quiet; every clerk stood playing with the store's offerings, and most of them made noise. Squeak-toys squeaked, electric cars and trains vroomed or tooted by, balls bounced and flew from sales clerk to sales clerk across the aisles. The young clerks' hands shaped Play-Doh with lightening speed, then held out the colorful clay creature for our approval, a battering of clacking Chinese words thrown out with it to convince us to buy.

A few blocks later we came to a row of restaurants. It was a little quieter now, but other senses were assaulted by big buckets of live snails set outside the eatery's doorway, so we could choose our lunch before we entered. Huge plate-glass windows turned out to be tanks full of live things. In one, the turtles and crabs were so thickly intertwined it took awhile to fathom what sort of sea creatures they were. Other tanks held slimy snakes, fish, and eels. Lobsters and crayfish writhed in a mass of claws and tiny white legs.

About this time, Linda remarked that she'd seen no sign of domestic dogs or cats, either loose or in cages. Despite the restaurants' best efforts, none of us were working up much of an appetite.

Ninety years before, the streets here were yellow dust. Carriages, wooden rickshaws and horses crowded the narrow lanes, and when the Mandarins went shopping, they were surrounded by their retinues: bald eunuchs in scarlet cone hats guarded the women who could barely stand on their mutilated feet; concubines and "singing girls," chosen for the day or just for the outing, followed the men in their richly embroidered silk robes.

We saw no traditional Chinese garments or fabrics on Wang Fu Jing street. I wondered if that reflected Chinese demand for Western wear, or just a matter of neighborhood. Perhaps the traditional clothing was only available elsewhere. One shop, far from the busy department store section, offered beautiful dresses made from velvet with delicate silk brocade sewn on in panels. Though the style was modern, the skirts were long and narrow, in the manner of a *Chiang Sam,* the form-fitting brocade dress familiar to window-shoppers in America's Chinatowns.

By now we had been adopted by an English-speaking older gentleman who offered to take us to a museum. He walked as quickly as we, and talked pleasantly about the rally and his life as a government worker, complaining that until he retired from his translation job to become a guide he never had more than ten days of vacation. After another ten-minute walk we came to our guide's museum —the sign in English said "Art Gallery." The building was a beautifully ornate example of traditional Chinese pagoda or palace architecture. Some student paintings lined the entrance, but on the upper floors, to which our guide now hurriedly led us, was an arts and crafts shopping center with prices far higher than the gift shops we'd explored within the Forbidden City. This sort of guide seems to pop up in every country, and they can sometimes be painful to dislodge. Linda simply told the gentleman firmly that we couldn't buy anything, we had a long journey ahead and had no room for anything other than essentials. He said, "No matter, I was coming here anyway," and left us in peace.

We stopped outside the "art gallery" to buy water and to consult our map. We'd come much further west than we'd anticipated, and it looked as if the Jingshan Hill, directly behind the Forbidden City, wasn't far. Sometimes called Coal Hill because it was made in the fifteenth century from the soil dug out from the Forbidden City's moat, Jingshan translates to View Hill, and offers the best view of the city. We walked for twenty minutes or more (we were farther from it than the map had promised), before we came upon a small kiosk outside the forested park's entrance. A woman there collected a fee—all I could read among the Chinese characters was the number three. I offered her a ten-yuan note, expecting to get seven change. The woman shook her head vigorously, so I showed her my money. She took the five-note and gave me back what looked like 5 one-yuan bills but was actually four yuan and one jiao—the cost was three jiao (one-tenth of a yuan). I had tried to pay her ten times the entrance fee.

Behind the gate the high-pitched nasal whine of a saxophone-type instrument accompanied several traditionally-dressed dancers in fur hats, prancing about with a litter on their shoulders. When they settled the litter to the ground, a young Chinese mother and child disembarked—it was an amusement ride. The dancers reached out to tempt us, but we hurried quickly up the hill (I wondered how they would cope with my 160-pound bulk).

The music accompanied us all the way up the steep stepping stones to the lowest of the five temples. The park contains five hills topped with five temples, with each inner hill progressively higher than the last, so the central hill is the highest and holds the grandest temple. *Feng Shui*—the science of winds and waters—and *yin/yang* considerations were involved with the creation of this miniature mountain range: rising directly north of the Forbidden City, the hills protected the emperor from the barbarians to the north.

From the bottom it looked only like a gently rising forest, though some of the green and red tiled temple roofs peeked through the trees. Once in it, we felt as if we had entered a Ming painting: gray-green foliage crowded gnarled gray rock, with our narrow path a brushstroke between them. The flagstone steps were so tiny I had to climb on the balls of my size-ten feet. In 1907, this park was for the exclusive use of eunuchs, palace ladies and the imperial family; tiny bound feet would fit these steps perfectly. The first temple, with a tiled double-roof rising over a circular colonnade, held only an empty pedestal. We climbed up the second, and it was empty too. Only one bronze Buddha is left; the four others were pillaged by foreign troops during the Boxer Rebellion.

We lingered at the Pavilion of Everlasting Spring—the temple at the top—to enjoy the 360-degree view of Beijing. Southward, the curved golden roofs of the Forbidden City cascaded in perfect alignment, north-south and east-west—the geometry was clearer here than on my Precious Remember. We only found out later that we'd had a very rare experience: a relatively smog-free day. Though skyscrapers and high construction cranes crowded every angle, we could see the shadow of the Western Mountains, the craggy range that had caused the 1907 Peking-Paris raiders so much difficulty.

As soon as they arrived in Peking, Prince Borghese, his wife and her dear friend (a countess) had gone on horseback into the Western Mountains. They each carried a bamboo stick cut to the exact width of the Itala, to see firsthand if the big car would clear the gorges. If the way was only slightly too narrow, crews of coolies would be hired to hack them wider. If the gorges were impassable, a new route had to be found. They covered the 160 miles between Peking and Kalgan, on the Mongolian border, in six days.

We had to circumnavigate the Forbidden City's eastern exterior wall to make our way back to our hotel. At the base of Jingshan Hill, streetside woks heaped with steaming noodles and veggies looked delicious and smelled temptingly of soy and ginger. We were hungry, but we feared the bacteria of these roadside kitchens and decided to keep walking.

The street turned out to be residential. High exterior walls disguised crowded rabbit warrens of low-ceiling houses, remnants of the traditional *hutongs* that had once constituted the typical Beijing habitat. Each one is walled, of course, but the gates are always open. If you look beyond that first gate, you see another wall, this one for the ghosts. Chinese ghosts can only go forward, so a short wall blocking a house's main entrance will keep them out. Though the rules of cosmic geometry must have contributed to these constructions, they lost any semblance of order by force of a natural rule: no one's wall could block another resident's path to water. The Mongolian word for well or horse-trough—*hut* or *hot*—gave these complexes the name *hutongs*. As new residents added their humble abodes onto existing hutongs, the paths became circuitous and narrow, just wide enough to let a single rider pass. Now, instead of horses, bicycles choke the alleyways, piled haphazardly one atop another. Relics of modern life have crowded the alleys too: washing machines, small rusty fridges, and piles of metallic miscellany infringe on the already tiny pathways.

Once closer to Tiananmen Square we came to a big restaurant, distinguishable by a seven-foot-high white plastic duck in a green tuxedo and matching hat. The foyer held a bank of live tanks on one side, and a nice clean grocery-store refrigerated display—just like a Safeway—on the other. No one volunteered to help us, so we sat ourselves at a table, and watched for a while as others ate. The place was clearly a popular businessman's eatery. A group of five or six green-uniformed girls with green-and-white cartoon duck-head paper hats stood as if at attention and stared at us, but made no attempt to take our order. We made motions and pointed to nearby tables to indicate "we'll take that," but nothing seemed to work. The girls smiled and nodded but showed no sign of comprehension. Finally we said "English? English?" and after much scurrying back and forth a woman was found who had a little more English than we had Chinese. With her help we finally realized that we were to pick out our choice of stir-fry or soup ingredients from the cellophane-wrapped packages or live tanks on display. The young uniformed girls then brought us frothy white drinks, a sweet rice mixture, and the food soon followed, hot, fresh and delicious.

The men of the 1907 Peking to Paris were fed their native fare in the foreign legation dining rooms. They were not the type to sightsee, but they were forced into idleness awaiting the Wai Wu Pu, the Grand Council of the Celestial Empire. Even though the French Foreign Office had received a telegram from its Chinese minister stating "The Peking-Paris race is authorized by the Chinese Government" back in March, by June, with the raiders within the city walls, the Council refused the French minister's request. What if these foreigners were spies? What if this newfangled Western machine, which the Chinese dubbed *chi-cho* or oil chariot, caused havoc in the streets?

The French and Russian ministers again appealed to the Wai Wu Pu, and their renewed effort convinced the anti-Western Council that these foreigners must indeed be spies; there must be a political agenda, a new conspiracy against China. The Wai Wu Pu declared, "The chi-cho must not pass," and refused to issue passports for the raiders to travel through Mongolia, the only practicable route west.

Prince Borghese was still out on his survey expedition when the news was handed down. He returned to find a dispirited group of Frenchmen. Five days before the start date, the men gathered to decide what to do. The De Dion-Bouton men were ready to give up; Godard declared "Whether I have a passport or not, whether I go alone or in company, I intend to drive the Spyker out of Peking on the day agreed, the tenth of June." Borghese, in his customarily dry, even tone, said "Gentlemen, whatever conclusion you come to, my own decision is made, and nothing can change it. I shall start on Monday."

We joined three ralliers from Arizona for dinner: Dick Taylor, Dave Pierce and Larry Davis. Dick, a tall silver-haired man in his early fifties, turned out to be chief of this crew that called themselves "three-guys-in-a-jeep." Their 1962 Willys Jeep was one of four 4-Wheel-Drives in the "Classic 4-W-D" category. This category hadn't existed when Linda first signed up. The classes then consisted only of Vintageants (pre-1951) and Classics (1951-74)—both divided into smaller classes by engine size—and the non-competitive Touring category. When she had asked about that Toyota Land Cruiser and been refused, she had assumed that it was the vehicle's four-wheel-drive, which would give a distinct advantage on rugged terrain, that had caused Philip to reject it. Now we wondered if it was simply the fact that the vehicle was Japanese.

We instantly hit it off with the three-guys-in-a-jeep. Though Dick had plenty of money, he was very casual and unpretentious, a "regular" American guy. The youngest jeepster at thirty-four, Dave Pierce had come along as riding mechanic; and the quietest of the three, almost withdrawn compared to his outgoing co-drivers, was Larry, who turned out to be the hardware man. His company in Arizona manufactured printed circuit boards, and he was in charge of the team's satellite telephone, digital camera, and laptop computer. The Arizona *Republic* had asked Dick to send in regular reports with photos, and it was Larry's job to make sure the machinery worked.

Though it was our second night in the main hotel restaurant, there was still a bit of cross-cultural confusion. We ordered a wide variety of courses, including steamed rice. The young woman who took the order never spoke; she simply nodded and smiled. The dishes arrived in odd spurts, until eventually everything we'd ordered inhabited the center of the table, except the rice.

Dave poked at his food with his fork (there were no chopsticks in sight), but didn't touch the food. "I wonder where the rice is. Do you suppose they forgot about it?"

Dick waved one of the waitresses over and convinced her to bring the rice. He had poured out the last of our bottle of "Dynasty" wine—"Would you like another glass of 'Nasty?" he asked—when the young waitress returned and offered Dick the menu. She opened to the very last page and pointed.

"Dessert?" Dick asked, then looked down. "Look at this! The menu says 'Food!'"

Our young server wanted to know if we would like "Food," items that the Chinese knew Westerners would want to eat, but didn't know where to put, like steamed rice. Dick politely declined.

"Next time," he said, "I'll have to remember to order the 'food' first thing."

On the elevator up to our room, we met three American journalists. I had received a call from a woman named Chris McKenna before we'd left; she'd identified herself as a writer for Discovery On-Line's Peking to Paris web page, a site on their award-winning net magazine. She was much younger in person than I had gathered on the phone; she and her photographer, Drew Fellman, were fresh out of the Columbia School of Journalism. They were both thin and pale, as if they'd spent too long in a New York City cellar. Mike, the hardware man, looked sturdier.

Chris had interviewed me for a profile, and afterward I asked her what kind of equipment she planned to bring along on the event. I had just been warned by two separate visa agents not to bring my laptop computer: customs officials in many of the countries along the route would charge me exorbitant fees and possibly even confiscate it, they said. Chris said they'd be bringing their computers, customs or no. I planned to do some reporting, firing messages back to Ann for posting on our P2PGALS website, so I had asked Chris if I could share their equipment. She hadn't confirmed it one way or the other, so there in the elevator I asked again, and all three graciously agreed to let me send my dispatches via e-mail on one of their two laptops.

Many of the two hundred participants were reporting to someone back home, like Dick Taylor to the Arizona *Republic.* I seemed to be the only one who opted for the Barzini method of writing my journal and dispatches out longhand. Everywhere I turned over the next six weeks, state-of-the-art computers and communications equipment emerged from hiding places among the cases of oil and toilet paper stuffed in odd crevices in competitors' cars.

Don Jones, who partnered Carl Schneider (the man Martin Swig had introduced me to in Italy), used his satellite phone to check in almost daily. Like us, Don and Carl had a web page, but they had been at it longer. They set out from New York City on July fifteenth, and drove their 1954 Packard Clipper across the USA to San Francisco, from where they had it shipped to China. Just as the Peking to Paris commemorated the 1907 event, Don and Carl were celebrating the Around the World Race of 1908.

The 1907 race had created a firestorm of international publicity, but to the shock and dismay of the editors at *Le Matin,* all the glory went to an Italian! So they decided to do it again, this time all the way around, and they enlisted the aid of *The New York Times.* They set the start in Times Square and the date for February, in the middle of winter, thinking that the cold would freeze over the Bering Strait, making it possible for cars to drive from Alaska to Russia. Until then, crossing the United States had only been accomplished by a few automobiles in the summertime. Three entries arrived immediately from France (including Charles Godard and Auguste Pons, this time with a four-wheeler), and one each from Italy, Germany, and the United States. At the very last minute a second American car entered, a Thomas Flyer built in Buffalo.

The route led to Chicago in the midst of blizzards and record snowfall. One car even got so far as the docks in Alaska before they persuaded the organizers that driving beyond—Alaska had no through-roads at all, much less one across the liquid straits—was impossible. Gathered back in San Francisco, the four cars that remained went by boat to Japan, then drove northwest into Siberia, along a route similar to Borghese's, until finally arriving in Paris. Only three cars made it all the way; the Thomas Flyer, the only American left in the event, won.

Two-hundred-fifty-thousand people crowded Times Square at the start of the Great Race of 1908. Not nearly so many cheered Don and Carl off when they left New York City, but millions watched them depart through the cameras of NBC's *Today Show.* Thousands more followed the race via the Internet. Almost every night since that first day in New York, Don hooked his cell or satellite phone up to his laptop and called in a report that could be read as text or downloaded as audio, or listened to the old-fashioned way by calling a toll-free number. Don had made a fortune in telecommunications, and his expertise was evident. Their web page had accumulated 8,400 hits by the time they left San Francisco, and on the day Yahoo named them "Site of the Day," they logged hits from fifty-two different countries.

Don, who had visited Beijing twenty years before, noticed the tremendous changes that had taken place in the city. "China in 1978 was sort of a colorless and somber place, sort of impoverished," he said. "The contrast today is startling. China and Beijing appear to be prosperous, colorful, vibrant, a lot of construction and modern buildings, a lot of large satellite antenna systems on tops of buildings, just like in North America. Young people under thirty all have pagers, and cellular telephones are pretty common. These are extraordinary shifts from what China was like in the 1970s."

∽ 6 ∽

On certain journeys it is better never to settle things. Any settling of plans is a deplorable act of presumption; it is an attempt to limit and direct Fate. Fate would avenge herself and humble our pride.

TIANJIN
[WEDNESDAY, SEPTEMBER 3]

The dock in Tianjin was a two-hour drive from Beijing. Ann set out for a day of sightseeing while Linda and I and the other contestants boarded buses that would take us to the docks and our Hillman.

Once out of the Beijing sprawl, the buses rolled onto a newly built expressway, four lanes wide and nearly empty except for a few military vehicles and trucks. After about an hour, our bus pulled over at a wide spot featuring a drab cement building. I recognized the Chinese characters for men and women above the building's two doors. Nearby were two carts on wheels, one with a woman in a large sun hat selling Popsicles, the other with a man selling icy bottled water.

The men piled out of the bus and stomped right over to the WC. The women hovered, wondering, until one brave soul went in. A few more followed. I bought a strange greenish Popsicle—from the wrapper I guessed it to be creamed mashed peas—and watched the brave faces going in and the disgusted faces coming out. Occasionally the women exiting warned the ones going in, "Just holes in the floor! Can you imagine?!" I was pleased to see that Arlene Kleptz, the woman who'd never peed in a bush, handled it just fine.

There were only about thirty women, mostly wives or daughters of their co-drivers. One amazing Yorkshire, England crew contained a husband and wife, David Bull and Angela Riley, and Angela's mother, Helen McGugan. Helen may have been near seventy, but she wasn't the type to be put off by holes in the ground. I could easily imagine her driving British soldiers around Egypt in rugged jeeps during World War II.

The cars were stuffed bumper to bumper in warehouses spread over several acres, a mile or two outside of the major port city of Tianjin. All we could see of this city of seven million was a line of new high-rises in the distance. In 1907, the city Westerners then called Tientsin harbored "concessions"—like the legations in Peking—neighborhoods designed and run by foreigners. The Raiders awaited the arrival of the ship delivering their automobiles in a club in the British Concession.

As we made our way through the sea of automobiles, I was incredibly nervous; I was certain some disastrous pile of mechanical mess awaited us. We found the Hillman in the farthest building, its insides piled high with stuff we'd never seen before and didn't remember asking Tom to get for us: sleeping bags, camping equipment, rally stuff like number stickers and hundreds of Navigator's bags (large red plastic zipper envelopes to hold maps and road books). It was all Philip Young's and the rally staff's stuff.

After all my faxes I couldn't wait to open the trunk and examine our tool supply. Linda pulled out the keys and lifted the lid. I couldn't believe it; it was practically empty! They'd ignored all my requests; no socket wrenches at all, only one set of crescent wrenches; not even a spark plug wrench! We looked at our fluids—some octane boost (which meant our engine had not been de-tuned for poor quality gas) and carburetor oil for the SUs (the dash-pot style carburetors required that the level of oil be maintained), but no motor oil except one small, half-filled plastic bottle marked "Synth" in permanent marker.

"Synth?" I asked Linda, "Does this thing have synthetic oil in it?"

Linda shrugged.

Great, I thought. We're supposed to work on this thing and we don't even know what kind of oil it's using. That's like a doctor planning to conduct transfusions without knowing the patient's blood type.

Engines were starting up all around us, and we were anxious to start ours. My fingers were shaking as I reattached the battery cables (they'd been disconnected per the shipper's requirements). A split second later Linda turned the key. It started! It worked! We both practically levitated.

But we still had to rearrange things in the back seat; we were trying to figure out what was ours and what wasn't. I was so enraptured with our own longed-for beauty, I'd barely noticed the car next to us until it started up its engine and rolled forward. The red open roadster crashed right into us, wedging its high motorcycle-style fender under our open rear door. I jumped back, yelling. I swore with auto shop eloquence, and the man in the driver's seat of the roadster looked back aghast. "Reverse, reverse!" I screamed, but he'd killed the motor, and when he started it up again—great puffs of putrid smoke blowing into my mouth—he continued forward, pulling our door with him and twisting the metal. "Stop! Stop!" we screeched.

He dismounted now, a late–middle–aged man with a full head of black hair streaked with gray and a weathered, very tan, Mediterranean face. He spoke British English but with an unusual accent, and a very deep gravelly voice. This was David Arrigo from Malta, and his car, now joined to ours, was a 1948 Allard.

"Oh dear," he said with typical continental understatement. "Maybe we can lift it off." He tried to lift the door. "Can someone help us here?" he called.

I should have stopped him. I should have insisted that he put the car in reverse, or push the Allard backward, out from under the door the way it came in. But the group of men that gathered followed Arrigo's instructions, and while he restarted his car, the men together lifted our door and thus the Hillman high in the air. The Allard pulled clear, then drove straight out of the warehouse. When the men released the door, the combined force of the hit and the lifting had twisted it so severely out of shape it would not close.

I had known forcing the door up would make it worse. Now my anger at Arrigo was doubled by anger at myself—I should have stood up to him. We had a rear door hanging open, and we hadn't even made it out of the warehouse.

Cars had left on both sides of us now, so Linda settled into the driver's seat. We had to get the car out of here, twisted door or no. She turned the key; it revved with the satisfying crackle and pop of the exhaust, the song of a hopped–up engine. But it didn't move. I bent down and looked in. "What's wrong?"

"I—can't —," Linda grunted as she muscled the gear shifter, "—get it into gear."

I watched her push it up, then push it down. She got out. "You try."

I got in, shoved the stick up, nothing. Shoved it down. Nothing. Turned off the key, started it again, pumped the clutch, nothing. "It's in neutral, let's push."

The group of men that had gathered to twist our door had been watching us, so now they helped. These five or six Chinese men, dressed in cotton shirts and slacks, looked like office workers on lunch break. The car rolled easily out of the warehouse, and we let it come to a stop far enough out not to block anyone.

"See if you can figure it out," Linda said. "I'll go find out about the license plates."

"We may have to get one of the mechanics to give us a hand," I said. I hated to say it; I hated to resort to help so soon, but an unshiftable gearbox wasn't one of the mechanical problems I'd asked Chris how to fix. Still, powered by anger and embarrassment, I sat in the driver's seat, and kept trying. Turn on the key; shift. In gear, then turn on the key, pop the clutch. Try reverse now, key on; key off. Back to first. It became a rhythmic motion: shift-key-rev-pop, different gears each time. I pounded the dashboard, and sat puffing, pissed and upset, then tried it again. Shift-key-rev-pop-shift-rev-pop and lurch, the car began to roll backward. Reverse worked. Shifted again, first. It worked! For the hell of it I drove twenty meters, then stopped. I would've driven donuts if there had been room.

I got out and looked at the twisted back door. Three of the Chinese men walked over and looked at it with me. I pointed with my finger at the twisted hinges, then held firm to the side of the door and tried to twist it back with all my might. Nothing budged. I shrugged. The men then each took a turn, then all three

together. Still nothing. I smiled and said "thanks anyway" in English, but I was disgusted. I didn't think anything short of a body shop with a body vice and dent puller would do it.

Linda came back and handed me the two black Chinese license plates. "Now I've got to go get our driver's licenses," she said, and disappeared again. Two of the three men wandered off as well. The third, holding a camera, hung around and watched me.

I examined the plates. The number "069" was inscribed in the center, and the English words "Beijing to Paris Motor Challenge 1997" appeared on the bottom; Chinese characters presumably saying the same thing ranged across the top. I was pleased at the number—the astrological symbol for Cancer, my zodiac sign. I don't normally take it seriously, but on the verge of an uncertain adventure I wanted all the good omens and tokens I could get (I'd been given a hand-woven crystal necklace by a good friend at home and I was hoping to find a miniature Kwan Yin, the ancient Chinese mother goddess, to take along as a mascot). Aside from being nice souvenirs, though, those plates and our driver's licenses were supposedly the treasure purchased by the exorbitant fees paid by Philip Young to the Chinese government—something in the ballpark of ten-thousand pounds per car. Normally, tourists in China can only hire cars with drivers; to be allowed to drive our own vehicles was a special privilege. I wasn't surprised that that privilege cost plenty.

While I removed the screws from our British plates and mounted the Chinese ones, my new Chinese friends reappeared with two-by-fours and bricks. One made the motion of lifting the car.

"Jack?" I guessed, and dug the bottle jack out of the trunk. When the men saw it they nodded vigorously.

With the car in the air and the two-by-four wedged between the twisted door and the sill, the three men put all their weight against the board. After three or four attempts, with grunts and groans and trial door closings, it finally worked. The door shut once again.

Linda had come back before our primitive body work was complete, and by the time it was finished we were so pleased with our recovery, we took turns taking photographs standing with our friendly helpers.

Door fixed, gears unlocked, we drove about two hundred yards away, where we were forced to stop and wait in the hot, humid sun for over an hour. Then we drove another couple hundred yards across the main street to a gas station, where we waited in line for fuel. Our special oversized tank took fifty-four liters, enough we figured to get us about four hundred miles. Then we waited for everyone else to fuel up, so we could all drive back in convoy. The Chinese police finally took off, leading us to the long, straight superhighway back to Beijing. The police cars set the pace at 70 mph, about as fast as our car liked to go (beyond that it screeched and vibrated; it was loud even at 60). We were glad of the pace. For our first real driving in the car, we were fortunate to be on a nice, super-modern, almost empty highway.

Linda drove, and I watched the kilometer markings on the road and compared them to the red-lit figures ticking by on our trip meter. This was the navigator's odometer, or mileage recorder, though in our case it was recording kilometers, to the hundredth place. Since the idea in a Time-Distance rally is to get to the next Time Control (TC) at exactly the right time, the navigator needs to keep track of every kilometer to the tenth or hundredth, and must constantly recalculate the average speed needed to make up for stops (for fuel or mechanical failures or slow traffic or whatever). I discovered that we had a tenth of a kilometer error. I read the trip meter's instructions on how to calibrate it, but I couldn't make heads or tails of it. An error of a tenth is pretty big; it would make the math more difficult. Unless the recce car had also been off by a tenth, in which case we'd be right on.

It was important—some said critical—to calibrate the trip meter to match the recce crew's; in the States, there's a special one-mile area marked off by the recce car at the beginning of the rally that each car can drive over slowly, specifically to allow competitors to match their trip meters to the recce car's. There was no guarantee that the kilometer markers posted on this Chinese highway were anywhere near the kilometers measured by the original recce car. So there didn't seem to be much point in worrying about our tenth-of-a-kilometer error.

Besides watching the trip meter, the navigator also has to watch the clock—set each morning to the officials' clock—and read the road book, which provides the kilometer-by-kilometer breakdown of every stretch of the road (or is supposed to, anyway). In case the road book is inadequate, the navigator has to have a map handy and be able to find herself on it quickly. There's also the time card book, and calculations to figure out what time you're due at the next TC. So the navigator juggles the road book (a thick 8-1/2"x11" spiral-bound affair), the time card book (about 5" x 8" card-stock spiral), pencils and highlighters, a calculator, and several folded, crumpled, and refolded maps.

Linda and I had purchased twenty-odd maps from various mail-order suppliers covering every inch of the route. As soon as we got the road books (which ran to three volumes), we sat down at Linda's kitchen table and spent over ten hours marking out the route. It gave us both a chance to get familiar with the books, the route, and the schedule.

From a navigator's point of view, there's plenty to do. Professional rally drivers are aware of this, but amateur drivers often discount the value of the navigator. In their view, all the navigator has to do is read a map and watch the clock. Some navigators denigrate their drivers, saying all they have to do is steer and shift and listen to the navigator. In reality, of course, they have to work together.

Linda and I figured the only way to find out which job was really harder was to do them both. We agreed to alternate, one day driving, one day navigating, throughout the course of the rally. Other teams had set roles. Team Retromobile was one. Once we were back at the hotel, we joined the four members of that team in the bar. The pianist up in the alcove pummeled out another jazz standard, rendering it unrecognizable, while we talked.

Two were from Birmingham, Alabama. Vic Zannis, forty-eight, sported a trim beard and usually looked serious; he was the shop foreman and crew chief at Precise Restoration, a company owned by his co-driver, Ted Thomas. Round-faced Ted played the jovial good ol' boy, but not a dumb one—he had "Boss" written all over him, the kind of boss who treated you fairly, but lost his temper easily. Besides the restoration shop, Ted also owned a very successful aviation insurance company. Ted planned to drive, and Vic would navigate, the #23 Ford Club Coupe.

The other Alabaman was Andy Vann, a wiry man who smiled easily under a bushy white mustache. He was from Trussville, near what he called the "Red Neck Riviera," and he ran a race car prep shop. His shop built the engines, transmissions, and helped Vic develop the suspensions for the two identical Fords. Andy would navigate car #24 for John Jung, who was clean-shaven, with short, dark hair and wire-rim glasses. His accent was much less southern—Dallas, tempered by long stays in San Francisco, where he kept a second home. John owned what sounded like a large and successful chain of stereo stores. Ted, John and Andy were all in their fifties or older.

John and Ted had met at the famous Carrera Panamericana Mexican road race. The Peking-Paris, like most classic T-D rallies, would require fairly slow average speeds of around 30 mph. The Carrera is the last classic car event that allows cars to go full speed on regular roads—every October, cars from 1950-54 gather in Mexico and fly two thousand miles across the country, reaching 150 and 200 mph on the special speed stages. Of all the Americans we'd met, these guys were the most serious racers. They'd be a good match for the only other serious racers we'd met so far: the Iranians.

That second-to-last night in Beijing there were two parties: one put on by the British embassy for Brits only (we heard a few grumbles from both Americans and Aussies at this touch of chauvinism), and another for everybody hosted by Prince Idris Shah of Malaysia. This particular royal turned out to be a vibrant and funny fellow who spoke perfect English; in fact, he has a house in Marin County, where he keeps a couple of Harley Davidsons. The Hard Rock Cafe was sponsoring the Prince's 1932 Ford Model B, which he and his co-driver Richard Curtis had decorated with the words *Humpty Dumpty* above the rear window. Richard explained that it took "all the king's horses and all the king's men" to get Humpty Dumpty ready for the rally.

The cavernous Hard Rock bar differed little from the neon rock 'n' roll mold that has made the joints popular with tourists around the globe. At first the music was incredibly loud recorded rock classics, which played as we helped ourselves to the huge buffet that lined the central dance floor. The steam trays held everything from miniature cheeseburgers and french fries to Chinese specialties, French cheeses, even European pastries.

The music didn't get any quieter when a band of white people, Heroin-chic pale with long hair and British accents, began playing old American rock classics like "Horse with No Name." Over the din, I heard someone say that two cars had already had to drop out of the rally due to mechanical problems. We left soon after; I didn't realize at the time that this unlikely band had provided the last rock music I would hear for the next seven weeks.

CHAPTER

∾ 7 ∾

*Our machine . . . had lost all trace of luxury, or even of comfort—all sign of its origin
as a means of enjoyment. It seemed framed for attack, meant to be hurled against some
powerful enemy with the full impetus of its own blind might.*

BEIJING
[THURSDAY, SEPTEMBER 4]

We spent the next morning sorting out the car at the Agricultural Center, a sprawling fairground marked by huge pagoda-like meeting halls and well-tended gardens. Our *parc fermé* (French for closed parking, our specially-guarded lot) was surrounded by simpler shop-style buildings; possibly the gardeners' work sheds. The journey from Tianjin had given us some feeling for the car and we were both pleased and relieved to find that it ran so smoothly.

The packing situation was much less pleasing. I was upset about the oil. On the one hand, I knew that the advantage of synthetic oil is you don't need to change it as often. Since we had a ten-thousand-mile journey, I'd planned to change the oil three times—every three thousand miles—or more, if the roads were unpaved. Did Paul Jackson and Tom Coulthard really think we'd need less than four-ounces of Synth over the whole journey? I managed to beg some regular engine oil from the organizers, but unfortunately, I had no proper container to put it in. The only thing at hand was a plastic water bottle, which I filled and tucked in the trunk beside the small tool box.

The lack of tools was equally irksome. We couldn't even find a tire iron at first. Finally, once we unloaded all the organizers' junk from our backseat, we found one strapped under the spare wheel. That was a relief, but I really wanted a set of socket wrenches. This may sound picky, as regular crescent wrenches might have been adequate, but I knew that socket wrenches would give me better leverage, making it easier to dislodge difficult bolts. Michael Veys was nearby, unpacking Mr. Christiansen's Rolls, a huge 1965 Silver Cloud crouched under a heavy roof rack. Michael had to unpack just to see what was there, and when I asked him how it was going, he laughed. "There must be at least two of everything here!"

"Really?" I said. "Even socket wrenches?"

"Definitely. Look at this." He unrolled one complete set, then pulled another from a box. We sorted through, and he kindly loaned me one of everything that was double; the only one we'd have to do without was the half-inch, since Christiansen only had one. "Don't tell Eric," he whispered as I wrapped up my booty. "I'm not sure he'd mind, but . . . "

"Mum's the word," I said.

Our Hillman was parked next to a 1934 Rolls Royce painted in metal-flake pink. Linda immediately christened the car "Mr. Sparkle." Four very proper British gentlemen were its crew, probably accountants: the accounting firm Coopers & Lybrand, clearly a sponsor, was painted on the car. One of the crew was also connected to the London *Financial Times,* so the pink paint was in honor of that journal's paper color.

That Rolls reminded me of a long-forgotten memory: there used to be a white Rolls Royce in my hometown as big as Eric Christiansen's. When I was ten or so, I would squeal with delight whenever it drove by. I thought I was squealing at the wealth that car represented, not at the car itself, but now I wonder. Though I've been living with a car guy since I was seventeen, my passion for classic cars crept up on me. The Fiats I first met as a teenager weren't yet classic; they were odd and eccentric, but the oldest, the 1959 Multipla, was no older than I. Chris's passion for autos came naturally from his father, and thanks to his mechanical abililty, grew into a fascination with and talent for internal combustion engines. Some of this has no doubt rubbed off, but to this day, steel, aluminum and gasoline fail to excite me.

Old cars, though, speak to me of the past. When I see an old car, I immediately wonder who sat there in that driver's seat. Who sat there beside her? Where did they take this hunk of metal and cloth? Did they have to wrestle that huge, wooden-spoke wheel off its axle and repair the tire? Was rain pounding on their heads and pooling on their laps? Did they drive fast in a race, or did they honor the early speed limits, as low as eight miles per hour. When they gazed out the window, what did they see?

Classic cars grew into even more of a passion when I realized that their beauty was entirely unnecessary. One can go just as fast or efficiently in an ugly car as one can in a fluid, glistening sculpture. That's why the classic Italians, and some of the early French cars, always win my personal automotive beauty contests.

Looking around that parc fermé in Beijing, I found the cars assembled to be surprisingly unlovely. The 1927 Mercedes 630 SSK and the 1928 boat-tail Rolls Royce were exceptions: the Mercedes' long white fender flanks had luxurious grandeur, and the inlaid wooden veneer on the older Rolls' body had a surprising delicacy. The old $4^{1/2}$ and $3^{1/2}$ liter Bentleys were impressive, but not for their beauty; these open roadsters are the archetypal classic British race cars. Other than those, only the sleek 1960s Aston Martins—racy Italian-style coupes—really appealed to me. There were two old Italian cars, a '48 Fiat and a '64 Lancia, but the Fiat was a humble 1100 sedan and the Flavia was one of the less-pretty Lancias (though they won a lot of rallies). The rest of the automobiles were largely bulbous and utilitarian. Luckily, a nascent 1970s edginess saved our Hillman from that same traditional bulge. And I liked its stance: high on its axles, ready to pounce like a metallic cat, its throaty exhaust note when revved reverberating like a caged lion's roar.

It certainly was the widest range of classic cars I'd ever seen gathered in one place. The oldest went all the way back to 1907, an American-built La France. The newest was a 1974 Austin 1800, a car nicknamed Landcrab for the way it had handled tough roads in pro-rallies. The smallest was Burt and Rich's 600cc Citroën 2CV; the largest was another Rolls Royce, the 1967 Phantom V limousine that had served as Queen Elizabeth's state car on her visits to Australia.

Near the back of the parc fermé, I found the Jeepsters. Their bright red and white Willys wore the highest number in the rally: ninety-nine. I hadn't seen them at the Hard Rock Cafe, so I asked them how they'd spent their evening.

"It was awful!" Dick told me. "We were driving along in the convoy, almost all the way back to Beijing, when we suddenly realized the Jeep's oil pressure had dropped to zero. We had to pull over and check it out—it was just a short rubber hose to the oil filter. A lousy five-dollar brass fitting had broken loose, so all the oil got pumped out right over the engine compartment and onto the pavement."

"At least it won't be hard to fix," I said.

"But that's not the half of it," Dick went on. "While we were parked there on the side of the highway, a big Chinese police car pulled up behind us, apparently to offer help, but they didn't stop! It was bizarre—they crashed right into us. Look at this! The tailgate and the bumper are all crushed! They had to bring us in last night on a hook."

The Jeepsters weren't the only ones frantically fixing mechanical problems there at the Agricultural Center. A pair of Portuguese businessmen were upset about their 1933 Ford Model B; it was one of the ones I had heard about at the Hard Rock Cafe. The engine had had a catastrophic failure—a thrown rod, or busted piston—and was completely out of commission. They were arranging for another engine to be shipped, but it didn't seem likely they would receive it in time.

As I circled back to our Hillman, I walked by our main competition, the other women-only team. They had gathered a crowd of reporters and video-men, so I stood on the fringes and watched. The Honorable Francesca Sternberg and Jennifer Gillies, wearing short-shorts, matching Chinese coolie hats, and waving Union Jacks, were perched atop their 1964 Volvo Amazon. The British video crew was interviewing them, and I stiffened when I heard the British reporter ask them how it felt to be "the only female team." I didn't catch their response; later, we discovered most of the British participants had no idea another female team existed. The Gulls (British pronunciation for *girls,* which Linda and I instantly adopted as their nickname) were clearly better at generating publicity than we were; whether they were better at rallying remained to be seen.

The other big crowd of media surrounded two classic Buicks, parked nose to bumper. Business-suited folk from General Motors, including the head of the Buick Division, Robert Coletta, came to greet their two sponsored entries: Pat and Mary Brooks from Iowa in their beautifully restored 1949 Straight 8 "Woody," and two British-born gents from Singapore and Hong Kong, Richard Clark and Ken Hughes. Their all-black 1948 Buick Special sported tasteful script in English and Chinese on both fenders. Both cars were powered by Buick's strong "straight 8-"cylinder engines, but the Special was a right-hand-drive that had been exported to England, then driven extensively in Kenya. GM China was using their sponsorship to publicize the fact that the Shangai Automotive Industry Corporation had signed a joint-venture agreement to begin manufacture of Buick sedans in China.

This kind of commercial effort also underlay the original 1907 race. At the time, the public considered the motor-car little more than a toy for the rich. A few knew it had the potential to be otherwise; one, Russian Prince Khilkoff, Minister of Roads and Railways, had introduced motor-truck transport to Crimea, but the disastrous Russo-Japanese War killed the effort. Two years later, Khilkoff had plans for building miles of wooden-plank motorways over the Siberian mud. He told a French reporter when the raiders finally arrived in Moscow that "Thanks to *Le Matin* the legend of the automobile solely as a distraction for sportsmen has vanished . . . your raid has proved what the most murderous speed-races on prepared enclosed roads could never do."

When the Wai Wu Pu blocked the race, the De Dion-Bouton drivers—car salesmen back home in France—were less disappointed than the rest, for the simple reason that their two 10HP motor-cars could be quickly sold to a willing Mandarin, as the first of what they hoped would be a long, lucrative line of exported French automobiles.

The Navigators' meeting was scheduled for 3:00 P.M. back at the hotel. Drivers didn't have to attend, but since Linda and I would be sharing duties, we both wanted to go. We took a taxi back, arriving just as the meeting started.

Young introduced the organization staff, from young and pretty Sarah Catt, who would handle all the accommodations arrangements, to the Marshalls or Clerks of the Course: John Vipond, Martin Clark and Colin Francis. Each man was in charge of one leg and all three had years of experience driving, navigating and clerking in rallies, classic and otherwise. Another head staffer, Michael Summerfield, a barrel-chested Brit with close-cropped white hair, looked familiar; he had clerked on the London-Sydney Marathon, and I'd seen him in that nervous-making video.

It quickly became apparent from the questions being asked that by far the majority of participants had never rallied before at all. The organizers answered a bit impatiently, often repeating that we should all re-read the regulations. Many questions pertained to abbreviations in the road books (S/O for straight-on, SP for signpost, etc.); Linda and I had figured out all the abbreviations except one. I raised my hand and asked what PSB stood for. Philip answered, though he made me feel like an idiot for asking: Public Security Bureau, bureaucratic Chinese for police.

Another great area of contention was the accuracy of the maps posted on the wall of the rally office. Linda and I hadn't yet compared our markings with those in the office, but others had noted a number of discrepancies. Which are correct, someone asked, the posted maps or the road books? John Vipond stressed that the road books are "gospel," and apologized for the errors, assuring us that corrected China and Greece maps would be up tomorrow.

As for rewards, everyone who made it to the end would receive a "Finisher" medal. Gold medals would go only to those who had met every TC within the two-hour-lateness window, and had received a stamp from every TC and PC (passage control, a checkpoint that didn't depend on the clock. This was a device used to insure participants drove the proper route). Silver medals would go to those who missed one or more stamps, and Bronze to those who at least gathered "in" and "out" stamps at the beginnings and ends of each major leg: Peking to Kathmandu, Kathmandu to Istanbul, then Istanbul to Paris. There'd be no penalty for early arrival at any TC, as long as we waited twenty-five meters or more before the TC, until the proper time. This would make life a lot easier; in the States, most rallies penalize those who arrive early and stop anywhere within 100 yards of a TC. For the Peking to Paris, we'd be able to drive as fast as we wanted and relax at the TC, instead of having to watch our speed all the way down to the last kilometer.

Arriving early was one thing, but checking in too early at the TC would earn double penalties—one minute early counted as two penalty points. The idea was to arrive early but not get your stamp until exactly the right moment.

There'd also be a few special prizes, including one called the *Coupe des Dames*. The Women's Cup has a long history in rallying. Women had been navigating in the Monte Carlo Rally since the first one took place in 1911, but no women drivers, or all-women teams, registered until the fourth Monte Carlo in 1925. That year, a Madame Mertens drove her Lancia from Tunisia to Monte Carlo and came within five points of first-overall (points were not figured by time alone; an arcane system of handicaps awarded extra points for every passenger; thus a six-passenger Renault finished behind Mme. Mertens, but took first prize). The following year a woman in a Citroën took third overall (three points behind second) and another *femme-pilote* finished fourth overall. In 1927, the organizers decided to recognize women with their own cup, creating first, second, and third place *Coupes des Dames*.

In France at the time (unlike in most of the rest of the world) women were not excluded from most forms of motorsports, so the new cups caused little controversy. Only later did the existence of the Women's Cups—and separate series of women-only races—become an issue of debate. Some say they demean women competitors by setting them apart, implying that women would never otherwise win a "real" trophy or a "real" race; other women believe the Cup is one of the few forms of recognition women receive in a sport still overwhelmingly controlled by men, and those women-only races redress the balance a little by giving women more track time.

As I sat in that meeting, I remembered the Gull's morning interview. Did they assume they'd win the Women's Cup by default, as the only women-only team in the rally? If so, they were in for a big surprise.

Our second big meeting followed at 8:00 P.M. This "drivers' meeting" was required of all participants. The grand ballroom of the hotel was now filled to capacity, as just about everyone had finally arrived.

Young started the meeting with the ominous news that twenty-one separate landslides resulting from the recent monsoons had closed the border between Tibet and Nepal. Crews were already at work trying to clear it, he said, but he couldn't guarantee the road would be cleared in time. Talking quickly, Young spent the next few minutes describing the rest of the route. The serious climbing would start in Golmud, the trading town that marked the eastern edge of the Tibetan plateau, but that would be nothing compared to the stretch after Lhasa. There would be two high passes in the one day between Xigatse and Tingri, both over sixteen thousand feet. Assuming we could all get out of Tibet on schedule, there would then be twenty-two Nepali rivers to cross, and thanks to those same monsoons, only nine had bridges.

Then, abruptly changing his tone, Young launched into a scathing diatribe decrying the excess baggage packed into every car. "You are all overweight! You'll never get up the mountains with all the garbage you're carting along!" He strongly suggested everyone cut their loads by half before Saturday's 6:00 A.M. start.

Then he introduced the staff: the clerks we'd met earlier, plus the twenty-odd other people who would be serving as timekeepers, mechanics, and emergency crews. These included "Jingers," an ace mechanic who always wore shorts; Mike Leahy, a young mechanic with a degree in urology; Tony Fowkes, a Paris-Dakar veteran; Mark Thake, a mechanic and paramedic from the Royal Army Medical Corp; Mick O'Malley, an ex-pat Brit who lived in Kathmandu; and Rick Bate, another paramedic-mechanic from Wales. These men would be driving the route in four brand-new four-wheel-drive Vauxhall Fronteras (Vauxhall is the British division of GM) and one Land Rover Discovery, all equipped with medical and mechanical gear, including heavy-duty towing poles. There were strict rules about using the mechanics' time: no more than ten minutes' assistance to any one vehicle per day. Otherwise, Philip warned, the crew would never get any sleep, much less have time to drive the full distance. That meant that if a breakdown was serious, all we could expect would be a tow to the nearest town or TC. Philip allowed a short question and answer period, but Vic summed that up in his journal: "At the navigator's meeting several questions were asked and the organizers said 'We'll cover that at the full briefing tonight.' Then the same question was asked at eight and the response was 'that question was asked and answered at three. Let's move on now.'"

David Burlinson, British representative of the China Travel Service and the man responsible for making most of the arrangements with Chinese officials, then offered a description of Chinese traffic laws—110 kph (68 mph) speed limit on highways, 80 kph (50 mph) regular roads, 40 kph (25 mph) on urban—and police attitudes. We should always honk and flash lights before overtaking, he said. Chinese trucks have no mirrors and won't be looking for us in any case. Most pedestrians won't expect cars at all—they're still a rarity in rural China—so never assume someone will see you and move out of the way. In fact, children would be likely to run *at* us, he warned, unaware of the grave danger they faced.

Then it was the doctor's turn. Greg Williams gave us a long list of danger signs for altitude sickness. Linda and I had obtained vaccinations for tetanus, polio, hepatitis A, typhoid, meningitis and diphtheria, and we brought along prescription preventatives for malaria and altitude sickness. We also had a suitcase full of every kind of over-the-counter pain reliever and first aid item we could think of. We were well prepared, but the doctor double-stressed the seriousness of watching for altitude sickness's warning signs. I'd just read Jon Krakauer's *Into Thin Air,* (sent by my father, of course) in which altitude sickness and bad weather had overcome most of a group of twenty climbers when, in their pursuit of Everest's summit, they'd ignored the signs. Five climbers had died, a sixth was horribly frostbitten. I carefully wrote down all the signs.

[FRIDAY, SEPTEMBER 5]

Drew Fellman, the Discovery photographer, wanted to get a picture of all the American competitors in front of the huge portrait of Mao in Tiananmen Square at 8:30 Friday morning. Only thirteen of us made it, including Linda and me, Burt and Rich, Team Retro, Pat and Mary Brooks, and Chic and Arlene Kleptz. Carl Schneider's co-driver Don Jones was there; it was one of our first opportunities to talk. We laughed about our respective sizes—he being bigger, in every dimension, than me and everyone else, hence his nickname, "Too Tall Jones." The last man in the picture was Casper Noz, an expatriate Dutchman who lived in California.

Casper was still angry about Wednesday. His dad's 1928 Ford Model A Pickup had overheated trying to keep up with the too-fast pace set by the Chinese convoy leaders. "How did they expect the old cars to drive that fast?" he protested.

We were due for official check-in at the rally office at 10:30 A.M. The walls of this hotel conference room were lined with all the maps, put together contiguously so you could follow the route, almost without break, by walking around the room. Competitors stood shoulder-to-shoulder, marking their own maps; it seemed crazy to me that they hadn't done it before now. Linda and I had only had difficulty with two sections—one in Iran and one in Greece—so we double-checked these while we waited our turn.

Once checked in, we packed everything except the few items we'd need for that last night and took them back to the Agricultural Center. It didn't take us long to pack the car. Even now, with almost everything in, we had far less cargo than everyone else. This made me nervous. Were we making a big mistake traveling so light? Clearly the men who prepped our car had taken lightness seriously; perhaps that's why we had practically no spare parts.

Borghese, on the other hand, had packed his Itala with a large fitted tool-case crammed with spare parts and had another complete set of spares shipped by railway to Omsk, Siberia, about four thousand miles from Peking. He carried a dozen tires and inner tubes strapped to the Itala's rear, and had Pirelli send further consignments of tires to Irkutsk (on the western shores of Siberia's Lake Baikal) and to stations every one thousand miles between there and Paris. This turned out to be overkill—two of those standard Pirelli tires ran for five thousand miles each.

The problem of weight did not occur to Borghese until he had scouted the first 160 miles of the route and confirmed that the car could not pass without the assistance of porters—men and oxen—to pull it up and hold it back on steep descents. At the Italian Legation, he watched the gang of laborers he had hired attempt to pull the Itala. Using bamboo poles, planks and crowbars, the group barely lifted the two-ton car off the ground before they collapsed. The gang's foreman demanded that the car be lightened. Borghese immediately had his mechanic remove the entire upper body, the two extra fuel tanks, and the heavy tool-case. They loaded the gear into three carts, and Borghese arranged for it all to be delivered to the point approximately seven days away, on the other side of the mountains. The Itala had been lightened by about one thousand pounds.

Weight was a critical issue for Burt and Rich in their Citroën 2CV. The two-cylinder car's tiny 600cc engine simply couldn't push the car fast enough weighted down. Leaving Tianjin, they'd discovered that their top speed fully loaded was only 45 mph—a slow journey on the flat, a crawling, miserable pace climbing any mountain. They jettisoned considerable weight, asking us to carry a case of oil for them. We complied, shoving their case behind the driver seat.

Philip's diatribe at the meeting certainly had an effect: everyone—except us—disposed of huge quantities of stuff. Team Retro eliminated over one hundred pounds. The pile of jetsam at the Agricultural Center grew to twenty feet long by ten feet high.

Once we'd convinced ourselves not to worry about the Hillman's weight, we began to worry about the Nepali rivers. Everyone was talking about it; twenty-two rivers with water as high as two meters. You'd never make it across, everyone agreed, without a snorkel for the exhaust, some kind of tubing to get the end up out of the water. We were also warned to disconnect the fan and cover every electrical connection with plastic or rubber. We already had a semi-permanent booty over our distributor, the only major electrical item that hung low in the engine compartment. But we didn't have anything

for the exhaust, so the snorkel made sense.

Burt and Rich took off their Citroën's tiny exhaust pipe; our much bigger pipe wasn't so easily removed, so we drew a circle the proper size onto a piece of paper. We had the rally's Chinese assistant write the characters for exhaust pipe beside it, and set off with Rich for Nansanlitun Lu.

Someone had told Rich the street name, and shown it to him on the map. We found a street lined on both sides with auto parts stores, narrow but deep shops with their doors open to the street. These were all small family operations; men, women and children lounged in the warm summer air in front of their shops, or snoozed behind the counters inside. Some of the women were still cooking, eating, or cleaning up lunch, mounds of noodles in big woks on hot plates sitting on the pavement right outside the shop doors.

We stopped whenever we saw rows of rubber hoses, in bins or hanging from the ceiling, using our notes and sign language to test out the various sizes. I had an odd sense of déjà vû—despite the Chinese sounds and smells all around me, it reminded me of going to Italy the first time with Chris to buy parts for our old Fiats; our Italian was minimal so we had to point to pictures in the parts books to explain what we wanted. Linda and I couldn't find a hose that fit, but we decided to buy a beaded seat cover. We had examined velvet cushions lined with alabaster beads in a shop behind the Forbidden City; the beads were amazingly cool to the touch, and somehow stayed cool when one sat upon them. We hoped the cheap plastic ones would work as well.

After dinner that night, I called Chris and the kids. I had made sure Chris had all the phone numbers for the hotels along the route so he could call me, and I promised to call every rest day. Calling home from far away is hard for me; it makes me miss my husband and children so terribly to hear their voices. On this last night before the race, though, their relaxed, happy voices soothed my anxious nerves.

Still, I was anything but relaxed. The alarm was set for 4:00 A.M. The buses would depart for the Agricultural Center at 5:00, and we were supposed to be on the road to the Great Wall at 6:00. There was no way either Linda or I would sleep without help. She took a Halcion and I took a Melatonin, but I still lay awake until after midnight. I couldn't believe it was finally going to begin.

CHAPTER

8

I followed it on foot, running and shouting, uselessly, "Stop! Stop!"

BEIJING TO ZHANG JIAKOU
[SATURDAY, SEPTEMBER 6]

W ell before 3:00 A.M., the electric teapot in our room began its nightly
explosions, shooting boiling water and steam up through every open-
ing. The noise woke me, and I tossed and turned and sat up to look at
the clock just as the alarm rang. Then a wake up call came at 4:15—the organizers must have asked the hotel to ring everyone up. I was down at breakfast by 4:40;
Linda was already there. We were ready for the bus by 5:00; it was still dark as we
walked down the hill to board. Ann had risen early too; a separate bus would take
her and other crews' family members off to the Great Wall. Since we would have
to get our cars from the Agricultural Center, our relatives would beat us there.

With our overnight bags thrown in, the Hillman suddenly seemed over laden,
and I worried that we had, after all, packed too much. But there was no time to
do anything about it. We were slated to drive out of the Agricultural Center two
cars at a time in one-minute intervals. The press and the Chinese thought our
starting line would be at the Great Wall of China later in the morning. That was
actually just a ceremonial start; the real start was right here in Beijing. We were
waved out at exactly 6:54.

Linda drove, I navigated, though there was no navigating to do (other than
academic kilometer calculations) since we were all in close convoy behind the
PSB. We got out of Beijing quickly on a major boulevard, passing miles of skyscrapers, huge apartment buildings, and new construction spreading out from
the city. The roof line finally fell to suburb levels, then the first signs of hills and
trees presaged our first view of the *Wan Li Chang Cheng,* the Great Wall. It
wound in chunks around the hills; it didn't seem continuous. Finally we popped
through a series of arches (which our road book declared to be replicas), past a
life-size "Plastic Policeman"—he certainly looked real from a distance, which

64

was obviously the point—and just past a Kentucky Fried Chicken restaurant into our first Time Control.

In 1907, Borghese's car had approached the first grand arch of the Great Wall behind a mule, a horse, an old white donkey, and a crew of coolies. Borghese, his brother the Italian ambassador to China, and Barzini rode alongside on donkeys so short their great overcoats completely enveloped the animals and skimmed the dusty earth. Ettore the mechanic stood upon the car, aiming it and hooting the horn to instruct the crew: one toot for go, two for stop. Behind them on horseback rode their translator, an Italian from the Legation. He wore a ribbon-bedecked hat that Barzini said "acquired the coquettish look of a lady's hat *Directoire* style. . . . Surely no odder cortège than this can have ever filed through the narrow passes of the Chinese Great Wall."

Ninety years later, the parking lot at Badaling was packed full of Chinese press and well-wishers as our own odd cortège filed through. This is now the most visited spot in China—the portion of the Wall closest to Beijing—and therefore probably the tackiest tourist trap in all Asia. Still, the high granite-gray wall behind our sea of colorful cars vanquished the souvenir shops and T-shirt vendors with its undeniable grandeur.

Since no one was sure exactly when we were going to take off again, we all gazed longingly at the Wall, but did not climb it. The main route up was blocked in any case; speeches were being made at the top of the grand staircase. Some twenty VIPs stood behind Philip Young at the microphone, and hundreds of media people and spectators filled the steps that ranged down to our parking lot. A huge red banner of tied-together balloons formed an arch over car #1, Lord Montagu's 1915 Vauxhall. Traditional Chinese musicians and drummers accompanying a dragon dancer circled Montagu's car; their atonal music clashed horribly with a modern marching band of some sixty young Chinese, blaring on horns just yards away.

Our cars were parked, fender-to-fender and bumper-to-bumper, in numerical order. Behind us, Nigel and Paula Broderick drove #52, a 1965 British Ford they called "Arnie the Eco-Flow Anglia." Their mates John and Simon Catt, a father and son team, were ahead of us in the #50 Ford Cortina sedan. These four Britons would bracket us for the first few days, as the Chinese kept us in a convoy in strict number order. Paula, with short dark hair and pretty blue eyes, was friendly but serious. She and her husband Nigel, producers of magnetic fuel-saving devices in Cornwall, were veterans of several tough English and European rallies. Though they weren't technically a team, they'd become friendly with the blond, athletic Catts in #50 at some of those events. "You won't mind if we overtake you now and again, will you? So we can ride together?" she asked, laughing. "Of course not," I answered. It is a strict rule (sometimes unspoken) in any rally or race, that slower cars must courteously allow faster competitors by. Blocking a pass is very bad form.

Nearby we found Rich and Burt in their #41 Citroën. Burt stood atop the small car, taking photographs of the incongruous meeting of classic cars and ancient wall. I wondered where the Jeepsters were, and if they'd found a replace-ment for their five-dollar brass fitting. It seemed like we had plenty of time, so I gave my camera to Ann and asked her to get some parting shots of the three guys from Arizona. Soon after she'd gone, people started getting in their cars. Motors started up and the cars started leaving. Philip waved to us, and said "Pull out!"

"Wait!" I yelled. "My mom has my camera!" I jumped out of the car and ran back toward where Ann must be—I'd forgotten that the Jeepsters were #99, the very last car. I found her, grabbed the camera, gave her a hug goodbye, and turned around.

The Hillman was gone. Linda was gone. Completely. Not just pulled over . . . gone.

I ran like a maniac down the hillside and under the balloon arch, swearing at the rally cars passing me on the right and left. My sandals were flapping— I hadn't thought I would need running shoes—the camera banged my chest and I was getting winded even though it was down hill. I couldn't keep run-ning. I turned around and planted myself in the middle of the lane and waved my arms frantically.

The car that screeched to a stop in front of me was a Chinese-marked station wagon. I didn't know if it belonged to the organizers or the PSB. I yelled, "You've got to take me down the hill, my co-driver left without me!" I climbed in next to a Chinese man with a walkie-talkie. In the front passenger seat, thank God, sat David Burlinson, the tour guide. He translated for me, and the Chinese man rat-tled into his walkie-talkie trying to find out if the red #51 had turned around to get me or was still ahead. Nobody knew. Burlinson couldn't believe she'd gone ahead. "I'm sure she's back there waiting for you," he said, and started to tell the Chinese driver to turn around.

"No," I shouted, "She's ahead. She's right in front of a bright yellow 2CV. Look for the 2CV!" I shouted from the back seat. The yellow 2CV was #53, and it belonged to a couple of Italians. At that the Chinese driver stepped on it, and he had no fear. He overtook one rally car after the other. I couldn't believe how far behind I'd already fallen. Finally, a spot of yellow appeared in the distance. Everyone was flying, but somehow our speeding Chinese station wagon, driving mostly in the oncoming lane, caught up.

The driver pulled the car out beside the Hillman, matching Linda's speed as he stayed in the oncoming lane, and Burlinson leaned out his window.

"Are you missing something?" he yelled.

Linda looked over, utterly surprised. She drove on a bit, then pulled over. I jumped out, yanked open the passenger door, and jumped into the Hillman. I was still panting noisily—from the run and shock—and Linda said nothing. Her face betrayed no emotion. Nothing at all. She immediately pulled back into the traf-fic, behind car #90, an Australian Chevy.

After what seemed a long silence, but may have been no longer than a nano-second, she said, "I was trying to figure out how to tell everybody I lost my co-driver. I figured you'd find a way to catch up."

I sat quietly for several hundred kilometers.

I supposed she had no choice. When Philip and the PSB say go, you go. But I did find out later that another car had been told to go without its co-driver. It was Phil Bowen and his partner Jane King/Rosie Thomas in a Volvo Amazon. Jane is a best-selling author (Rosie Thomas is her pen name) in England. Phil was her driver/mechanic, and Jane was in the loo when he had to take off. But Phil circled around and picked Jane up. The PSB were annoyed, but Jane didn't have to jog six kilometers and jump in front of a speeding station wagon to catch up.

Still, it was a good lesson for me: *never let your co-driver out of sight!* I forgave her by the time we hit the first TC.

Later, Linda told me that as she drove down that hill alone, she was angry too—what a chaotic, disorganized way to start the rally! And we'd been cheated out of a chance to see the top of the Great Wall. Was this a sign of what the next forty-three days would hold?

Once my heart rate was back to normal, I was able to enjoy the view. The sunburnt strip malls—low brick buildings, often black from coal—grew progressively thinner the farther we got from Beijing. Several towns were simply extended coal depots: huge mounds of black rock and dust, black-sided low buildings; men, women and children covered in black dust, carrying black burdens on their backs or heads (the weight-bearing straps pressed against their foreheads), the street black mud. Twenty kilometers out of the "trucker's stop" of Huailai, the road book alerted us to "Satanic Mills on left." The twin cooling towers looked like a huge steel plant or nuclear power plant in the dim, polluted air. More towers, belching orange-black smoke, lined the remainder of the road into Zhang Jiakou, our stop for the night.

Just before the town we had to stop—with the whole convoy—for gas. The coal dust air had cleared a bit, and the arid mountains were now clear; the topography was reminiscent of the Superstition Mountains on the outskirts of Phoenix, Arizona. The weather was similar, too: incredibly hot, though more humid here. The wait, while all ninety-three cars got free gas (part of that ten-thousand pounds per car), stretched over several hours. We were entertainment for the locals, some of whom had boxes full of bottled ice water or Popsicles, mounted on their bikes. I tried a strange-tasting purple Popsicle this time—perhaps creamed eggplant?

After we'd filled the tank, we waited again while the police lined us up for the convoy to the hotel. We drove very slowly through the throng of people crowding the entrance to our parc fermé, a dirt soccer field in a low area behind our hotel. The people were held back at the gate by at least ten policemen; one policeman opened the gate to let us out while the others struggled to keep the townspeople from squirming through. The crowds had started to build in the larger towns after we cleared the worst of the coal region, where everyone had been too burdened with their loads to register our passage. By Zhang Jiakou, the PSB were kept very busy managing the crowds.

The exterior of our ten-story glass-and-steel hotel looked great, but inside were filthy rooms. Ours wasn't that bad, except for the two inches of dirty water on the bathroom floor. Many of the participants were vocal in their disgust; the Iranians, for instance, vowed to sleep in their cars.

We set out to explore Zhang Jiakou, a medium-sized city of 600,000. We were thirsty, so we stepped into the first shop outside the hotel. The saleswoman was prepared for us: liter bottles of warm beer stood ready on the counter. We walked around town drinking the beer right out of the bottle. The streets were wide, full of cycles and mopeds, the sidewalks full of people. Men squatted on the sidewalk playing checkers; others walked with larks and canaries in cages, airing their birds. Streamers and hanging lanterns decorated the streetlights, as if the town were preparing for a big holiday. Don Jones, whom I came to think of as Info-Don for his amazing store of demographic, geographic, and political information, had mentioned that the Party Congress was going to happen on September twelfth. This was the communist government's biggest deal, like our political party conventions, only proportionately larger given China's huge population. Perhaps the banners were in its honor.

Outside the hotel, the ralliers sat on the stairs and smoked, drank, and talked. Lord Montagu's mechanic, Doug Hill, worked frantically on his 1915 Prince Henry Vauxhall, car #1 in the rally. A fan bolt had broken off only five kilometers out from the Great Wall, shooting through the radiator and inflicting serious damage. Roy, the riding mechanic for Mr. Sparkle, lent a hand, but both mechanics were clearly struggling. Edward Lord Montagu of Beaulieu was the poster boy of the rally; he'd been instrumental in assisting on the diplomatic end of the political arrangements. His home in England, the Beaulieu Palace House, had been in the family since 1538; before that, the nearby thirteenth century abbey dominated the grounds. His father, the Second Baron Montagu, had been a motoring pioneer; his purchases were the foundation of the large collection now housed in Britain's National Motor Museum, a modern building just down the path from the Palace House.

I first saw Lord Montagu when we rode the same crowded Beijing elevator in which I spoke to Prince Idris Shah of Malaysia. I was asking the Prince if I could interview him someday when we were both back in California. The doors opened and we spilled out into the hotel lobby. The Prince pointed at a gray-haired, sixtyish man walking away from us and said, "Have you interviewed him yet?"

"No," I said. "Who's he?"

"That's Lord Montagu. If you write about cars, you should really talk to him."

I still hadn't spoken to him, and here in Zhang Jiakou, he looked utterly distressed about the fate of his automobile. Our interview would have to wait.

Another auto had failed only a few kilometers further than Montagu's. The Noz's 1928 Ford A Pickup, the same one that had overheated on the way in from Tianjin, overheated again, this time damaging the engine beyond repair. The father and son were sending the car home, but hoped to continue the rally somehow themselves. They were asking everyone in Zhang Jiakou for a ride. Without a back seat, Linda and I couldn't be of any assistance.

Car #2 carried a character who called himself Hermann the German. His was the oldest car, the white 1907 9400cc La France. This chain-driven open road-ster (a chain transferred energy to the wheels, instead of a driveshaft) rode on four wooden-spoked wheels that, if not soaked periodically, would shrink. Hermann Layher, owner of the Sinsheim and Speyer Auto-Technik Museums in Germany—amusement parks loaded with every kind of car, truck, train, and air-plane, along with video games and IMAX screens—was one of the most flam-boyant entrants in the rally. He wore white driving suits to match his white car, period headgear, and spoke loudly, joking and laughing often. The side of his car was painted with the word *Funkenblitzen;* when the side panel was lowered to gain access to the engine, the words *Oh Shit!* appeared in the same gothic script.

After dinner at the hotel, we sat with Michael Veys and Eric Christiansen drink-ing beers at a sidewalk cafe right across from a row of outdoor pool tables. The pool looked like serious business; the balls clacked and the Chinese players laughed and shouted out their syncopated syllables throughout our stay. Earlier, Vic, Andy, and Ted of Team Retro had shot a game of pool against the local pool shark. "We all lost," Vic said, "but we drew such a crowd we had traffic tied up in the streets."

CHAPTER

❧ 9 ❧

The great longings of the Western soul, its strength, the true secret of all its progress, is embodied in the short word—faster! Our life is pursued by this violent desire, this painful insatiability, this sublime obsession—faster!

ZHANG JIAKOU TO WEST BAOTOU
[SUNDAY, SEPTEMBER 7]

The following morning, out in the lobby on the official Rally message board, Linda and I discovered that, along with the regular notices of road book changes and start times, there was a memo from Philip. This note once again harped on the weight theme, and then added:

> *This suggestion has been taken quite seriously by the ladies team in car #51. To ensure maximum lightness, the two have agreed to share one tube of toothpaste and one toothbrush.*

Philip had never spoken to either of us about toothpaste or anything else—this was his idea of a joke. I heard about the note before I saw it, when I introduced myself to David and Sheila Morris, Welsh drivers of a beige '56 Austin A90 they called Mr. Blobby. Sheila said, "Oh! So you're the one with the toothbrush are you? I wondered if there was another ladies' team. I think a lot of us didn't know about you two."

Jokes aside, Philip wasn't complaining about weight for nothing. Several cars were incredibly over packed with many questionable items. Mark Fortune, for one, admitted that his mom and dad must've been batty when they packed the car. Their '55 Chevy Bel Air, loaded back home before they'd had to drop out and pass the torch to Bud Risser, contained a Warehouse-Club-size package of toilet paper—twenty-four rolls. They had over three hundred rolls of film, enough toiletries to stock a drug store, and sufficient food for a forty-five-day camping expedition. Much of this had to be jettisoned and donated to the locals. Some items, like their battery charger and oxygen generator, CD players and a large selection of CDs, stayed. They had a full selection of tools that

was the envy of every mechanic on the event.

I was envious of that CD player. Linda and I didn't even have a radio.

Out time that morning was 5:30 A.M., "due to unforeseen circumstances," the posted bulletin said. Rumor had it that meant the PSB didn't want us sticking around. We weren't certain what was bothering them; everywhere we went, the people seemed pleased to see us; we didn't seem to be creating any political difficulties. Perhaps it was the simple fact that we had the ability—in our own private vehicles—to go whereever we wanted, when we wanted. Rushing us out early and insisting we remain in tight convoys lessened that ability a great deal.

Thanks to the convoy, several TCs were canceled, and we'd been warned to stay with our cars, as the police could "restart with little notice and expect everybody to follow promptly." It was slow going at first. West of Zhang Jiakou the roads deteriorated, becoming dirt through the villages and over the many road construction sites. We were now entering the province of Inner Mongolia, and along both sides of the road, the housing was exclusively low, crowded *hutongs*. Sometimes we could catch a glimpse of the interior; behind the bland mud-colored outer walls, bright whites, reds, and golds sparkled in the sunlight. Barzini had noticed this same phenomenon back in 1907: "The outer walls of their houses are rough, all alike, bare and grey, because the Chinese never displays his wealth to the passer-by. But through every open door we could see the interior of spacious gay-looking courtyards . . . long spirals of brightly-colored dragons and monsters . . . all the showy display of figures and words which in China have the duty of repelling ill-fortune and of welcoming good."

Now that the grubby coal towns were behind us, the landscape became beautiful. The terrain was grassy and treeless, and climbed continually over a 4,500-foot summit, but then settled down at about three thousand feet above sea level. Signs of the old China became visible—Mao suits on older people, barley fields worked with single-blade ploughs pulled by oxen—and the first signs of darker-skinned Mongols and other minorities. The terraced grain fields climbed hillsides, camels appeared, often saddled and employed as work animals or for transportation. Women, children and men crouched together, working in their wheat fields along the Yellow River, which we followed most of the afternoon. Our effect on these farm families was amazing. They dropped their hoes, and ran up to the road to get a closer look at us. Smiling happy throngs of people met us in every town, usually crowding so close that we had to crawl at three or four miles per hour. Beautiful children shouted thousands of "Hellos"—Chinese are required to take six years of English in school. They must have relished this rare opportunity to practice.

This was my first day driving, and Linda's first navigating. The road book was useless until we got to a toll booth; three-quarters of the day was basically unnavigable. It mattered little, since we were in convoy, but Linda was upset.

This was her first-ever rally, and she'd been told repeatedly that the road book was "gospel." How could she learn to navigate properly if the gospel couldn't be trusted?

It wasn't just the navigation that upset her. Differences in our personalities were now becoming evident. I'm a talker in most circumstances; when I'm on the road, I talk all the time. I've always traveled with others (never in big tour groups but always with at least one to four other people) and I'm used to filling the silence with innocuous conversation, saying things like, "Wow, look at that camel!" It's thoroughly useless, wasted breath, I admit, but Linda's the first travel companion I've ever had who found it irritating. When the road book proved itself completely wrong for the fourth or fifth time—saying "Right" instead of "Left," or having ridiculously wrong kilometer figures—I started to joke about it. She got very angry.

"I have a tendency to babble when I drive," I explained.

"You'll have to stop it," she said.

"You'll have to tell me when it irritates you."

"No! I'm not going to be a taskmistress."

Okay, okay! I thought. I'll just have to train myself to shut up. *Good luck!* I almost said out loud, but I stopped myself.

All of a sudden an unmanned toll gate signaled the beginning of a brand-new, elevated expressway; three wide lanes going straight to the western horizon. The police at the head of the convoy stepped on it, and all the postwar cars followed apace. We ended up riding for several hundred kilometers with the big cars: Don and Carl in the '54 Packard, a British couple in a '49 Cadillac, the three Iranian Peykans, all of us flying as fast as we could go, 75 or 80 mph. I rejoiced in the earsplitting wind noise. It made my innocuous, irritating conversation unnecessary.

Strangely, Chinese soldiers in their green uniforms appeared at regular intervals standing beside the expressway. Was this stretch of new road in need of defense? From whom? Us? Could all this really be just to prevent us from driving off in an unauthorized direction?

Too-Tall Don calculated that some five thousand army officers had lined our route that day. "Imagine," he said, "if you drove from Kansas City to Denver—similar terrain and a similar distance—and every three miles there was a police officer just standing there." His interpretation was that it was no more than an excuse for the locals to get in on the action. "Not very much happens in Inner Mongolia," he said. "The only significant thing happening was our Peking to Paris Motor Challenge. So we were an excuse for the local troops to get involved, to help us find our way and be sure we didn't get off the prescribed route." Since a significant portion of China's population—as many as eight million people—are employed as public safety officials, or are in the military, there were a lot of bored soldiers available for the job.

Prince Borghese experienced a similar kind of military accompaniment on his journey, but not until he neared Moscow. In 1907, Russia was in turmoil. The military disaster of the Russo-Japanese War added fuel to the fire of anarchists and revolutionaries who had already been plaguing the Czar for decades. The ignominious defeat at the hands of the Japanese caused formerly patriotic soldiers to desert or turn against their commanders and join what Barzini called "the revolution of 1905." Since then, the military had been in a permanent state of alert, and some of this energy was expended for Prince Borghese's protection. Barzini reported that "thirty versts from Moscow we meet two splendid mounted soldiers whom we take for Cossaks from the Kuban. . . . They are standing still, facing one another, by the side of the street. . . . At every hundred yards other Cossacks guard the road in the same way. It is not long before the conclusion is forced upon us that this guarding of the road is done in our honour, so that we may be sure to find the way free of other traffic, which the sentinels keep to one side of the road."

When Borghese was in Mongolia, the strong, squat horses that brought Genghis Khan to power were still much in evidence. Fascinated by the *chi-cho,* a herd of these horses charged at the Itala and its motley crew. "They seemed to want to annihilate us with one furious charge," Barzini wrote. "They ran with a peculiar mad stampede . . . like a hurricane destroying everything. But at ten yards' distance from us they would suddenly stop with stiffened knees. . . . Then they would start again, running by the side of the car; and would accompany us at a gallop until we had outrun them. . . . There were moments when we were running at a speed of thirty or thirty-five miles an hour. Never had Mongolia been traversed so swiftly."

Just as abruptly as it had begun, our empty expressway ended. It had taken us completely around the provincial capital of Inner Mongolia, Hohhot. In Mongolian *hohhot* translates to "blue city," though many of the majority Han Chinese (Mongolians make up only 15 percent of Inner Mongolia now) mistakenly translate it as "green city." Whether it's green for the grasslands—now mostly devoid of those famous horses—or blue for the clear blue sky, it works: it's the capital of the sunniest region in northern China.

We lined up back in convoy for the fueling and our parade into the industrial, blue-glass-filled town of East Baotou. A bridge across the Yellow River took us quickly into West Baotou, a metropolis with two million inhabitants.

I was tired, and relieved to pull into the grand Tian Wai Tian Hotel (the *E* was burnt out, reminding me of the "Hot–l Baltimore"). My legs were cramped and sore, and had been since about noon. I'd driven from 6:30 A.M. to 3:30 P.M. with only two short breaks, both too short to take the time to pee. And though the

Hillman's racing seats were comfortable, Paul never had succeeded in getting the seat adjuster to work. It was farther back than it had been on that short test-drive in England, but still too close for my long legs. As I splayed my legs wide to keep them on the pedals, my right thigh pressed hard into the high edge of the seat. I could feel the bruise that had already formed.

But this is a not a complaint: I love to drive, even cars built for short people. So I fell into bed right after dinner, exhausted but happy after this first full day behind the wheel.

Whenever we passed through a town we found people awaiting us in the streets to cheer us. We were preceded by the news of our coming. Even in the open country we were often recognized.

WEST BAOTOU TO YINCHUAN
[MONDAY, SEPTEMBER 8]

I started a new thing today. *I'm navigating again, which means I get to play with the calculator and scribble all over the road book. And since Linda doesn't like my small talk, I'm going to babble to my notebook instead,* I wrote in my road journal. It was a great idea, but as the road surface deteriorated, my cryptic sentences written in soft-lead pencil became a set of hash marks looking more like ancient Aramaic than English. The only legible words read:

Bird Nest Iron Gourds and colorful melons for sale in piles along both sides of the road out of Xinbao. Ladies in high heels on bikes. Adobe houses like SW, with ladders to roof. Tall white trees—poplars?—on both sides. Mayhem in Linhe.

It was another 5:30 A.M. start, and though my regular writing schedule makes me religiously opposed to early awakenings, I was actually beginning to enjoy the dawn. The land out of busy Baotou reverted to wide open farm fields, with corn, melons, sunflowers and a few trees, lit by the morning sun and blessed with some kind of ancient Asian serenity. Industrial activity appeared suddenly. The whole village of Xishanzui was caked in red brick dust, and the brick factory belched pollution into the sky. The people carted bricks on bikes, rickshaws, and camels. And then we were back in farmland, with low mud-hut villages; ladders led to wheat and hay drying on the roofs. Soon these changed to the traditional round houses of the Mongolians (*yurtas* in Russian, *gers* in Mongolian). In the villages, the *gers* were made of cement and glass, reminding me of fancy fruit stands in California's Central Valley. Out in the countryside, the *gers* appeared to still be made of clay and cloth or leather. These had not changed much since Borghese's day: "From time to time we saw a *yurta,* low and round, like a beehive," Barzini wrote. "That small grey cupola covered with felt is the habitation of the Asiatic nomad tribes,

of the Kirghese and the Turkomans . . . it alone would suffice to prove the common origin of all the races of the centre of Asia, their common descent from the Great Mongolian trunk."

The Yellow River, or *Hwang Ho,* which runs three thousand miles from its source on the Tibetan Plateau down to the Yellow Sea, was our companion for most of the day. When we drove close to its banks, the tall thin trees, white like poplars, birch or aspens, lined our route. When we rose high into the hills, the river remained visible far below.

The day developed into a battle against two forces: bad roads and huge crowds. In every town and village, we were up against what Don and Carl called the Great Wall of People. They later estimated that from one-half to a full million people stood by the side of the road along the route that day. In Xishanzui they'd been too preoccupied with their bricks to linger long over our parade. It built gradually through Xinbao and Wuhai; then by Linhe, 262 kilometers into the day, it was mayhem. According to our road book, Linhe's tree-lined streets were "colourful and bustling," but all we saw was a writhing wall of faces and hands. This crushing crowd of humanity wasn't hostile, just the opposite; they smiled and yelled "Hello!" and "How are you?" Hands reached into the open window to touch us, and pressed or slapped against the car. At one point, someone even yanked Linda's door open.

The faces of the people had changed substantially since Beijing. In the east, the light-skinned, round-faced Han were dominant. Now we were seeing all kinds of different skin colors and facial features mixed in with the still-plentiful Han, primarily the darker but still Asiatic Mongolians. Closer to the Ningxia region where we ended the day, the Arab- and Indian-looking features of the Muslim Hui became more prevalent. These people are descended from traders who came to China along the Silk Route. The Hui, Han and Mongolians are only three of China's fifty-six different "nationalities."

When crowds of people weren't a challenge, the roads were. About sixty kilometers out of Baotou we hit the first of many bad *wadies*—the Arab word for dip or gully that the British had long ago adopted. The road book instructions for a stretch of only thirty kilometers before Xinbao read:

> !! *BAD WADI* !! *into village*
> !! *Hump backed bridge* !!
> !! *Paved wadi* !!
> !! *Uneven wadi* !!
> !! *Two BAD bumps* !!

Even when they were paved, the roads were treacherous. Our buddies Burt and Rich dropped a wheel in a deep pothole that snapped a suspension joint. They were able to patch it together and drive on, but at a slant. Worse off were the Gulls, whose suspension system also failed—the shock absorbers apparently just gave way. It took some time and help from the mechanics and fellow competitors to cobble together a temporary repair. The Buick from Iowa also had a problem. Too much dust and dirt in the air filter was reputed to be the cause, but the smoke billowing out the tailpipe looked like something more serious to me. A black 1930 Stutz from Canada was out due to electrical problems, and the only Jaguar in the event was suffering from suspension problems. Ted and Vic's #23 Team Retro Ford broke its left-front sway bar mount just before the last checkpoint. "We made quick roadside repairs," Vic told us later in Yinchuan, " then found a small welding shop on the edge of town and fixed it. The shop owner refused payment, but we took our picture with us and him beside the car. The crowd of people that gathered around were *very* envious of him. He may run for mayor."

This was our first day let loose of the PSB convoy; we still had a phalanx of green-coated officers following us or standing along the route, but they no longer dictated when we could start and stop. The rally clock and our own average speeds would now determine that, and the Time Controls and Passage Controls would all matter. This was our first day of true competition.

The PSB had trained us well. We'd gotten into the habit of driving like hell, pausing rarely for very short breaks when the PSB dictated, then driving like hell some more. Now, Linda drove the same way, but our breaks were much longer, as we arrived early at each of the day's three checkpoints (Xinbao, Wuhai, and Yinchuan). Between Linhe and Wuhai, we crossed the Yellow River and rose to grassland intermixed with sand dunes. High atop one of these golden, wind-formed hills, a herd of camels rested with the clear blue sky above and the river snaking away behind them on the plain below. We bought some iced bottled water and more odd Popsicles—the temperature was in the nineties, though the air now was pleasantly dry—at the top of that camel-dusted hill.

We came into Wuhai, a "nothing-special unattractive industrial town," according to our road book, with fifty-six minutes to spare. The heat was intense; there was no shade. The bicycle-cart water vendors had all sold out. The curious residents were gathering in force. The clerks, probably at the strong encouragement of the PSB, took pity on us all, and gave us permission to drive on, rather than wait in the hot sun until our "due time."

From Wuhai, the road led through solid industry and pollution for the last 165 kilometers into Yinchuan, our stop for the night. There we discovered that Lord Montagu, whose #1 Vauxhall was now on its way back to England, had found a ride in the back of Australian John Matheson and Jeanne Eve's 1967 Rolls Royce Phantom V limousine. Our other hitchhikers, the Noz duo, found seats in one of the organizer-mobiles and in the back of the big '55 Chevy Bel Air.

Yinchuan was filled with 860,000 people, a cluster of skyscrapers, and smog. The organizers had advertised that the night's dinner would be something special: Mongolian Hot Pot. We took over a restaurant with large circular tables built around deep cooking pots—an outer pot containing hot water and inner pot containing hot oil or broth. The food was brought to the table raw, and we could pick and choose what we wanted to cook and eat.

There were huge noodles that grew so incredibly slimy when cooked, you couldn't lift them out of the pot once you dropped them in. The mackerel I tossed in cooked well; someone else at the table must have enjoyed it. Across from me, juggling chopsticks and slippery noodles as awkwardly as I, were the members of Team Chocky, an irreverent bunch of Britons driving Bentleys. Adam Hartley and Jonathan Turner piloted Adam's 1929 4 1/2 liter Le Mans. White stick-on letters on the car's British-racing-green door read *TO P? OR NOT TO P?* They were both handsome, not much over thirty, and inveterate jokers. They were apparently already involved in a practical joke war with their teammates, a much more sedate British couple driving a '55 Bentley Continental. Jonathan was also a charmer and audacious flirt; Linda nicknamed him "Dimples."

"Why Chocky?" I asked.

"Simple," Adam answered. "We were all sitting around on a cold evening, drinking hot chocolate, trying to think of a team name. We were holding it right there in our hands: Chocky."

In a moment the courtyard of the Bank seemed transformed into a workshop. Everywhere lay cans of oil and of fuel: screw-wrenches, hammers, tyres, spare parts thrown about in confusion. The cars exposed their shining mechanism to the eye through their open sides, and they gave themselves up meekly to the performance of their toilette.

YINCHUAN TO LANZHOU
[TUESDAY, SEPTEMBER 9]

It was my turn to drive again, and it had become apparent that Linda and I have very different driving styles. I generally wait longer to shift than she does, and it clearly annoyed her. I tend to wait until I can hear the engine tell me it wants to shift. I've noticed my tendency before, when I've tested new cars that are too quiet to hear. Driving by sound is the mark of an Italian car owner—they're the noisiest cars in the world, on purpose (ask any V12 Ferrari owner). The Hillman had a very noisy engine; so noisy, in fact, it reminded me of my husband's favorite Fiat, a 128 he set up for autocross (a type of racing where a twisty course is defined by cones on a large parking lot, and drivers are timed as they drive through the course one at a time. The fastest time wins). The Hillman had a high raspy exhaust note that meant business, and for me, psychologically, it was very comforting.

On top of the shifting issue, I kept forgetting about the overdrive, a thin metal stick that stuck out behind the steering wheel where I was used to finding things like headlight switches and wiper adjusters. This odd stick turned out to be like a fifth gear (our floor-mounted gearshifter only had the standard four plus reverse). From fourth gear, if you flicked that little stick up once, the transmission would drop into overdrive—a nice cruising gear that put less strain on the engine at high speeds. Flick it once downward, and you fell back into the normal fourth gear. I'd never driven a car with a column-mounted overdrive before.

I supposed by now all the other drivers and navigators were ragging on each other about shift points and forgotten overdrives. I wondered if husbands and wives were worse, or better. For me, these discussions were extra tough, because when Linda would say something like "Why don't you shift?" or "Overdrive! Overdrive!" I'd launch into a long explanation. She really didn't want to hear it—she still wanted the car quiet—so then I'd realize belatedly I should just shut up.

When I finally understood how the overdrive worked, I really got into it. We discovered that it worked just as well in third gear, giving us gradations that made the car much more responsive at a variety of speeds.

Linda also acted frightened whenever I passed, and the day was filled with slow trucks and steep grades. I often didn't blame her; she was in the "death-seat" in our right-hand-drive Hillman. It would be an advantage in Nepal, India and Pakistan, where they drove on the left side of the road, but here in China, RHD was a real pain. We had one interchange when I asked "Is it okay to pass?" as I began to pull out. I heard what she said as "Go!" What she actually said was "No!" I stepped on it, then slammed on the brakes and pulled back in, almost shaving the oncoming truck.

"Next time," I said, still recovering, "say 'Stay!' instead of 'No.' Stay, doggie, stay!"

We both laughed at that one. Overall, we seemed to be getting more comfortable with each other. In my journal that night I wrote "Today worked well. Linda only yelled at me once."

We left the Great Wall of People behind in Yinchuan and followed the Yellow River up toward its source, onto sand dunes and mountains, climbing perpetually now on our slow ascent to Tibet. Across the river was the Tenngar Desert, a southern outlet of the great Gobi. We'd skirted the Gobi's southern edge ever since Zhiang Jiakou. This section of high desert reminded me of the Mojave, though there was nothing so grand as a cactus; only scrub, grasses, and sage-like gray-green brush. Still, it had a stark, serene beauty.

When we began to follow the Yellow River back in Baotou, we departed from the route Prince Borghese and his French followers had traveled ninety years before. To avoid the Himalayas, impregnable by any but the hardiest silk-traders, they had to choose a northern or a southern route, and, by force of language and politics, Russia's Siberia was the logical choice. So the 1907 raiders drove directly northwest into what was then Outer Mongolia and is today the independent country of Mongolia, while we modern ralliers followed the old Silk Route and the Yellow River.

In this desert-like stretch, it was hard not to think about Auguste Pons and his troublesome three-wheeler. On the seventh day of their race, all eleven men overnighted together—the first time they had been alone in each other's company—camped on the Mongolian plain. Pons and his co-driver had arrived last, their 6HP Contal having stopped them completely several times the prior day, putting them far behind. They had all agreed back in Peking to convoy as far as Irkutsk (Siberia) so that they could assist each other with any breakdowns or health problems, so Pons' slow speed and continual breakdowns were delaying all the participants. To get a head start, Pons set out at 3:00 a.m. the next morning, straight toward the Gobi Desert. Godard and the two De Dion-Boutons left together a little later. Borghese was last out that day, delayed by his efforts to secure his luggage, which kept falling off the car due to the continual bumping.

The Frenchmen soon caught up to Pons, and they all stayed together until a wide expanse of short-grass prairie tempted the drivers of the larger cars to put their feet down. These conditions were perfect for the Itala, too, and Borghese soon overtook the leading Spyker. Later, Godard reported that Borghese had assured him, calling out from his Itala as he passed, that the Contal was close behind, doing fine. Barzini, however, reported that when they had passed the tri-car, it was stopped. "Pons and his companion had alighted and seemed occupied in the working at something in the engine. The Prince, who was driving, slowed down in order to give help if needed. But after an exchange of greetings Pons told us to go on, saying he did not require anything... and so we got up speed again." In fact, Pons had run out of petrol. The tri-car drivers waited by their car, assuming the others would turn back when they noticed their absence.

That day, though, all the raiders separated, getting lost each in their turn when they lost sight of the telegraph poles that delineated the route. Each assumed that the others had gotten back onto the right track ahead of them. When the four cars gathered at the day's end, they agreed that Pons must've turned back. When that could not be confirmed by telegraph, Jean du Taillis, *Le Matin's* correspondent and Godard's co-driver, arranged for the Chinese telegraph operator to hire horsemen to go back and find the Contal.

Pons and his companion soon realized the situation, and lacking water, began walking. Thirty-six hours later they had walked forty miles, found no food or drink, and collapsed. The nomadic Mongolians found them some hours later, took them to their huts, and nursed them back to health. The Contal was left rusting on the plain.

The Frenchmen, from the day of Pons' disappearance forward, knew that the convoy agreement was effectively void; they were now each on their own. Barzini wrote on the night of Pons' disappearance, "We had no sort of anxiety as to the fate of Pons and of his companion; they were still in the inhabited zone, and could, no doubt, easily find hospitality and help." He and the Prince only learned how close Pons and his companion had come to death upon their arrival in Paris.

As I piloted our Hillman through the desert on the paved but bumpy road, two-humped (Bactrian) camels strolled about on either side of us; these seemed wild, compared to the saddled beasts we'd seen the day before. Yak, those plush, long-haired, long-horned cattle, also began to appear. Out here, most of the people we saw seemed to be involved in roadwork of a very crude sort. Groups of women and children squatted at the side of the road with small hammers, chip-chip-chipping at big rocks, making gravel. Teams of men painted lines down the middle of the road using a piece of string and a board to measure the edges. Where major work was underway, hundreds of men, women and teenagers stood on either side of the raised road, shovels in hand.

Our midday TC was at Zhongwei, a peaceful market town known for the Gao temple, a hodge-podge of wooden towers and statues honoring all three Chinese religions: Buddhism, Confucianism, and Taoism. As we climbed away from the town—our high point that day would be eight thousand feet—the road grew worse, with bad bumps and dips and wadies. I noticed our gas was low, and when Linda, reading aloud from the road book said, "Fuel on right at end of truckers halt," we decided to stop.

The "truckers halt" was not a village, just a broad dusty plain at the top of a long hill, with a few blue Chinese trucks parked on either side of the road. The gas station held two gas pumps, but we couldn't figure out what octane either one was. Free gas was due to be available much later on, but we weren't sure we'd make it through the next long stretch without fueling up now. We filled the tank, gave the helpful woman a handful of Yuan, and immediately on take off the engine pinged so loudly it sounded like pebbles exploding in the carburetors. We had no power whatsoever. I pulled over immediately and dumped a bottle of octane booster in the tank. It helped, but we only had three bottles on board, and if the quality of this gas was a sign of things to come, we'd be needing a whole lot more.

Getting gas was a major trial for Burt and Rich in their Deux-Chevaux. They'd had to abandon the use of their second fuel tank due to the fluid's excessive weight relative to the rest of the car (with both tanks full, the front of the little car lifted right up off the ground). That left them with only a five gallon tank, and even with the car's admirable mileage (probably 40 to 50 mpg unladen), that still limited their range. On that long strange "expressway" on the way to Baotou, when we'd been cruising with Carl and Don's Packard, Burt and Rich had run out of gas repeatedly. The PSB had acted as go-fers, shuttling one of them to and from gas stations with their portable gas can.

Before Lanzhou, the terrain leveled out into wheat-growing plains. But that long sandy stretch had been a trial for at least one of the American teams. The Kleptzes in their Marmon had pulled off the road on what they thought was hard surface, and the heavy motorcar sank right into what turned out to be sand. The support crew towed them up, but a little later their drive shaft broke. The car came into Lanzhou on the hook.

The Lanzhou Legend was a first-class hotel and convention center complex. Lanzhou, the capital of Gansu province, was for centuries a major staging point on the Silk Route. After the Communists put through the railroad, it became a major industrial center. The population of five million (almost the size of Chicago) is crammed into a twenty kilometer stretch of narrow Yellow River valley, walled in by steep mountains on both sides. This means that fumes never escape. Don Jones claimed that Lanzhou has the worst air pollution of any city in the world. "A very successful Chinese businessman, whose hometown this is," Don said, "has vowed to tear down a mountain to allow the wind from the north to come into the city and clean out the air. One of the mountains here is in the process of being washed down."

Lanzhou would host the first of our seven rest days: a chance for rest and repairs before tackling the Himalayas. So breakfast Wednesday morning was the most leisurely since Beijing; I drank more coffee than I'd had since California, and talked with Mary Brooks (of the smoking Buick) and Carl Schneider. Mary was the first person to ask me about my family; I obliged with pictures of my beautiful children and handsome, far away, husband and she in turn showed me pictures of her grown children. Eventually our conversation turned to the rally: what made us do it?

Mary figured we were all adventure seekers and exploration junkies. "I was so disappointed when I learned in third grade that Christopher Columbus had discovered the New World!" She explained, laughing. "I mean, would there be any new worlds left for me to discover when I finally grew up?"

Carl, who was sixty-six, mentioned a writer he'd read as a child, Richard Halliburton, the inventor of the travelogue and author of *Seven League Boots* and *Seven Wonders of the World*. "You read those books," he said, "and you're marked for life."

I had read neither, and in fact, I'd never heard of Halliburton. I had always loved to read about far away places—thus my choice of international relations in college and business school—but my real motivation for the Peking to Paris came from a passion for road trips.

My first road trip was hell for my mother, heaven for me and my three brothers. We were escaping Maryland, where our parents' marriage had failed, and heading toward Beach Boys' paradise: California. I was nine, my brothers were three, six, and eleven. We fought and sang across the USA, counting license plates and dodging our mother's random slaps backward. We had the time of our lives.

Then, at seventeen, I set off with my boyfriend (now husband) Chris in that funky Fiat Multipla. We took what little money we had—my college financial aid check and his bike-shop-mechanic savings—and drove as far north as we could go, to the Arctic Circle in Alaska. We spent four months, wandering as far east as Montana, before turning back toward home.

I had entered college nine months before with the notion that I would go into the Foreign Service. When graduation rolled around, I no longer considered leaving Chris a possibility. We settled down into jobs that allowed us no more than two weeks of travel per year. We filled those with long bicycle tours—several times up or down the California coast, once on a loop around England—or with auto-parts buying trips to Italy.

When our son came along in 1990, the traveling ended as I focused on writing and motherhood. After our daughter, born in 1992, entered preschool, the traveling resumed, though now I was leaving Chris and the kids behind and traveling with a photographer, in search of automobile stories. Though all this travel required some driving, it was too much like work: short jaunts between appointments, always worried about getting somewhere on time. By the time I met

Karen—and thus, Linda—I was ripe for a new, longer road trip.

Many love driving for the physical thrill of it—power over machine, terrain, direction. My own love of driving is so mixed up with my love of riding that I never thought of it that way. It's not the power I love as much as the movement itself. I am happy in a micro-car that barely tops 55 mph; I've been thrilled, too, to careen around a track in a 478HP Ferrari F40. I like the slowly unfolding scenery of the former, the blurred impossibility of the latter. I like the concentration required in the driver's seat, but also enjoy the mind-wandering relaxation offered by the passenger seat. I like elegant cars for their luxury (who wouldn't rather wear velvet than burlap?) but I'm happy driving an economy car because I know that if I toss it around a little recklessly, I can fix it without going broke.

What driving often affords that other forms of transportation don't, is unpredictability and freedom. If you have a full tank of gas, you can go wherever the road leads. Even when you know your final destination, you may not find what you expect when you arrive; you never quite know what you'll come upon next. Virginia Woolf wrote: "What I like, or one of the things I like, about motoring is the sense it gives one of lighting accidentally . . . upon scenes which would have gone on, have always gone on, will go on, unrecorded, save for this chance glimpse. Then it seems to me I am allowed to see the heart of the world uncovered for a moment."

One doesn't arrive "accidently" on a commute or on any too-familiar road. So it's not just any driving that inspires my passion, it's *touring* in its original sense. Auto touring was long ago defined as the opposite of track racing: on tracks you go in circles, on tours you cross some country. Driving to somewhere new, unknown, or unpredictable—that's what you need for the perfect road trip.

I thought it was interesting that Carl Schneider had been inspired by Halliburton; it reminded me of Allen Andrews' book, *The Mad Motorists,* which had inspired Philip Young to bring us all here to this grand hotel in China. Though I was already primed for a road trip when I began reading Luigi Barzini's book, it made a big impression on me. My own trajectory through life had some odd similarities to the paths its two protagonists followed: like Prince Borghese, I'd studied diplomacy; like Barzini, my love of words is matched by my love of travel; like them both, I've studied several languages. I'm no princess or front-page correspondent, but Barzini's book put the Second Peking to Paris into a personal and historic context I couldn't resist.

Out of wonder, or sheer obnoxious curiosity, I spent a good part of that rest day in Lanzhou—when I wasn't under the Hillman—asking people why they had decided to tackle the Peking to Paris. It also gave me an excuse to properly introduce myself to the Gulls, Francesca and Jennifer, later that evening. Francesca credited no particular book; her answer was short, sweet and somehow British in its ambiguity: "Seemed like the thing to do, didn't it?"

She was tired, though relieved, after a long day of struggling with the car. Their Volvo—which they'd nicknamed Gordon after Gordon Bennett, an American who'd moved to England and made a name for himself as a racer—had been lucky enough to get one of the four garage spots available in Lanzhou. Their list of troubles was long. Aside from the serious suspension problems already noted, they had an antifreeze leak and a fuel feed problem (when they filled up, they had to rock the car up and down to get the gas to flow down, a slow and exhausting process). So far, they'd been late seventeen minutes at the various TCs. Since each minute counted as a penalty, they had dropped down in the posted rankings to tenth place. Every rest day the official rankings were posted in the hotel lobby. At Lanzhou, I read that fifty-four cars (including our Hillman) remained unpenalized; fifty-four contestants were tied for first place. So though seventeen minutes and tenth place doesn't sound so bad, the Gulls were now behind sixty-three other cars.

A few others had suffered equal or worse penalties. The Kleptzes' dive into the sand had cost them four hours and twenty-four minutes, putting them second to last (only the Canadian Stutz, which had now retired and gone back to Beijing, had more penalties). The Marmon's drive shaft lay spread out on the pavement behind the hotel when I caught up with Arlene; Chic had been off for several hours, looking for someone to fabricate a tiny joint it needed. "The only plastic piece on this 1919 car," she said, "and it breaks. Go figure!"

Linda and I needed more octane booster, so we hired one of the hotel's concierges to go out looking for it, using our empty bottle as a translation aid. Then I got down under the Hillman and did a visual check. The rough roads had jogged everything loose and we were hearing all kinds of noises; I wanted to make sure nothing serious was getting ready to fall off. All the welds and brackets were intact, but I found the source of our loudest rattle: the exhaust pipe had loosened itself where one section slid into the other. There didn't appear to be any way it could loosen any further, so I let it be. We tightened many hose clamps—they had all worked loose. Every car has a fuel filter, but we had an extra large one with a clear glass bottle attached, so we could keep track of how dirty the fuel got, whether from road conditions or from poor quality gas. The bottle had a wing-nut screw on the bottom that, when loosened, would let the heavier dirt particles drain out. I accidently unscrewed it too far and dumped a gallon or two of gas on the ground, no big loss since it was that rotten seventy octane anyway.

We then raised all four tires' air pressure to forty pounds, checked our two carburetors' oil levels, and rerouted the accelerator cable (one of the Iranians pointed out that its unnatural angle might cause it to rub and break). We examined the contents of the car for anything we could jettison—detritus from other cars now included a portable refrigerator, a complete tool box, and a long, heavy tow chain—but decided we were fine. We were all done with our ministrations by 2:00 P.M.

I treated myself to tea and cake for lunch, sitting on an elevated dais above the lobby, where I could watch the ralliers coming and going. When Rich and Linda reappeared, we set out for a walk. Blocks and blocks of high-rise apartments defined the neighborhood, many trimmed at ground level with row after row of outdoor ping pong tables. We came to the market section and wandered through the sensory overload of its many lanes. After seeing so much fly by at speed, it was a treat to immerse ourselves in the colors, scents and sounds of the market. At first it seemed all a jumble, then we realized that each street or half-street was a "department"—produce here (bok choy and incredibly long string beans, every kind of leafy green); the butchers just down there (their clanging cleavers beat out a morbid rhythm); around the corner for the fishmongers, and seventeen different varieties of egg, from tiny quail to huge speckled things. A whole street of noodles and tofu in unlikely shapes, piles of spices, bright fabrics, and box upon box of buttons, stacks of women's panties and bras, shoes, and on and on.

Every night at dinner, an odd dance took place: ralliers stood or paced slowly with their buffet plates full, wondering where to alight. We'd been on the road together for four days now, and we had yet to form concrete cliques; we were like electrons, shifting about in search of the nucleus. Most, like Linda with her biker buddies Rich and Burt, had at least one pre-existing friend in another crew, to form the core of their first group (though not necessarily their last). Nationality and language were natural attractants, but these lines were still very fluid.

There in Lanzhou, Linda and I ended up with a Dutch woman named Lisa Klokgieters-Lankes, driver of a yellow and black '51 MGYB that we nicknamed "Bumblebee." Somehow she'd accumulated a large store of gossip, and entertained us with her tales. First, she said, two older guys had accidentally switched false teeth. Then one of the older ladies lost her false teeth on an elevator. True or false? Lisa didn't reveal her sources, and it became an ongoing aspect of the journey, trying to determine if a rumor were true or false, especially if it bore upon the running of the rally, or what the organizers were up to. Since Philip himself was known to propagate lies—e.g., our shared toothbrush—it would turn out to be a continual challenge distinguishing fact from fiction.

Lisa also told us this one, which I confirmed later was true: Roberto Chiodi and Fabio Longo from Italy stopped their 1964 Lancia Flavia at a toll gate they thought contained the TC. Fabio walked up, but there was no rally staff, only a group of smiling PSB officers. So Fabio asked "Do you know where I can get the stamp?" in English. The Chinese policeman was thrilled to help, and said, "Of course, I must take you in my car." So the policeman drove Fabio off to a post office three kilometers away. By the time Fabio realized what had happened, the policeman had driven away, leaving Fabio to walk all the way back to the Lancia and his anxious co-driver.

CHAPTER

∽ 12 ∽

The Mongolian people have a poetical superstition, by which they believe that the wind in waving that paper and those flags shakes the written prayer out of them and bears it up to Buddha. In passing over this place the air would therefore be filled with prayers as it is filled with perfume when it passes over flowers.

LANZHOU TO KOKO NOR CAMP
[THURSDAY, SEPTEMBER 11]

Koko Nor is a beautiful and fascinating place. Ten-thousand-six-hundred-twenty feet high, according to the altimeter on Rich Newman's fancy watch, in what used to be the eastern province of Tibet named Amdo, and was now the Chinese province of Qinghai. The current Dalai Lama (the four-teenth) was born in a small village nearby named Takster, just northeast of our stop for the night.

We'd been climbing up the Tibetan Plateau all day, up and over four separate ranges of the Qlian mountains. By evening I could feel the elevation—first in my chest, then a little in my head—though the dull ache might've been caused by the beer I was offered on arrival.

For the first time in the rally we had to struggle to make a TC on time. That morning, we'd come out to our car to find a Lanzhou Legend Hotel key card for room #2104 with a note scribbled on it:

Linda—go like the wind today. Lots of uphill. Today could sort out the leader board. Foot down! I have tightened up rear shock absorbers—can slacken off tonight if too hard. P.

The P. was Philip Young, of course. We didn't know what to make of it. Was this just an impulse to be helpful? Was he developing something of a crush on Linda?

He was right about the day's drive, though. Until now, we'd always been able to maintain a pretty good speed, 55 to 75 mph, except in towns where we had to crawl because of the crowds. Navigation had been simple too, even though the book was miserably unreliable; the way had been made obvious by the thousands

of uniformed police officers lining the route. Today, though, road construction slowed us down dramatically, and 220 kilometers out of Lanzhou, the PSB led us astray. The instructions very clearly said "S/O"—straight on—into the busy provincial capital of Xining, but the policeman standing in the middle of the road forced us left. We turned, law-abiding as we are, and I swiveled around, and watched the Cortina #50 behind us swoop right around the policeman and continue straight.

Now what could we do? Traffic was terrible—the narrow road was thick with trucks, donkey-carts, those three-wheeled half-tractor half-chopper things that carry anything from huge haystacks to twenty or thirty people gripping each other like acrobats. We were completely off the road book. Another policeman waved us off yet again, and at some point I realized they were sending us completely around the town, rather than straight through it.

Linda and I were both upset, but she was driving and she did what any panicked rally driver would do: she stepped on it. As I watched the minutes tick down on the trip meter, she passed for all she was worth, on the left, on the right, zigzagging around slow trucks, taking one long stretch up a hill passing everyone on the dirt shoulder that might've been a sidewalk if Xining had such a thing. She'd gone into motorcycling mode, watching for openings and weaving through without hesitation. We made the checkpoint with only two minutes to spare.

The adrenaline charge of that assault kept us wired through all 240 kilometers of the next stage. Linda kept her foot down full speed all the way to Koko Nor. We were the fourth car into the camp spot, a full hour ahead of our due time. We averaged 72 mph on that last stretch, through blustery rain, over peaks as high as twelve thousand feet. Not bad for a thirty-year-old "fedora on wheels."

There had been plenty to see as we flew down that road. Thirty or so kilometers out of Xining, we trundled over stalks of wheat piled onto the roadway, laid there on purpose for the traffic to thresh. Twenty more kilometers on, in a village named Huangyuan, a herd of shaggy yaks blocked the road. We crawled slowly through them, then took off again. Near the village of Daotanghe, huge haystack tepees lined the fields, and fifty kilometers on, we spotted our first prayer flags, tied to a triangular structure in the distance. Just before the TC, a tiny village named Heimahe consisted of mud huts set back about twenty-five yards from the road on either side. Pigs lived in a muddy area, full of holes and rotting vegetables, between the huts and the road. Two yaks were saddled and tied up on the edge of town, like a bus waiting at the station.

It rained steadily as we set up our tents. Even so, the campsite had a spare, desolate beauty. Rolling moss-green pasture carpeted the ground to the horizon, interrupted only by the slash of silver created by the huge salt lake called Koko Nor by the British, Qinghai by the Chinese. The lake lay a short distance across the road from our campsite. When I squinted, I could just make out a slight shadow above the lake: Bird Island, a breeding ground for gulls, cormorants, sandpipers, extremely rare black-necked cranes, and bar-headed geese, known to fly as high as 30,000 feet in order to reach their winter home in India. The birds had already flown south; their only season at Koko Nor is spring, and perhaps the sense of desolation was created by their absence.

Scattered herds of sheep and yaks speckled the nearby fields, and it wasn't long before shepherds came to visit us. We had finally traveled beyond the dominance of the Han Chinese. The people around Koko Nor are darker-skinned nomadic Tibetans from tribes with names like Golok and Khampa, and faces made red and leather-like by the harsh weather. First came a few men, then a few families. The women wore long black wool skirts trimmed with bright, multicolored edging and tied at the waist with bright magenta or chartreuse sashes, topped by felt hats with decorated bands or hair sculpted in amazing, elaborate braids. The men wore their heavy wool, fur-trimmed jacket with one arm in its sleeve, the other draped over the shoulder so the sleeve fell straight down the back. Most had a small decorated scabbard tucked into their bright green, orange, or red belt.

A trio of troubadours appeared next, serenading our colorful gathering of classic cars with unfamiliar string instruments. They settled for a while near the two Team Retro Fords. Inside #23, Vic Zannis wrote in his journal:

> To the south is a range of hills, but the distance is difficult to determine because there are no trees, anywhere. The sheep and yaks look like salt and pepper sprinkled on a crumpled pile of faded green velvet. Halfway up, a curl of smoke comes from an unseen camp. Farther up, the hills are capped with snow. I see clouds wrapping themselves around the mountaintops like white-gloved hands. The sun is going down in the west and the temperature is dropping by the minute.

Vic also noted that one of our ever-present military contingent wasn't too happy about the locals; using a bullhorn he announced something that probably meant "go home."

It didn't work. A whole school of children arrived at once, led by their schoolmasters. They all wanted something, and many of the teams had things to offer: pens, postcards, pins, Polaroid photographs. One little girl took a liking to Linda and me, even though we had no trinkets. She may have been ten or so, a very stubborn age. After most of the other children had left, she kept coming back. When she came back after dark, I finally gave her the pen I'd been writing with.

The Hillman's overdrive had quit on us that day. Despite my early reticence, I'd become hopelessly addicted to it now, as had Linda. When we mentioned it to David Drew, who was camped nearby, he immediately got down on the ground and started crawling under the car.

"I didn't mean you had to—" I started.

"Might as well as not," he cut me off, "I'm already in me wet grubbies, ain't I?" He'd been working under the 1972 Rover 3.5 that he maintained as mechanic/navigator for Jonathan Lux. David had prepped the bulbous silver "businessman's saloon" in his shop in England. Lux said, "How'd ya do" in posh-accented English between puffs on his cigarette. He seemed nice enough, but David really swept me off my feet. Not with his looks, or anything even vaguely sexual, just his honest, no-nonsense helpfulness. David was the type who never thought twice about dropping what he was doing to help someone, doing the thing because that's what he wanted to do, not because somebody told him to. He was a talented mechanic, and all the Brits knew him as "Mr. Fix-It". It was only our fifth day out and he'd probably repaired something on all three Rovers and any number of other British cars already.

It didn't take him long to fix our overdrive; the problem proved to be electrical, our first of many. While David still fettled under the car, I tried to turn the mixture screws on our SU carburetors. Thanks to Fiats, I'm more familiar with Weber carburetors, which require you to change your jets to adjust the air-fuel mixture to the appropriate richness or leanness that the engine needs at different altitudes. (As the air thins, there's less oxygen to help with combustion, so you need to lessen the fuel commensurately, or "lean" the mixture.) It's not an easy job changing Weber jets, and Paul Jackson had assured us that the SUs would make our life easier: "Just adjust these two little screws as you climb." I was having a hard time getting the stuck suckers to turn; Michael Veys took pity on me and did it for me (there's a reason why mechanics have such strong hands).

Poor Michael looked absolutely exhausted. He'd been working too hard keeping the trouble-prone Rolls running, and he wasn't sleeping. Eric Christiansen turned out to be a very difficult person to drive with, and sleep was nearly impossible because he snored so horrendously. Michael grumbled about it in his almost inaudible mumble, but they were getting along well enough in public. Eric praised Michael quite publicly that night at dinner, which was held in mess tents erected by a busy crew of Sherpas.

At that same dinner we heard that Hermann the German was out. His old open La France had been acting up—rumors attributed this to swallowed valves or a broken piston—but it turned out mechanical problems were the least of it. The support crew found him ranting hysterically in a Tibetan family's hut, suffering from pneumonia and altitude sickness. He was flown home to Germany, and his car began the long trip back to Beijing.

For this and our next four nights of camping, David Burlinson's company had provided two crews of young Nepali and Sherpa men—one for evenings, the other for mornings. They set up big tents, including a pretty white one with Tibetan-style decorations which served as the TC and rally office, and several blue ones for the mess halls. Long tables inside sat about twelve of us in each tent. Since we still numbered nearly two hundred (six cars had officially retired, but Montagu and the Nozes held on), we had to be fed in shifts; when we got our final stamp in the Tibetan TC tent, we were assigned a seating time.

Once the sun set, the rain stopped but the wind was bitter cold. The dinner tents gave us a measure of warmth, as we sat shoulder-to-shoulder on the long benches. The Sherpas served us hot soup, followed by a good hot meal: curry and rice, beef stew and noodles, or pasta and greens. It was basic, hot and surprisingly

PRINCE BORGHESE'S TRAIL

good, with hot tea, beer, or hot lemonade or hot orange juice to drink. I'd never had hot juice before; it tasted great and felt much healthier than beer, which after that first one, I decided to avoid.

Back by the car, our nylon tent felt cozy. I stripped off my heavy pants, jacket and two shirts, and in my soft thermal long johns, climbed into my sleeping bag. Linda climbed into hers completely clothed and was out immediately. I lay still for a while, listening to the wind whip the light nylon wall, exhausted but amazed: I was lying on the Tibetan Plateau, almost two miles up, halfway around the world from my home.

❧ 13 ❧

We are seized by a strange intoxication; it is the reaction against the long silences and the depressing slowness of our recent mode of journeying. And we are conscious also of a new joy—the intense and inexpressible satisfaction of doing a thing that has never been done before. We experience the inebriation of conquest, the exaltation of triumph, and with it all a kind of astonishment, a sense of unreality, because of the strange thing this is—the running of such a race in such a country!

KOKO NOR TO GOLMUD, TIBET
[FRIDAY, SEPTEMBER 12]

Everything dripped ice water. My euphoria from the first night's camp-out wore off sometime in the middle of the night, after the rain had pounded and the wind threatened to push the tent over, when I innocently brushed against soaking wet nylon. At dawn, we scrambled out of our soggy bags and rammed them into their stuff sacks. I lifted the lightweight tent and shook out as much water as I could. Sun glinted off the frost-covered grass, and though it did nothing to dispel the cold, its glittering beauty cheered me up. I folded the tent and stuffed it away, still wet.

"At least there's a hotel tonight," Linda said, scowling. "Anything'll be better than another wet camp."

Breakfast in the mess tent was hot rice cereal. I liked it, but Vic of Team Retro called it "some kind of unidentified white porridge. There're too many yaks and goats and sheep around to try it." He had toast and two fried eggs instead.

We learned that morning that Pat and Mary in the #22 Buick had never made it to the camp. A rear main seal had blown, which meant major bottom-end work. The car, and the friendly couple from Iowa, were now on their way back to Beijing. This was the first retirement that really saddened me. I'd been looking forward to many more long talks with Mary.

Leaving our pasture land campsite, after a night of heavy rain, meant that we created our own nasty mud bog. After one or two cars tried to drive up the steep embankment onto the road, the pathway they'd used was destroyed. The Team Retro Fords left before us; we watched as Ted, in #23, threw mud up behind his tires as he roared up onto the road. Behind him, John in #24 got stuck. While other rally cars created pathways around them, one of the Chinese Toyotas attached itself to the stuck Ford, and with Vic and Andy pushing, up to their ankles in mud, the Ford was moved onto the road. I avoided the muddy ruts by driving out onto the untouched pasture.

The sun shone with incredible intensity. As I drove, I remembered people talking about the special clarity of the high mountains; perhaps this was it. Or maybe it was just the freshness of the rain-washed air; or the ecstatic pleasure of travel—awesome, unlimited vistas, purposeful movement to somewhere undiscovered. We drove up toward the closest snowy mountains—the A'nyêmaqên range—with the lake and salt flats on our right, a curvy but gently climbing route through the first of the four mountain passes we would cross that day. If we'd had a 3-D topographical map it would've been too jagged to hold. We were riding between sixteen and seventeen thousand feet peaks. We didn't have an altimeter in the car—we'd been trusting Rich Newman's elaborate tell-all watch for that—but our hearts beat faster, our breaths grew quick and shallow. We were really climbing now.

Abruptly the mountains seemed to end. We came down a long shoot of a grade onto a wide flat plain, still ringed by high mountains, but now far in the distance. Two rows of spindly trees—the first in ages—signaled the town of Qinghai and our TC. Afterward, there was nothing but wide high plains filled with sand and dirt, a barren sea-bottom of grey rock and brown dust. In odd lumps we'd see high stacks of dirt topped by tall dune grasses. I told Linda they looked like camel-humps, and this time she agreed with me, and didn't tell me to shush. I was driving, she was navigating, but there was not a lot of navigating to do. The road seemed infinitely straight, those immensely tall peaks still surrounding us, but so far away, only their jagged white tips were visible, and then only if you forced your eyes to pick them out against the stark bright sky.

The road seemed flat but climbed and climbed, the kind of mountain climbing I'd hated as a bicyclist, because the straight road gave the illusion of flatness so effectively that my leg muscles would refuse to pump. The Hillman loved it, zooming steadily along, hour after hour. Linda said little, and she may have dozed. Barzini wrote eloquently about the stupor that overtakes passengers on journeys like ours and Borghese's: "The oppressive aspect of a journey like this for those who are not driving is inaction. You first observe, then you let your fancy roam at will, and at last your tired mind loses itself in vague wandering: no vision wakens it any longer. You remain in a state of tacit insensibility. Your brain is drowsy and filled with the sweet wanderings of sleep."

Rich Newman later told us that he had fallen asleep on this stretch. "When I woke up I thought, Oh my God, I've been asleep for two hours and I'm still sitting here in this 2CV, next to Burt. He's still driving but we haven't gotten anywhere. It's the same flat expanse of dirt in every direction! I've died, and this is Hell!"

Golmud wasn't Hell, but it may have been China's closest terrestrial relative. Even our road book's description, which I discovered later was lifted from the *Lonely Planet* guide, said "This town is a pioneering post in the oblivion end of China. Even the residents will tell you that from here to Hell is only a local call." The city itself was everything people had warned me Third World countries would be like: dirty, overcrowded, chaotic, greedy, too many traders of questionable items vying for everyone's attention. The city's *raison d'être* was one large intersection: the Qinghai-Tibet Highway, Qinghai-Xingjia Highway, and the Dunhuang-Golmud Highway all met here, along with the old Qinghai-Tibet railway. China's two great rivers, the Yellow and the Yangtze, originated nearby. Our road book also stated that Golmud's claim to fame was its potash plant about sixty kilometers from the city. There are only two others like it in the world: one in Salt Lake City, and the other in Israel's Dead Sea. The city itself was a mass of decaying communist constructions and crowded karaoke bars. Thankfully, the peaks of the Kunlun Mountains in the distance compensated for the uninspiring skyline.

The main hotel with our parc fermé sported odd, globular architecture, very modern, but as the Retro guys would say, "not quite right." It looked huge, but it could only take a fifth of us. The Yin Bin, *our* home for the night, didn't sport any kind of English sign. We'd driven past it and come to the edge of town, then turned around and realized it had to be the building with one of the rally Mercedes parked in front. The place was a dump; hiking up the three flights of stairs—at almost ten thousand feet—took our breath away. With hearts pounding, trying not to smell anything or register the contents of the odd buckets lining the hallway, we let ourselves into our rooms. The beds were funky, with heavy rice-hull pillows; we decided to sleep in our sleeping bags. The bathroom was filthy. We closed our eyes, kept our shoes on, and took hot showers.

We were jealous of the "A List" people who had registered—and paid—their Rally fees earliest (that turned out to be the only criteria for placement on the list): they got to stay at the main hotel. Turned out they were envious of us when they found out we had hot water; they had only cold.

None of the five different hotels in Golmud hosting ralliers could be recommended, but we certainly weren't the first travelers to experience substandard lodgings. Back in 1907, Borghese and Barzini "wandered about the desert roads in search of an hotel and found one—the worst and dirtiest hotel in Siberia." This was in the town of Kainsk, on the Om river, an inhospitable place indeed. Barzini recruited a young local there to take him to the telegraph office. "We knocked," Barzini wrote, "and heard an irritated voice crying behind the door:

"'Who is there?'

"I gave my name and described myself.

"'Come back tomorrow.'

"'I cannot. I am leaving at dawn and I have a telegram to send off.'

"'Go away!'

"'I have a telegram to send to the Governor of Tomsk.'

"'Go away.'

"The voice had grown threatening. I insisted. The man on the other side of the door called out something which I did not understand, but which the youth who had come with me understood and answered by precipitate flight, making a sign to me to follow him. I asked him:

"'What is the matter?'

"He replied with the action of one firing off a gun, and with these two elo-quent monosyllables: 'Boom! Boom!'

"My paper must be left that evening without news of our race. 'Well,' thought I to myself, 'better without news than without a correspondent.'"

As we walked to dinner, we were caught up by a trotting, distressed Lord Montagu. "Is this—? Do you know—? I'm supposed to be in the A-group—" and he hurried off, like Alice's white rabbit. When we found the restaurant, I noticed Montagu only a table away. Linda and I had inadvertently infiltrated the A-group. The food was a combination of Chinese entrees, some familiar, some not—the strange stuff usually turned out to be a different kind of noodle. Suddenly, french fries began to appear—manna from heaven! Someone had figured out how to order them, and soon all the tables were brimming with french fries. They were snapped up as quickly as the young servers could bring them.

On the walk back to the Yin Bin we listened to ear-splitting karaoke singing re-broadcast onto the streets by competing bars, the loudest of which was right across the street from our hotel. Back in our room, we discovered that the toilet had overflowed. Since it ran continuously anyway, it kept overflowing all night into the floor drain. That meant we had to pee in the sink, brush our teeth out the window, and make awkward but necessary use of the strange looking pot on the floor, which I'd figured out by morning was a spittoon. (The Chinese have serious health problems caused by public spitting; they do it constantly.) I felt bad for the poor woman (probably) who would have to clean the place up.

Cleaning clearly wasn't on the normal list of services available at the Yin Bin. Instead, there was every indication that the establishment offered more intimate services. I hoped the languid young working girls lounging in that filthy lobby didn't have to double as custodial staff.

The authorities had sent six soldiers to guard the entrance to the Bank, with orders not to let anyone in. This was a grave mistake, for a Chinese soldier naturally has a certain number of friends, relatives, and creditors, to whom he owes a debt of good nature and kindness, and whom he allows to pass whenever he mounts guard. But the number of creditors, relations, and friends of six Chinese soldiers is equivalent to the average population of a town; for which reason, through a door bolted and barred and guarded by six men, there flowed in upon us a stream of people like water from a jet at continuous pressure.

GOLMUD TO TUOTUOHEYAN
[SATURDAY, SEPTEMBER 13]

Our start wasn't until 9:07, the latest yet. Those 5:30 and 6:00 starts required by the nervous PSB had trained us to get up early, so we had plenty of time to rearrange the car in Golmud. Huge crowds had been trying to get into the fenced parking lot ever since we'd arrived the night before, and the uniformed guards at first kept them out, then started to let small groups trickle in. There was some kind of hierarchy—party officials and family members of the guards got in, while lowly functionaries didn't. But in the morning, either the system broke down, or the day-shift guards had larger families and more creditors. The parking lot was inundated. Children seemed to be everywhere, asking for pens and autographs. We gave a young girl in a pink sweater our Gatorade—instant packets that neither of us had ever bothered with—and she left, ecstatic. Then she came back with a small greeting card that featured a photo of little European children playing dress-up, with the central child blowing out candles on a birthday cake. Inside she had carefully printed a note:

> *Dear Friend:*
> *My name is Li Xian, I am fourteen. Today is my birthday. I'm very happy. My English name is Jane. I'm in No. 1 Middle School. Best wishes! Good luck!*
> *Your friend: Li Xian.*

I took her picture standing with Linda by our car, and Linda took one of her with me. I promised myself I would send copies of the photos to her when I got home, care of the Golmud Hotel.

Other than the Gatorade and some accumulated garbage, there wasn't much else to eliminate. We decided to toss the button seats; the buttons were falling off now, and we certainly didn't need them for cooling anymore; the air temperature hadn't been higher than forty degrees Fahrenheit since Lanzhou.

Golmud was the last bit of "modernity" we were to witness for a while. We would soon enter the Tibet Autonomous Region, the euphemistic name imposed by the Chinese when they took control in 1951. Modern in this sense meant simply no hotels; our next two consecutive nights would be camping. After the hotels in Golmud, many of us thought camping would be preferable.

The other modern convenience that began to disappear was asphalt. Dirt isn't so bad, or even gravel, but mud, literally, sucks. And the asphalt that remained rolled in waves—frost heaves—as high as four feet. You could really get airborne, if you didn't mind slamming your car's nose and exploding its suspension on the crest of the next three-footer on the descent.

It was to be an incredibly difficult day. We all knew that no one back home would ever understand how tough it really was. As Don told the web via satellite phone on his nightly report, "It's hard to believe some of these things until you actually have them happen to you, or you see them yourself. We wonder how our friends and family are possibly going to believe it."

The roads out of Golmud were decent at first, with stone bop dots to prevent passing. The climb steepened immediately, with the terrain growing ever more desolate. Prayer flags on poles topped almost every high mound, near and far. Where did the people live who constructed these things? Were they built by pilgrims on their way to Lhasa, or were homes hidden somewhere on the barren dirt plain? The answer is both: the structures are erected by the locals (if I strained my eyes, I could make out low, mountain-colored tents in the distance), but pilgrims and travelers add their prayers as they pass. Every flag or "wind horse" contains one, if not many, prayers (typically *om mani padme hum,* often translated as "O hail the jewel in the lotus") and every gust of breeze sends the prayer galloping heavenward.

Along with flag structures, we began to notice mounds of stones. They reminded me of those little stacks of stones I was taught to make on Girl Scout hikes. But these are not simple trail markers; they are stone versions of prayer flags. The jagged but flat chunks of slate, sandstone, and sometimes yak skulls, have prayers carved on them. Called *Mani* stones, they are piled at hilltops and peaks—closer to heaven—and sometimes grow so large they become shrines in themselves, places that pilgrims circumambulate before continuing on.

Arriving at the Kunlun Shankou Pass was cause for celebration, even though we hadn't yet reached the TC at Glacier Plateau. We joined the Australian Rolls, Bud and Mark in their overloaded but strong and sturdy Chevy Bel Air, and a number of Chinese truckers. Everyone had to climb down from the roadway to have their picture taken before the two monumental white statues—a bird and a dog or lion. The two huge figures were separated by about fifteen feet, and in the center stood a monolith with a startlingly white marble headstone carved with round Tibetan swirls, and red-painted Chinese characters carved down the front. Weathered prayer flags decorated the two characters, and prayer flag poles tilted haphazardly

over the side of the wide, stepped pedestal.

The Chinese-script-covered monolith seemed somehow not to jibe with the prayer flags and mythological figures. I wondered how much of the monument was a latter-day communist contribution. Perhaps only those ragged prayer flags were truly Tibetan. It didn't matter. We were thrilled to have climbed the 4,930 meters (16,022 feet) it represented.

The checkpoint was still 102 kilometers on, so we couldn't linger. We surfed the waves of asphalt and arrived with a comfortable margin of time. The Brodericks of Cornwall (in the #52 Anglia) and the Catts of Oxfordshire (in #50 Cortina) were there ahead of us. We'd become something of a threesome, with similar vintage cars, similar engine capacities, and tendencies toward lead feet all. We spoke contentedly about the rally. "The times are fairly generous," Paula Broderick remarked. "But it's still better to be early. You never know . . ."

It was the pause before the storm.

It's not as if the Chinese didn't maintain the road. Some stretches were beautifully "made," and we passed a fair number of shovel-wielding men and women, working away at piles of rocks lining the shoulders. "Road workers' settlements"—government compounds that looked more like prisons—were the main landmarks in the road book. According to my *Lonely Planet* guide, they probably were prisons, as this region was famous as the "Chinese Siberia, where common criminals as well as political prisoners are incarcerated . . . including victims of the Cultural Revolution, supporters of the Gang of Four and opponents of the present regime."

The problem turned out to be water. Any sort of creek or river intersecting our path caused the road to disappear. Then we had to traverse the mud and water and the obstacle course created by stuck, sometimes abandoned, vehicles.

We learned that when the road book said, "Road uneven - THEN unmade!" that meant dirt or gravel, if we were lucky; or ferocious, river-bottom, slime-sucking, axle-breaking mud if we weren't. We weren't very lucky that day, nor were the Chinese truckers. In the first place, they were incredibly overloaded; they had been, ever since Beijing. Sometimes a mountain of hay would come at us down the road, and only when we met would the overburdened truck underneath become visible. Loose loads—boxes, bricks, bags—were stacked up to twenty feet high, causing the top-heavy vehicles to tilt dangerously to the side as they rumbled down straight sections of well-paved road. Imagine these things on mud. They sank or overturned on contact, spilling their loads and often injuring their occupants. At one scene, some fifteen people had tumbled from the top of the truck on which they'd been perched. Mark, the rally's paramedic, tried to help them as much as he could. A little further on, the arm of a truck driver hung limply from his crushed cab; a group of men wept on the roadside nearby. If the drivers weren't injured, they went off to wherever discouraged nomadic truck drivers go (hopefully somewhere warm), leaving the blue trucks to sink ever deeper into the mire. Then the next truck, or hapless Western rally car, to come along had to find a new way around the sunken hulk, picking and choosing a path among the many muddy crisscrossing ruts.

We were waddling our way carefully through one of these diversions—Linda was driving, slowly—when we had to get around one very deeply sunk, scarily tilted truck. The road workers and soldiers waved us on, over the same churned-up mess of tire ruts that had almost swallowed the rally car in front of us. We were too advanced to pick a different course, so Linda accelerated slowly, and we sank. I hopped out, and we all started pushing—at fifteen thousand feet, every shove took all my air—and together with the helpful road workers, dislodged the car.

Linda lurched the Hillman forward, and I jogged—pant, pant, pant—to catch up. She slowed, loaded me in, and we tried the next wet patch—and sank. I hopped out again, but this time the rear wheels spun, shooting mud up in flamboyant disregard of our distress. She slid the clutch mercilessly, trying to get first gear to engage. Finally, with several shoves, it caught. Forward once more, a couple of yards, and then—stuck again.

This time the engine had died, and the car wouldn't start. When I got back in, the smell of hot asbestos was intense.

"I think you smoked the clutch!" I told her between gasps for air.

"Why won't it start?" She asked, frazzled. "Every time I tried to release the clutch, it just died, and now it won't start!" She turned the key; nothing, no sound. Then she turned the key again, and the engine went *urrrrump.*

"That sounds like a dying battery," I said, "not enough juice." Could it be some kind of high altitude vapor lock? I wondered. I didn't say it out loud because I didn't have enough breath for the extra words.

Linda tried a few more times while I sat there, trying to get enough air in my lungs to stop panting. It didn't seem possible—was this hyperventilation? The other rally cars made slow, wide detours around us; they seemed to be moving in slow motion. We watched them leap effortlessly up the embankment that led to the heavenly dryness of the "made" road.

I started to get my breath back. Linda tried the key again.

Uuurrrrrump.

I got out of the car and went to open the hood. Just then, David Drew appeared. "What's she at?" he asked.

Linda got out and waved him into the driver's seat. "It won't start."

He sat down, did something to the pedals, and turned the key. The car started right up. "I'll get it up on the road for you!" he shouted as he gunned the accelerator and we jogged—pant, pant, pant—behind, watching our mud-encrusted red beauty leap onto the roadway.

David jumped out and into his Rover. Jonathan took off in a hurry, dust and gravel spraying out from the big car's rear tires.

But somehow our Hillman stalled again. And it wouldn't start. Linda tried the key. Nothing. We sat.

"Look," I said, fighting for breath again, "let's just relax a bit. Maybe it needs to cool off." It got very quiet. The rally cars we had been traveling with had now passed us by. A few trucks still grumbled around, and the road workers shoveled. I looked at the road book and contemplated calculating how many kilometers we had left, and how little time. But I wasn't sure my brain would grasp the numbers with so little oxygen—and I wasn't sure I wanted to know. Finally, my breathing slowed, though my heart continued to pound alarmingly.

"Okay, maybe try it now."

Linda turned the key; the engine started. Greatly relieved, we motored off to the checkpoint. We got to the TC thirteen minutes late, earning our first penalty. Thirteen minutes on September thirteenth.

Borghese's Itala had first succumbed to mud in China, on the banks of the Hun Ho (the Romanization then of *Huang He* or Yellow River); his coolies pulled him out. The second time was just out of Mongolia's capital city, Urga (now Ulan Bator). They left that city at 5:00 A.M., and within an hour they were bogged in mud. Borghese had released the coolies back in China, so the three men—Borghese, Barzini and Ettore the mechanic—debated returning to the city for help. Before they had made up their mind to perform that humiliating task, a band of Mongolians appeared and accepted payment to fetch planks. By levering all four wheels, the Italians and Mongolians managed to lift the heavy car to solid ground.

The third time was that same day, with some three hundred miles still to go before the Siberian border at Kiakhta. They had grown suspicious of abandoned paths, but when they came to a wide plain covered with green bushes and tall grasses, they didn't notice that the vegetation was acquatic. "Suddenly," Barzini wrote, "we noticed that the road seemed to be abandoned, and we scarcely had time to exchange a swift word before the car sank and stopped. It had entered a turbid slime, the crust of which, dried up by the sun, presented all the characteristics of solid earth."

This strange crusted soil was a kind of quicksand. "It was obvious that below the slender surface there were depths of water. . . . We understood that the mass of mud would swallow up our car if we did not succeed in saving it at once."

First the axles, then the running boards sank below the surface. The men desperately unpacked everything, hoping that lightening the Itala would slow the sinking. At the rate it was sinking, walking off to get help would be fruitless; by the time they returned it would be gone. The unloading didn't seem to help, and they had given up hope when, miraculously (since they were on an abandoned road), a Russian Buriat tribe "on the trek" appeared, with carts and horses enough to pull the car out. These were the first Russians the raiders had come across: "We

PRINCE BORGHESE'S TRAIL

felt the affinity of our race with theirs, here in the heart of Mongolia." Then Mongolians on horseback arrived. The Buriats refused Borghese's first payment offer, and when the Prince offered more, the Russians said, "It cannot be done," but stood by, watching. The Mongolians accepted Borghese's offer, rode off at a gallop, and returned with oxen and planks. After hours of labor, the Itala was freed. "We generously distributed a large number of roubles among the Mongolians, and they received them with enthusiastic exclamations. . . . The Buriat chief approached and put out his hand too. Prince Borghese said to him, smiling:

"'No work, no money.'

"The Buriat drew back his hand with a surly glance, and replied:

"'I have no need of your money.'"

Borghese was still pleased when he finally reached the Russian border, but he was sorry to say goodbye to the helpful Mongolians.

Seeing the gaily decorated TC tent at Tuotuoheyan was such a relief, I almost didn't mind the biting wind and icy sleet. I put on every piece of clothing in my bag and grabbed a mugful of hot orange juice. In moments the juice was cold. I offered to do gas filling duty once the "bowser" (British for gas pump) arrived. This tanker truck had been following us, and since it had negotiated the same mud pits all day, it didn't arrive until two or three hours after most of us. Since there was only one hose, waiting in line was a long ordeal each night. I sat inside the car, sheltered from the wind, and crept forward now and then, sometimes letting the car idle, sometimes turning it off and starting it up. I was afraid to turn it off at first, after the stalling earlier, but the Hillman seemed to have recovered. I sat for hours, using the time to write in my journal. Linda came to relieve me when she realized the Sherpas were shutting down dinner. Outside the car, the air temperature had dropped dramatically; it could not have been more than ten degrees.

I stamped my feet under the table through dinner, trying to stay warm, and then climbed into my sleeping bag, fully clothed. Outside, on the Roof of the World, sleet pummeled the tent. Inside, though the doctor had warned us that the high altitude might make it hard to sleep, I was out in minutes.

CHAPTER

~ 15 ~

We came across a penitent pilgrim, with shaven head and wearing a long, grey tunic, who went upon his way in continuous prayer, kneeling down by a vow at every three steps to kiss the earth . . . . It suddenly flashed upon our minds that we too, after all, were bent on a strange pilgrimage. We, too, had vowed a strange vow, and were faithfully keeping it. If the genuflecting pilgrim had in his turn inquired of the reason of Prince Borghese's journey, he would no doubt in his wisdom have greatly wondered on hearing it.

TUOTUOHEYAN TO NAGQU
[SUNDAY, SEPTEMBER 14]

The night's camp at Tuotuoheyan was on tundra-like pasture land just beyond an army barracks. Though the name translates to "village on the Tuotuo" river, there was no sign of any inhabitants other than the military. The Tuotuo river nearby is the source of the Yangtze, the world's third longest river at 6,380 kilometers. Don Jones measured the temperature in the morning, when we emerged from our ice-encrusted tents, at a crisp eight-degrees Fahrenheit (minus-ten degrees Celsius). We shook off the ice, crammed everything in the trunk, fetched some hot food and drink, and set off.

Back in Golmud, we'd started dosing ourselves with Diamox to ward off altitude sickness. We'd been warned about the drug's side effects—tingling in the hands and feet—and I'd noticed it before, but now gripping the steering wheel seemed to exacerbate it. I found my hands cramping up—the cold, the Diamox, the altitude, the competition, just a little stress. The road book made it clear that road conditions today would be no better than those we'd endured yesterday; given the continual climbing, they'd probably be worse. The drug was also a severe diuretic, which led to frequent unscheduled stops.

Today we were driving across the Roof of the World. No other rally drivers had ever done as much. Our stop at Tanggula Shankou (5,180 meters or 16,835 feet) would go into the *Guinness Book of World Records* as the highest rally TC ever. There was some controversy as to the actual altitude. Rich Newman's miraculous watch failed to measure anything higher than 13,000 feet, but the organizers' Vauxhalls carried Global Positioning Systems that used satellites to calculate altitude. All three Vauxhall GPSs agreed that the elevation here was 17,600 feet, an even better record. There was no heavy stone monument to mark the spot, only tattered prayer flags and a light dusting of snow on the wide open plain. A few

shepherds with their yak and sheep popped out of nowhere to see what the commotion was about.

About two kilometers before the TC there'd been an elaborate gateway over the road. The square columns and lintel were recently painted white and decorated with many bright red Chinese characters. Across the top flew new-looking flags—not prayer flags; there was no writing on them—in white, brown, blue, red, yellow, orange and green. The road book said "Gateway—for no obvious reason!!" Perhaps this gateway was in honor of Tanggula Shankou, our highest point.

The last two days had been hard for everyone. We'd earned our thirteen minutes the day before, but that was nothing compared to some of the other competitors. The Gulls had lost their shocks again, and by the time we reached today's destination, Nagqu, they had racked up two hours and forty-two minutes in penalties. Burt and Rich in the 2CV simply had no speed, and with their continuing gas-fill problems accumulated an hour and eight minutes in penalties. The thinning oxygen slowed the already-slow Jeepsters by robbing their engine of power, and the rain created an irritating problem when they came upon a slow truck—the acceleration needed to pass it reduced their engine's vacuum so drastically their 1962 vacuum-operated windshield wipers quit.

Carl and Don's Packard wasn't faring well either. Their exhaust manifold broke, causing fumes to circulate in the car and, of course, tremendous noise. Their tires kept going flat, and their on-board air compressor failed. It's required to maintain the Packard's air suspension system (hailed as an amazing innovation back in 1954), and without it the car practically rode on the ground. It took them over an hour to find a source of air for their four tires. Together with carburetion and spark plug problems, they'd suffered nine hours and twenty-two minutes in penalties.

Several more cars were now out of the rally. Rumor had it we were down from ninety-four to eighty-two. No one had seen the Jaguar in days, and some cars weren't showing up at the night or morning TCs. The black Buick from Singapore did show up in Nagqu, on the back of a Chinese flatbed truck. They had lost a main seal and dumped their oil, just like the Buick from Iowa, but somehow the PSB didn't force them to turn back. They were able to pay a trucker to haul the six-thousand pound car to Lhasa, where they hoped to find a shop capable of doing the necessary repairs.

The mud got the Queen's Rolls, too. The big black Aussie limousine struck a huge boulder buried in mud; the impact shot a spring straight up through the chassis. We heard the Germans driving the #5 Rolls—the wood-trimmed 1928 boat-tail roadster I'd admired so much in Beijing—had given up; the car had suffered ten punctured tires in one day. The smallest of the oldest—a 1928 Bugatti and a 1932 Aston Martin International, both powered by less than 1500cc's—were both suffering. The Bugatti's fragile chassis was being shaken to bits; the Aston Martin had been reported as missing.

For us, the road to Nagqu wasn't so bad. A crystalline sun came out, and the rain stayed away. We had several stretches of unmade muddy road, and it was Linda's turn now to jump out and push whenever the mud sucked us under. She came back each time more breathless and upset: "I'm dying here! I can't do this anymore!" she said, panting. Luckily, that was our last mire. We made it to both TCs mud-encrusted but "clean"—rally-speak for penalty-free.

The final Nagqu TC, for some bizarre reason, was about six miles beyond the town, another camp on the open plateau. As we drove past the bustling little yak- and sheep-trading center, we noticed a high-rise hotel (by Tibetan standards, maybe five or six stories) in the white cement and blue glass communist fashion. Why weren't we stopping there? we wondered. Some lucky few, mostly the organizers, did stay at the hotel, but most of us camped in the cold.

We had to be warmer, tucked in our nylon tents, than a few souls we saw crawling along the road that afternoon. Four men and women in the well-weathered pink robes of Buddhist pilgrims made their slow progress; hands sheathed in wooden mitts, they clacked their hands down on the road, prostrated their bodies full down, tapped their foreheads on the earth, rose to their knees (burlap aprons covered their fronts), then stood and clapped their wooden hands together in front of them. One step forward, clap down again, on and on.

In *My Tibet,* the Dalai Lama writes of pilgrimages:

> *Pilgrimage by prostration takes a strong sense of motivation and purpose, which results in great accumulation of merit for the pilgrim. Khampas from eastern Tibet sometimes take years to complete a long pilgrimage, prostrating every foot of the way. When you walk a circular pilgrimage route, your feet touch the earth with big spaces between them, but when you prostrate, your whole body connects with the sacred ground to close the circle. So, you see, it is not just the hardship that brings the extra reward.*

I wondered how many days it would take these pilgrims to cover the 212 miles to Lhasa.

Once Prince Borghese crossed into Siberia, leaving Mongolia behind, he expected smoother sailing. The Trakt, or cart-track, across Siberia was a well-established road; it had once carried substantial wheeled traffic, and driving in midsummer over steppes and forested plain should have posed no serious difficulties. As it turned out, the Trans-Siberian Railway (mostly complete by 1903) had by 1907 put the road into complete disuse. Many of the bridges were crumbling, and long stretches of the roadway were abandoned. The weather, too, conspired against the raiders. The rain began in June and never ceased—it rained every day of their journey through Russia—so what might have been dusty but negotiable roadway became a morass of mud.

Their first day's drive northwestward was uneventful, except for the challenge of getting the heavy Itala up onto river ferries designed for the light Russian carriages known as *telegas*. The evening of June 26 they arrived at a major turning point: at Verkne-Udinsk, they ceased their northward journey and turned directly west. Up at 3:00 the next morning—they were far enough north now that it was already light—they rode off toward Lake Baikal in steady rain. "After an hour's advance," Barzini wrote, "we were on the point of turning back: we found ourselves before a short climb which at any other time we should scarcely have even noticed, but which to-day proved indomitable. This kind of obstacle always roused us to perfect fury. We should have preferred a river, a mountain, a precipice, any other respectable and considerable difficulty. Nothing of the sort! Here was a hundred yards' stretch of the most innocent-looking road. But it was covered with that greasy, slippery mud, on which even a man's foot is unsteady and slides with an irresistible tendency to go backwards rather than forwards, and our wheels felt the same tendency; they revolved in vain; the car was marking time."

"And to think," they exclaimed as the rain poured down, "that half an hour's sunshine would turn this into an excellent road!"

CHAPTER

~ 16 ~

We had wondered whether there could be in the air or in the water of that Asiatic centre, some mystic power to draw men away from the world. The greatest among religions arose in Asia; they came like sparks out of the flames of that land of ideals destined to spread over all the world. The conception of the soul, which is perhaps the highest conception ever attained by man, and in which lies the origin of conscience, virtue, and goodness, is an Asiatic conception. Our skeptical materialistic civilisation, flowing back again into Asia, beats against a great contempt of worldly things like the waves of the sea against the rock.

NAGQU TO LHASA
[MONDAY AND TUESDAY, SEPTEMBER 15 AND 16]

Linda was driving, and we had a new enemy to add to the mud: altitude. It didn't make sense, since we'd been cruising above fifteen thousand feet for days. But this time, the ascent to the Kyogche La pass (15,925 ft) was a steep climb up into the Nyainqêntanglha range. As we left Nagqu, the dun and gray mountains rose steadily before us, our ribbon of a road snaking up its sides— no more long, straight road on the gently rising plateau.

If there'd only been the grade, and no mud, we would've made it. We could pull up the grade slowly on a decent surface, if we got a good running start. And we could get out of mud on a rise if the slope was gentle enough. But we couldn't pull out of mud on a steep rise. The oxygen that our engine needed for fuel was so rare now, only traveling at speed forced enough air into the carburetors. At low revs and low speeds, the Hillman gasped and sputtered and would not accelerate.

For the first time, we had to resort to the towrope. Two friendly South Africans, David Tremain and Carolyn Ward, were competing in the "Classic 4WD" category with Carolyn's 1961 Land Rover. This kind of terrain was their element. They gladly pulled us out of our first mire.

Later, the official mechanics in the organizers' new Land Rover stopped to assist us. Our engine was struggling so badly for air that it barely moved the car—maybe half-a-mile an hour—and we'd pulled over and opened the hood and were examining our SU carburetors.

"I've already opened the mixture screws as far as they go!" I told Jingers in exasperation.

He suggested we try taking the pistons completely out of the carburetors' dashpots so that nothing would block what little air was available. It seemed to make a difference.

On one muddy diversion, we bogged down right near a large party of road workers. The laughing men came running over right away to help push. We had to reverse, so they pressed their huge smiles and ruddy faces up against the windshield, and laughed and strained as they pushed us backwards. It must've seemed absurd to them, these crazy Westerners driving their fantastical automobiles way up here. We suspected their amusement doubled when they saw we were both women.

The short tow and the huffing and puffing got us to the TC at Damxung on time. Though we were climbing again through the narrow pass under the 23,276-ft Nyainqêntanglha Feng, the road had improved remarkably. We followed the Kyi Chu river down its narrow gorge, the mountains rising on both sides. Now, instead of arid walls of rock, the mountains were lush and green, thanks in part to some ingenious irrigation canals.

These were the Himalayas of picture postcards. No more moonscape, dusty seabottom desert, or rolling pasture land. This was a proper mountain gorge, with jade-colored water babbling below and slate-gray granite outcroppings above, as we followed the contours of the river on a decent road built into the mountain's side. Occasionally we'd notice footbridges over the river that looked as if they were built with thousands of little sticks. If I allowed my eye to follow the path as it left the river on the other side, I could barely make out a well-camouflaged village, nestled in the mountain's lower crannies. As we neared Lhasa, these complexes grew more numerous, and their decorations became more fanciful—whitewash instead of earth tones, with colorful interlocking swirls or square designs painted in bands around the eaves.

The timing now seemed generous, but perhaps it was just the better road that made the difference. Required average speed was only 35 mph, and we were able to amble at a comfortable 45 to 50 mph down the long valley. The temperature had risen too, and at one point we simply stopped, for no reason other than to enjoy the view, take a few pictures, and eat some peanut butter and crackers (our staple on camping days; on hotel days we'd gotten into the habit of making sandwiches with the toast and meat offered at breakfast, or taking hard boiled eggs and fruit, and spiriting it all out to the car in a napkin or ziploc bag). As I sat there gazing upward, the rocky promontories rimmed by grasping vegetation looked to me exactly like the artwork on ancient Chinese scrolls, with wispy clouds decorating the upper reaches.

Back in the car we came up behind a slow truck. While we followed along, waiting for an opportunity to pass, we realized that his cargo, peeking above the high tailgate, was none other than the Queen's Rolls. John Matheson's and Jeanne Eve's heads bobbed up and down and side-to-side as the truck bumped along the road, like those little hula girls and puppy-dog-heads on springs that sat in the back windows of cars in the 1960s. Linda and I both laughed out loud and almost couldn't contain ourselves when Jeanne waved as we passed, her white-gloved hand rotating in an absurdly displaced royal wave.

As the Kyi Chu valley flattened, several large white chortens—conical or domed

Tibetan shrines—announced our return to an urban world, and before long we were flagged over to the side of the road by PSB officers. Once about ten of us gathered, they convoyed us into Lhasa on a wide, modern highway interspersed with short segments made of large square cobblestones. The police delivered us to the Holiday Inn, a large hotel capable of holding us all. Aside from the main restaurant, the hotel offered the Hard Yak Cafe, featuring yak steaks and burgers.

Linda and I had sworn that we wouldn't wash the car until we got to Paris, but our Hillman had grown so filthy we couldn't get anywhere near it without having mud, dust and oily grime rub off on us. So we spent our first hours in Lhasa at the local car wash, watching a woman in a house dress and Easter hat wash our car. Her son came to help, and the two of them took a good hour. While we waited, another rally car arrived, #39, a 1963 Rover P4. Crew members David Brister (a retired Concorde pilot) and Keith Barton sat with us; we hadn't had the chance to talk before. When our car was good-luck red once again, the woman accepted payment (the US price worked out to about a dollar fifty) and we headed straight back to the bar.

Others didn't pay at all. Burt Richmond told us that the woman who washed his 2CV refused the money, saying "You Americans have been good to my Dalai Lama, so I want to do something good for you."

Lhasa, of course, had been the Dalai Lama's winter home until 1959, when he fled Tibet with some eighty-thousand others after the Chinese crushed their rebellion.

Most Westerners, including most in our group of ralliers, believe the Chinese grabbed Tibet for sheer political, ideological and economic gain. The Chinese, on the other hand, argue ancient linkages and believe they "liberated" the Tibetans from a "feudal serfdom under the despotic religion-political [sic] rule of lamas and nobles, a society which was darker and more cruel than the European serfdom of the Middle Ages." Their efforts to convince us of their righteousness in Tibet were evident in the English language newspapers we read in Beijing and later, along the route. One headline read "Prisoners Say Life in Lhasa is Good."

Buddhism arrived in these high mountains back in the third century, and combined with the ancient animist religion and Indian influences to create the unique religion called Tibetan Buddhism. The Dalai Lama is considered the reincarnation of Chenrezi or the Bodhisattva of Compassion (also known as Shayamuni), who first appeared to Tibetans, after several reincarnations in India, in 1391. The country had been ruled by secular kings until Mongol hordes caused their decline (as they did all over the Eurasian continent), and political authority reverted to the Lamas. From the early seventeenth century on, the Dalai Lama or Ocean of Wisdom ruled the country as its god-king. Upon each lama's death, a young boy believed to be the prior lama's reincarnation was sought out, brought to the palace, and trained to be the next religious and political ruler.

In spite of this local authority, China considered Tibet a remote protectorate. Officials and soldiers had been stationed there ever since the early eighteenth century, but the country's sheer inaccessibility prevented the emperor in Peking from having much of an impact. The country evolved slowly, the spirituality of daily, difficult living taking precedence over technological development and international politics.

When in 1904 the British decided to establish trade with Tibet as a means of building a buffer against Russia, they signed a treaty that seemed to recognize Tibet's sovereignty. But two years later the British signed a treaty with China that acknowledged China's prior claims over Tibet. By clouding the issue of Tibet's sovereignty in the international community, England essentially gave the Chinese all the ammunition they needed to later claim rightful ownership.

The fall of China's Qing dynasty in 1911 prevented the Chinese from exercising any authority in Tibet, so the Tibetans seized their de facto independence and expelled every Chinese official and soldier, and a fierce period of reactive isolationism followed. No foreigners, apparently, entered Lhasa, the true "Forbidden City," until after the death of the thirteenth Dalai Lama in 1933. The Chinese were the first back, setting up an office to keep an eye on things. World War II brought a small group of Westerners—the two Austrians of *Seven Years in Tibet,* a handful of Americans downed in a plane crash, then a British wireless operator.

Once China recovered from its own revolution, the Maoists re-asserted their "ancient" claim, and this time backed it up with anti–Western Liberation rhetoric. By the time Tibet appealed to the international community, it was too late to overcome the years of isolation and the ambiguity set in place by the British. The People's Liberation Army easily beat a weak Tibetan force in 1951. Resistance grew and culminated in the rebellion of 1959, but once again, the Tibetans were overwhelmed. The fourteenth Dalai Lama has lived in India ever since.

In modern Lhasa you see many happy Tibetans, and also marching columns of serious Han Chinese soldiers. So whose city is it really? The Han now represent the majority—70 percent of Lhasa's 203,000 people, by some accounts. Free speech does not exist. Tibetans (and Han, for that matter) can be seriously punished for saying anything negative about the ruling Chinese. So it was not something we could discuss with the hotel staff.

But having driven 4,049 kilometers (2,514 miles) across China, we had a unique perspective. As I became aware of the diversity of "nations" of people as we drove west, I couldn't help but be reminded of my own country's history, and the many nations that once peopled our equally large land mass. The colonizing Europeans arrived in the east, and pressed ever westward, mowing down or relocating any inconvenient natives that got in the way of their "Manifest Destiny."

The Han Chinese have their Manifest Destiny, and as my American forefathers called ours Progress, so the Chinese call theirs Liberation. In my opinion, it's simply the dominant group's ever-pressing need to expand into new territories, to colonize ever-more-distant lands, no matter how harsh or high, and reap whatever economic, political, ideological or spiritual gains they find along the way.

The process started long ago. Borghese and crew did not come to Tibet, but in the upper reaches of Mongolia, Barzini reported that "the Chinese emigrants overflow into these regions, and their agrarian instincts attach them to the land. They represent agriculture invading little by little the land of nomadic tribes. This is a greater force than that of armies, because the nomad does not . . . defend the land. He withdraws towards the free spaces; he yields without knowing it. The Chinese people are spreading now towards the west."

Ninety years later, with China's population pressures—cramming roughly six times as many humans (1.2 billion) into a landmass actually a bit smaller than that of the entire United States (China measures 3.6 million square miles to the U.S.'s 3.7 million square miles)—it's a miracle there are any Tibetans left at all. They are disappearing fast. As the fourteenth Dalai Lama, Tenzin Gyatso, says in his elegant English, "All six million Tibetans should be on the list of endangered peoples. This struggle is thus my first responsibility."

At 12,500 feet, Lhasa is the second highest city in the world (the highest city is Wenquan, Tibet, at 16,575 feet, just north of the Tanggula Pass). By now we'd grown comfortable without all that extra air. We spent the morning checking over the Hillman, tightening bolts and hose-clamps. Afterward, Linda wanted to relax—we had both certainly earned this rest day—but Rich Newman and I were ready to explore. We set out for the Potalla Palace.

Our Holiday Inn was clearly in the Chinese part of town, and the shops and administrative buildings were reminiscent of the uninspiring architecture of Yinchuan (a little less blue glass than Golmud and Baotou). Our view of the high Potalla was blocked at first by two huge golden yaks set way up on a pedestal in the middle of a busy roundabout, with taxis, trucks, and tuk-tuks (motorcycle-powered three-wheeled pickups) whizzing around the base. Their monumental scale suggested a communist source. According to *Lonely Planet,* the yaks were "erected in 'celebration' of the 1991 anniversary of the Chinese takeover . . . they have slightly more appeal than your average Mao statue, and that's about the most that can be said for them."

It felt great to be on my feet instead of sitting in the car, and as we strolled, Lhasa made me feel happy. The Tibetans, despite their political situation, seemed to be perpetually smiling, happy people. The Buddhist theory that all things are relative clearly had its effect here: "Inner peace is the key," the Dalai Lama says. "In that state of mind you can deal with situations with calmness and reason, while keeping your inner happiness."

Thousands of steps climb up every angle to the Potalla Palace, the Dalai Lama's former home, a terraced white, ochre, and burgundy marvel of Tibetan architecture. In the West, people, even devout ones, would balk at the prospect of walking up all those stairs. Someone would've put up a glass elevator complete with ugly rigging and would be charging twenty bucks to ride it. Rich and I had been so infected with Tibetan happiness that we actually started to climb right up.

Inside the seventeenth century structure is the Red Palace for religious functions and the White Palace for the Dalai Lama's living quarters. There are literally thousands of rooms, shrines, and statues, as well as the jewel-bedecked tombs of previous Dalai Lamas. If the monks will let you up, the roof offers an incredible view.

Only a few steps up, though, we were thwarted by a kind gentleman who pointed to a sign that said (in several languages) *closed*. We had both been busy with our respective cars when it was open. We nodded sadly and turned back.

Below, the perfect photo of the Potalla Palace encompasses a lovely old building that had once probably served a dual guard and greeting function for the much higher palace. Now, however, a twenty-foot by five-foot Mobile One billboard carrying an ugly, very Western advertisement, had been tacked onto the top of the Tibetan building. Clearly, the Chinese are not the only ones who have invaded Tibet.

We kept walking, past the many radiant pilgrims happily clacking their padded hands and bare foreheads down on the pavement, and eventually wandered into the Tibetan side of town, and the famous Barkhor, an area defined by the circular pilgrim's path around the gold-topped Jokhang Temple. This is Tibetan Buddhism's cathedral, but it too was closed. We were happy to wander in the Barkhor's tremendous market, a kind of de-facto Tibetan stock exchange, jamboree, and swap meet. We saw and heard: the ever spinning and glittering brass prayer wheels, the cacophony of hawkers calling in many languages ("Lookee lookee good for you lookee lookee"), music from high-pitched ancient pipes and whistles and modern ghetto blasters; and came to the pungent food markets, housed under a dark canopy that kept the smells, sounds, sights and even tastes unavoidably close. From the tamer rows of vegetables we happened into the butchery row, and when I realized that the sound I heard was a man on the floor hacksawing a whole pig, I made a quick turnabout toward the safer soy products: tofu of very strange colors and a variety of impossible consistencies; jellied mounds writhing in the air; flies buzzing; noodle mountains elaborately braided to stay together; buckets of live things I didn't even want to think about. We eventually emerged onto a busy sidewalk chock-a-block with rickshaw drivers seeking customers.

We declined, preferring to walk, and turned back round toward the Potalla.

More market stalls drew us in—clothes and hats and souvenirs now. Rich had a grandson to buy goodies for. I'm a terrible shopper—my children have to tell me exactly what to get them or I'm likely not to bring them anything—and I recognized too many items as the same "made in China" stuff we see every day in California. Rich commented on the incredible prevalence of his home team, the Chicago Bulls and, of course, Michael Jordan. What would his grandson think about a Chicago Bulls cap brought all the way from Tibet?

Rich didn't find anything satisfactory before the stalls ran out in a large open area, where a Chinese fighter jet turned out to be an amusement; a lady sitting and knitting nearby took your money if you wanted to climb up and look inside. Little motorized kiddie rides—one a very ragged tiger, the other a weird Santa-on-a-Reindeer-thing (where does Saint Nick fit into communist ideology?) were popular with the little ones. A dad had paid his yuan, set his little girl on the saddle of the tiger, and jogged along with the raggedy thing, desperately trying to prevent his teetering toddler from falling off onto the pavement. We ate white Popsicles (coconut!) and listened to a Strauss waltz.

The powers that be were pumping Strauss through street-light-affixed speakers. I read later that video cameras were up there too, keeping an eye on Tibetans and foreign tourists alike. This same square had been crowded with ancient Tibetan homes until the early 1990s, when, in the name of urban renewal, the Chinese brought in heavy equipment and mowed them down. Knowing this made the barren paved plaza, ragtag amusements and classical soundtrack doubly surreal.

As we finished our Popsicles we noticed two young Tibetan monks—there were monks in red robes everywhere, of all ages and sizes—who seemed so awestruck with the view of the Potalla, I thought they must be pilgrims from another part of Tibet. In the manner of tourists the world over, they took turns posing for a picture with the palace behind them. One of the earnest young fellows approached me holding out his camera. I thought he wanted me to take a picture of the two of them together, and nodded ascent.

After signs and smiles and much waving, I understood he wanted to get a picture of me, the Peking to Paris Rally woman, with his friend, and with himself. I laughed, embarrassed, but sat on the side of the cement fountain for my photos. We repeated the process with Rich, and then Rich volunteered to take one of the three of us, so I sat with these two small, red-clad fellows close on either side of me, and smiled broadly into the camera. I was trying not to laugh, not just because of the sweetness of their attention and the earnestness of their efforts, but also because of one monk's Chicago Bulls backpack, and the other monk's Ray Ban sticker shining brightly—and blocking part of his vision—on the lens of his new sunglasses.

Spirituality does not preclude a hip look and a crush on Michael Jordan, or even a classic car collection. The Dalai Lama is something of a car guy himself. When he moved to the Potalla Palace, he discovered that he had inherited three motorcars from his predecessor:

> There were two 1927 Baby Austins, one blue and the other red and yellow, and a large 1931 Dodge, painted orange. . . . They had been carried over the Himalaya in pieces and then reassembled. However, they had not been used since [my predecessor's] death and had stood and been allowed to rust. I longed to make them work. At last I found a young Tibetan who had been trained as a driver in India, and with my eager

assistance he managed to put the Dodge in working order, and also one of the Austins, by borrowing parts from the other. These were exciting moments.—My Tibet

Unfortunately, they all broke down again. The steep road up to the palace was too much for them.

There was besides in our work something more unnerving than this physical strain—there was anxiety. Times of uncertainty, often of great strain, attended our progress; then, there were the continual vivid impressions we received; our discouragements and our moments of buoyant hope; times of obstinate resolve, the ups-and-downs of an apparently useless struggle.

LHASA TO XIGAZE
[WEDNESDAY, SEPTEMBER 17]

Most of the American teams were holding up well. The Jeepsters had time in Lhasa to replace their damaged rear inner tubes; Team Retro once again eliminated several hundred pounds of stuff. ("We've purged the cars three times now and they still seem full," said Vic.) Ned Thompson—he of the very thorough packing list—and Bill Binnie, both from the Northeast (Maine and New Hampshire) had some electrical trouble with their 1928 Bentley 41/2 liter. Vic and Andy from Team Retro helped them trace it to a bad master switch. On the rankings posted on the Lhasa rally board, the American Bentley Boys, Bill and Ned, were running a close three minutes ahead of the British Bentley Boys, Jonathan and Adam (one hour forty-three minutes for the Yanks and one hour forty-six for the Brits).

Vic and Andy also helped out the Packard with timing and high-altitude carburetor adjustments. Don and Carl's accumulated penalties now topped ten hours, fifteen minutes.

We met another amazing American competitor. The appropriately named Ray Carr was well into his seventies, and he'd already been in the *Guinness Book of World Records* for driving across North America three times: first in a steam-powered 1907 Stanley from Anchorage, Alaska, to Bar Harbor, Maine; then in a 1912 Baker electric car from Astoria, Oregon, to Atlantic City, New Jersey; and finally in a gas-powered 1902 Northern from San Diego, California, to Georgia. Peking to Paris in a 1939 Ford V8 Convertible must have seemed only natural to Ray and his affable assistant, Mike Wyka, a recent emigré to the States from Poland. They'd only had a few delays—enough to accumulate one hour and sixteen minutes penalties—but were ready to roll the morning we pulled out of Lhasa.

We should probably have put a little more time into figuring out our Hillman's

carburetor problem. As we prepared to leave, we thought Jingers' advice about removing the dashpot pistons had done the trick.

A major change in both the route and the timing was announced in Lhasa. Originally, we Classic cars were supposed to cut up to Gonggar and Gyangze via a smaller road. Philip Young's account of this section for the road book made it sound tempting.

> *Later cars run over a high mountain pass, pass a lake with extra blue due to the effects of thin air and the high altitude. The corners are many, some are tight and big cars will have to negotiate the hairpins with some skill. The surface was well graded when I drove this in a very tired old Toyota. It did not stop things like the headlining collapsing around us, the wiring coming out of the dashboard (the dashboard was held in by my right foot), the windscreen wipers fell off, the seat brackets broke, the radiator rattled loose until it was held in by the hoses, and the battery swung from the earth cable just as the spare wheel dropped off the back, taking the bumper and exhaust with it. We have told you before about the One Eyed Yellow Monster to the North of Kathmandu ... it is still running with only one headlight. The road surface is better than this suggests, honest! It's a drive you will not forget.*

About the valley route originally intended for Vintageants only, Philip wrote:

> *Less mountainous, and a good two hours shorter than the later Classic Category... this route is typical Tibet. It's a challenge, there are off-road excursions to avoid some of the rutted stuff, there are some fine views. With good ground clearance you should have a reasonable run but it will shake up everything, so hopefully you have done a spanner-check and all is bolted down.*

The PSB disagreed with Philip's assessment of the road surface on the Classic route (Philip had driven it a year earlier), and declared the high road off-limits. Whether there were landslides or other hazards, or the PSB just didn't want to have to follow us up there remained unknown.

By now, the Chinese authorities were very upset with the rally organization for their lack of control over participants. Every night we were warned in the bulletins that "everyone must report in!" Several cars, like the Singapore Buick and the Queen's Rolls (both on trucks) and some of the participants in the non-competitive Touring class, were driving at their own pace, either far ahead or far behind the rest. And the PSB was very unhappy when the organizers couldn't tell them exactly where everyone was.

And there were all those cameras. Photography is technically illegal in the Tibet Autonomous Region, and every one of us had a camera, if not three (some participants had one digital, one video, and one standard camera). The officers left most of us alone, but they were furious with the Discovery Crew and the British videographers from World Action Sports, the production company that had been following and filming us all since Beijing (ostensibly for a BBC special). These journalists had gone to considerable expense and difficulty to arrange special visas that allowed them to photograph in China, but apparently those arrangements didn't extend into the "special" region of Tibet.

So thanks to the PSB, our route for the day was expected to be much easier than originally planned. It was still plenty tough. It was my turn to drive, and though the first stretch out of Lhasa was smooth—and mostly deserted, though we passed a painted Buddha carved into a rock wall in the distance—we began to climb again just before the first TC, named appropriately Yak Track (a herd idled on the shoulders and in the road beyond the stop). The log building that housed the TC took us by surprise, and when Linda went up with the time-card book to get our stamp, she endured a dressing down from Michael Summerfield about parking twenty-five meters before the TC. When she got back to the car and told me about it, I re-examined our position and judged us to be well beyond twenty-five yards. I figured he was telling everybody.

From the Yak Track on, the scenery grew stunning: steep rocky gorges occasionally crossed by wire-and-stick bridges, waterfalls, and streams. We were in the drainage path of the unpronounceable Nyainqêntanglha range as we approached the Tsangpo River (called the Brahmaputra when it reaches Nepal). Unfortunately, all those streams created mudflats, watersplashes, and landslides that had to be dodged or forded. A sampling of the road book's instructions include:

!! Rocky section over landslide !!
!! Road collapsed !!
!! Big DIP across stream !!
!! Damaged section!!

We were supposed to pass through all this at an average speed of forty-seven miles per hour.

We were late to the final TC by thirteen minutes.

About seven kilometers into the next stretch, we were suddenly back in the middle of sand dunes. I'd thought we'd left these behind back in the Gobi, but now the sand blew over the road surface for well over two miles. Then the surface settled down into a long suburban road as we neared Xigaze. Suburban, because a well-paved grid of roads began long before the town's buildings, resembling housing developments in California, where the roads are completed long before the houses are built.

This "easier" day turned out to be tough on everybody. Only seven cars still had zero penalties (coming into Lhasa there'd been twenty-five). Team Retro got their first penalties. "We're no longer first—I messed up," Vic wrote in his journal. "They reduced the time for the middle leg today and I forgot to refigure my average speed. We picked up nine penalty points and dropped to seventeenth position overall and third in class. I'm not happy with myself."

All this talk about time penalties requires a little more explanation. The Vintageants, all the pre-1951 cars and four-wheel-drives, carried a blue time-card book, and Classics, 1951 and later, carried yellow time-card books. Time allowances in the blue books were generally greater, in some cases as much as an hour greater than the time allowed to the Classics for the same distance. Required average speeds were therefore much slower for the older cars.

This stage, where both our Hillman and the Team Retro Ford got penalties, is a good one to use as an example. We got our penalty by taking sixty-five minutes to cover the sixty-five kilometer stage, thirteen minutes over the stage's required fifty-two minutes. Team Retro's nine minute penalty meant it actually took them eighty-seven minutes to run the same sixty-five kilometer gauntlet, but since their allowed time was longer (seventy-eight minutes) they got a lower penalty. Our Hillman beat them to the TC by twelve minutes, but got four extra penalty points.

In Tibet, nobody worried much about this kind of nitpicking. But as the days wore on, these little things became major irritants.

Xigaze (or Shigatse) is another holy city, the home of the Panchen Lama (considered to be a reincarnation of Ambitabha, the Buddha of Infinite Light) whose headquarters is the Tashilhunpo Monastery, a gold-roofed palace on the city's mountainous edge. The Panchen Lama is not quite as important, traditionally, as the Dalai Lama, and the tenth Panchen Lama, who died in 1989, had lived what some called a puppet existence mostly in Beijing since the 1960s. The search for his reincarnation created an international incident. After the tenth Panchen died but before Beijing could act, the Dalai Lama nominated a boy named Gedhun Choekyi Nyima as the new Panchen; the Chinese spirited away this six-year-old boy and his family and nominated their own successor instead. This proved to many that the Chinese still intend to control and direct the practice of Tibetan Buddhism, despite their claims that Tibetan "religious beliefs have been protected; we have built many temples."

That should read re-built, as it was the People's Liberation Army who demolished thousands of monasteries in the 1950s. The Tashilhunpo was too important to destroy, even then. It houses the twenty-seven-meter-high statute of the Maitreya Buddha and the tomb of the fourth Panchen Lama, encrusted with eighty-five kilograms of gold and a mass of jewels. It draws pilgrims from all over Tibet.

Linda and I saw the golden towers from the long line at the gas station outside of town. I'd read a little about it and hoped to visit it, but once we got back to the hotel, the day disappeared in car duties. Our left strut (a shock-absorber combined with the upper part of the suspension) was leaking hydraulic fluid—no surprise, considering the punishment of these roads—but worse, our front tires were practically bald on the inner half. They'd been brand-new heavy-duty Avons at Beijing; even a punishing road won't wipe the tread from a tire in less than 3,000 miles. This was the fault of our suspension setup, and could only be stopped by a full realignment. A computerized alignment like we'd expect in the West wasn't available, but Nigel Broderick of the #52 Anglia offered to help us do a visual alignment.

But first we had to replace those two worn-out tires with our two spares. Only one of our spares was mounted on a wheel, so we had to dismount one of our worn tires and mount the spare on the wheel. Nigel Broderick and another Nigel—the long-time-gone Nigel Webb of the Jaguar that had been reported as officially out of the event; he and his co-driver Derek Radcliffe had fixed their problem and driven straight through for several days to catch up—assisted, driving the Anglia over the old tire to pop the bead, then using irons to pry it from the wheel. It took quite a while, and then we drove out to a tire store Nigel Broderick had located earlier and had them mount our spare.

When we got back, we realized that the spare had developed a huge bulge in the side. Our brand-new Avon had a bad sidewall. The Tibetans had no tires of the proper size, so we made a deal with the Brodericks to borrow one of their two spares (the Ford Anglia and Hillman used exactly the same wheel and tire size) until a proper-size tire could be found in Kathmandu.

By the time the tire swapping routine was done, there wasn't time to explore the town. We were hot and tired, and a shower followed by a cold beer sounded perfect.

The hotel in Xigaze was grand in a scrubbed and barren way. A wide marble staircase swirled upward toward the second floor. The halls were long and dark, but the room was pleasant, with an electric hot water kettle and tea bags set out on a tray waiting for us. Once clean, I descended and joined fellow competitors in the large lobby bar.

Most of us were there; it was just about sunset, and we poured Chinese beer from large brown bottles into glasses. Vic and Andy from Team Retro and Carl Schneider all had time to go for a walk, eventually hitching a ride on the back bumper of Dutchman Bart Rietbergen's bright green Volvo (which everyone called Kermit) up to the Tashilhunpo Monastery. "There was one big Buddha inside," Vic said, "over eighty feet tall, all gilded." He and Andy are both devout southern Christians, and seemed to be amazed at the energy and strange activities devoted to this special brand of Buddhism. I could imagine them shaking their heads at the grandeur and oddness of that immense icon.

I shared a glass or two of beer with Michael Kunz. Michael is a jovial, heavy-set New Yorker transplanted to Hong Kong, where he practices law. He was navigator to short, thin, jockey-like Jonathan Thomason, in Jonathan's 1963 Triumph Vitesse (#47), a cute sport sedan. The contrast in size between these two crew members earned them the nickname Little & Large from the support crew. The Triumph seemed prone to mishaps; Jonathan spent every evening fixing something.

I also talked with Gerry Crown, from Australia. He piloted a Holden, an Aussie-built Chevy, with another Austalian named John Bryson, who was considered one of the world's best rally navigators (he'd competed in the original London to Sydney back in the 1960s). John always wore a tie. I thought it was meant to show us he took navigating seriously, but it turns out he'd made a deal with his boss back home in Sydney: he could have the seven weeks off if he promised to wear a tie every work day. John's clipped and colorful speech was charming, but for some reason I developed a strong sort of daughterly affection for Gerry. Maybe it was the twangy way he called me by my full name—"Hey! Gene-vay-eve!"

I ran into Linda and Michael Veys in the hotel gift shop. It was a narrow room with shelves on both walls and a long table down the center. We'd seen many spooky silver souvenirs in Lhasa, everything from intricate Buddhas to jewel-encrusted daggers and silver-lined human skull cups. Here the offerings were more modest: small silver Tibetan good luck charms, prayer wheels, and Buddhas. I was hoping to find a tiny—no bigger than thumb size—Buddha to go with my Kwan Yin, but everything was too big, so I decided instead to get postcards and stamps. The individual postcards were nice, but the books of ten all seemed to have one or two good photos followed by dismal, out of focus sunsets, yaks and deer shots. I bought a packet anyway (I wanted to get all my postcards written and mailed at once). Before I could give the shopkeeper my money, the room was plunged into blackness. The power had failed. There was a wave of worried noises from our cohorts still at the bar, and all of us standing stranded in the shop. But moments later the shopkeeper's big lantern-style flashlight came on. He smiled broadly and shrugged, counting out my stamps. It was business as usual.

The power went on and off many more times that night.

At the time of Prince Borghese's visit, Urga, the capital of Mongolia, consisted of three cities—Chinese, Mongolian, and Russian—arranged in a triangle. The Grand Lama, reputed to be only slightly less important than the Dalai Lama (this may have been the Panchen Lama, or a lesser one), lived in a great white palace within the Russian sphere. As soon as Borghese and his crew arrived, requests came in from both the Mongolian Governor and the Grand Lama to be given rides on the motor-car. The Governor arrived first, at high speed, his palanquin's four poles resting, unsecured, on the saddlebows of four galloping Mongolian troopers.

"The Mandarin," Barzini wrote, "most pompously clad, with enormous silk sleeves which covered his hands . . . wearing a hat adorned by two peacock feathers, first walked right round the machine inspecting it with great care. Then he mounted, while the Prince took the wheel."

The Itala started and the Governor climbed aboard. He "seemed completely enraptured. His little pigtails fluttered in the wind, and the men of his suite thought perhaps for a moment that their lord was being kidnapped. They threw themselves upon their horses . . . and dashed off after the diabolical engine, shouting."

The car left the terrified troopers in its dust, but soon returned with the Governor intact. Later that evening, a message came from the Grand Lama; he would need several days to decide whether to "grant the privilege of beholding his countenance."

"'But how is that?' we exclaimed. 'He was so anxious to see us.'

"'Oh, that's understandable,' somebody murmured. 'He is offended.'

"'Who?—the living Buddha?—and why?'

"Because of the Governor's ride. He is punctilious about priority, and he dislikes the Governor.'"

It was left to the French contingent to entertain the Grand Lama. After Prince Borghese's crew had already left town, the De Dion-Bouton drivers were called to his palace. A courtier-monk asked the Frenchmen to look at a motor-car that had been given to the Lama but had never functioned. One of the De Dion-Bouton drivers answered bluntly, "Not interested. We haven't come to see a car. We want to talk to the living god. Tell him that if he doesn't come out in person we'll go away without looking at anything."

They waited a half-hour, and the Lama arrived with his full retinue. When the time came for a ride, the Lama declined, instead offering the seat to one of his courtiers. He laughed as he watched his man ride around the courtyard. Then he again implored the Frenchmen to take a look at his car.

It was a box with wheels, and though the wheels had the right shape, it was no more than a shop-front dummy, the kind used for advertisements.

"The best thing I could tell you to do is to buy another," said the De Dion-Bouton driver, who was also a De Dion-Bouton salesman. "It's a wonderful little machine, ten horsepower, very strongly built, economical, will go anywhere, and I can let you have it for . . ."

He had difficulty translating francs into the local currency, and then noted the Grand Lama's distant smile. Alas, there would be no motor-car sales in Urga that day.

CHAPTER

∽ 18 ∾

Then came a crash. We stopped. Prince Borghese jumped down to look at the wheel,
and uttered an exclamation of real grief. "We're done for. We can't move another foot."

XIGAZE TO EVEREST CAMP
[THURSDAY, SEPTEMBER 18]

I read the road book as we headed out of Xigaze that morning. "Tough challenges all the way to Kathmandu," was noted at kilometer number eleven, and forty-six kilometers later this sentence: "Villages known collectively as 'Ne'." Knowing the recce was done by Brits, I could only think of Monty Python's *Holy Grail* and "The Knights who say Nee!" Were they serious? Or was this a joke? There was no English sign anywhere to prove or disprove it.

Comic relief was welcome. The road conditions were not amusing. We had six kilometers of asphalt starting there in Ne, in fact. All the rest was mud, rocks, ruts, or dust. Today, the dust would do us in.

After all the drop-outs and time penalties before Lhasa, we were now running with a different group of cars. The Catts (#50) and Brodericks (#52) were way ahead of us, up with the Iranians and a few others who still had no penalties. Down in the twenty-six minute (penalty point) range, we were joined now by #45, "Maurice" the Morris Minor. (The name was painted on the fender, and pronounced "Morris the Morris" in a proper British accent). It was a cute car driven by a honeymooning British couple. The woman had an impressively trim, muscular body thanks, apparently, to a demanding exercise regimen, and she showed it off with skintight aerobic-wear. She wore thick red lipstick and black lines around her eyes, drawing attention to her heavily lined face. The contradiction between body and face made guessing her true age impossible. Her husband was tall and thin, with the haggard look of a small-town parson. The irreverent support crew had nicknamed this unlikely pair The Vicar and the Tart.

Linda drove us out of Xigaze even though she was feeling rotten. She'd contracted a head cold, and had rummaged through our first-aid kit and picked out a remedy or two. We were already taking Diamox; I wondered what kind of effect the combination might have. She gamely proclaimed to be up to the task of driving.

Right out of town the road book said "12,800 ft rising steadily." Within a mile "Z bends" began. Linda handled the wheel fine as we zig-zagged parallel to the Tsangpo River, sometimes with sheer cliffs dropping off a thousand feet to the river below. Above us on every rise were prayer flags, and we passed two monasteries, one in ruins, the other a dun-colored complex flush against the mountain in the distance.

We crawled around and through a fresh landslide at kilometer ninety-five. It slowed us so much I began to worry about our timing. We passed the five thousand marker: small white road markers had staked out every kilometer since we left Beijing. "NOW road starts to climb steeply," the book said redundantly about ten kilometers later. We'd been climbing for hours. We were going far too slowly, I knew, but I wasn't sure what to say, if anything. I had come to appreciate Linda's required silence, even treasure it. We had both grown to find the quiet a comfort. It meant all was well.

Of course it was far from quiet. The car's engine, rattling exhaust, rattling everything else, all made a huge racket. We had our new tires on, but our strut was still leaking and the left side of the car bounced much more prominently than the right whenever we hit a rut. Linda tried to favor that side, but it was impossible. From time to time we'd hit a pothole WHACK smack dab in its middle with the left front tire. But then from my seat on the left side, I realized, these potholes were much more obvious. I scolded her at least once, reminding her about the strut, and she slowed our overall speed in response.

Now the road, when it wasn't wet with mud, was rutted in what the road book called corrugations. We could move along faster than on the erratically-rutted dirt, but the car still bounced and jounced violently, with our tires playing a deep rhythm as if passing over a huge granite zither.

When I glanced at the clock and realized we only had five minutes left, I blurted it out. "We only have five—"

I heard our overtaker before I saw him. The car whipped around us, a blazing white cloud of dry impenetrable dust, but we were leftward bound, out of control (from my perspective on the passenger side) before a second car's blinding rear curtain had fallen. I think the first one was #76, a Peugeot manned by two serious rally drivers, one British, the other French (the only Frenchman in the bunch. Odd there was only one, I thought as the car went out of control, since the original 1907 event had been such a French to-do). I didn't see the second car—I'm not even positive there was a second car—but something seemed to make the dust cloud bigger, louder, more blinding.

We hit something—BAM! Black rubber, mud and shiny metal shot up through the floor. The twisted wheel, stripped rubber and shredded flooring pinned my ankles. Mud welled up in what had once been the foot well and was now a big hole in the floor.

"We're finished!" I shouted. "We're history!"

The car slid down, plowed under, finally stopped. Linda said, "We're still here." Then a moment later, "You're not hurt are you?"

The dust settled and the sky slowly emerged. A rumbling—no, mumbling—of voices, not engines, filled the sudden silence. A crowd had gathered. I tested my feet, pressed by the wreckage but not, amazingly, injured. I opened the door. It scraped along the top edge of the mud. I climbed out and rose to my full height, conscious of the stares of the amazed Tibetans. A village wall was less than six feet away. We'd been lucky we hadn't hit it, in our blind trajectory. Instead, the deep muddy rut had swallowed us up.

I walked around the car. Linda was already up and out. We shook ourselves, hugged.

"Go ahead and cry if you want," Linda said.

It was the last thing I wanted to do. I was too angry. First at Linda: I would've slowed down but not veered, I told myself oh-so-confidently, as if I had any idea what I'd really do in the same situation. Then at myself: "If I hadn't been looking down I might've been able to warn you about that culvert," I told Linda, who scoffed and said, "There was nothing you could do, it was driver error." The only thing I was really sure about was how angry I was at those other rally drivers.

In a daze, I circled the car three times; got my camera and took pictures of the wheel, the car, the gathering crowd of locals.

While pacing I figured out what happened. When we careened leftward, we'd run into a cement culvert over a drainage pipe on the edge of the road; that's what sent the wheel through the floor. Back at the car, I opened the trunk and got out our folding shovel. Once I started digging around the wheel, the locals got the idea, and men and boys stooped to join me. Someone motioned to us and Linda got in and put the car into reverse. It went back far enough to dislodge the front fender from the deepest part of the mud. I went back to digging—a young boy of maybe nine and I were using our hands now, pulling wet gritty masses off the exposed hub—but then more hand signals were exchanged and a group of twenty-odd men, including some green-coated military (where had they come from?) surrounded the car. They were chattering wildly, smiling broadly, and they all bent and grabbed onto the car's lowest edges. Then a sing-song chant, something like "chung ching" or "lay lung," rose up joyfully into the air, and they heaved the car up out of the mud and onto the road.

Once on the road I got the wheel off and starting taking the mud off the brake calipers. They looked okay. I got under and saw that the steering control arm and heavy cross bar or link in front of it were both severely bent. Despite the bend we replaced the destroyed wheel with the spare, just to see. Linda tried driving it. Her high-revving low-speed crabwalk across the dusty lane (the right wheel drove while the left wheel was simply dragged across) had the locals slapping their knees in laughter. At least the car was now well out of the line of oncoming traffic, and more visible. "No good," I told the ever-helpful Tibetans, then took the spare back off and waited for the organizer's mechanics crew.

We were lucky that they weren't long in coming. I had contemplated trying to disassemble the bent pieces myself, but the Land Rover arrived before I'd convinced myself to do it. Tony Fowkes and Jingers, in his customary shorts, had it apart in minutes and the U-shaped control rod on the vice on the Rover's rear fender soon after. It took them some finagling with a pipe to straighten it, while Rick the paramedic tested my ankle for injury. "It's fine," I told him. He asked Linda if she were all right, glancing at his stopwatch.

"Are you working at one of the time controls today?" I asked him. He had thick ringlet-curled black hair and a handsome Welsh face.

"No, I have to keep track of the lads' time, ya know. Ten minutes max per car."

I'd completely forgotten that little detail, and the shock, the thought of being left there with a half-bent-back rod because we'd run out of time, must have shown on my face.

"Sometimes we can bend it a little," he whispered, as if Philip Young himself might hear. He handed me a rope to hold—to keep the Tibetans away—and by now along with our locals we'd gathered a nice little crowd of rally hangers-on: more PSB officers, and a Chinese Toyota carrying Number One, his lordship Edward of Montagu (or Eddie of Monty, as Linda and I called him in the privacy of our Hillman). He wielded a nasty little video cam that caught me laughing at the scene of the crime.

I was greatly relieved by then, as the rod bent obligingly back and in the crew's adept hands flew back onto the steering linkage in a jiffy. I don't think we exceeded their limit by much, and the Land Rover Lads were off again in no time. Before we set off, we decided to reward the friendly locals with the only prizes we had handy: rolls of Lifesavers. We gave our dozen or so rolls to all the children (there weren't enough to give any to the adults) and headed to the TC at Lhaze.

Our penalty came to one hour and thirty-one minutes—a half hour to spare under the two-hour-maximum-lateness. Our total penalties now added up to one hour and fifty-seven minutes, but we still had another 153 kilometers to go, and the bulletin issued back in Lhasa had warned that the last seventy-five kilometers between Gyatso Pass (16,965 ft) and Everest Camp (only sixty-five feet lower) was so muddy, there'd be no TC at the end. Instead, the TC had been moved up to the pass itself, a short thirty-four kilometers from Lhaze. We only had twenty-nine minutes to get there.

Linda insisted on continuing with her driving duties after the accident, but she seemed to be possessed, driving sometimes incredibly slowly, then too fast and bashing our bruised suspension into unavoidable ruts. I might very well have done the same. I didn't realize until the next day how difficult it was to handle the car with the steering so completely tweaked. Once I thought she might be crying; then I realized that the sniffling was probably due to her cold; I figured the altitude was making it worse.

As we climbed up to Gyatso, our engine lost all power again; our carburetors simply would not function. We tried all Jingers' tricks and nothing worked. We were stalled awhile, intermittently starting the car up: it simply groaned and rolled forward at one or two miles per hour, if that. By the time a Land Rover rounded the bend behind us, we were ready with our tow rope. It turned out to be the British video crew.

They were happy to hook us up and film us at the same time. Linda was manically happy at their arrival, and more than willing to talk. The cameraman joined her in the Hillman and I rode in the Land Rover. We both ended up reciting our respective versions of our accident while the Land Rover's driver barreled along. He got going so fast, I think he forgot the Hillman was there. Linda blared on the air horn.

"You're going too fast!" I said, "Our car can't take these bumps."

If there had been a way to dislodge the tow rope at speed, we wouldn't have needed to be towed more than a hundred yards: once we got the Hillman's speed up to 15 mph or so, the airflow into the carburetors increased enough to give us some power. But the Land Rover barreled on into the TC, towing us a total of about fifteen minutes. I rushed out with the time-card book and up to the desk, where Michael Summerfield said, "I do not see a tow rope."

I laughed. "What tow rope?" Linda and the camera crew were busy untying our two vehicles. Mike's tone had been playful, but I wondered if we'd broken a rule: I didn't remember reading that you couldn't be towed into a TC, and towing (and trucking!) were certainly legal in every other instance. Three days later all was made clear when bulletin #10 stated clearly "All cars towed into a control will be deemed to have missed the control and will receive the appropriate penalty."

We'd been penalized anyway; the delay caused by our gasping carburetors and the tow cost us forty-seven minutes, dropping us to a total for the day of two hours forty-four minutes in penalties. That would put us down somewhere near fortieth place. Thankfully, each TC had a separate two-hour-maximum-lateness window; so though the day's total exceeded two hours, we'd still be in the running for a gold medal. We still had some seventy-five kilometers to go, but at least those would be un-timed.

An hour later, we hit another bad rut and bent our rod again. This time we were aided by the same crew who'd first come to our rescue: Rick, Jingers and Tony. We had the wheel off and ready for them, and endured their lectures: "You're driving too fast! You gotta slow down! This rod's not gonna hold up."

"I know," I assured them, "it looks like a noodle now."

"You'll need to weld some extra metal on there as soon as you can, tonight if possible." I took that to mean they'd have welding equipment available at the camp.

We drove very slowly—15 to 20 mph—toward Everest Camp, a spot some four days' walk from the beginning of the North Face ascent of the world's highest mountain. From here, Everest (29,029 ft) sits with two sister peaks, Xixapangma (28,209 ft) and Cho Oyu (26,749 ft). Everest's Sherpa name is Chomolungma (spellings vary, as Sherpan is not a written language), which means Goddess Mother of the Universe. An angry apparition awaited us as we drove onto the tundra-like campsite, but it wasn't anything like a goddess: a big man with a large belly and a floppy, wide brimmed hat stood with hands on hips and legs spread, silhouetted against the gorgeous, luminous mountains.

It was Philip Young. "I heard you were speeding," he said, "going seventy. What did you do?"

"Seventy? No way!" Linda said, then explained. Philip was not pleased, but left us alone to park and find dinner. Some ralliers set up chairs to relax and enjoy the view. We, however, had work to do.

I was determined to find that welder, so I sought out the support crew, camping far on the edge of the field. The welding reference had been to someone else's kit. The mechanics were sure somebody—the Alabamans? the big Chevy Bel Air?—had a welder. But I couldn't find the Alabamans (Team Retro), and anyway I didn't know how to weld, and neither did Linda. But I was fixated on getting the thing fixed; I was determined to do something to strengthen the car, or at least lessen the likelihood of another bad bend.

Linda, for her part, was fixated on a glass of gin. In my welding-apparatus search, I'd discovered that the Bentley boys, Jonathan and Adam, kept a full flask and were willing to share. Linda disappeared for a while, reappearing with a smile on her face, and her camp mug full. She poured a therapeutic dollop from her mug into mine.

As luck would have it, David Drew, our miracle Rover repairman, and Jonathan Lux, had parked right next to us. But they didn't set up any tents. They'd decided to ditch camping and go to a little inn nearby with a yak-dung burner for heat and a mud floor. David slipped under our Hillman for a quick look at our bent noodle. He said "All you've gotta do is . . ." and so, while Jonathan smoked and took pictures of the changing light on the mountains, David and I removed the sump guard (a mud-encrusted bitch with nuts, and we had no vice grip) and then disassembled the steering arms, putting it all back together in a slightly different way (by moving various arms and bushings), in an effort to get the wheelbase back where it was supposed to be.

The Jeepsters were camped nearby, and Dick Taylor offered a hand, helping to push the whole left side forward. It had been pushed back by the impact about four inches, even popping out the windshield. Linda and I hadn't realized that the glass had just been resting loosely in its frame all afternoon.

Dick went back to the Jeep for dinner, but we gathered up a new crew—still David Drew, but with help now from two Michaels (Veys of the Rolls and Kunz, the American from Hong Kong) and Canadian Captain John O'Neill and his Cypriot co-driver, who were camped beside us with their #46 Volkswagen. These guys decided we shouldn't remount the too-worn spare, so they dismounted and mounted the tires, the same laborious process we'd endured in Xigaze. That job stretched on after dinner until ten-thirty or so.

While the Michaels messed with the tires, David devised an elaborate device with string that set the windshield back in its weatherstripping. It all went back in just right, except for the top right corner. David climbed atop the car while Michael Veys and I applied counterforce from inside, but the car was too tweaked and the last corner refused to set. We finally just applied multiple rows of duct tape.

Other than David Drew, we never asked any of these guys for help; they'd all heard about our accident, of course, and it was clear from our Hillman's appearance that some major work needed doing. Their generosity, when they could have been lounging and enjoying the view, amazed and humbled me.

I was acutely aware that, as women, we were perceived to be more dependent on the support crews and the kindness of our fellow ralliers than others. The Gulls had already taken some ribbing for their heavy use (some said abuse) of both the support crews and other ralliers whenever their Volvo gave them trouble. In fact, I realized early on that I knew far more about automobiles—both history and mechanical theory—than many of the male participants. Yet that knowledge didn't make me a capable mechanic, and I literally lacked the arm and hand-strength necessary to muscle the suspension into place, or even to dismount a tire. Yet, there at the base of Everest, it was clear that these men wanted to help not because we were women, but because we were fellow ralliers. We were confederates; we'd become friends. And this was borne out over the full length of the rally: whenever someone was in trouble, it was as likely to be another rally car that stopped to help as one of the support crews. This kind of cooperative camaraderie is the thing classic car ralliers treasure most; it's one reason they prefer classic events to pro rallying, where cooperation outside one's own team is taboo.

David Drew had been helping us now for hours. The sun had set in a phantasmagorical display on the Sisters' glorious flanks—red, orange, yellow, white, silver, deepening to purples and warm grays. By now, Jonathan was really fuming. He'd been waiting to take David with him to their hotel. I told David he should go; we'd manage, and it was clear the Michaels and others would help. David just muttered in that inimitable British way—something about bastards and buggering—and kept working until the fluorescent full moon had risen high in the sky.

Thanks to David, the two Michaels, and a batch of other generous souls, Linda and I were able to collapse into our sleeping bags satisfied. We had a straightened steering rod, a new tire on a decent wheel, a taped-up windshield, the torn metal banged out of the way of the wheel, and the hole in the floor taped.

All this, and the world's highest mountain.

Borghese, Barzini, and Ettore the mechanic never really conquered the Siberian mud, but they mastered several ingenious methods of extracting a motor-car from it. Wood was far more plentiful in Siberia than it had been in Mongolia, so the forests were thinned for the cause. With that problem at least managed, a new one presented itself: all the bridges around Lake Baikal were crumbled, or about to crumble. The rivers were swift and deep and impossible to ford. The only bridges of any strength were those in use by the railway.

Borghese applied to the stationmaster at Missowaja, on the banks of Lake Baikal, for permission to drive his Itala on the railway line. Not *in* a railway car—that was strictly against the rules agreed to in Paris. The local authorities resisted this fantastic notion, but Borghese was armed with several letters bearing official stamps from St. Petersburg. The bureaucracy (then as now) was slow moving, so they had to wait several days for a decision.

The permission finally came, and they set off with two planks to serve as ramps up onto the rails. Once upon them, they settled the Itala's left wheels over the right-hand rails.

"The sensation of this motor journey was at first delightful," Barzini wrote. "That superb, even, level, clear road was full of attraction after the ruts, the woods, and the ditches of the other." But eventually the route grew punishing: "The sleepers, though very near each other and covered with a layer of sand, made the car sway and gave it a motion as of a slight, gentle gallop, but if we went faster the gallop became violent and ended in a terrible jarring, a wild jerking and shaking which it seemed must break the machine."

After a few miles of this "horrible dancing," they came to a station, and descended. The master there warned them that a train approached, and would not let them back on the rails. He recommended the old road, which he claimed was still in use.

"We had been scarcely more than half-a-mile when we came to an old wooden bridge . . . over a torrent about ten feet deep," Barzini wrote. "Ettore slackened speed and stopped for a few seconds to look . . . in this spot we had a moment's hesitation, a fleeting foreboding of danger; but it was only for a moment.

"Prince Borghese gave the order to Ettore.

"'Go on, slowly.'

"The car advanced on the planks, which trembled, cracked a little, swayed as so many others had done under the weight of our machine. . . . The front part of the car had already traversed more than half the bridge. . . . Every danger seemed over. . . . Suddenly we heard a frightful crash. The planks had given way under the weight of the hind part of the machine.

"The car . . . fell in backwards with a sudden heavy movement . . . it raised its front wheels up in the air and plunged with its back towards the abyss . . . it plunged deep into the torrent—to the very bottom of it—carrying all three of us down amid a terrible debris of broken, wrenched, smashed planks and beams. . . . With the slowness of some uncouth great animal, the car had accomplished a kind of backward somersault."

Barzini had been sitting high atop the luggage and therefore fell the farthest. "I

was under the bridge in sudden and ominous shadow, catching on to the ropes of the luggage; the car was still falling and breaking more timber. I felt as if I would never arrive at the bottom. I just allowed myself to be dragged along, bending under the storm of broken wood which beat upon me. . . . I remember noticing with a certain satisfaction that I felt no great pain. . . . The part destined to hold the oil was now perpendicularly above my head, and was flooding me. . . . I could feel it pouring over my face."

The Prince and the mechanic had been thrown from their seats. "I heard just above me cries of pain coming from Prince Borghese. I saw his feet kicking desperately above my head, and also dripping with oil. His cries ceased almost immediately. At that moment Ettore appeared at my side."

The strong mechanic pulled Barzini and the Prince free of the wreckage. "We all three found ourselves on our feet facing one another, each asking the other how he had fared, and exchanging expressions of great relief. Looking back at the position in which the car stood, we exclaimed: 'It is incredible—surely we were saved by a miracle!'"

Linda and I weren't the only ones who had had an unlucky thirteenth day. Don and Carl accumulated more penalty points as they "skied" across the Himalayas on their airless suspension, and I couldn't find Team Retro and their welding gear because they didn't make it into camp until almost midnight.

The trouble didn't begin until the day's second stage, that thirty-four-kilometer stretch where Linda and I had resorted to the video crew's tow. "That was some of the roughest, most inhospitable terrain I've ever seen," Vic said. He and Ted were in car #23. "We got hung up by a road crew, a policeman, another competitor being towed, trucks, you name it. We missed our time by less than ten seconds, so we were penalized one minute."

John and Andy in #24 made it through clean, so #23 now had ten penalty points, and #24 had eight. The last stretch was untimed, but about forty kilometers from the last TC, #23 hit a ditch, damaging the steering center link. Vic took the whole thing apart right there on the side of the road. When John and Andy arrived with the welder, they pushed the car off the elevated road, perpendicular to it, so they could get under it without jacking it up.

But the welder wouldn't work. A passing rallier mentioned that the hotel back in Lhaze not only had a welder, but another rally car was already there taking advantage of it. So Vic and Andy took the steering pieces and headed back in the #24 car. When they got to the hotel, a group of German trekkers told them that the welder had just left. Andy spotted a Toyota Landcruiser going around behind the building and, on a hunch, followed.

"There," Vic said, "in the middle of Tibet, behind one of the worst hotels I've ever seen, was the Bugatti, being welded on by a Chinese man. He had no other tools but the welder and two hammers. He cut pieces of angle iron by burning them with the welding rod, hammered them into place, then welded them, somewhat skillfully, into place. Since the owners of the Bugatti had decided to stay in the hotel overnight and rejoin the rally early in the morning, they interrupted the man so he could repair our center link. He did a pretty good job. When we tried to pay, the Bugatti owner said that he would take care of the bill if we would use our satellite phone to call his shop in England, and ask them to ship a frame stub to Kathmandu."

Next they needed fuel. There was a gas station just across the road, but it was closing. "We begged the attendant," Vic said, "and he finally agreed to let us in. Andy gave him a T-shirt, and we got our gas and started back to the disabled car, where Ted and John were waiting."

"The moon hadn't risen yet," Vic continued, "so we stopped the car, turned out the lights and looked at the stars. At fifteen thousand feet, with no lights for hundreds of miles, the stars were spectacular! We made it back to the broken car just as the moon was coming up. We crawled under, installed the repaired piece and in no time we were on our way—dirty, dusty, tired and hungry. We picked our way through the ruts in the dark. A few kilometers from where the campground was supposed to be, a jeep-type vehicle pulled up, motioned for us to follow, then led us to the campground."

For one Dutch couple, Renger and Gerda Guliker, the thirteenth day was their last on the rally. Their '56 Chevy Pickup, fancifully painted with the entire route all around the pickup's bed, went off the road (apparently blinded by overtakers in a situation similar to ours) and could not continue. They had also received sad news from home: a much-awaited grandchild had been born with severe health problems; a good enough reason to return to Holland, even if the truck had been repairable.

It had been our toughest, most exhausting day. And yet, when the Diamox woke me in the middle of the night, and I rose out of the tent into the icy night air, I stood still, in utter awe. The sky had fallen. Stars rested on my shoulders, skimmed the top of my head, glittered along the shadowy ridge of Everest and her immense sisters. I could almost hold one in my hand, if I reached out just. . . so.

I had never been so close to heaven.

❧ 19 ❧

Every morning at the time of starting we felt strong and ready for our journey, because
we had lost the exact remembrance of our experiences of the day before. A beneficent mist
spread over past suffering, and at our departure we always imagined every difficulty to
be over. Oblivion and hopefulness were our strength.

EVEREST CAMP TO CHOKSAM
[FRIDAY, SEPTEMBER 19]

We broke camp in the cloudy, cold morning and set off for "Choksam" or Nyalam, the location of our last night's stop in Tibet. It was my turn to drive. Before we'd left Lhasa, we'd been given a special bulletin covering route changes all the way through this day, and I'd gone carefully through the road book to mark the changes. We had an hour and eight minutes to complete the first sixty-two kilometer stage, a required average speed of fifty-five kph (thirty-four mph). The second stage up to the La Lungla summit (16,413 ft) was much shorter—only twenty-six kilometers—and though the required average speed was about the same, everyone was calling it a "speed stage." It seems like a misnomer but it's not: thirty-four miles an hour over tight hairpins and up steep inclines with sheer cliff edges is dangerously fast.

Being extra careful about our left front, I tried to keep the speed up between thirty and forty mph, but for many bumps we had to slow to a crawl. When I didn't, thinking the road was smoothing out, we'd inevitably hit something hard and deep and worse on the left. Then Linda would scold me just as I'd scolded her the day before. We came into Munboch, the day's first TC, with a seven-minute penalty.

The tape and hemp floor mats we'd used to patch the hole in the floor didn't keep the water out when we forded the two rivers that day. Everything was technically downhill now, and the waterfalls, streams, and landslides made it clear that the road was no impediment to that gravitational pull. All that water also created more vegetation. The landscape became greener and more lush with every mile, and the road book warned us to watch for "hares." It was a nice change after so long on the cold, gray-green tundra.

Linda still suffered from her cold, and she was in a bad mood that grew worse as the day wore on. "We'll never get up the mountain," she'd say. "This car is a piece of shit!" Whatever happened to her cherished silence? Now she was driving *me* crazy. That night I noted in my journal:

> *I don't remember what exactly she said that was too much, but at one point I said, "Linda, you have every right to be pissed off and negative, but don't ruin my positive mood. Think it, but don't say it." It seemed to work.*

We were fifteen minutes late coming into La Lungla, but that penalty wasn't just due to the road and our weakened suspension. Just before the summit, we had to stop. On one side of the road stood a big blue Chinese truck, on the other, the black Mercedes #70 with a three-man German crew. The Germans were distraught and someone was lying on the ground, obviously hurt. Linda jumped out of the car and ran over, thinking her nursing training might be of some assistance.

The downed man was the Chinese truck driver. Apparently he'd stepped out right in front of the Mercedes, which had been flying along, probably at 35 mph or faster. We stayed until the rally support crew, including a medic, pulled up. The Chinese man looked like he had a bad concussion, Linda said, and probably broken bones.

We drove on, reaped our fifteen-minute penalty, then continued the eighteen kilometers toward what the road book called the "Choksam Hotel." If Linda spotted "Milarepa's Cave," a seventh-century Buddhist poet's cave the road book said was near kilometer seventy-three, she didn't tell me. Perhaps I'd shushed her too adamantly. We were descending rapidly now; this Po Chu river valley would lead us all the way to Nepal, with ever-steeper drops and ravines falling off on our right.

When we parked along the rock wall that marked the "hotel," we discovered a derelict warehouse, apparently once home to roadworking crews. We had already been told we'd be camping, so we weren't sure what to expect. It turned out there were a few "hotel rooms" available, but they were so dark (no power), and dank (dripping wet), most chose to camp. Vic said the place seemed "like something from a Stephen King novel."

Linda and I set up our tent under a semi-permanent awning over the garden. It had been sprinkling on and off, so we thought it would keep us dry. This "garden" proved to be a pig yard; we heard rooting and snorting outside our tent throughout the night.

Inside the huge open room that served as lobby and dining hall, we all sat around on a mismatched assortment of chairs, drinking. Burlinson's Sherpa crew dragged in a long extension cord, attaching a single socket to their generator out in their truck. This single light-bulb swung from the ceiling, providing the only light as the sky outside darkened.

I sat alone writing until it was too dark to continue, then joined various groups of drinkers. Most, like me, held onto bottles of Chinese beer provided by the Sherpas; others nursed flasks from their private stocks. All four of the Bentley boys, Jonathan and Adam from England and Bill and Ned from New England, were at the top of their form, sharing Scotch and laughing uproariously. But I wasn't feeling well. I was coming down with Linda's cold. She, on the other hand, had completely recovered from her blue funk, and was chatty and happy and over her cold.

Amazing what a touch of gin can do for one's outlook.

I talked quietly for awhile with David Tremain, of London and South Africa. It surprised me to learn that the vintage Land Rover he was driving was actually owned by his navigator (and sometime driver) Carolyn Ward, a pretty blond woman with a husband and children at home. He hadn't known her well before the rally, but had been chosen through a network of friends when Carolyn's first choice had been unable to make it.

Team Retro hadn't had an easy day of it. They'd had to install the last of their spare rear shocks that morning at Everest Camp (Ted called out on his satellite phone and ordered eight more), and they had to struggle to make the 45 kph required average (10 kph or 6 mph slower for the Vintageants than for us Classics). They weren't worried since they'd been told the day's last TC had been canceled because of the Mercedes' accident. If that was true, Linda and I were due back our fifteen minutes. As it turned out, we had to keep our penalty, but the next day's TCs were all canceled.

Rumors filled the air. When we'd first pulled up at Choksam, the two British gents in the '67 Camaro said, "Are you the ones that hit the Chinese man?" Apparently our accident the day before made us the most likely suspects. Most in that cavernous room believed the truck driver was dying or near death, and that the Chinese had arrested all the Germans. Linda thought it possible, remembering the rattly sound of that truck driver's breathing and his one dilated pupil.

Rumors were also flying about the fate of the journalists. I'd overhead the British video crew talking about their Discovery Online colleagues. They said Chris, Drew, and Mike had all been arrested before they could leave Everest Camp. The British journalists hesitated for only a moment before climbing back into their Land Rover and setting out for the border. Dick Taylor of the Jeepsters clarified what happened in his report to the Arizona *Republic*:

> *As we break camp, I overhear a loud argument involving one of the Chinese policemen and an American photojournalist who has paid to come along to film the rally. Despite having a valid Chinese visa, and having pre-paid for the entire two weeks in China, the police insist that he cannot go on with us, and must leave China immediately or be imprisoned. I volunteer to take the only action available to aid our fellow American, and agree to smuggle him under our sleeping bags and camping gear through to Nepal! For the rest of the day we are constantly alert every time a police car approaches, but we get our contraband photographer close to the Nepal border, and then put him on a German tourist bus, under a tarp covering the luggage, to cross the border safely into Nepal. He couldn't stay with us, because*

*we must camp one more night before reaching the border and he would surely be
caught. We thought we were to be rally drivers, but end up smuggling a photographer out of China!*

The full story was later revealed on the Internet, in articles the crew prepared
for the Discovery website. The young journalists hadn't been arrested; in fact,
Chris was able to travel openly to the border with the rally support crew. She
wasn't in trouble, she was only a writer; it was the cameramen and their hardware the Chinese were after. Mike eluded the PSB and found a willing smuggler
in a competitor's '55 Peugeot 403, then joined Drew under that same tarp in
the German tour bus. The hardware made it out in various rally cars.

PRINCE BORGHESE'S TRAIL

CHAPTER

∽20∾

Our right-hand wheels travelled on the very brink of the abyss. It was a matter of an inch or so. The manoeuvre possessed no technical difficulties for a driver of unremitting attention and a steady hand, but it was impossible at these moments to help feeling a slight instinctive thrill which made you clench your fists, and keep your eye fixed on the front wheel as you went over the narrow way on the edge.

CHOKSAM, TIBET TO KATHMANDU, NEPAL
[SATURDAY, SEPTEMBER 20]

We had a routine morning, rolling up our sleeping bags and tent, but not so Dick Taylor of the Jeepsters. Dick wrote:

As I get out of our tent in the dark for an early start on what proves to be our most difficult day, my foot catches on the tent door, and I fall forward into what appears to be mud. My entire right side and back are covered with "mud," but as I try to clean it off without any source of water, its smell immediately tells me that I have fallen into feces dumped by two pigs seen near our tent the night before. Since I can only wipe off with hand tissues, my aroma in the car the rest of the day doesn't make me popular with my traveling companions.

According to the road book, the day's run totaled only about 140 kilometers, or 87 miles, between Choksam in Tibet and Kathmandu, Nepal. Our shortest ever—less than my typical drive from Santa Cruz to San Francisco, which takes no more than an hour and a half with heavy traffic. And because of the accident the day before, the competition had been canceled for the day—no checkpoints, no stamps, no clock watching. How could such an easy, non-competitive distance be, as Dick wrote, "our most difficult"?

The first twenty-four kilometers were fine, slow but steady going to the border town of Zhangmu, a precipitous pile of buildings that literally rise one atop the other, separated only by the road's zig or zag cutting straight down the mountainside. The border guards were stationed here, as were the huckstering Nepali rupee-hawkers and Chinese yuan-traders. We were processed and then, escorted by the ubiquitous green-coated PSB, led down to the muddy truck ruts of "no man's land," eight kilometers kept almost impassable by the weather and perhaps

politicians—it creates a deterrent to unauthorized border crossing.

In this one day, we would descend from 16,000 feet to only 3,200 in Kathmandu; most of that drop happened within sixty miles of very twisting road. As narrow as six feet in places, the road was carved into the side of the mountain, and followed the deepening canyon of the Po Chu river. The drop off our right was said to be as much as three thousand feet. Even the organizers, veterans of rallies around the world, said this is the worst road in the world.

Thanks to the recent monsoons and landslides—as many as twenty-one separate slides—the surface of this narrow lane was sloppy mud and bare rock. It took most of us ten or more hours to get to Kathmandu. That's an average speed of less than nine miles per hour.

Dave Pierce, the young mechanic at the Jeep's wheel, told me later that he'd been driving for all he was worth, almost scraping the rock wall, constantly concerned about clearance on the right. At one narrow point, he asked taciturn Larry, "How's it look on that side?" Larry, looking down, saw the right half of the tire supported by nothing but air, the sheer drop to the river directly below his shoulder. Larry swallowed, looked back up and said simply, "Clear."

Dave, thinking Larry meant "fine," breathed a sigh of relief.

It was again Linda's turn to drive. In our right-hand drive Hillman, she now had the worst of both worlds: the wheel and the sheer side of the road. Her solution was simple: Never look down.

On my cliff-hugging side, the ride was painfully slow and nerve-wracking, but less frightening. On several occasions I had to climb out of the car, jog ahead to help clear the road (chucking the biggest moveable boulders aside), and help push the cars that stuck, repeatedly, in front of us. Then I'd balance on the edge, cheering as Linda muscled the car across the torrent of water that had made the road its riverbed. I snapped pictures, then trudged through the mud and water to catch up.

A good deal of those ten hours we spent waiting, parked in a snaking line of vintage and classic cars clinging to the muddy mountainside. Down below us, a huge boulder had fallen between two competitors, miraculously missing them both; it took a crowd of drivers, PSB, and locals to wedge the monstrous stone off the edge of the cliff so the cars behind could continue.

We crept forward, trying not to slip in the mud. Just ahead, we all had to drive under a torrential waterfall. A Medusa's head of tangled steel rebar jutted from a decaying concrete mass above, the remains of an effort to direct the waterfall's flow outward and away from the roadway. I heard later that this engineering failure— or testimony to the incredible force of moving water—had lasted less than a year. We watched as #32, the little white BMW 328, an open roadster from the 1930s, prepared to pass under: the Austrian driver and his daughter lifted high their bright yellow souvenir Chinese Travel Service umbrellas. Linda and I laughed nervously at the ridiculous sight, and then our turn came.

Linda hit the accelerator, and we revved right under, hooting and hollering as several hundred pounds of water pressure slammed down onto our taped-up windshield. We were now soaked from above and below; the tape over our accident-ripped floor only kept the thicker clots of mud out.

Alongside the anxiety there was a delirious sense of accomplishment as we crept down the incredibly steep mountain. We knew there was nothing like it anywhere in the world. No amusement park could simulate this experience, no video could capture its essence, not even virtual reality could evoke the contradictory combination of incredulous insanity (what the hell are we doing here?), personal mastery (over ourselves and our automobiles), and sheer terror: a single mistake, a freak landslide, a fatal slide, and it would all be over.

When the path widened to more than ten feet, an amazing tent city lay claim to the very edge of the precipitous roadway. Men, women, children, and dogs crouched under tattered blue-and-white striped awnings, and muddy lean-tos perched on any available flat surface, filling the rim between the traffic and the sheer cliff. This tent city appeared to house the roadworkers who'd just finished clearing the landslides; they had erected impromptu markets and "restaurants," and when they weren't working the road, they worked the traffic: men and boys stretched their hands out toward our slow-moving cars, some offering to sell rupees or yuan, others simply begging.

Now we began to see birch, oak, and rhododendron growing alongside the road, and the air grew hot and humid. Suddenly, we were in Nepal. The Friendship Bridge didn't feel like a bridge at all; the throng of cheering, happy humanity on both sides blocked any view of water. We received a hero's welcome as we passed under a huge, decorated arch bearing the words "Nepal 98 A World of Its Own." Foreign video crews (American and European journalists who'd been denied permits to enter Tibet) joined the locals waving Red Cross flags. The clothes, the faces, everything was so different from Tibet. It was clear that little, except Buddhism, has truly been shared between the two countries in centuries.

While we stopped briefly for Linda to run an errand on that busy Kodari street, I noticed several groups of German and Japanese tourists getting off their tour buses. They schlepped their heavy backpacks and started hiking up the steep hill toward the border. I wondered if some other conveyance would carry them over that eight-kilometer gauntlet, or if they'd have to walk. After our drive, it seemed to me walking might be safer.

Back on the road, green-terraced rice patties alternating with the thin-trunked trees climbed up the hills as we descended. By comparison to the "no man's land," the road here in Nepal was a pleasant drive, though we still had many waterways to cross, sometimes with pebbly pavement under only a few inches of water, other times with natural river rocks and gravel in depths up to two feet. As we forded one of these, a piece of gravel wedged into the Hillman's left front wheel; now every turn of the wheel produced an earsplitting screech. We talked about what might be happening: the stone might be carving grooves into the brake rotors, or scraping the linings off the pads. We decided to stop, not just to look at the brakes, but to eat, pee, and pull off several layers of clothing.

Linda pulled over beneath a large shade tree. At first the area seemed deserted, but once we'd parked we realized an old man was sleeping peacefully in the shade.

He stayed asleep, so we took turns going into the forest. By the time we'd re-emerged, a young boy on a bicycle had ridden up and stopped, watching us inquisitively as we rummaged through our food box and put peanut butter on crackers for our lunch. The old man woke up, and more young people gathered. We felt as if our every move was their entertainment.

I thought about doing something with the wheel—taking the tire off, inspecting the brakes—but I felt uncomfortable with the ever-growing audience. So we started the car up and took off, and as luck would have it, the stone had dislodged itself. We were back to the relative quiet of our raucous engine, the omnipresent wind, and the duct tape flapping against our windshield. I kept my hand out the window, holding the top edge of the flailing tape down.

The children along the roadside were just the advance guard. Every village greeted us with an overhead banner, and hundreds of people lined the narrow road as we approached. The mayor or head of the local sports society would stop our car in the center of town, shake our hands, and press a brochure or letter into our hands, with charming and sometimes distressing phonetic English spellings.

> Dear Participant,
> "Peking - Perish old Timer Car Rally"
> We Heartily Wel-Come to You
> We wish all the Best
> for
> Your Travel & Your Mission.
> Bel Prasad Shrestha, Mayor of Dhulikhel
> Ashok Byanju, Deputy Mayor

Girls and boys offered bundles of bright red or yellow tropical flowers, and some pressed a quick thumb to our forehead—I learned not to flinch—plastering good luck goo, some sandy red substance, over our third eye. The waving Red Cross flags appeared again and again. It turned out they had something to do with the Pink Rolls Royce crew, whose work with the accountancy firm Coopers & Lybrand and the *Financial Times,* was tied to a fundraiser for the Nepali Red Cross.

The road grew wide and heavily-trafficked as we neared Kathmandu. At one point a torrential downpour hit us, lasting all of ten minutes; when we mentioned it to others later, they'd missed it completely. Kathmandu's architecture is a hodge-podge of old and new, with some of the high-rise buildings oddly top-heavy; the floors tapered inward as they neared the ground. I was surprised there wasn't a more distinctive look. I'd heard so much about this city from the dreamy paean of the old Cat Stevens song to New-Age reverence, I expected something fantastically exotic. Instead, the jostled-together low buildings of wood and cement block with corrugated plastic and aluminum roofs, seemed remarkably ordinary.

The Birendra Convention Center, though chunky and colonial, had a noble kind of grandeur. As we drove under the main entrance's great overhang, Nepali officials presented us with more pink forehead goo and flowers. Linda hollered out the window, "We made it! Can you believe it?" Both of us were ecstatic after our exhausting day. A smiling man rushed up to Linda, who hugged him. It took me a moment to place him in context: Paul Jackson, our Oxfordshire mechanic, from the Brightwell Garage. Then I, too, was thrilled. And relieved.

We pulled down into the main parking lot and showed Paul all the damage. Buses were waiting to take us to the Yak and Yeti Hotel; filthy from Choksam and camping, we couldn't wait to get to hot showers. The fancifully named luxury hotel welcomed us with a rose. Nepal seemed to be a land filled with flowers.

Once clean, we all headed for the bar. We found several of our cohorts there: Ted Thomas and Vic Zannis from Team Retro, Michael Veys, and Michael Kunz from Hong Kong. It was our first chance to trade stories since Lhasa.

Everyone had a stuck-in-mud story, but Michael Kunz's was unique. His rally car—co-driver Jonathan Thomason's 1963 Triumph Vitesse—was overweight and underpowered, and so it had seemed to stick continuously in Tibet's treacherously muddy roads. Since Michael is no lightweight, at each sign of mud, he'd alight from the Triumph and hike up to the next spot with hard ground or a more level surface. Thus Michael had to hike and pant his way across numerous diversions, difficult work anywhere, but exhausting at high altitude. On one of the longer diversions, Michael knew he couldn't make it to the end on foot in any reasonable time without passing out from the exertion, so he decided to see if he could hitch a ride.

He flagged down an oncoming Chinese truck. The driver understood Michael's sign language, but when Michael headed back toward the cargo hold, the driver waved him into the truck's front seat. Michael opened the door, only to see the seat cushion occupied by a large, dead pig.

Michael balked, but the driver cheerfully spread a towel over the carcass, patting it briskly in the universal sign language for "Sit! Sit!"

Michael sat. "I was riding high on the hog," he said, amid groans.

The Retro boys' stories weren't as much fun. In fact, Vic was more than a little worried; they still hadn't heard from their teammates, Andy and John, in the #23 Ford. A little later, when we joined Vic and Ted for dinner, news had come in that the two were stuck in No Man's Land with a broken steering center-link, the same failure that had delayed car #24 on its way to Everest Camp. Vic was hard on himself in his journal:

I feel guilty, not because the steering broke (it would have held under 99% of the

roads in the world) but because I wasn't there to help. Andy was there for me. Now
he has to remove it, find a welder, repair it, go back to the car (how and with who?)
reinstall it and worst yet try to make it in to Kathmandu in the dark!

He brooded through dinner at the fancy Russian restaurant named Chimney. The rest of us, Ted, Michael Veys; Nigel Challis and Tony Jeffries (partners in a '55 Land Rover that had been in Nigel's family for thirty years) celebrated, drinking French wine, eating the good food. Linda, in particular, seemed amazingly cheerful. The double gin on the rocks probably helped—she'd given up on finding a real martini—but more likely it was sheer joy at having completed such an incredibly difficult week. We'd completed a third of the rally; more than five thousand kilometers of the worst roads in the world were now behind us.

John and Andy didn't make it in to Kathmandu until almost midnight. The steering link had broken right in the middle of one of those streams crossing the road. The big 1950 Ford was immobilized, with the right front wheel turned ninety degrees to the right. "To get out of the water and everyone else's way," Andy told me, "I had to hold the right front wheel straight by holding the rear of the fender and the bumper, and pressing my knee against the tire. As John eased the car forward, it jerked and flipped my knee cap to one side. I straightened my leg and pushed it back in with the palm of my hand. Then, I used the other knee and we got the car to a semilevel place."

There, Andy jacked the car up and removed the broken pieces. He didn't trust the heavy car for long on their light-weight jack stands, so he bent down to roll a large rock under the front cross member, hurting his back in the process. By now, all the other competitors had gone, but John was able to stop an old Chevy van carrying two Swiss tourists. Andy hitched a ride with them, but before the border they came upon David Arrigo's red Allard—the same one that had twisted our Hillman's door back at the docks in Beijing—stuck in a water crossing. The Allard's exhaust pipe had broken, and was tangled in the wheel spokes. Andy helped jerk the exhaust pipe free, hurting his back even more.

Finally at the border, Andy couldn't find Ted and Vic, but Eric Christiansen was there, and he loaned Andy some Nepali money—he'd left without a cent, neither rupee nor yuan. He then caught a ride with Theodore Voukidis, the Greek Doctor in car #58, a '55 Chevy. Theo drove into one after another Nepali town and construction site, until they found a welder, about sixty kilometers from the border. Theo left to continue the rally, and after the welder repaired the piece, Andy asked him about a ride back up.

"He told me about a man with a taxi, but when I found his house, the taxi's engine was out. So I went back to the welding shop, and he said to take the 4:30 P.M. bus. I found the bus but didn't have enough money to bribe the driver to leave early. Back at the welding shop, the owner told me that for some amount of money, he could take me back on his motorcycle. I only had half of what he wanted, but he agreed. I thought it would be something big like a Harley; it was a 125 Honda! As we drove back, I had to get off and hobble up the hills, wade through the water crossings, all with my hurt knee and back."

At the border once more, Andy was waiting for the welder to get custom's clearance to enter Tibet when John Vipond and Mike Summerfield, two of the rally marshals, found him. When he pointed out the little motorcycle he'd been riding on, the marshalls, who had one of the four-wheel-drive Vauxhalls, said "Get in!" They took Andy back up to John and the car. The marshalls asked how long the repair would take.

"About forty-five minutes," Andy said.

"You have thirty minutes," Vipond said, "the border closes at dark."

The marshalls said they would have to leave, and John and Andy would have to spend the night there on the side of the road. "That was a big incentive!" Andy said. "I fixed the car in about twenty minutes. We crossed the border just as they were lowering the gate on the Tibetan side."

On the way back, they stopped at the welding shop and gave the man the other half of his money. From there to Kathmandu, Andy rode in the back of the repaired Ford, on top of the luggage, with his leg held out straight.

Still, Andy and John weren't the last to arrive. Don and Carl's Packard "sled" had trouble in No Man's Land, too. "The '54 Packard attempted to do it," Don later reported, "but in the course of doing it the undercarriage was damaged, the clutch to the vehicle became tight and generally, as Carl would say, this Packard has had more use and abuse in the last two weeks than it has in the previous forty years of its life." The men cleared the border just before closing, then realized that the car would never make the five or six hour drive to Kathmandu on its own. They decided to load it onto a transport cargo truck. "In quite a remarkable scene," Don reported, "about fifty people got behind the six thousand–pound Packard and pushed it up a pair of planks onto this transport truck. At times, it seemed to me while I was driving the vehicle onto the truck that the people were actually lifting the car off the ground to get it in." Once on the truck the going was slow, so by the time they reached Kathmandu, the Packard was the second to last car into the hotel. "It was about 2:30 A.M. Peking time when we arrived," Don said "but clock time was 12:15 A.M."

The Chinese have a unique way of dealing with time zones. The entire expanse of the country, including far-western Tibet, runs on Beijing Time. Thus our crossing into Nepal jumped us two hours and fifteen minutes into the past. Those fifteen minutes are apparently Nepal's effort to remain distinct from India; when we crossed that border, we'd lose the other quarter hour.

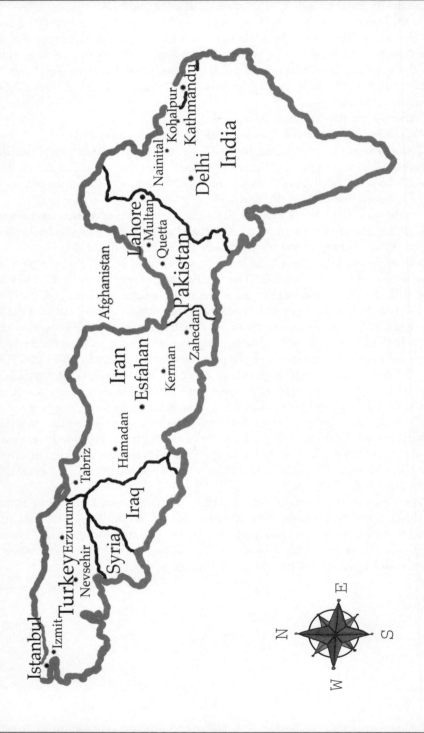

KATHMANDU
TO
ISTANBUL

CHAPTER

~ 21 ~

We indulged in a delightful period of repose. Repose is really a rather exaggerated expression, but to rest often means no more than changing your occupation.

KATHMANDU

[SUNDAY, SEPTEMBER 21]

Kathmandu would be the site of our longest rest period of the rally: two full days off the road. The traveler in me was anxious to explore, but the classic rallier knew that our first order of business lay with fettling the Hillman. Though Paul Jackson was there to do the major work, both Linda and I wanted to be at his side, easing the operation, nurses to his surgeon.

The Hillman was filthy, inside and out. It seemed as if we had smuggled huge quantities of Tibetan soil across the border, and no inch of the car was free of dust, dirt, mud, or sand. My idea of putting oil in a plastic water bottle had resulted in a horrible oily mess in the trunk: something had punctured the bottle, and 20/50 covered everything. Our first task therefore was custodial: a complete unloading, item-by-item cleaning, then repacking.

We settled into our spot behind the huge conference center. Mr. S. Pabitra, the Brahman master of ceremonies for things mechanical, soon came to greet us. The Brahmans—the traditional Hindu priest caste—dominate Nepal's Hindu upper class, and this handsome fifty-something gentleman had an aristocratic air, with wispy gray hair that settled on the collar of his clean, off-white worksuit. His English was excellent, and he noted our needs as a waiter might our dinner choices: "Welding? Certainly. Paper towels? No problem." He then went on to the next car—David Bull's big black Rover (#59) had parked beside us—and wrote down their order as well. "Leaking petrol tank? Of course." We all had the feeling we were well in hand.

Many hours later, Linda and I still awaited paper towels, and Paul had had to muscle his way into the welding line. Two portable welding kits were making the rounds, and only one really worked properly. We'd used up all our own paper towels scraping oil off everything, so we'd had to get creative with soap, water,

142

newspaper and cloth scraps. At midday, we raided our food box for lunch, smearing Ritz crackers with peanut butter. The Peykan team generously offered the spare parts we needed for Paul to reassemble our steering system. Eventually both welding kits were working on our car. Two young Nepali men welded our floor back together, while another attached our straightened control arm to a piece of angle-iron.

Suddenly, someone realized that the liquid pooling around the bare knees and feet of our welders was not the water Linda and I had spilled during our cleaning, but gasoline pouring down from the nearby Rover's leaking tank. In a panicked flurry we dumped buckets of water on the spill, then tried to sweep the fluids away from our car. The sweeping—or dumb luck—worked: nothing exploded.

Later, Paul decided the young Nepali's welding was inadequate and redid the control arm himself. Paper towels (a huge bundle of six rolls, far more than we needed) appeared just as Linda and I decided to give up, around 5:00 P.M. Paul stayed to do a tune-up, getting back to the hotel sometime after seven-thirty.

Prince Borghese did not have the luxury of a rest day in which to repair his Itala, but remarkably, the fall through the bridge did little damage. One strong beam of the crumbling bridge had slowed the fall, holding the car's heavy front end up in the air and keeping it mostly off the passengers. In the rear, the dozen India-rubber spare tires cushioned the Itala's landing. "If the beam had been just a little further off, or the tyres had been strapped elsewhere, our race would have been over," wrote Barzini.

It took the Italians three hours to right the Itala and drag it from the river. Ettore the mechanic said joyfully, "She seems quite safe," and, after wiping the oil from the surfaces of the points, cranked the starting handle. The engine fired right up. Still, Ettore insisted on carrying out a thorough inspection that stretched for two more hours, but the Prince and his crew were back bumping along the railway ties by 3:00 P.M. the same day.

Barzini, though, was seriously injured. He could barely walk and had to be lifted up into the car. He made light of it, scarcely mentioning what must have been his incredible discomfort as the Itala continued its "horrible dance" westward across Siberia.

In our last official bulletin, we'd been warned that our attendance was expected at an official reception planned for this evening in the Convention Center's ballroom. The Kathmandu Governor, and possibly the Crown Prince of this, the world's only Hindu monarchy, were expected. I rushed to catch the tour buses awaiting us in front of the Yak and Yeti.

It was a sad affair. Many ralliers (including Linda) opted to skip it, and the officials never arrived: the government was in mourning, we learned, for the "Supreme Commander of the popular movement," a man named Ganesh Man Singh, who had just passed away. Our small crowd of scrubbed and dressed-up ralliers munched curried hors d'oeurves and sipped sodas, talking mostly amongst ourselves, in the large, barren ballroom.

The architecture of this and other grand buildings was distinctly European neo-classical. I blamed it on the British, but in fact Nepal had historically resisted the British longer than their neighbors in India. When the British East India Company declared war on the kingdom in 1814, a large portion of territory was lost to Imperial India, and the British won the right to keep a "resident" in Kathmandu, but that resident was not permitted to leave Kathmandu Valley. In 1846, the king was overthrown by his Prime Minister Jung Bahadur Rana, who then ruled that the office would be hereditary. He called himself Maharaja, and he and his heirs ruled for 104 years. Jung Bahadur traveled extensively in Europe and brought back a taste for the white-stucco neoclassical style that still dominates official buildings in Nepal.

The monarchy was restored in 1951 by a people's revolt led by the Nepal Congress Party. Ganesh Man Singh was instrumental in bringing a form of democracy that contains a constitutional monarchy, a bicameral legislature, and multi-party elections. At the time of our visit, the "ruling party" was the Communist Party of Nepal (UML), but that apparently didn't satisfy the Maoist guerrillas who increasingly make their displeasure felt (as my father's e-mails had pointed out). The English-language newspaper, *The Kathmandu Post,* was filled with condolences for Singh, like this one from the Prime Minister of Pakistan, "Not only Nepal but the whole of South Asia has lost a political figure of great stature."

[MONDAY, SEPTEMBER 22]

On our second rest day, we were all required to attend a rally meeting in the large basement dining hall where breakfast was served. Since Kathmandu marked the end of the first stage and the beginning of the second, newly arrived Touring Category crew members had to be formally indoctrinated. More importantly, we all wanted to know about those twenty-two rivers we'd be crossing.

Philip Young did little to dispel the unnerving rumors, claiming that the water level at some crossings had been reported as high as two meters. By now, I'd realized that he relished these reports; he took some visceral pleasure in scaring us. He recommended we use condoms to cover our electrical connections. (Even Ned Thompson's comprehensive packing list hadn't included that.) He was livid that someone had used their satellite phone to tell the world via the Internet that the Chinese man hit by the German Mercedes had been killed. In fact, Philip said, he had no more than a broken leg and would be back at work in four weeks.

Since neither Philip nor the Chinese were entirely reliable sources of information, we never did find out the truth.

Philip claimed that, other than high water, the bad road conditions were now behind us. "Be decisive overtaking, and use your horn," he said. He apologized for the errors in the last book, claiming that the directions in volume two would be better. He warned again that high speeds were not only dangerous, but unnecessary. "The average speed required in the blue group is only eighteen miles per hour!"

Mike Summerfield then took over, warning us not to abuse the support crews: "The lads've been working overtime! Twenty cars maximum, fifteen minutes each per day, from now on!" Fuel would now be our own responsibility (no more Chinese bowser truck), and Mike warned us not to let the tank drop below half full. With temperatures expected to reach ninety-degrees-plus, he cautioned us to carry lots of water, more than enough for both ourselves and our cars.

At my breakfast table were the two Germans who drove the #3 Bugatti, and the Bugatti specialist they'd flown in from England. Their car needed a complete, frame-up restoration. One was a professional photographer, the other a dentist. One of the early rumors held that the dentist had used a vise grip to pull another German competitor's aching tooth out, near the shores of Koko Nor. He confirmed now that he had indeed performed this service.

I took a leisurely walk from the hotel up to the Convention Center and the car. Though I was nowhere near the main tourist attractions, some of the native architecture was evident; Kathmandu translates to "wooden temple," and occasionally mysterious painted eyes gazed out from decorated eaves, keeping watch over the jostling, horn-blaring traffic. The streets held almost as many walkers as scooters, trucks, taxies, rusted old cars and overloaded tuk-tuks. Some of these three-wheelers were used as buses, with ten or more people crammed inside the covered beds. Linda and Rich Newman had warned me about the Indian-built TATA trucks (TATA is India's state-owned car manufacturer). The word had become a cry of terror on their motorcycle tour of Rajasthan. The TATA trucks and buses wore fanciful decorations but belched diesel and drove like lunatic behemoths, oblivious to anything in their path. I was glad to be walking instead of driving.

I was suffering physically from my cold, and emotionally from a load of car-based guilt. I thought I'd been brought along to play mechanic, at least partly, and felt guilty about leaving the car worries to Linda. This was self-imposed; when I offered to help she shooed me away. I wandered around the Convention Center complex and watched Paul Jackson helping the Iranians. They'd devised a unique method for straightening their damaged suspension: they tied bright red tow straps into a huge loop, stringing one end around the wheels on the Peykan with a bent front-end, attaching the other ends of the loop onto a different car, then accelerating away at a ninety-degree angle. It seemed like it might do both cars more harm than good.

At the other end of the convention center from the repair stalls, a craft and food fair had been set up. The local classic car club had come out to join us, and I was thrilled to see a Fiat Multipla, just like the one Chris and I had driven to Alaska. *The Kathmandu Post* had announced the fair and our presence in a large ad, calling it a "National Event." Despite the publicity, there were few locals on hand, because the entrance fee was too high for most Nepalis to pay. Aside from the soldier/guards and some women and children who appeared to be the guards' families, only a few well-dressed residents attended. The crowd thickened suddenly in mid-afternoon, when a big black Mercedes roared in amidst a convoy of police motorcycles. It was the Crown Prince, come to make his official appearance. Journalists surrounded the Prince as he walked with Philip Young. The Prince strode quickly and purposefully, glancing at the cars, then stepped back into his Mercedes and drove away. We smiled at the fact that the Royal Mercedes was old enough to qualify for the rally.

At the craft fair, I purchased the largest souvenir I could allow myself—a beautiful cloth-painting of Lokeshowr, the goddess of craft workers, a many-handed, many-headed deity. I walked back to the hotel, window shopping, and within a block of the Yak and Yeti, a smiling shopkeeper leapt out of his shop at the sight of my six-foot-three-inch frame. "Miss! Miss! Extra, extra long, made specially for you!" He took me into his small shop, and showed me a tunic and pant set made from batik-like fabric of tan and navy blue. I held it up and couldn't believe it—it actually did have long-enough legs! I had to buy it. I rewarded the shopkeeper later by dragging Linda back there with me. We'd both decided some local clothes might make it easier to cover up in Iran. The price, translated into dollars, was something less than twelve dollars. Linda found a black-and-white set similar to mine.

When I talked to Chris and the kids on the phone that afternoon, Chris was greatly relieved to hear we were all right. He read to me from a rally office fax he'd just received:

> *Linda Dodwell's Hillman Hunter was reputedly in trouble yesterday when one of the car's front wheels was forced through into the floor pan after a heavy landing at 70 mph—this having been repaired by Tony Fowkes and one of the Iranian Peykan (=Iranian Hunter) crew. She is motoring once again!*

I was angry about that 70-mph crack. Philip knew full well that high speeds were impossible on that horrible stretch of road. It was one thing to tease us in person, but quite another to unnecessarily alarm our friends and family back home. It was just like him to have a nasty bit of fun at our families' emotional expense.

At dinner, the Jeepsters bought us beer. When Dick, Dave and Larry marveled at the chaotic Kathmandu traffic, Linda only laughed. "When I was in India last February on this ancient Enfield motorcycle, I was almost pinched by the front corners of two TATA buses going in opposite directions. If I'd been in a car, I never would've made it. The traffic there is insane—you ain't seen nothin' yet!"

As we departed, Linda and I promised to buy the guys beer next time. We had forgotten that alcohol would soon become a very rare commodity.

We caught up with Team Retro later that evening, our last in Kathmandu. They'd had an incredible day, getting their cars fixed and dealing with Nepali customs. Rather than using Mr. Pabitra's services at the Convention Center, they had located a shop on the way into town. There, they found the American Bentley boys, Bill and Ned, with their mechanic, who had flown in from Philadelphia. While Andy and the locals serviced both Fords, one of the shop boys drove Vic, with the steering pieces that needed strengthening, on the back of his motorcycle to a welding shop. The machinist turned out to be a young barefoot man of about twenty, wearing wire-rimmed glasses with a cracked lens. "This guy was rebuilding ball joints, taking them apart, remachining them, reassembling, rewelding. This is a disposable part anywhere else in the world, but not here!"

This young man took Vic down to a nearby body shop, where they found John Thomason's Triumph Vitesse having its front fender straightened. Every auto shop in Kathmandu must have had at least one classic car in it.

"In one corner of this yard," Vic said, "there was a guy building a jeep—not rebuilding, building. They were making everything by hand—no power tools, no shears, brakes or slip rolls, only a hammer and chisel, dollies, and blocks of wood. They sat there in the dirt and hammered out every bead, every curve, every crease and made an automobile!"

There, Vic's young welder tacked the reinforcement at one end of the center link, shaped it with the hammer, then reinforced the entire length by welding and hammering. "No sign of a welding hood or even any kind of goggles," Vic said. Finished, the young man asked for two hundred rupees, only about three dollars and twenty cents US. Back at the first shop, repairs on both cars were finished by 4:00 P.M. The total bill came to one thousand rupees, or about seventeen dollars for the day.

The mechanical work was complete, but now they had to get their shock absorbers, ordered by satellite telephone, out of customs. "Here began the most amazing thirty-five minutes of my life," Vic said. "We went blindly to the cargo area of the Kathmandu airport. The atmosphere was like the farmer's market—people everywhere—loading bales of different commodities into VW transporters. I walked into the first office and asked if anyone spoke English—only blank stares! As we left, a skinny local came up to me and in broken English said he would try to help. I told him what flight the shocks were on, the airline and the time. He asked for copies of the way bill—lost. Almost impossible, he said, but we will try. Into our waiting cab to another part of the airport—'we hurry,' was his repeated cry. Up four flights of stairs we hurry. Two offices later we find the list on a desk piled with papers. We hurry down four flights of stairs to the waiting cab and we hurry to another part of the airport—customs. Another area of total confusion: junk cars sitting around the perimeter, an overpowering stench from sewage running across the brick pavement. Our guide told us to pay twenty rupees (thirty-three cents) upon entry. We hurry to a dozen offices, in each one Ted has to sign his name. Finally we came to the big cheese's office where he demanded Ted's passport—left at the hotel! I volunteered his passport number— I made one up— and they were happy.

"We hurried to six more dark and dank offices, Ted signed his name, paid some more money and we hurried to the warehouse. The warehouse man was gone for the evening. Our guide talked to someone, they disappeared and came back a few minutes later with another man who had a key. He asked Ted to recite his passport number, of course, he couldn't! Then we pointed out the 'Team Retromobile' logo on our T-shirts—the same name on the waybill, and everything started up again. The lock was removed and doors slid back to reveal a mass of boxes and bales and packages all piled inside. After searching awhile, to no avail, a young boy yelled out that he had found one. He ran outside clutching the bag containing the shocks while others tried to wrestle it from him. He was like a hyena trying to defend his meal.

"We hurried to two more offices, signed names, then the customs man came and opened the box to make sure there were actually shocks inside. Then we had to go to pay the duty—seven thousand rupees—we only had fifteen hundred. Finally we talked them into taking US dollars—$125, then $135, then $145— signed more papers—hurried to the police checkpoint—the kid still following us, clutching the bag containing the box that had our shocks inside—sign name, pay twenty rupees and out the gate. Our guide told us to give the boy one hundred rupees—he demanded two hundred—we paid—he relinquished his death grip on our shocks—we got in the cab and left. We made it!"

Team Retro had set a rally record: they did in those hurried thirty-five minutes what other competitors spent as much as a full day doing. Some spent that long and still weren't able to retrieve their parts.

There had been further attrition. David Drew, our Rover mechanic hero, had to fly home to England from Kathmandu due to health problems. Jonathan Lux, his co-driver, decided to go on without him, even though the crew change relegated him to the Touring Category.

Michael Veys was still having trouble sleeping and getting along with Eric (whom I'd heard call himself a "rich, old, grump") but that morning as we prepared to leave Kathmandu he was even more upset than usual. "My whole life's gone!" he told me. He only had one personal bag, and somehow it had disappeared between the hotel and the parking lot.

The official rally count now was some seventy-five cars, including the non-competitive Touring class. At the time, it was hard to tell who was in and who was out, as cars that had disappeared for days would suddenly reappear, like the

Queen's Rolls Royce. Remarkably, that car was still in the running. In the official rankings posted at Kathmandu, it was listed in last place, with five days, nine hours and nineteen minutes penalties. Carl and Don's '54 Packard was ahead of them eight places, with forty-eight hours, six minutes in penalties. The Jeepsters and our Hillman were practically tied at three hours, ten minutes, and three hours, twelve minutes, respectively. Team Retro had, luckily, timed all their breakdowns for non-competitive stretches, and thus were still ranked in the top ten (seventh and eighth) with only eight and ten minutes of penalties.

❧ 22 ❧

The masters have brought their school children on the road in a line, to see this car which has come from Peking—an excellent incentive to the study of geography.

KATHMANDU TO KOHALPUR
[TUESDAY, SEPTEMBER 23]

The Nepali Ministry of Tourism had spared no expense publicizing our rally. The front page of the September 21 *Kathmandu Post* featured the headline "Battered & bruised, Beijing-Paris motor rallists reach Kathmandu," and the next day's issue featured a story on page eight titled "Motor rallists strive to break political frontiers." Philip Young was quoted: "The rally aims at sensitizing the world that political frontiers could be made redundant and also to activate the government of the respective countries through which we pass to make their road conditions better."

Though it's hard to imagine those exact words coming from Fleet-Street-trained Philip's mouth, the sentiment was more appealing than that offered by two headlines directly below: "23 Killed, 17 injured in Kashmir bus accident" and "Over 20 drowned in Bihar," thanks to a capsized river ferry.

Once we hit the road, it was clear the publicity campaign had worked; it seemed as if they must have declared a two-day school and work holiday. As we traveled through this small country of twenty million people, thousands lined the streets waving Red Cross flags, or hand-made placards that read "Wel-come," "Peace," and "Thank you to come to Nepal!" School children in uniform, dancing girls and drummers in traditional dress, mayors and local VIPs, everyone came out to see our parade. Don Jones estimated that between three and four hundred communities placed banners across the highway, and that 300,000 people lined our two-hundred kilometer route. By his calculation, in the course of our travels so far we had probably waved at about a million people.

Leaving Kathmandu, it was my turn to drive. Linda got to inaugurate our second road book. I threaded through the heavy traffic, following Dutch Lisa's Bumblebee, the bright yellow-and-black '51 MG sedan. Lisa Klokgieters-Lankes had already made a name for herself as a very aggressive driver (her co-driver, a quiet British man named James Wheildon, was reputed to be an excellent rally navigator). Once again Linda quickly grew flabbergasted with the road book, and I was concerned that if I lost sight of Lisa, we'd be hopelessly lost. I stuck to her bumper through the tuk-tuks and TATA trucks, bumping and slamming over the rough road, driving as aggressively as she.

Linda held on, quietly fuming.

Conditions improved once we cleared out of the city. I slowed down considerably, which earned us a fifteen-minute penalty at our first TC. Green tropical countryside, bamboo trees and terraced rice fields, rustic grass-topped shacks, and the colorful, never-ending stream of humanity pulled us westward through the country. Sometimes, the handmade signs (some mounted on cardboard, others on wood) were thrown at us and came through the windows, hitting our arms and shoulders. The autograph seekers, handshakers, and tica pushers (that bright yellow or red good-luck goo) created an exotic, exhausting gauntlet.

In the distance, we could see the Ganesh and Manaslu Himal, the major peaks between Kathmandu and Nepal's second largest city, Pokhara. We followed the Trisuli river westward to Mugling. Here, the road book warned "Do NOT accept invitations from ladies!!!" The town is bustling but very poor, and dominated by the Magar people, traditionally farmers and stonemasons. The Magars and Brahmans are the majority "ethnic groups," though that term is actually just a convenient euphemism for Nepal's sixty or so tribes, clans, castes and races—the Himalayan Sherpa, Tamang, Rais, and Limbus; Kathmandu's native Newars and aristocratic Hindu Chhetris like the royal family; Muslim Musalmans and more, all scattered about the small country.

From Mugling, we turned to follow the Naryani river, one of the major tributaries of the Ganges. There were several water crossings, but nothing too serious. At one point, we stopped in a sparsely forested area. It seemed deserted enough to allow us to pee in peace. I hiked into the greenery while Linda did the door trick, which had always afforded adequate privacy in Tibet (we'd open the front and back doors on the shoulder-side of the road, and crouch right there, sheltered by the doors). Within minutes, two kids on bicycles arrived, and stopped to watch. When we were back in the car ready to go, I turned the key.

Nothing. The starter wouldn't catch.

This had happened once or twice before, but on those other occasions the second or third try always brought the starter to life. I tried again. Nothing. A couple more times: click-click-click. The two kids stood still, watching us. I crooked my finger at them, motioning for them to come over. Linda got out, and the three of them pushed. I popped the clutch, and we were on our way. Sometimes it helps to have an audience. We still ended up with a six-minute time penalty at Bhalu Bang, the day's second TC.

The evening's stay, our last night camping, was in Kohalpur, near the Royal Chitwan National Park. We were now in Nepal's lowland Terai, an agricultural region that used to be malarial swamp, with an average elevation lower than 1,600 feet. Now that malaria is under control, 47 percent of the country's population lives here. Still, when we put our Diamox away at Choksam, we began our malaria prophylactic, just to be safe.

We'd been warned that there was a man-eating tiger loose (the few surviving tigers are protected here). There'd been reports of attacks in the nearby villages. We saw no stripes, but the land was noticeably wilder, very hot and humid, with long grasses, tall trees, and monkeys. We drove into the campground at about five-thirty, and I pulled in next to the Triumph Vitesse. I rolled a bit too far; the car's front end sank into a depression in the grass. "You miss the mud that much?" Michael Kunz said, looking up.

The heat and the jungle brought bugs. Swarms of winged and jumping creatures settled down upon us as the sun slowly descended. We marveled at the extremes our five days camping had offered: wind, rain, snow, ice; now jungle heat, humidity and bugs.

Thanks to the infestation, the blazing fluorescent tubes strung out above us for our safety, the sticky heat and the roaring portable generator that powered the lights, many of us never slept at all that night.

We drove on, winding over the beds of torrents, over paths carved out by the waters. As we advanced along the bottom of a broad river-bed, the slimy soil impeded our progress. The wheels revolved in vain, splashing mud, ploughing it up, sinking into it.

KOHALPUR, NEPAL TO NAINATAL, INDIA
[WEDNESDAY, SEPTEMBER 24]

We shook out our dew-drenched tent at dawn, and in the already hot air, sampled the minimal breakfast provided by a Kohalpur caterer (Burlinson's Sherpa crew were now much missed). A row of sinks had been set up on the edge of our camping field, along with tent shower stalls equipped with water buckets. The Europeans, like Mr. Dichtl, a Rolls Royce driver from Austria, and the father-and-son team of Josef and René Feit (in a hot-rodded '67 VW Cabriolet), were untroubled by modesty. They walked to the faucets in those tiny European swimsuits that make straight American males (like my husband, anyway) blanche. They doused themselves, merrily scrubbing away with bar soap, the elder men rubbing their ample bellies. Seventeen-year-old René was a skinny, pale, smiling boy with a single earring. In my twisted memory, they're all singing Wagner arias together as they march triumphantly back to their cars and tents. The Feits then emerged fresh and clean in their matching bright-red driving suits, Mr. Dichtl all scrubbed in a nice tweed suit. Red-cheeked Thomas Noor (the envy of all as his luxurious '66 Mercedes convertible had room for a large cooler, which he filled with fresh ice every morning) stood in a spotless white terry-cloth robe, his gorgeous French wife, Maria Bouvier-Noor, in a one-piece bathing suit.

We too-modest Americans just stayed in our clothes and went on sweating.

Today was to be the dreaded river-crossing day, and it was again Linda's turn to drive. The car was easily dislodged from the hole I'd parked it in, and we set off without doing any special waterproofing to the engine; we'd been driving with

our distributor waterproofer in place the whole time. The first seventy-six kilometers over the Mahendra Highway led us to the Kanali bridge, an amazing, modern white high-rise suspension bridge donated by Japan; it seemed as if it had been dropped by spacecraft into the middle of the jungle. Before the bridge the road had been rough, with three watersplashes. On the first, Linda bogged down and stalled. The Land Rover waiting on the other side happily took our proffered tow rope and pulled us across. Before we set out across the next river, I read aloud Philip Young's "River Crossing Tip Sheet" from the road book:

Slip the clutch. Keep revs up, speed down. You need lots of revs to make sure water does not creep up the exhaust pipe. Whatever you do, do not stall the engine as water will be sucked right up inside the engine, bending valves, or even con-rods. Talk to Tony Fowkes (the mechanic who had done the Paris-Dakar) on his Safari experiences, and don't become the next chapter in his book, Great River Disasters I have Known.

On the banks of the second river, I coached her: "Clutch in, okay now, rev it! Slide the clutch! Keep the revs high!" It worked, and we got across. We were both happy then, and Linda seemed to be getting the hang of it.

After the Kanali bridge, though, the road literally disappeared. River rock and boulders defined the route for six kilometers, and we had no choice but to trundle and bump slowly behind the rally car in front of us. By now, I knew we were running way too late. I was annoyed at the organizers: why did they make these times so tight, after all those lectures about going slow and taking it easy? To make matters worse, the TC was not where it was supposed to be. According to the road book, it should have been at the Kanali bridge. My kilometer figures had been right on (I'd gotten used to compensating for our trip meter's 0.10-kilometer error) and the TC just wasn't there. So we kept going, crawling behind other rally cars over the jumbled river-stone pathway that couldn't be negotiated at anything more than 10 mph. When we finally came clear of the gravel and boulders and onto a regular surface, we spotted the TC, and I yelled at Linda to "Step on it!" I was determined to keep our penalty down to the ten or eleven minutes that we'd already accumulated.

Michael Kunz leapt in front of our Hillman, waving his arms frantically. He was shouting something—what? I thought it was maybe "hurry, you'll make it." Linda swerved around him, pulling up to the TC. I jumped out of the car and slammed down the time card book. Angela Riley, standing there with a surprised look on her face, said "No, no, wait, wait! You're okay."

"What?" I said.

Michael Kunz said, "Uh oh, somebody didn't read their bulletin. Tsk Tsk!" His voice was pleasantly teasing, but I didn't take it that way.

"What bulletin?" I asked, alarmed.

"Your book's down," Michael Summerfield interjected officiously. "I gotta write it down. That's nine-oh-three." He wrote in our arrival time with a flourish. Then Michael Kunz and Angela explained.

"Yesterday's bulletin—didn't you see it? They added over twenty minutes when they moved the TC. You're not late, you're early!"

Great. Early penalties counted double. Our eleven minutes late were actually seventeen minutes early, and would be counted as a thirty-four-minute penalty!

I felt—and must have looked—like an absolute idiot. I had made a fool of myself running past everybody. I should have realized what was up. Everyone was calmly parked, killing time; the changed TC location; Michael's frantic waving. Back in the car, Linda said, "Oh! That's right! I got this yesterday morning in Kathmandu." She fished a folded piece of paper out of the zipped navigator pocket. "There was no way I could read it with the car bumping up and down out of Kathmandu."

"Why didn't you tell me about it?"

"I forgot."

As usual, Linda betrayed no emotion. I don't know if she felt bad about it or not. I wanted her to. But it was my fault as much as hers; it's a navigator's responsibility to keep track of bulletins, whether her driver hides them or not.

I got over it. As she knew I would.

The river crossings—there were many more that day, thirteen total before the last Nepal town of Mahendranagar—weren't nearly as bad as Philip and rumor had made them out. Some competitors, I heard, had been so nervous about the rivers they'd opted to take a completely different route, with the corresponding penalties that would accrue from missing TCs altogether. Being late or early at a TC still left one in the running for a gold medal. Completely missing a TC dropped one to silver medal status.

The rivers actually got to be quite entertaining. The locals lined the banks cheering us on, sometimes breaking into applause when we revved the car dramatically as we plowed out of the water onto the opposite shore. It was hard to resist those genuine smiles, the beautiful faces, especially the beaming faces on all those children. Those were the ones that pierced my heart, reminding me of how much I missed my own.

In the end, there was a positive side effect to our early arrival at that TC. Sixty miles later, when we crossed the Band river that divides Nepal from India, we were well ahead of the rest of the rally. Just on the western side of this luscious green riparian corridor full of curious gray and black monkeys, was the official border station. We were only the seventh or eighth car in. It was a blessing, because the incredibly repetitive paper processing hadn't bogged down yet. It only took the Indians two hours and forty-two minutes to write down our names three times, copy our passport numbers four times, and copy every detail off of Linda's Carnet (the Hillman's official "passport"), all by hand, three more times.

Right after the border, Linda was surprised to meet her motorcycling buddies Patrick Moffitt and Jahdeep, a Sikh motorcycle guide. Both men had accompanied her, Burt Richmond, and Rich Newman on their February motorcycle tour of Rajasthan. Burt had written to them about the Peking-Paris, but they hadn't come to meet us; they were on their way into Nepal and were as surprised to see Linda as she was to see them. Linda wanted to spend some time, but I was still upset about our latest penalties, thinking "How can we socialize when we're running against the goddamn clock?"

Perhaps I was taking the competition too seriously, but so far that day we'd racked up more penalties than any day since our accident. And we had less than three hours to cover the 159 kilometers to our destination, the mountain resort of Nainatal.

Linda reluctantly pulled herself away from her friends and got back behind the wheel. Once again the border brought with it instant change: twice the people, and twice the traffic, not just vehicular. From Tanakpur to Haldwani, the unique Indian attitude about roadways became apparent: people walk, stand and sit upon the dirt or asphalt surface. Animals amble in herds or singly, sometimes shepherded, sometimes just idling in their sacredness. Twice the trucks and buses, all TATAs, and as many trishaws (tricycle rickshaws), tuk-tuks and tractors as Nepal, plus ox-carts and scooters carrying as many as five people on their tiny two wheels joined us on the roadway.

The towns, visible behind the lines of men and boys—no women—alongside the road, were jumbled low buildings of wood, stucco and corrugated metal. Occasionally, a Hindu temple's tower would rise above the jagged rooflines.

From Haldwani, we began to climb into the Kumoan Hills. Pine trees, chestnuts and rhododendrons replaced the tropical flora, and the letters "HP" appeared on the brick or stone walls banking each hairpin turn; Linda complained that her arms hurt from turning the wheel constantly lock to lock. The town at the top, Nainatal, had a distinct colonial feel left over from the British Raj: whitewashed Georgian architecture joined the stately domes of grand Indian buildings in the town center. Buildings climbed from the banks of Lake Nainatal up the steep hills on three sides. The lake had so tempted a British Sahib back in 1840, he'd arranged to have his yacht carried up the 6,299-foot mountain. Nainatal had been a resort destination ever since.

Our parc fermé turned out to be a sports field in the center of town surrounded by grandstands, far above the lake. We were a couple of minutes late, but our Indian welcomers insisted we drive around the field in a big circle, as if parading for judges, before they let us park. Then it took a few more frustrating moments to find the timekeeper, who was hidden behind business-suited officials, several women in fancy-dress-saris, and a marching band. This added another seven minutes to the day's disastrous total.

Somewhere an announcer blasted away in Urdu and English over a loudspeaker, telling the gathered locals all about us and our car. After I got the book in, the women in saris performed a small ceremony, dabbing our foreheads with red and yellow tica and handing us flowers.

We had to wait around quite a while for other competitors to arrive, before a mini-bus finally took us up the steep village roads to the main hotel, called Manu Maharami (busy young boys plastered the hotel's stickers all over our car). We discovered that, once again, we were relegated to a different hotel, and eventually found the second shuttle which took us even further up. This time the road, cobbled in jaggedy red brick, was incredibly narrow, and the tiny van careened up it at full speed; looking back down toward the town gave me vertigo. At our hotel we joined the Gulls, the Tinzls from northern Italy (they switched fluently between German, English, and Italian) who were driving a '63 Peugeot sedan, the Italians with the troublesome Lancia Flavia, Michael K and John, and the Wong father and daughter from Malaysia.

I felt much better after a shower, forswearing annoyance for the rest of the evening. I was greatly cheered to hear that the day's TCs had all been canceled, because the delay at the border (for those who followed behind us) had climbed to five or more hours. Dick Taylor and the Jeepsters were among the unlucky; their crossing took nearly six hours. The delay forced many of the rally cars to drive the difficult, hairpin-filled stretch in the dark. Indians rarely use any kind of light on the road, certainly not the walkers, loungers and animals. Even trucks and buses often keep their lights out until they spot oncoming traffic, then flash it on with blinding brilliance when the oncomer is already upon them.

When the Jeepsters were about six miles from Nainatal, they came upon several cars stopped on the side of the road. An antiquated tow truck had its tow cable extended over the edge of the road, down the mountainside. They drove on, and when they got to Nainatal after 10:00 P.M., they were told that #96, the classic Land Rover driven by Nigel Challis and Tony Jeffries, had gone over the edge down the mountainside. Miraculously, pine trees on the steep hillside caught the vehicle and stopped it from plunging further down the slope. The two men were reported to be injured, but not too seriously; their Land Rover was reportedly totaled.

Oblivious to the Land Rover accident, Linda and I drank beer and chatted with the Italians. The hotel's lovely patio overlooked the town, and the air was comfortably warm—not hot, thanks to the altitude. Monica Tinzl brought out fancy Italian snacks she'd packed along, and then we ate from a buffet of excellent, mildly-spiced Indian food. Perched on the hotel's patio near the upper rim of the horseshoe of mountains surrounding the lake far below, we watched the colorful lights of the city sparkling on all three sides. The real stars paled in comparison.

The next morning, after being bused back down the mountain to the parc fermé, we heard about Nigel and Tony, the two gentlemen we'd dined with back in Kathmandu's Chimney restaurant. We both looked at each other, and Linda said, "Nigel's the one who gave us that Bible, isn't he?"

"Yes," I answered, trying to remember where I'd stashed the tiny *New Testament* Nigel had pressed into my hands in the early morning, only a few days before.

Everywhere, indeed, we find that boys are our most assiduous admirers. . . . Our journey must appear to these youthful imaginations enormously greater than it really has been.

NAINATAL TO DELHI
[THURSDAY, SEPTEMBER 25]

We had a very late start, so we had a lot of time to hang out in the parking lot. Once again a big band, dancers and announcers regaled us, and this time they let the public in; young Indians seeking autographs were everywhere. We'd been flattered and amazed when the first Chinese autograph-seekers had approached us; by now, it'd grown tiresome, and we struggled with polite ways to refuse.

All the ralliers were talking about Nigel and Tony. There seemed to be as many possible scenarios for what happened as there were rally cars, though most of us believed Dick Taylor's report; he'd driven by the scene, at least. In an e-mail about a month after the rally, Nigel told what really happened:

We were forced off the road by a lorry failing to keep to the left. We scraped our right side down the lorry as our left wheels went over the edge, and we ended up in a gully no more than twenty to twenty-five feet down, where the bumper ploughed into a soil bank. We did not roll, nor were we thrown out as "Discovery Channel" reported. After we came to rest, the engine was still running and the lights on. We both had to release our belts (to which we probably owe our lives) before we got out. We then climbed back to the road believing that we would be able to continue. However, the Indian "recovery" team put paid to that. As the LR was winched up to the road they let her roll against a sharp rock edge which dislodged the spare wheel from the engine cover and flattened the windscreen and hood and bent the steering wheel - as well as breaking off the doors! Had a crane been used to lift her back up to the road the apparent damage would have been very different. To make matters worse, overnight in the police yard, the LR was pillaged. We lost our clothes, some of our camping equipment, our tools, jerry can, and spare oil, indeed everything of any value; even the horn and

lights were unscrewed and the driver's seat taken out! Mr Jain (the general manager of the Manu Maharani Hotel where we stayed) advised us not to press the police too hard in respect of the stolen items or we would find that we would not get the necessary papers to release the vehicle. The police maintained that "what we were missing must have fallen out at the time of the accident." If you get to see the "Discovery Channel" photograph, like us, you will wonder how anyone could have come out of the LR alive, but it wasn't like that when we left her.

It was shocking and scary, but in one sense not surprising. The drivers and traffic in India are unlike anywhere else in the world. The fact that the rally's first injury accident happened to a Land Rover added another odd twist for those who'd been grumbling: there are some situations where four-wheel-drive offers no advantage.

The Retro guys had also come in after dark. Vic and Andy had been working hard keeping up with the repairs needed by the two identical cars, #23 and #24. A shock mount broke on #24, so Vic had to install a new one amongst the bugs at Kohalpur. Then he reset the carburetor to run at low altitude, just to climb back up past six thousand feet for Nainatal. Finally, that night John had arrived twelve minutes late, partly because his Halda rally clock had quit working, making navigation difficult. Vic spent the morning fixing that and a bunch of other little things.

The Packard was back with us, Don and Carl having completed major repairs in Kathmandu. They still had a laundry list of problems: almost no suspension system, four bolts holding the front wheels on instead of five (one had disappeared), windows that wouldn't close and broken doors that had to be wired shut, plus a gas leak. But they were carrying on, taking fourteen hours to drive the four hundred-kilometer day to Nainatal. Don noted wryly that they were at least keeping ahead of the shipping broker, who "hangs around like a mortician, waiting for people to give up and quit the event and have to ship their car home."

When our 9:49 A.M. start time finally arrived, it was my turn to take the wheel. It was not to be an easy ride. That night I wrote in my journal:

Linda's a terrible passenger. Hates it when I drive fast. Complains if I drive slow. Thinks I pass too recklessly, hated going down the twisty mountain from Nainatal. She's been single too long, traveled solo too many miles. Doesn't want me to talk, and tells me to speak louder. Can't win. Says I don't shift quick enough. Says I need to be in low gear, ready to "get out of a situation" a la motorcycles. I've always thought in terms of stopping in an emergency situation, not speeding up to get out of it.

Despite Linda's pale face and imminent car sickness, I had fun on that fast, curvy stretch, full of HPs (hairpins), down from Nainatal. We arrived at Corbett Lodge (India's first national park, named after British tiger hunter Jim Corbett; now it's a tiger preserve) thirty-four kilometers and forty-four minutes later—ten minutes late. I thought that was pretty good. Ted Thomas in his Ford Club Coupe made it two minutes before their time was up, but since the blue book gave them fifteen minutes more than we had, I actually beat Ted by three minutes—Ted, vintage racer extraordinaire in a much more powerful car! (Though I had to admit that the Ford was a lot heavier and probably a lot more difficult to maneuver.) Linda said, I think complimentarily, "I don't think anyone could have driven it any faster." I told her that at least one man would've done it *much* faster: my husband Chris. He would've loved that road.

When you're driving that kind of road and trying to go fast, you don't see much of the scenery, but beyond the walled HPs I glimpsed thick and tropical forest; it reminded me of the movie adaptation of *The Jungle Book*. Once outside the forested reserve, we settled onto the great Indo-Gangetic Plain that spans the two great rivers, the Indus (in Pakistan) and Ganges. We would cross the great *Ganga* in about two hundred kilometers, but first we had to deal with the traffic.

Driving in India was everything Linda and our cohorts had warned of, and worse. I liked Don Jones' description: "Driving in India I would describe as sort of a human pinball machine. It makes the machine pinball kind of dull. ... We've attempted also to do it at night, which is like playing the pinball game blindfolded." Driving was hectic enough—at least, being right-hand-drive, we could see to pass—but now, for us, it turned out that parking had become dangerous, too. For the first time in more than 6,000 kilometers of rally driving, our gender put us in jeopardy.

We arrived early at the checkpoint in the crowded but unremarkable town of Moradabad. Linda left the car with the time-card book and walked maybe several hundred yards—out of my sight, anyway—up to the TC. I was parked in what I considered an unsafe place: perched on the side of the road at the end of a long line of other rally cars, too near the lane full of TATA trucks, tuk-tuks, carts, everything. I figured I should stay with the car and move it up as space became available.

I sat in the car waiting, on an angled bit of dirt shoulder. Fine dust blew up when traffic passed, but otherwise the air was heavy and still. It was just after noon, over ninety-degrees, and the sky was white with heat. I looked down the dirt slope on my left to a low area with trees, perhaps on the banks of the Ramganga river we had just crossed. On the other side of the road, a line of low buildings included a market with produce out front. Before I could quite register what was happening, my view was blocked by the mass of male humanity that had quickly gathered around the Hillman. With my windows down, they pressed their hands and faces in, asking for autographs or just wanting to talk (though, as in China, we rarely got past "hello"). In order to eat my lunch, I had to roll the windows up (I'd pocketed some snacks from Nainatal's breakfast buffet). The men pressed their face against the glass, fascinated to watch me peel and eat a hard-boiled egg. The heat had curled the sandwich I'd made into cardboard bread around a strip of Naugahyde. I couldn't eat it, and by now I couldn't breathe. The closed car had become a furnace.

I rolled my window back down. Immediately, the men shoved their arms and hands in, and one short fellow even tried to stick his head through the window, his white teeth flashing. I pushed him out, and decided to open the door and stand up.

It was a mistake. I felt I had to get out, just to get some air, and at first, my ploy seemed successful. The mass of men backed away as I rose to my full six-foot-three-inch height. But that only lasted a few seconds. They laughed and pressed in again, and my height attracted even more—boys came running over now from the market across the street. I didn't know what to make of this. These men and boys weren't sinister, they weren't "copping feels;" they were smiling and curious, but they pressed ever closer, forcing me back against the Hillman.

I started to panic, and searched over the mass of heads for help. I saw Michael Veys striding back toward Eric's Rolls, not too far up ahead. He had two orange sodas in his hands.

"Michael!" I shouted. "Michael!" He turned and saw me, but didn't register my panic. I couldn't move my arms to wave at him—the boys had me pinned.

"What?" he mouthed.

"Come here!" I ordered, and now he realized I needed help. Some of the Indians had to back off to let him approach. He thought I wanted his soda—in fact, he gave me one and I thanked him profusely—but I kept him there, talking about nothing, just to have his bulk between me and the mass of Indian men. When he left, I had to push the men away to get back in the car, and then I just turned the key and started creeping forward—the cars ahead had finally moved—almost expecting to run them over. They didn't budge until the car was practically rolling over their bare feet.

The Gulls had suffered a similar experience. We were told their clothes had been pulled at and ripped. Instead of calling a nearby rallier for help, though, they violated the twenty-five-meter rule and drove straight up to the TC; instead of being penalized, they were allowed to check out early. They were exempted from waiting at any TCs for the remainder of the rally's stay in India. Linda and I never found out if the waiving of the rules extended to us, so we continued to honor them.

The Indian habit of crowding around a curiosity came into play for some of the men in our group as well. Too Tall Don Jones was surrounded, and Carl told me how "one particularly elderly gentleman who was probably about four-foot-three stood alongside of him. Don picked him up and carried him around and the people applauded and laughed."

We crossed the Ganges just before the town of Garh Mukteshwar. The broad brown expanse of calm water lay under a relatively modern bridge; no bathers or temples were visible in the distance, no structures other than humble lean-tos on its banks. The river is said to flow from the locks of the great Shiva, Creator of the Universe in Hindu mythology. We were far north of the city of Varanasi, where thousands go daily to ritually bathe in the Ganges' "purifying" (though unfortunately polluted) waters. Here, the only sign of the river's holiness was a sign that said "No Photography Permitted." This was not to please Shiva, but the government: photographing bridges, airports and military establishments is strictly forbidden in India.

By the time we got to the "dual carriageway" into Delhi—which sported autos and oxen; bicycles and mopeds; TATA trucks, buses, and tuk-tuks going in both directions despite the fact that there was a separate carriageway beyond the wall—Linda was a nervous wreck. Traffic density grew steadily as we neared the capital. Beyond the rails of the highway we could see ramshackle urban sprawl spreading out in all directions. We both bashed constantly on our air horn; the navigator has her own horn button between the bucket seats, and the driver has one on the column. Horns are not just recommended, they're required: the back of every fancifully-decorated truck and bus is lettered with "Please blow horn!"

But long before Delhi—160 kilometers before, in fact—our horn died.

That was the last straw. Linda freaked. "Slow down! Oh my god!" She was almost in tears.

I slowed way down. Very slow. Now unable to honk to alert the slow traffic ahead that I intended to pass, I simply couldn't. I hovered behind one slow, fume-belching truck after another. Here's how traffic in India flows: the truck directly ahead of me would edge right, then I'd see that he was trying to go around a truck in front of him, but *that* truck was also moving right, to go around a bicycle in front of it. Then the bicyclist would stagger rightward too, avoiding a sacred cow. The whole line of traffic would fill the dual-carriageway, all lanes, all attempting to pass in the same direction at the same time.

I didn't blame Linda, I was frightened too. But after breathing great lungfuls of diesel for kilometer after kilometer, I grew braver. I'd be damned if I was going to hitch our nose onto the slowest, stinkiest TATA truck bumper in India and let it practically tow us into the city just because our horn was out.

So I decided to get nasty. I started passing, silently. It was horrifying. Linda was paler—when I could steal a glance—than I'd seen her yet. But it was working; we were making progress. Twice I told her that she could drive—the only solution I could think to offer, which of course would have been more punishment than appeasement. It didn't calm her down. Fed up, panicked, but determined to get to the goddamn hotel, I finally said, "Don't you think I hate this, too? I feel like I've had my tongue cut out!"

I don't know if it made her feel any safer, but I think she finally understood that I wasn't driving aggressively just to make her mad. It was the only way I could see to get through that insane mess, with some speed, in one piece, without a horn.

We reached the Hotel Ashok before our due time of 16:44, by forty minutes. We thought we'd barely made it—Linda had calculated our due time to be 1604—she'd added fifty minutes and fifty-four minutes and forgot that 104 minutes is one hour forty-four minutes, not 1:04. Such are the pitfalls of navigational math.

The horn problem was too serious to ignore, so we barely took a break. We checked into our room in the cavernous hotel, then immediately returned to the car. The hotel parking lot was alive with a big reception that had been prepared for us, featuring media from Europe and India, a decorated elephant and rider, dancers (one in a horse costume), drummers, and local classic car clubs on display. Each car was greeted by the dancers, who pulled and prodded us into joining them. Some joined with pleasant abandon; I saw Bud Risser of the '55 Chevy dancing, and the Yorkshire family from the big black Rover. Linda and I declined, worried about our Hillman.

First to come to our assistance was Rich Newman. We found him hanging around the 2CV, which Burt was busy fixing. Richard, feeling non-essential there, volunteered to help us diagnose our horn problem. In the process, we realized that our headlights were out, and the evening deteriorated into the kind of electrical nightmare often decried in the British car world as the Curse of Lucas, Prince of Darkness. We were joined by two of the Iranians, and together we stayed until well past dark in the parking lot, rewiring the horn directly to the battery (this was Rich Newman's suggestion, which worked), and putting in a headlight switch bypass (the Iranian mechanic's suggestion). Unfortunately, I never got that fellow's name straight; it was either Hamayoun Kamal, Vahid, Roozben, or Ramin. Mohsen, another Iranian with excellent English and relatives in San Francisco, also helped out. These guys really had become like team members to us.

By the time the electrics seemed to be working again, it was after nine. Linda and I grabbed some food and crashed: the next day's start time was scheduled for 4:00 A.M.

We seemed at times to be almost pushing the car ourselves with our assiduous longing; we accompanied it so intensely with our will that its work caused in us true physical exhaustion.

DELHI, INDIA TO LAHORE, PAKISTAN
[FRIDAY, SEPTEMBER 26]

The 4:00 A.M. Delhi start time was wicked punishment for having dared to rally into India. Philip Young and company had reportedly paid some tremendous sum to the Indians to provide "expedited" border service, consisting of several extra workers to speed processing. Then, a week before we arrived from Nepal, the Indians supposedly demanded an additional five thousand pounds per car. When Philip refused to pay up, they pulled their workers. No one knew what to expect at the hostile Pakistan border, but since it closed promptly at 4:30 P.M., the early start time was the only way to insure that all of us, including the slowest Vintageants, would get through.

Delhi has lovely decorative street lights, but in the pre-dawn blackness, none of them were lit. The morning's first stage—just getting from the hotel to the start at India Gate—caused a great deal of navigational grief. Luckily, I'd taken the time days before to highlight the route in the city map provided at the front of the road book. It helped immensely, and with Linda driving, we arrived at the gate before our 4:18 start time, leading a few other cars who'd apparently gone astray.

We parked at the base of the 136-feet-high India Gate, the All India War Memorial; its marble arch looked stark and modern in the eerie indirect light from our automobiles. India Gate dates back to 1911, when New Delhi became capital of the British Raj, and it defines the east end of the Rajpath, a mall-like area of lawns, fountains, and canals. On the other end of the Rajpath is the grand Rastrapati Bhavan, or President's Palace.

Though Delhi dates back to the Pandava civilization of the sixth century BC, it first appears in recorded history in the twelfth century. The "seven cities of Delhi" that first earned renown throughout Europe were seven medieval citadels in the vicinity. Some of those citadels remain, but thanks to our border problems, we

would see none of them; only India Gate, a shadowy relic of one of the city's most recent incarnations.

Many of the Vintageants had trouble seeing in the dark; their old cars had weak, practically useless lights. As we sat there idling under India Gate, our Hillman's headlights quit; the night's fix hadn't taken. Only the brights worked, when Linda held the flasher switch on, and our "gumball" roof light, which had amber lenses. Since that roof-mounted light flashed, it gave the impression that it was rotating like an emergency vehicle's light. So Linda drove out of Delhi holding our flashers on for headlights, with our gumball flashing. We repeated our earlier Pied-Piper performance, leading several of the Vintageants out of town. Our flasher intimidated the local traffic, cutting a swath through the early-rising truckers.

The road surface, sometimes dual-carriageway, was much improved over the previous day's, and in the two hours before the sun came up, traffic was light outside the city. After the sun rose, though, traffic doubled, speeds increased, and the sacred cows began to roam.

Everywhere we saw evidence of recent head-on collisions. We called them "Dead Elephants"—not real animals, but huge, overturned or crushed TATA trucks that littered the highway, their payloads spilling out, abandoned by their drivers. Team Retro's Vic saw one such aftermath where "the driver got out, took his bedroll over to the side of the road and went to sleep." Rich Newman told us he watched one truck pass another; each truck was so overloaded their cargo-loads bulged at the top. The passing truck shaved the side right off the burlap sacking holding the second truck's cargo, causing grain to spew down onto the road. Both trucks just kept rolling along, oblivious, while the 2CV danced around the treacherous new road coating.

When we stopped for gas, I got out to do the pumping. The young British Bentley boys were there, and their Bentley had some kind of fuel leak; gas seemed to be everywhere. Dimples didn't have the right kind of rupees; he was laughingly upset that his Nepali ones were now worthless. Linda fished out some of the right-colored "frugals" from her stash (she'd purchased a handful of every kind of currency she could get before we left; she couldn't keep their names and exchange rates straight so called them all "frugals"). While we paid for all the gas, a crowd of young Indian men once again surrounded the Hillman. I jogged off a hundred yards to a stand selling cold sodas, and while I was gone, the men leaned into the car, as they had at Moradabad. When one began hacking with a deep, tubercular-sounding cough, Linda rolled up the windows. They laughed and pounded on the car, tormenting Linda, until I returned.

Just then the Jeepsters pulled in. Dick, Dave and Larry jumped down from the bright red-and-white vehicle, distracting our tormenters. The Jeepsters pulled off their rear wheels and confirmed their suspicions: the Jeep's rear brake shoes had worn completely through. They had a spare set of shoes, but no way to remove the brake drums. As we set off, they told us they would have to find an auto shop.

We re-entered the traffic dance heading northwest into Haryana, an agricultural region that has been invaded by industrial monoliths. These giant complexes grew even more frequent after we entered the Punjab, India's troubled northwestern state. There, the city of Ludhiana holds one of the world's biggest bicycle factories. It's also a large textile center, so uncovered trucks loaded with long skeins of brightly colored yarns trundled along in their own smog. It amazed me that the colors were visible at all: sometimes the trucks created clouds of diesel so dark it was hard to tell whether the vehicle was coming or going. All this industry—West Punjab is also India's steel region—and the diesel expulsions from not-dead-yet TATAs combined to create dense, thick pollution I could taste. I had to hold my shirt-tail over my mouth and nose.

This was our second direct experience with intense pollution; the first had been the drive through China's coal region. The level of industrial pollution was sadly no surprise; though the technology exists for steel mills and coal-burning smoke stacks to clean their effluents, I know enough about international politics to know that neither China nor India feel they should be forced to pay the high price those new technologies cost. In their view, global environmental restrictions are a classic case of the Haves telling the Have-Nots "do what I say, not what I do." When we were talking about it later, Andy Vann told me about his grandfather. "He was a milkman in Birmingham, which was Alabama's big steel town. He'd go out every morning in bright white clothes, and come back every evening black as a coal miner. We've cleaned it up some, maybe these folks'll get it cleaned up soon, too."

More troublesome thoughts plagued me as we drove through India's thick acrid air: what sort of message were we sending by driving classic cars halfway around the world? I had been forced to think about it months before. My sponsorship efforts had been dismissed by several companies on environmental grounds: Classic cars are polluters.

That is true, and in a global sense there is no denying it. And yet, I wanted the world to know it does not *have* to be true, and in my personal life, my husband and I do everything we can to make it not so. Our old Fiats were economy cars in the first place (with 20 to 50 mpg), and since we keep them in tip-top running shape, they burn cleaner than many late-model cars and use far less fuel than any modern SUV. My husband's efforts to keep old Fiats alive by providing parts and service is a daily act of conservation, and we're both active environmentalists in every other sense of the word. And Linda—she didn't even *own* a car in California. Her motorcycles do far less environmental damage than almost any car.

Yet here we were, two die-hard environmentalists, driving a Hillman Hunter. Our rally car had been prepared for power, not for clean air; our dual-carburetor, throaty-exhaust engine was a classic late-1960s hydrocarbon-spewer. And all of the cars in the rally were the same or worse (in some very early cars, oil is poured *over* the engine, leaving slicks in the car's wake). Though none of our cars polluted with the abandon of a TATA truck or bus, we certainly were not sending a very environment-friendly message.

The last Indian city before the border was Amritsar. There, somewhere beyond the veil of smog, lay the seventeenth-century Golden Temple, in this "Reservoir of Nectar," the holy city of the Sikhs. The only crew in the rally that visited it was Gerry Acher and Bruce Young, two British accountants in the "baby" 1928 Aston Martin International. They had arrived so late at the border, they knew they could not pass, so they took their time visiting the sights, spending the night in Amritsar and heading into Pakistan the next morning.

The rest of us wanted to get through, and we all wanted to get through at the same time. It was not a pretty sight.

Prince Borghese technically only crossed four borders: between Mongolia and Russia, then from Russia into the German Empire, into Belgium, and finally into France. But throughout the Russian Empire, the crew was often stopped by officious bureaucrats protecting some petty personal or village empire. Three weeks past the Mongolian border, a man with an official-looking register chased after the Itala as it started to leave. "We knew these little village despots by this time," Barzini wrote, "who give themselves airs as if they were put there to direct even the course of the rivers and the blossoming of the meads, who take advantage of their position of authority in order to give all possible annoyance to their neighbour. They are ignorant and greedy people, who on other occasions had asked us our name, surname, profession, nationality, demanding explanations of every kind, and transcribing our answers solemnly in a little notebook, and looking at us with the severity of judges. A stranger, from the mere fact of passing over their territories, is treated by them as a criminal."

Prince Borghese was at the wheel, and he drove steadily on, ignoring the man who ran after them, crying "Stop, in the name of the law!" Barzini, perched high atop his fuel-tank seat, turned around and "seriously, gravely, looking over our luggage, made the most horrible face at our persecutor. Just the worst face I could remember having learnt in the far-off time of my earliest school career. He stopped, disconcerted at so much daring; and we gaily continued on our way."

Many of us lingering long at India's Attari border station dreamed of honoring our rally's history by attempting a similar escape, but our officials were not so easily shrugged off, and this border was not so inconsequential as that invisible line near Siberia's Om River. Ever since 1947, the line dividing Hindu-dominated India from Muslim-dominated Pakistan has created incredible tension. Our "village despots" had long, sad political and religious agendas to defend at this border.

As a result, our crossing was exhausting. Linda and I were in the middle of the pack. It took a miserable six hours to show our passports and carnet again and again. All TCs had been canceled so we weren't watching the clock, but still tempers were high. Mike Summerfield had asked me to tell people not to worry about what order the cars were parked in, just to leave them and come in on foot, but he'd told Linda to move our car up, to prevent any gaps. Our Hillman was behind the British-crewed 1930 Delage; the father was nowhere in sight and the son sat slumped in the passenger seat, sleeping. Linda went to move our car around the Delage to fill the gap that had developed, but the father came rushing up, screaming in outrage, "How dare you jump the queue!"

We had to abandon the cars for the duration anyway, to stand in a series of interminable lines, in small hot rooms, then finally in one big hall. Here there were six or seven long lines leading us to one long table filled with agents. Persistent warm-soda and warm-water salesmen had been following and bothering us since we first stopped the car. "Please buy, only one US dollar, please buy, soda soda, water water?" pulling on our sleeves.

Linda and I were both feeling under the weather, and she was getting angry. She had almost yelled at one of the first customs officers. I said something like, "Calm down, it won't do any good to get angry," and she took it well, calming for a bit. But now, into our third or fourth hour and with the constant yammering of the sellers, she really let loose on one of the water guys.

"Would you leave me alone? How many times do I have to say no? If I want water I'll buy water, goddamn it!"

Everyone backed away, the water seller and the other competitors, but I was relieved; better to let it out on this poor sucker than on some self-important customs official.

I narrowly averted my own disaster a little later. It was finally my turn to be processed at that long table. The woman handling this stage shuffled my papers, and I noticed, just barely, a small piece of paper flutter to the floor. She ignored it, so I assumed it wasn't important. She finished writing in her ledger, shoved my papers back at me, and gestured me toward the next room. There, the next person asked for our papers. We handed them over and the man rifled through them and said to me, "Where is your exit slip?" I looked at the tiny paper Linda had, and ran back to the other room, cutting through to the front of the line. "My exit slip fell to the floor," I told the woman. "It's under your chair." She looked for a split second, refusing to see anything, and shrugged. I insisted, and finally the fellow next to her looked under his chair and handed it over, holding it between two fingers as if it were a used Kleenex. I rushed back, handed it over, and our papers were finally approved.

The Jeepsters had been delayed by their brakes and traffic—in one town they were gridlocked for nearly twenty minutes—and so they didn't arrive at the border until 4:15 P.M. They were told that the Indian Immigration Services closed at 4:00, though the fellows discussed the hour of closing for another half-hour, finally agreeing to allow the Jeepsters through. "As a special favor," Dick said, "the authorities told us we could not take our 2,500 rupees in Indian currency with us across the border. Instead, they graciously agreed to take the money from us. We gladly parted with the rupees—equivalent to about seventy dollars US—in exchange for being allowed to escape to Pakistan."

The Pakistani border guards, clad in elaborate, long green coats and high-feathered red caps, went out of their way to be solicitous. They took every opportunity to say things like "You will have no trouble here like you had in India."

We hit the road, essentially in convoy since we'd become so backed up, and threaded our way over and alongside a series of canals. We almost missed a ninety-degree left turn, and after the turn a chicken attacked us, jumping at the fender. I think it lived, but the road was so narrow there really hadn't been room for both the Hillman and the chicken.

The roads and the canals both widened as we neared downtown Lahore. The canals had been built by the British to bring colonization to this arid plain beginning in 1860. By 1892, the lower Chenab Canal opened, transforming the Punjab (or Panjab) region (now split between India and Pakistan) into an agricultural breadbasket. The most ambitious project, completed in 1917, joined Lahore's Ravi river with the Chenab and Jhelum rivers to irrigate the desert southwest of Lahore. Today, wheat, rice, fruit, sugar, tobacco and cotton are all grown around the canals' green paths.

We crossed the Canal Bank Road and spotted the Avari Hotel. It looked like it extended for three city blocks; three separate high-rise towers connected at angles. The parc fermé was a well-guarded, immaculately manicured grass lawn. Our welcomers laced our necks with garlands of deep-red perfumed roses and offered each of us a glass of cold orange juice.

It was a long walk to our room, past several bored-looking machine-gun toting guards, one or two for every floor. Linda said she was hungry, but I was exhausted and felt queasy; I'd been fighting the effects of Delhi Belly all day. I said I didn't think I could handle any more than soup or rice. Linda suggested I order room service and then disappeared. The next few hours went by in a complete haze. The food came and I ate it, but I was asleep soon after the last bite. I woke briefly when Linda came in and said she'd gotten a separate room, picked up her stuff and left.

As I went back to sleep, I thought how nice it would be to have the place to myself for two nights—the next day was a rest day. But in the middle of the night, I awoke alarmed, thinking *Where am I? Where is Chris?* I saw the empty bed next to me and thought, What happened to Linda? Then I remembered. When I settled back down, Linda was no longer in my thoughts. I dreamed I was home, sleeping with Chris and both kids, in one great big comfortable bed.

CHAPTER

∽ 26 ∽

We watched over the working of the car with an anxiety that was not unmixed with affection. We had ended by loving that obedient machine which carried us.

LAHORE
[SATURDAY, SEPTEMBER 27]

I t felt like I'd slept in, even though I awoke at six without any alarm. For the first time since Lhasa I felt rested, thanks to that wonderful bed—both the mattress and pillows were incredibly comfortable—and my dream of home. Vic had a similar dream the next night. We'd been away too long.

I found Linda at breakfast and we were both ready for the Pakistan Motor Sport Club man at 8:00 A.M. He led us, the first batch of mechanically-needy ralliers, into the city to auto shops; in our case, one that featured a fully-computerized alignment setup. This was what we needed to stop the inexorable shredding of the inner third of our front tires. In addition, we hoped to solve our intermittent ignition problem, figure out the cause of a new clicking sound (turned out to be a loose generator mount) and, of course, we needed the electrics sorted.

Carl Schneider came along with the '54 Packard, as did Ivar Moe from Norway with his bright yellow 1969 Morgan Plus 8. Ivar was tall and handsome. Paula Broderick teased him by saying in a loud voice whenever he neared, "Here comes Ivar, watch your daughters!" His co-driver Tom was shorter and rounder, and reminded me of Bob Newhart; they both had excellent, slightly accented English. Their car had been suffering terribly throughout the rally. The British Morgans became famous in early motoring for being fast on three wheels; they came out with an almost identical-looking four-wheeler in 1935. The cars kept their 1930s look throughout their lifespan, so the high-powered eight-cylinder cars that came out in the 1960s (like Ivar's and Tom's) still have flat front radiators and cycle-type fenders beside long front hoods. Morgans are very low to the ground, and the Norwegians had gone to considerable expense to raise their suspension; but it wasn't enough for Tibet's tough roads. The whole wooden subfloor had come up, dumping baggage on their heads. They'd cobbled the car back together, but

then overheating and radiator problems began.

Watching Ivar and Tom struggle was particularly painful for Paula and Nigel Broderick, the British couple in the #52 Anglia, because they knew that Philip Young had given Ivar and Tom a terrible time about entering the Morgan. Philip swore the Morgan would never make it out of China. By now, everyone, even the few who'd liked and respected Philip before the rally, was irritated with his imperious arrogance. What delicious payback it would be for the Morgan to prove Philip wrong. We all wanted that car, as much as our own, to make it to Paris.

Ivar was very discouraged that day in Pakistan and irritated with us in particular, I thought. Our Hillman got quicker service than either his Morgan or Carl's Packard, and Ivar was very upset, as his Morgan needed much more intensive work than our car; the Morgan had hit a pothole on the way into Lahore that had broken three of the four radiator brackets right off. I reasoned that it made sense for the crew of six or seven young men to tackle the simpler job first to get it over with. I suspect the Pakistanis took ours first not because it was easier, but because it belonged to two women. No feminist has ever argued that the old pedestal doesn't have its occasional benefits.

We realized early on that there was one master mechanic and all the rest were apprentices. The club man had to go back to the hotel to find service for the next batch of ralliers, so we were left with only one young man who spoke a little bit of English. It seemed to take the crew forever to rotate our tires back to front, balance the wheels, then move the car to the only spot that was hooked up to the alignment computer. That whole process took even longer, as a man was needed on each of the four wheels, all working at the same time. Our "custom" suspension, using those specially-made bushings we'd had shipped from Australia, had given Paul a lot of trouble back in Oxfordshire; he told us in Kathmandu that he'd set up our steering so the car would track straight, not realizing that it would eat tires. With the additional damage caused by our accident, the Pakistanis had a difficult job to do. They did the best they could and finally released us, to Carl and Ivar's great relief.

Now we just needed our electrics fettled. A helpful fellow led us to another shop a few hectic blocks away, down a hot dusty alley. We pulled halfway into a tight, narrow driveway. A small dark hut housed an older man who was obviously the electrical guru, along with his many young apprentices. We tried to explain about the headlights, and he seemed to take a long time replacing the burnt-out turnsignal bulb in the front left assembly—a minor problem compared to the switch, which he finally, belatedly realized. No one spoke anyone else's language, so it took a lot of energy to get them to understand our priorities. Back in Delhi, the Iranians had pulled the Hillman's headlamp switch assembly out and rearranged the wires, leaving the switch, partially taped up, hanging there. Our expert in Lahore put on a second, toggle-style switch. So now we had two assemblies, both tacked onto or hanging off the dash, and we weren't quite certain that either one would work. At least now all our turnsignals worked, as if anyone in South Asia ever paid attention to such things!

It was incredibly hot in the sun, standing around while the young apprentices watched the older man work. They brought us funky old chairs to sit on, setting them in a tiny patch of shade. The yard was crowded with rusted old cars spewing masses of tangled wires. Beyond the space our Hillman filled—its rear end jutting out into the dusty alley's lane—the yard was filled to capacity.

All our work was done and paid for by about one-thirty, so we rushed back to the hotel, hoping to catch a 2:00 P.M. sight-seeing tour. I quickly washed my face in the lobby restroom and went straight to the bus. Linda followed, just in time, picking out a seat a few rows ahead of me.

The comfortably air-conditioned bus took us all around the city. Everywhere were banners reading "Red & White Classic Car Parade." At first I thought Red & White must've been the nickname for the Pakistan Motor Sports Club, but it dawned on me after seeing a few billboards that it was a cigarette company. It was interesting, too, that we were called a parade. The name change apparently reflected the fact that Pakistani law prohibited any form of automotive competition on open roads. Ironic, considering that some of our toughest special stages were due to take place out of Multan two days later.

I sat back in the bus and enjoyed our guide's voice-over. He made earnest speeches about Muslim religious tolerance: "We have many Sikhs, Hindi, and even Catholics!" (Only 3 percent of Pakistan's 108 million people will admit to anything other than Muslim, though.) He pointed out the British colonial buildings in the Mall, and the big old cannon named Zamzama, (also called "Kim's Gun" after Rudyard Kipling's *Kim,* set here). Next he pointed out the "old town," which he claimed has been inhabited continuously for 200,000 years. Legend says that the city was founded by Loh, son of Rama, the hero of the Hindu epic Ramayana. My *Lonely Planet* called this square kilometer "a fantastic place to get lost," but from high up in the bus it looked less than inviting: a mass of mud hovels with odoriferous livestock yards around low, crumbling buildings.

The bus then drove on to the much grander Lahore Fort (some say the city's name comes from Loh-awar, which means "Fort as strong as Iron"), restored to the era of the Moghul emperor Akbar (1548-1598). From here, Akbar ruled an empire that stretched from the Arabian sea eastwards to Bengal, from Kashmir in the north to the Deccan Plateau in south India, encompassing 150 million people. The broad brick edifice had elaborate elephant mosaics on the outer wall, and mazes of rooms and courtyards inside. The grandest rooms sat on the highest level, offering a view of the city in all directions. One narrow room was covered from floor to ceiling with a mosaic made of tiny mirror tiles. Lovely in daylight and at night, with candlelight, the walls and ceiling would create brilliant golden patterns, a fitting background for the court's royal pleasures.

Back in the bus, we were taken to the grand Badshahi Mosque. Completed late in the Moghul period (1676), this towering brick mosque is one of the world's largest, holding sixty thousand people in its cavernous central courtyard. We all removed our shoes and stepped tentatively on the matting that led us onto the stark white cement floor of the courtyard. An experimental touch of my toe revealed the necessity of the matting: it was unbearably hot. Thus we followed each other single-file into the cooler recesses of the intricately mosaicked interior, under arches still exposed to the weather. I wondered if a hidden, fully enclosed interior awaited worshipers, somewhere off-limits to infidel tourists.

Last, after a longer drive in our cool bus, we came to a beautiful garden. Here was the sandstone mausoleum of Emperor Jehangir (father of Shah Jahan, who built the Taj Mahal), and nearby the tomb of his empress Jur Jahan. We were given more sodas—cool ones!—and the serenity of the grand park with its lovely shade trees and squared-off, manicured lawns offered a glimpse of the peace possible amid the frenetic pace we'd come to expect in South Asia.

By the time the bus returned us to the hotel, we had just twenty minutes to get dressed up for "Tea with the Guv'nor." Some treated it as a formal affair—Lord Montagu and a few others showed up in black tie—but all I did was go to my room and wash my face and brush my hair. Carl, in a suit and tie, told me about his afternoon as we rode along on the bus to the Governor's Palace. After the Packard was repaired, one of the auto shop's regular customers, a classic car fan, invited Carl on a quick tour of Lahore in his Toyota. After visiting some of the same sights we saw from our tour bus, the man took Carl to his home for a drink. "I never expected to see the inside of a Pakistani home, and I certainly didn't expect to be in one that had fourteen bedrooms, ten servants and a flock of peacocks wandering all over the place!"

A select group of rally cars—a couple of the Rolls Royces, a Mercedes and the Cadillac—greeted us at the palace entrance. We were not to go inside, but out onto the large manicured lawn. Several dozen servants, in flamboyant traditional costumes (turbans with high white crests, like cockatiels), stood at attention along narrow tables covered in formal china, silver service and trays full of tea-time treats, mostly sweets.

But we were not to touch them just yet. Instead we were directed to sit in chairs ringing a central, empty plaza about a hundred yards from the tea tables. Finally the Governor arrived, and delivered his speech alongside Philip Young at the far distant end of the empty plaza. We were posed for group photos for the Pakistani press, then we were released and allowed to eat. It took talent to hold the hot, delicate, tea cups as the liveried servants poured, then balance a tiny plate of tea cakes in the other hand.

Linda, sweltering at the opposite end of the garden, listened not for the first time to a jolly Brit declare that hot tea is just the thing to cool one down in a hot climate. I found it all very awkward and British, occasionally making an effort at desultory, inconsequential conversation with one of the friendlier Aussies or Brits. As the sun went down, hundreds of little black birds came out of the towering trees surrounding the outer edge of the lawn. Their sudden twittering was so raucous, their looming black presence—gathering, swooping, dispersing—so supernatural against the orange-purple glow of the darkening sky, it brought to mind Hitchcock's *The Birds*.

"Lovely," the British murmured. "Simply brilliant."

The day passed similarly for the other Americans. Team Retro had gone to the Mitsubishi dealer, where they made some minor repairs on their Fords before helping Richard and Ken, the Singapore/Hong Kong Brits with the big black '48 Buick, replace their rear main seal. The Buick had been losing substantial quantities of oil since Tibet. The Jeepsters completed their jeep duties early, and relaxed in the comfort of the air-conditioned hotel room watching the Ryder Cup golf matches.

Dinner was a buffet of excellent local specialties, arranged around the pool. Music and dancers entertained us, but the music was too loud, so we retreated to a table in the back with the Jeepsters. I spent a long time talking to Dave, and Dick teased us about not being able to repay him the beer we'd promised. Alcohol could only be consumed in the rooms, and then only after providing your passport and signing a statement declaring you were not Moslem.

Back in my room, I looked over the little bundle we'd been handed along with our rose garlands when we arrived. I untied the white ribbon and found miniature versions of the Hotel's Anniversary menus, celebrating Pakistan's fiftieth birthday, the "Golden Jubilee." India had been celebrating their fiftieth too—fifty years since their independence from the British. Here, Pakistan celebrated the anniversary of their independence from India, an event that resulted from the departing British's "Lahore Resolution," creating the new Muslim state and a new word— Pakistan, an acronym of the major provinces: Punjbab, Afghan, Kashmir, Sind and Baluchistan (plus, it means "land of the pure" in Urdu, the national language). Within weeks of the declaration, as Hindu and Sikh pulled up ancient roots to cross the new border into India and Muslims did the same to relocate in Pakistan, something like a million people were killed in one of the bloodiest mass migrations in history.

The text accompanying the meal descriptions in these special menus was the most ardent Islamic propaganda I'd yet seen. Each menu had a title and theme: "Pioneers of Freedom" for The Fort Grill honored the "Muslim leaders of the sub-continent who contributed to the freedom movement for Pakistan" and featured this rousing quote from Quaid-e-Azam Muhammed Ali Jinnah's 1945 speech:

> Remember, Muslims can never be crushed. They have not been crushed in the last 1,000 years by any power. . . . Our religion, our culture, and our Islamic ideals are our driving force to achieve independence.

"Artisans of Pakistan" appeared on the room service menu; "Long Live Pak-China Friendship" celebrated the Silk Road and the country's alliance with China for the Chinese restaurant named Dynasty. "Defenders of Pakistan" featured aggressive pictures of gun-toting soldiers in the menu for The Samovar Lounge, and finally Kim's, the main restaurant, bore the title "A Nation is Born" and featured nineteenth-century etchings inside the menu. On the back of this one was a color-coded map of the subcontinent circa 1947, with Muslim-majority areas designated in bright green.

Like most Americans, the only thing I knew about Pakistan before I signed up for the Peking-Paris was that little bit about their bloody independence, and the lingering hatred of India it engendered. My father's e-mails had tried to bring me up to date, as did the book he'd sent, *The World's Most Dangerous Places:*

> *Pakistan is still the classic adventurer's paradise, a wild mountainous region (to the north) and an arid wasteland (to the south), inhabited by fierce warring tribes and squabbling minorities. The isolation and poverty are positively biblical in the smaller towns. The big cities make Bladerunner look like a Caribbean resort. Sensory-numbing amounts of noise, dirt, poverty, temperature extremes, crime and general mayhem send most travelers fleeing to New York seeking peace and quiet. But as many Pakistanis point out, don't forget India is worse. Pakistan offers natural, archaeological and historical sites, as well as a wealth of interesting backwaters. Amazingly, amongst this Third World development disaster, the Pakistani people are some of the most handsome, generous and engaging to be met on this planet ... despite their constant warfare and banditry.*

This seemed a more comprehensible hazard than that posed by Iran, whose fundamentalist religious zealousness frightened us Americans, male and female, agnostic and Christian alike. Islam is taken no less seriously in Pakistan, but where tourists are concerned, there seemed to be a great deal of tolerance. And Pakistan has the amazing example of Prime Minister Benazir Bhutto, who ruled for a stormy twenty months back in 1988. Ms. Bhutto was not only the first-ever female Prime Minister of an Islamic state, but at the time was one of only five female premiers in the entire world. Pakistan's constitution prohibits discrimination on the basis of gender, and it was written a full forty years before the United Nations' declarations on women's rights.

That's probably why I decided to wear shorts the next morning.

*We began to feel that we must have passed the branching point—and to have completely
lost our way.*

LAHORE TO MULTAN
[SUNDAY, SEPTEMBER 28]

We had a very late start time: 10:45 A.M. By nine, it was one hundred
degrees with surprisingly high humidity, and even in my shorts and
tank top I suffered. Loading the car, we were accosted by a new set
of Americans in the parking area. Robin and Ben were driving a brand-new
black Jeep Wrangler, carrying serious video gear and making the rounds interviewing everyone about the first third of the journey. Once the cameras were
down I asked them what they were up to. Robin spoke with a rapid-fire
Philadelphia accent; Ben was quieter, a laid-back African-American. They'd been
hired by the intrepid Ray Carr, the elderly gent from Pennsylvania in the '39
Ford, to document the trip for his grandkids. I was disappointed; for one wild
moment I'd thought maybe a major American TV channel might have taken an
interest in our quaint little competition.

Robin and Ben had had a wild ride on their own. Their new Jeep was supposed to have been delivered to Beijing; instead, the shipper sent it to Antwerp.
There wasn't time to ship it again, so they decided to drive it down, following
the route in reverse. They drove straight through, trading off to sleep, talking their
way through the border crossings, finally catching us at the India–Nepal border.

I sat in the Avari's mercifully air-conditioned lobby, killing time by writing
in my journal. I also bit my nails, worrying about driving; I was back at the
wheel today. I wondered if the car would start; none of our Pakistani mechanics had even looked at our intermittently fitful ignition switch. I read and re-
read the road book. It gave the impression that today, crossing the Moghul's
Grand Trunk Road, would be easy. In my journal, I noted the pattern that had
developed:

It's odd how Linda keeps getting longer days with more kilometers and tougher driving. I've told her to look ahead a few days in the road book and decide if she wants to switch off, or go half days, and so far she's being stoic, but complaining a bit. I told her it's the "middle" doldrums and that it should get better soon. She swears she'll never do another rally, and in fact I don't think she will. Whereas I actually enjoy the driving and the navigating, she seems to dislike both—though she seems to hate navigating more. She claims it's because the book is so bad, and I can't tell if the book is truly worse on her navigating days or if she just can't get the hang of reading it and adjusting for the errors (some caused by our mis-calibrated trip meter). So far we seem to get there no matter how frustrated she becomes, so I should stop complaining.

Funny that I wrote those words that morning. Because shortly after setting out, about six kilometers down the road we got really lost for the first time. We took a left where the road forked, mistaking that left fork for "S/O" (straight-on). We took comfort in the fact that "Maurice," the little Morris, had followed us, so we kept going—too far—before we realized we were completely off the book. Suddenly the street narrowed, brick and wood buildings rose on both sides of us: we'd come into a village. A horse cart clopped in front of us, then paused to let a dozen mud-encrusted water buffalo pass. Cross streets appeared, but buildings and traffic blocked our view; we were both completely disoriented. Ahead of us the street disappeared beneath currents of black, foul smelling water. We watched the horse cart cross it in front of us; the black stuff rose to its high-wheeled axles. Using river crossing techniques, I revved across, terrified that if I let up on the accelerator we'd be mired forever. The stuff splashed high on both sides, spraying through our open windows, sprinkling us with shit—literally, horse, oxen, water buffalo and probably human sewage.

There was no going back now; I refused to cross that mire again. Forward looked like more foul-smelling ruts, so at the first crossing I turned. I may have yelled something at Linda like "Which way?" but I didn't wait for her response. I immediately regretted my turn, which took us straight into the heart of the crowded town. We crawled to a stop in the gridlocked people, horse, oxen, cart, and bus-packed traffic. Finally we crawled forward until we were cheek-by-jowl with a brand-new Mitsubishi Pajero going the other way. I yelled at Linda to yell out the window at them.

"Can you help us?" We both yelled. "Can you tell us which way is Bhai Pheru?" I tried, having seen those words on the map. The two men clearly didn't understand. "How about Pattoki?" we tried, having found that further town's name in the road book. After we'd held up our map, they understood, and said in English, "Follow us." They waited while we turned ourselves around—I did a three-point turn right in the middle of the grid-lock, a maneuver no stranger than the stopping, starting, and zigzagging of the locals—and then we both sped out of town, our Hillman clinging to the Pajero's bumper.

We were now headed the opposite direction of the way I'd originally turned, and my innate sense of direction, which usually doesn't lead me astray, was completely baffled. The Pajero driver stepped on it, and we flew by poor Maurice, stopped on the side of the road—I couldn't stop since we had no way of communicating with our saviors up ahead—and drove for miles and miles on tiny one-lane dirt roads, sometimes along canals, with man-high grasses and grains growing on either side of us. Out of the village, we rarely encountered any other traffic, except for one tractor, which caused the Pajero-driver not a moment's hesitation—he simply powered around it, so I followed, my heart in my teeth (if any other vehicle emerged from that blind turn ahead, I reasoned, at least the Mitsubishi would take the first impact). The Pajero never slowed for our benefit; he sped at 70 mph on these unbelievably narrow paths and we followed, our windshield tape rapping with brain-rattling intensity, percussive counterpoint to my heart, pounding away in fear of losing sight of him at any moment.

When we finally emerged from the high grassy fields to find ourselves at a major intersection with a stop sign, the Mitsubishi waited for us to pull up alongside. The driver said, "Left here, Pattoki." He handed Linda his card: S. Najam-ul-Hasan, Workshop Manager for Sigma Motors Ltd., a Land Rover dealership in Lahore. She handed him one of our P2PGALS stickers—we had very few left, having given most of our one hundred stickers to other competitors. They took off just as Ivar and Tom's Morgan sped by in front of us. Yes! We were back on the route, eighty-three kilometers from the morning's start!

We made it to the time control at Canntt only one minute late. No help from the road book—it said "TC In Restaurant on RIGHT" and the restaurant was, of course, on the LEFT.

The rest of the roads into Multan were sweet nothingness—uncrowded modern dual carriageways along grassy fields made green by the canals. We were fascinated by the road book notation that said "Military Dairy," amusing ourselves wondering if they were Army, Navy, Air Force or Marine cows. The reality was an anti-climax; a worn sign beside the road read simply "Military Dairy." No cows in sight of any stripe.

Multan was a busy brick-colored city reputed to have "four gifts: heat, dust, beggars and burial grounds." For a change, the directions to our parc fermé were clear, and we were welcomed with cups of cool juice at the final TC. We left the cars in a grassy field surrounded by a high fence with heavily armed guards, and rode a bus to the Holiday Inn. The guards were for the Iranians; their Peykans had been vandalized in Lahore: windows broken, hostile graffiti spray-painted on the sides of the cars. Clearly the hostility between these two countries hadn't lessened since that e-mail my father had forwarded back in April.

Inside the Holiday Inn, we were rushed into a side room off the lobby, where a troupe of men dressed in bright orange and yellow clothes with green turbans danced frenetically to pounding drums and the earsplitting soprano wail of an oboe-like woodwind. This performance was our special welcome, which was really a shame: after the long day's drive few of us could stand the din long enough to appreciate the tribute. Instead, we cringed, shoved the finger-sandwiches into our mouths, gulped the cold orange soda, and left at the first opportunity, grabbing the proffered rose—this one a long-stemmed, fragrant beauty—on the way out.

Linda and I cleaned ourselves up and went right back to the car. We'd rotated our tires in Lahore but had decided we'd be better off with new ones. The Brodericks, still waiting patiently for us to replace the Avon they'd loaned us back in China, had spotted a shop earlier. Their #52 Anglia was habitually the third or fourth car in, still with only seven minutes of penalties, close behind their friends the Catts in the #50 Cortina, who were leading the whole rally with only three minutes.

The hole-in-the-wall tire shop didn't have any Avons, so we bought two "Federals," made in Taiwan, and had them mounted and put on the rear. We got gas, then gave the Brodericks back their spare in the parking lot. We joined John Jung in the hotel's Chinese restaurant for dinner. We'd expected to eat with the whole Team Retro crew, but awhile after John and Linda and I settled in, Ted, Vic, and Andy arrived and sat at a different table.

John is surprisingly different from Retro's Alabama three. From Dallas instead of Birmingham, he was unmarried at age sixty-three. He spent a great deal of time in San Francisco and seemed to share some of the liberal attitudes characteristic of that city, almost opposite the conservative southern aura that accompanied his crew members. They seemed like an oddly-matched bunch.

Back in the lobby, we had time to check the official rally board for standings and bulletins, and a batch of articles that had been put up, reprints of Montagu's reports to the London *Times*. They seemed to feature, almost exclusively, photos of Francesca and Jennifer's Volvo. Some of the Gulls articles were posted, too; they'd been writing for the Saturday *Daily Telegraph*. Everybody, it seemed, was a journalist.

Moments later we ran into the Gulls themselves, as they were rushing out of the hotel. They were off to go shopping with a local fellow and invited us to join them. "Come along, it'll be fun," Jennifer said enthusiastically, and introduced us to our guide, who handed me a card. "Shahzad Mansoor, Executive Sales. Deals In: Tajima's Imported Vinyl Flooring Tiles; Dulastic Imported UPVC Doors; Forte Tiles & Senitry Ware."

Shahzad, who looked to be about twenty-five, was a showman and a trickster, too, and he relished the role of escort to four Western women ralliers. We piled into his tiny Suzuki and he drove us all over town, stopping at five or six places, calling out his window at each. "This is my brother's house," he'd tell us, then honk his car's tinny horn and holler "Hey, Brother, Come see!" Then the same routine at "my uncle's house!" *Honk honk.* "My cousin works in this shop!" *Honk honk.* "You must come home with me for a drink!"

At that we insisted, "No, we want to shop. Take us to the dress shops before they close!"

He circled back around to the shop where his cousin worked. The sign above the door said "SHE." Inside we found a wide variety of colorful tunic sets, all in the style of the traditional *salwar kameez*: a long overshirt and baggy, draw-string pants, with a matching scarf to cover the hair. The fabrics varied dramatically, from fancy embroidered velvets to simple, loose-weave cottons. We tried a few more shops, walking up the street, but came back to Shahzad's cousin's to buy. I asked Jennifer's opinion—I remembered she worked in fashion—and bought the two she recommended, even though I knew the pants were hopelessly short. The price amounted to only about six dollars each. Linda bought two as well, and Francesca and Jennifer each bought several. Jennifer called Francesca "Pogs" or "P," and I realized then that the two must have been old friends from childhood.

The Gulls were already decked out in Nepali wear; they'd found flowery fabrics unlike anything I'd seen in Kathmandu (but I always have been a terrible shopper, and a rotten dresser, too). I heard later they'd commissioned their Nepali-wear in London, but never could confirm if that was true. Our talk revolved around the rally and our cars; they continued to have trouble with their frustrating Volvo. The competition fomented between us by Philip and others was ignored for the sake of camaraderie. We promised to join them for dinner some night.

I really wanted a chance to get to know them better. Jennifer seemed warm and open, Francesca more self-absorbed in a traditionally upper-crust way. I wondered—and still wonder—how much of Philip Young's talk in Paris was true. Were they really unaware of our entry until Beijing? And once they'd become aware of us, did they care? By the time we'd all gotten to Multan, our lead was two hours, forty minutes. Had they given up on the notion of winning the Women's Cup? Did it bother them?

If it did, they didn't show it, or say a word. The British, male and female, are good at that.

CHAPTER

❧ 28 ❧

"Why all these arms?" asked Prince Borghese. "You can't go out at night without weapons," replied the man. "The whole countryside is infested with highwaymen. They assault, kill, and rob everywhere."

MULTAN TO QUETTA

[MONDAY, SEPTEMBER 29]

That night, while Linda, the Gulls and I were out shopping, Don and Carl invited Ted Thomas to talk to the folks back home on Don's webpage phone report. Ted talked about Iran, which had been on everyone's mind. "Actually," he said, "I wasn't looking forward to going into Iran, but now I think I am. We've met a lot of Iranians here. There's six of them actually participating in the race. The Iranian government has advised us that they are going to pay for all of our fuel, they're going to put out extra support trucks with mechanics to help us with maintenance on the cars. So I think it will be a pleasant experience."

Ted, Vic, John and even the ailing Andy were long gone by the time our bus arrived the next morning to take the later-starting Classics from the Multan Holiday Inn to the car park. We sat under the front awning, waiting, with Ivar the handsome Norwegian. He looked exhausted and ragged, and several pounds thinner than the last time I'd seen him. The fence railing seemed to be holding him up.

"How'd the repairs go?" I asked him, remembering the bright-yellow Morgan and its long list of needs in Lahore.

"Worked all night on it. Haven't even slept."

I knew from his heavy-lidded eyes that he was telling the truth. His co-driver Tom was peppier; I hoped he'd be doing that day's driving. "All fixed now!" Tom said, countering his co-driver's exhausted pessimism. "We've rebuilt the whole car—everything but the engine, which hasn't given us a bit of trouble."

After the bus came and took us to the lot, we piled into our cars and drove the short distance back to the hotel, where the day's official start line had been drawn. Our good friend Shahzad entertained us all by riding up and down the street on a motorbike: once with no hands, then on his back, then standing, then upside down. I wondered if he noticed I was wearing one of his cousin's tunics over my

181

cargo pants. We weren't in Iran yet, but we knew it wouldn't be wise to show any skin in Baluchistan. I'd put away my shorts indefinitely.

Our late start time—9:00 A.M.—wouldn't have been bad on a short day, but today would be one of our longest yet: 624 kilometers or 387 miles. Bulletin #14, which had been distributed in Lahore, had shortened all the day's times considerably, so we knew we had "speed" sections and at least one hill climb ahead.

Still, we had no idea how bad it would really be. Months later, at home, I reread *Dangerous Places*. This time, these words jumped out at me: "Mountainous highways and insane drivers make Pakistan's roads a killing ground."

Exactly.

It was Linda's turn to drive, of course. The first leg was easy, crossing the huge Mississippi-like flood plain around the great Indus river; shirtless boys in baggy pants sold fresh coconut along its bank. Not far beyond the river, the land became more arid, and the road a bit disconcerting; it would eventually be a four-lane dual-carriageway, but was now an unfinished zig-zag. First we'd drive on one two-lane stretch, then abruptly the pavement would end on our side, so we'd cross over gravel to the other two-lane stretch. We landed at the first TC in Sakh Sarwar, a dry desert town in the foothills of the Sulaiman Mountains, with plenty of time. The only problem was the heat, which was well over a hundred already. The road book's warning that today "heat is probably going to be your main challenge" turned out to be spectacularly wrong, but waiting there at Sakh Sarwar, it seemed reasonable. The sky sparkled in the palpably hot air; distant silver-covered minarets blazed like torches. Traffic was already heavy with dazzling trucks—the Pakistanis glued everything and anything that glittered or made noise to their trucks, and painted every uncovered millimeter with fluorescent colors. Long chains formed a metallic grass skirt around the lower edges, mimicking the sound of breaking glass as they chinked and rattled by. Tassels, mirrored tiles (though nothing so practical as a rear- or side-view mirror) accompanied murals, painted praises to Allah and glued-on fetishes. Entertaining to watch pass by from the safety of the roadside, but deadly to meet head-on.

We watched the trucks rumble by—one even carried four camels in its open bed—and waited for our time at that first TC. This next stretch was to be the real test, a combination speed-trial-hill-climb, time for the organizers to "clear the leader board." Most of us didn't think the board needed clearing. There were still officially seventy-two cars in the competition, and only about a third of those, we thought, were still in the running for gold medals. What's wrong with handing out twenty-five gold medals? Some said Philip and the rally organizers were too cheap, and would never pay for so many. Others, some of the seriously competitive ralliers, thought it was about time that the event got tougher; too many people, they argued, were turning the whole thing into a long joyride.

Linda and I had decided ever since the accident in Tibet that the goal was just getting to Paris. We did watch and compare our times to those for #62, the Gulls. It would be nice to get the Women's Cup. So far, our two-plus hours felt like a comfortable lead. But it wouldn't be worth another crash to preserve it.

SCRAPBOOK

#51, our Hillman Hunter, next to the
1934 Rolls Royce (Mr. Sparkle) at
the Agricultural Center, Beijing

CHINA
September
6
BEIJING

CHINA

Yaks in the road near Baotou, China

Kjeld Jessen's 1929 Bentley 4-liter along the banks of the Yellow River

欢迎您到宁夏旅游观光

TIBET

Camping near Koko Nor

Prayer flags, Tibet

The 3-liter Bentley climbs into Tibet

Linda prepares to drive through a stream across no man's land road

No man's land between China and Nepal. We all had to drive under this waterfall. If you look closely, you'll see the white BMW 328 passengers with their yellow umbrellas raised.

PEKING TO PARIS
90th
ANNIVERSARY
SEPT/OCT
1997
MOTOR CH

Nepali welcome
banner in Kabhre

"We're toast!" Accident near Lhaze, Tibet

Bill Binnie's Bentley preparing to cross a river in Nepal; orange tube is his exhaust snorkel

Pakistani traffic, with truckload of camels

Rally cars in the lot at Palandöken, Turkey

Linda and Genny in
Iranian women's wear
(or Pakistani men's wear)

Monasteries in Meteora, Greece

2CV and Don & Carl's '54 Packard
convertible going through a cute,
peaked-roofed cottage
village in France

Linda standing atop
the Hillman in the
Place de la Concorde

FRANCE

October
18

PARIS

PARIS

Linda and Genny receiving the Women's Cup
at Peking to Paris awards banquet

1907 2nd 1997

97

SEP California

2 GALS 2P2

PEKING TO PA

Our "in" time, 10:55 A.M., arrived, and still we waited. What was the delay? We'd never been asked to wait *after* checking in before. Someone said there was a problem with the next stage —something about clearing the trucks off the road. We'd get to start again at 11:19 A.M. Twenty more minutes.

We were surprised to see the Jeepsters arrive then; the blue-book Vintageants and FWDs should have been far ahead of us. The #99 Jeep had been delayed right out of Multan. "A local driver backed across three lanes of traffic and bashed into our right front fender!" Dick explained. "Fortunately, a policeman witnessed the accident. We were allowed to go on, with an apology from the offending driver."

With ten minutes more to go, I checked the road book: "After the Time Control at Sakh Sarwar," it read, "there is a forty kilometer section up through a superb mountain pass . . . quite narrow in places. Not far from Khar is the old mountain Fort Munro built by the British." Fort Munro is the gateway to the desert province of Baluchistan. "After Khar," the book continued, "the road becomes very fast and straight . . . There's not much of a traffic problem in Quetta. . . . " I hoped some of it might be true, for Linda's sake. She deserved an easy day's drive.

Then I switched to math. We would have thirty-four minutes to climb the 45.5-kilometer "hill climb" to Fort Munro at the top of the Sulaiman Range. That worked out to an average speed of 50 mph. That would be very hard to maintain over any curvy mountain pass, even a perfectly paved, well-marked Western one. So we already knew we couldn't make it "clean." The plan was just to drive.

When we finally set off, Linda drove aggressively but carefully. There was only one lane, edged by sheer cliffs over deep canyons, and loose gravel tempted our wheels to break loose on every turn, most of them blind hairpins. The road was far from clear; we came upon more Vintageants, locals, trucks, camels (one-humped dromedaries) and more. Several places were completely blocked by road construction, or by oncoming trucks; we had to back up at one point, to clear a space wide enough for the oncoming truck to pass. As in Tibet, we had to go around construction sites on sand, mud, running water and gravel.

At the top of the mountain, I ran panting in to the TC station, and slapped my book down. We were twenty-eight minutes late. The TC workers, Peter and Betty, an older British couple who had joined the staff in Nepal, were clearly upset.

"Sign this! You must sign this!" Betty yelled, shoving a piece of paper at me, her blue eyes looking panicked. She was wrapped in blue Islamic cotton from head to toe. I tried to read it, but the place was a mass of confusion—locals and ralliers were rushing back and forth out of the dark room, conversations going on in several languages. I couldn't make sense of the paper. It said something like, "I understand that I have been told to wait . . ."

"What's this all about?" I asked. "You want us to wait here?"

"No! You've got to get going. Just sign it! It doesn't apply to you, only to the Vintageants. Go! You'll have to move your car!"—as if Linda and the Hillman were blocking traffic. Betty had a limited view out the open door of the roadside shack, but I knew she couldn't see our car; there were far too many other cars between the Hillman and the entrance.

I shrugged, signed, and ran back out to the car. As I ran, I noticed Ray Carr and his co-driver Mike fiddling with their '39 Ford; Howard Bellm climbing under his '67 Camaro—it looked like he'd had a crash. Other rally cars were scattered about, parked in distressed and disheveled heaps. Plenty of cars here—against the organizers' wishes? What was going on?

"We've got to go." I told Linda, deciding that clearing out was a good idea. The place felt like bad luck, and it looked contagious. "Go now. I don't know what's going on, but they don't want us hanging around."

Linda looked at me, surprised, but set the gearshifter in first and took off. I don't think she even had time to stand and stretch. No snack, no pee, nothing.

The road down the mountain was no wider or smoother than the one we'd just climbed up, and the trucks were more numerous, a never-ending, hallucinogenic convoy of bright flashing color against the brown dirt mountains. Once on the far side of the Sulaiman Range, the earth flattened and grew even more barren. Baluchistan is Pakistan's driest (less than fifteen centimeters of rainfall annually), hottest (average temperatures from 86 to 122 degrees F), and least populated province (only four million people live here, even though the province constitutes 42 percent of Pakistan's total area). A team of US geologists declared that Baluchistan's terrain is "remarkably like the surface of Mars," and a local proverb says that "Baluchistan is the dump where Allah shot the rubbish of creation."

There was nothing now but dirt and sand and the distant Toba and Kakar Ranges on the edge of Afghanistan. The road straightened, but it was not "very fast" as our road book had promised. Thanks to the trucks, we could barely increase our speed on this roughly-paved one-lane highway. At one point, we passed the Dutch-driven Citroën 2CV (there were three of the little French cars in the rally: Burt and Rich's American team, two Italians in the bright-yellow #53, and the two Dutch in a light-yellow car). They'd gone off the road and suffered serious suspension damage, and now the younger man, Johann, rode standing on the bumper as the older man Willem slowly drove; Johann's weight was needed to keep the car level.

About halfway to our next TC at Loralai, 192.5 kilometers from Fort Munro, I calculated our times, and realized there was no way we could make it on time. The organizers had again shortened the time allowance, and since we'd already stopped for gas and to pee, we could never make up the difference. I just hoped we could keep the penalty short.

It was a relief to switch places. I took over the driving and handed Linda the road book. The driving took all my concentration, trying for speed when the way was clear, but mostly it wasn't and we had no choice but to play an elaborate game of chicken: "Okay truck, are you going to move off the lane or am I?" We eventually learned that the trucks never moved. This was their highway, and Allah would be damned before they'd move their rattling, decorated hulks one inch. It became an elaborate, repetitive ritual: brake, then crawl over the soft sandy shoulder—at least one wheel had to be off the side to make room for the wide trucks—then trundle back over the rocky lane edge, spit gravel to accelerate away, then repeat the process around the next truck, bus, or tractor.

I drove straight into the setting sun, heat blasting our faces through the windshield. The desert, a dusty, treeless expanse, stretched out on all sides; we hadn't seen another competitor for hours. The piercing sun had given me a whopper of a headache by the time we reached the Loralai TC. We clocked in at 4:13 in the afternoon, one hour and twenty-seven minutes late. Some of our fellow ralliers were here, all of them angry and upset. The Brodericks' #52 Anglia had broken an accelerator cable, punctured a tire, and run off the road coming down from Fort Munro (the day's penalties ended up dropping them from third place to seventh). Ivar and Tom's Morgan had fatally overheated; the engine, the only part of the car they hadn't touched, had been destroyed. The Jeepsters, after getting hit right there in Multan, were skewered by a truck out of Fort Munro: "As I squeezed by this truck, with a precipitous drop to my left," Dick said, "the truck lurched into a pothole, and a steel beam across the back of the truck speared the Jeep through the middle window on the passenger side. The inside was showered with broken glass, and it took us several minutes of maneuvering to free us from the beam." Both rear passenger-side windows were broken and the B-pillar severely damaged.

Back in the navigator's seat at Loralai, I swallowed some aspirin and reexamined the numbers. We still had 262 kilometers to go, and the sun was beginning to set. I couldn't believe that one hour and twenty-seven minute penalty could be correct. We had driven aggressively, as fast as we could, and barely taken a break! My earlier annoyance grew into hot, irrational anger as I punched and repunched the numbers on my calculator. No, we had not made any math errors: the required average speed was 50 mph, same as the previous stage. But how could we have accumulated as many penalties in this one stage as we had in Tibet on the day of our accident? On a reasonable Western road 50 would have been a cinch. In this part of Pakistan, it was impossible.

Tired and upset, my head pounding, I gave up on navigation and settled into watching the road. The terrain was hillier now; we were in the foothills of those dry, twisted mountains that separated us from Afghanistan. Here, we first saw one of the most frightening, heart-rending sights of the whole journey: women covered by full *burqa,* those horrifying all-encompassing tents that Afghan and Pathan women (the Pathans live here in Baluchistan and in Pakistan's North West Frontier Province) must wear, with nothing but a tiny cloth grid allowing the sun to reach their eyes. They crouched in the dust, these mounds of faded pastel cloth. The sight made Linda and me both want to cry.

We'd been warned about Iran, and Islamic strictures regarding women's clothing, but this was our first sight of fundamentalist *Purdah,* the set of Islamic customs that women "keep" when they veil themselves. Urban Pakistan's relatively tolerant culture allowed women to "keep purdah" by simply covering their hair with a scarf or *chador* (a longer veil) and honoring certain kinds of social sexual segregation. Out in the countryside, especially close to the extremists in Afghanistan, purdah required absolute invisibility. All of Islam presents a mind-boggling contradiction to the Western woman: *Shar'ia,* or Islamic law, explicitly protects a woman's right to education and a livelihood, and allows her to own and inherit property separately from her husband. In practice, though, in Pakistan, Pathan women cannot own or inherit land or houses, they must marry without their consent, they cannot ask for divorce under any circumstances, and the punishment for adultery is death. Even a woman's rights to her own personal property, like jewelry and clothing, are subject to her male guardian's approval.

Some of these males stood near their shrouded women, each with a machine gun slung over his shoulder. They wore the striped turbans that probably belonged legitimately to some tribe (the Pathans are made up of many, with names like Wazir, Mahsud, and Khattak), but to us warned of banditry. As we drove on, we'd often see single men, walking a short distance from the road, always armed with at least a rifle, if not a machine gun. If not Pakistani tribesmen, perhaps they were Afghan refugees (they had been flooding the region since the Taliban took over that country). I took comfort in the fact that these gentlemen were wandering solo; packs of armed men would've been even more frightening.

The sun fell toward the bleak horizon, and police checkpoints—or check-points that looked like they should've been manned by police but seemed to be operated only by ragged men or boys—multiplied. At one, we almost drove into a wire placed about axle height, before I shouted and Linda stopped. It was dusk now, not yet fully dark. I yelled out the window angrily to a couple of boys that looked about ten years old. "Hey, we're with the rally! Let us through!"

They lifted the wire, laughing. We drove on.

Later, others were less fortunate. Bill Binnie and Ned Thompson came to one of these roadblocks in full dark, and were directed to leave the road by a gang of machine-gun toting men. In the pitch blackness, the Bentley boys drove their roadster over the rocky terrain, following a bouncing flashlight—they feared the worst: kidnapping, robbery—until they were miraculously led back to the main road, and waved on, their hearts in their throats.

This was our first time driving at night; back in Beijing, the marshals had promised that night driving would not be required. "If you have a breakdown, you may certainly have to run at night to catch up," one of the marshals had said, "but otherwise it will not be necessary." Back in 1907, Prince Borghese first drove at night in search of water, both for the Itala and for the crew. They were in upper Mongolia, and expected a river to cross their path at any moment, but it did not materialize. "We had no lights; at least, we had lamps, but they were not prepared for lighting," Barzini wrote. "We were amid lofty heights, and our path followed narrow valleys, climbed, descended, was scarcely visible . . . we strained our eyes to see it for fear of missing our way, and to our tired eyes under the spectral light of the moon, all things appeared to take on terrifying, uncertain, fantastic outlines. . . . In the night all that there is of the fabulous, impossible, and absurd in our fancy comes out and takes a place in the shadow."

At least, on our first night driving, the Hillman's headlamps were cooperating. Linda buzzed along, our windshield tape flapping, the night air cooling. I offered to take the wheel again, once my headache had cleared, but Linda declined. As our ribbon of narrow road disappeared into the black horizon, the landscape became fraught with scary moving shadows: trucks. They appeared out of the gloom like a psychedelic nightmare; our headlights would suddenly catch the fluorescent and mirror-tiled facade or unlit rear—flaming reds, yellows and oranges darting and whirling past our eyes as we trundled off the road yet again to get around. Sometimes the oncomers would flash their headlights—always too late, just as we were upon them—and the sudden blinding white beam would etch into our startled vision. We'd crawl past, shake our heads clear of these drug-like afterimages, regain the road, and try to gain some speed before repeating the whole surreal scenario over again.

Until we were stopped dead in a massive traffic jam. We could see revolving police lights in the distance. What could it be? Road construction after 8:00 P.M.? I was still indignant about the unrealistic timing and penalties, and I immediately assumed something bad had happened; perhaps an accident. Linda, more optimistic, said hopefully, "Maybe the police are going to escort us around all this traffic and lead us to the hotel!" We were only about twenty kilometers from the provincial capital of Quetta, the day's final TC and our hotel.

A little earlier, fifteen kilometers up ahead, John and Andy were driving the #24 Team Retro Ford into Quetta's heavy traffic. They had lost a headlight and a shock already that day, and had been late at a couple of the TCs, but not as late as most; it looked like they might make the final TC on time. Andy was reading the road book when he heard three consecutive backfires.

"I looked up as the white Volkswagen passed us on our right and braked hard, turned sideways and went straight on into the front of a bus parked on the side of the road, letting off passengers."

He yelled for John to stop, then jumped out and ran to the VW. It was car #72, the '67 convertible VW Bug driven by Josef and René Feit. "It was a horrible scene," Andy said. "I checked the young boy and couldn't find a pulse, but the older man had a strong pulse and was bleeding profusely from a head wound. I knew I needed some help. I turned and saw the Discovery Online Land Rover. I ran over and beat on the window."

"There's been a terrible accident," Andy yelled. "Does anyone know first aid? Anything? It looks really bad."

The Land Rover pulled over. Robert Thomas and Christina Bennett, the young reporters who'd joined us in Nepal, climbed out. "The bus with a crushed right fender was half way off the road," Christina reported. "Glass, metal and plastic parts crunched under our feet as we ran. The white VW convertible was barely recognizable: its entire front end was a concave mesh of metal and glass, and the hood was buckled like a folding chair. Both Josef and René Feit were pinned under the dashboard. The teen was already dead; his father was unconscious."

With the help of a crowd of Pakistanis, Andy and the Discovery crew dragged the crushed VW out from under the bus, then fastened a rope to the Volkswagen's hood and peeled the chassis open. "I couldn't get the door open," Andy continued, "so I broke the side window off and reached inside. I pulled the inside handle back and the door came open, but I couldn't get the older man free. He was jammed under the dash. Someone handed me a handkerchief; I folded it and placed it on the man's head, then tied my bandana around it. Then, with a lot of help, we were able to pull the steering wheel and the dash away and finally removed him."

Two young Pakistanis had come to help, and they spoke English, so Andy asked them how long it would take for an ambulance to come. They said an hour.

"How far to the hospital?" Andy asked.

"Ten minutes."

"Do you have a car?"

"We have a pickup truck."

They carefully lifted Josef Feit onto the pickup's tailgate. Andy crawled in under the camper shell, and gently pulled Feit forward, resting the injured man's head on his lap.

They couldn't get the pickup out by the road because of all the traffic, so the onlookers joined together and literally picked the back of the truck up and turned it around. The students drove off the side of the road, into a ditch, and then out of it with more help from the onlookers. "Twenty minutes of heavy traffic and severely bumpy roads later," Andy said, "we arrived at the hospital. They took Feit from the truck, and I told the two boys, 'Don't leave me here alone!' The hospital had poor conditions and no equipment. I talked to reporters and policemen for about an hour and a half before the son's body arrived. The police couldn't understand that I didn't know them or their nationality. I told them I thought they were either Dutch or German. It was easy to see why they didn't understand: I was covered with blood, had a back brace on, and a large Ace bandage on my knee. I explained and explained but it did no good. I kept expecting someone from the Rally to show up any minute. After about three hours, the Chief of Police of Quetta came and talked to me, asking the same questions. I told him that he needed to talk to someone in charge of the Rally. I was just another competitor."

The Chief of Police decided to take Andy back to the hotel to find the rally staff. "Wait," Andy said, "I want to see Mr. Feit again before I go." Andy and the students were led to Feit's side. "When I saw him, he looked much better, but he still didn't respond when I talked to him. As we left, we went through a parking lot with lots of people wrapped in blankets, sleeping in rows on the ground. I think they were patients."

Meanwhile, back on the road at about 8:45 P.M., our Hillman followed three other rally cars—Bud Risser in the Chevy Bel Air, South Africans Carolyn and John in their Land Rover, and Malaysian Mr. Wong in his MGA—behind the sirens and flashing blue lights of our police escort. The policemen drove us slowly past the stopped traffic. Five kilometers from the hotel, we crawled by what had caused the traffic jam.

"Oh my God," I said.

"Is it?" Linda asked.

"One of us? Yes." I could clearly see what was left of the Peking Paris decorations on the side of the crushed VW Bug. Then I remembered the German father and son, dressed alike in their matching bright red driving suits.

There was nothing, absolutely nothing, left of the passenger side. It had been sheered completely off by the bus; the overdecorated, pitch black hulk lay tilted only a few feet away. We knew there was no way the person sitting in the passenger seat could have survived. We nursed our hope that the driver had fared better.

We parked and I stomped into the Quetta hotel's luxurious lobby. I found the TC table, slammed down the book and said "Doesn't matter what time you put down, does it? They're going to have to cancel this one anyway."

The guy working the table—he was a young British man, deathly pale, and I'd never seen him before—looked like he was in shock. "I don't know. I don't think so," he said, "how about 21:03?" He was being generous, giving me a minute or two, but I was furious. I might have said something rude then, I don't remember. Mick O'Malley appeared, his familiar face calming me down a bit. He'd been working the rally from the beginning, and had a laid-back attitude possibly cultivated by years of living in Kathmandu.

I asked, "Did anyone survive?"

"The father's alive," Mick said. "The boy's dead. Killed instantly. Josef's in hospital."

My anger over the day's timing and penalties had been stewing for more than eight hours, and now it boiled over. In my mind, this terrible accident was a direct result of the day's crazy timing: if the times hadn't been so tight, if the marshals hadn't been so intent on "clearing the leader board," this insane accident might never have happened. How incredibly stupid to die fighting to make a TC at an outrageously unreasonable required average speed! I automatically blamed the organizers for this horrible, unnecessary tragedy.

Before I left the lobby to search for Linda and the car, a phone call came for Mick. His young assistant and I stood by and listened. "Is he? Yes, all right."

"Dead?" I asked.

"Josef Feit is dead, yes."

Andy carried the Feits' personal effects back to the hotel in a paper sack. He went looking for John, Ted, or Vic, to find his room and a blessed shower. He spent the rest of the night sequestered with the Quetta Police Chief and Philip Young's assistant, Sarah Catt, writing up an official account of the accident. "This just isn't fun anymore," he told Robert the next day in Zahedan. The words weren't necessary; it was obvious to everyone that the once happy-go-lucky man was emotionally and physically demolished.

The rest of us were in a state of shock. Every car that pulled into Quetta brought with it another accident or breakdown story. We heard at least a dozen that night. Later, when all were accounted for, it turned out that forty-one separate accidents or mechanical incidents occurred on the road to Quetta, by far the rally's darkest day. The Jeepsters, with their two accidents, didn't arrive until after 11:00 P.M.; they had driven for more than sixteen hours without stopping to eat. Carl and Don pulled the '54 Packard into Quetta at 2:00 A.M. after a long, long day fighting brake and shock absorber problems. The Bulls' big black Rover (#59) was hit by a tractor. An Army lorry rammed another Rover near Fort Munro, the two-tone green #39 driven by Concorde-pilot David Brister and Keith Barton. The accident completely destroyed the Rover's right front fender and damaged the radiator. They thought they'd fixed the radiator, but once they got going again, they discovered that the water pump was damaged as well; they had to stop every six or seven miles to add water. They never even made it into Quetta that night; they finally stopped in Loralai at 3:00 A.M. There, they found other beleaguered rally drivers: the baby '32 Aston Martin, the '36 Railton, and the Allard. The Germans in the Bugatti came into Loralai late too, but decided to soldier on; they arrived in Quetta at 4:00 A.M.

Even the expert ralliers suffered: the first-place #50 Cortina driven by the Catts lost twenty-eight minutes, dropping to third place (the new first-overall was a British-owned 1942 Willys Jeep). The Dutch-driven Citroën D19 had lost a transmission. Welsh David and Sheila Morris, in Mr. Blobby, broke a suspension piece and waited three hours in the desert. They had run completely out of water before a second, almost identical Austin A90 being rallied by a friendly pair of British gents named Fred and Tim, arrived with the crucial spare part. Even Philip Young's Peugeot was hit by a truck.

Despite the tragedy, the stories became so numerous and improbable, they began to seem almost humorous. Michael Kunz laughed incredulously as he told us about his and co-driver John's terrible day in the little Triumph Vitesse: they had had four separate accidents, hitting two trucks, a sheep, and later, in the dark, landing in a ditch while trying to avoid another truck. John had spent the time in between bash-ups tacking the hood and various other tattered body panels back onto the poor Triumph's chassis. As Michael finished the tale, John was still out in the parking lot, cobbling the car back together.

At midnight, we ate dinner at the Quetta Serena's restaurant with two British couples, David and Patricia Dalrymple with the big blue '49 Cadillac, and Chris and Janine Dunkley, with a '35 Bentley. Like us, they'd been lucky, coming through the day unscathed, but were as angry as we were at the day's ridiculous timing. They were able to clarify some of our confusion about the Fort Munro TC. The Pakistani police had apparently promised Philip they would close the "hill climb" road for us, but when the time came, some of the truckers defied the rally marshals. Who would pay for the rotted fruit, the truckers said, if their loads weren't delivered in time? They threatened the marshalls, and with no Pakistani police to back them up, the marshalls had to yield and let the trucks through. The tight times for that section would have been more logical—and far less dangerous—if the road had been cleared of all traffic.

I never did figure out what that piece of paper I'd signed signified, nor why

Betty had been so upset. One rumor had it that a fundamentalist Pakistani had taken offense at Betty's appearance. If so, she had changed, covering herself in blue cloth, by the time I saw her.

This was one night that really required a drink. Linda decided it was worth jumping through all the religious and bureaucratic hoops to get us a couple of glasses of gin. She called room service and placed the order. A young man arrived with a full, unopened bottle.

"Oh no! We just want two drinks. Two glasses. Not the whole bottle."

"Only like this," the server said.

"Well," Linda said, "can I open it up and pour out two drinks and then you take back the rest?"

No," the server said. "So sorry, you must speak to my supervisor." In a moment Linda was on the phone. After much back and forth, she figured out that not only did she have to hand over her passport, sign on the dotted line, and pay a substantial sum of Pakistani rupees, but she would be required to take the whole bottle; no good Muslim was allowed to touch the decadent thing once it was open. She poured us two tall ones; I thinned mine with a little lime juice.

The gin helped, but as I sank into bed, I was still a mass of conflicting emotions: grief, sorrow, anger that threatened to become a chronic condition, and embarrassment. I realized now that I had probably sounded to Mick like I was more concerned about my penalties than I was about the Feits. Over it all, though, was a layer of relief: by dumb luck or skill, our Hillman had come through undamaged, and Linda and I remained, so far, uninjured.

CHAPTER

~ 29 ~

We had so far cherished the illusion that each difficulty or danger we encountered would be the last. We had thought that the beginning of our journey must be the worst part of it, and that presently everything must become easier; but now we seemed to find that obstacles grew and multiplied before us.

QUETTA, PAKISTAN TO ZAHEDAN, IRAN
[TUESDAY, SEPTEMBER 30]

The next day, all we could talk about was the fatal accident. We learned more about Josef and René Feit. At seventeen, René was the youngest person on the rally; Josef had been celebrating his own birthday. We wondered how the rally officials were going to tell Josef's wife and three other sons. Their home in Waldkraiburg, Germany, was not far from our route two weeks hence.

In a reflexive and human rationalization, some ralliers quietly stated that Josef Feit was one of the most competitive and, by inference, reckless drivers on the rally. The rumor had been circulating that his VW was powered by a Porsche motor, so this was offered as evidence. "If anyone had it coming . . ." We all knew how the expression ends, but no one spoke the words aloud. I wondered if any of us non-German speakers had the right to draw any conclusions at all; the Feits had been friendly with all, but socialized mostly with the German and Dutch competitors.

Many considered Philip Young and the rally staff at least partly to blame, as I had in my early anger; the increased required average speeds were seen as encouraging reckless driving. With time, I came to realize that placing blame on the rally was unfair: anyone familiar with competitive rallying knows that risk of death in an accident is, and always has been, a normal part of the sport (indeed, a normal part of everyday driving). "By giving them average speeds," Philip told the Discovery reporter, "we are not telling people how to drive. It's all about how to pace yourself." Greg, the doctor, told me that two bodybags are standard in every endurance rally's medical kit.

Philip made a statement for the press, distributed by the Rally's press man, respected automotive journalist Graham Robson, which my husband, mother

and father received via the same Rally Fax Service that had informed them of our accident:

> We are all devastated by this awful event, which has deeply affected everyone else involved in the Challenge. Although it is the wish of the competitors that the event should continue, their mood will clearly be subdued.

None of us really wanted to talk about it, but we couldn't leave it alone. We all hoped and prayed that Frau Feit, at least, believed her two men had died happy, in the midst of doing exactly what they wanted to be doing.

Start time out of Quetta was 6:00 A.M. It didn't make sense—4:00 A.M. starts in China and Delhi, then ridiculously late starts on long hot days in Pakistan, now back to an early start, on a morning when we'd all had so little sleep we might as well have stayed awake all night. The gravity of the accident seemed to require something more than business as usual, but as far as we could tell, nothing was done, except the canceling of the following day's TCs. The logic escaped me: why remove the competition *after* the disaster, and still penalize people for having suffered *through* the disaster? It seemed both arbitrary and a case of too little, too late.

It was necessary, though, since a contingency of German competitors, led by Thomas and Maria Noor, planned to stay behind in Quetta to take care of contacting the family, to make arrangements to ship the bodies, and to pay the hospital and administrative fees. They also ended up bailing the bus driver out of jail; the Pakistani police had arrested him, even though there was no evidence that he did anything other than park his bus in the normal manner. Young allowed the Germans to stay without penalty, but warned them that they'd have to catch up with the group by the time we all left Zahedan, on the morning of October second.

Quetta was an oasis town, at a relatively high (and therefore cooler) 5,444 feet, facts we hadn't been able to register driving in at night with police lights flashing. In the morning, as we drove down clean streets through date palms and modern buildings, we learned from the road book that a major earthquake had leveled the town in 1935, killing some twenty thousand people. The town had since been entirely rebuilt, which explained the odd newness of it. Soon enough, though, we were back in the desert. Now there were no more gas stations, just roadside stands with fuel in plastic cans. Excellent quality, we were told, freshly smuggled from Iran.

It was a long, uneventful drive (of course it was my turn) through blowing sand and wandering camels, following the railway down to the Pakistan-Iran border. We were closer than ever now to Afghanistan, and at the Lak Pass twenty-eight kilometers out, we had a clear view of the Chagai Hills that defined the border.

Nearby stood an impressive mud-and-wattle fort, the first of many we would see at high points above the desert. By the time we reached Dalbandin, a dusty oasis town, about halfway through the day, the road had straightened out, and with truck traffic much lighter than it had been the day before, we could now move fairly fast. We still saw the occasional wandering, armed, tribesman, but the harsh desert and few towns kept them to a minimum.

Despite our "subdued" mood, we were almost ecstatic with relief to be crossing the border into Iran. Pakistan had been a fascinating, contradictory place; the people had been so helpful and welcoming after the crush and rush of India. Yet the harsh land with its painted, menacing traffic, haunted us now, three days later. We couldn't leave fast enough.

The border town on the Pakistan side, Kuh-i-Taftan, could hardly be called a town. The Palangan mountains nearby were a geologist's delight—folded and twisted stacks of dark red and black rock—but the settlement was little more than a military camp. Sprawling, haphazardly arranged buildings faced no particular angle and looked deserted; we relied on bright orange Peking-Paris arrows to lead us through the maze into the TC. We found Doctor Greg and Mike Summerfield sitting on folding chairs at a single table in an otherwise empty shack.

Greg asked us how many ralliers we thought might be ahead of us, and we said quite a few. We listed off the ones we'd seen, including Eric Christiansen and Michael Veys in the big Rolls. They'd dropped from the competition into the Touring class and were now leaving when they wanted instead of at their designated start times. Greg looked at his list and frowned. Most, apparently, were missing this hidden little TC completely.

It was impossible to miss the border itself, which lay only a few hundred yards away. I was nervous—after all my father's warnings, after all the talk about the clothing restrictions, after reading *Dangerous Places*—and I think Linda was too. We dutifully covered our heads with our Nepali and Pakistani scarves, then drove up to the guard. A gentleman from the Iranian Automobile Federation came to the window on the passenger side. He asked Linda for our passports and the carnet, then walked over to a building and shoved them through a tiny square window. We stayed in the car, and waited.

And waited.

The car ahead of us had long since gone through; it hadn't taken them this long (Vic later told us it took the Fords less than five minutes). I wondered if we should get out and go ask at that little window ourselves, then thought better of it. Instead we finally called the Federation fellow back and asked him to go check for us. A short while later, he brought back the passports and waved us through.

I wondered if they'd been waiting for a third passport, one from a man.

Just past the high border fencing—driving on the right now, a relief for most Americans but trickier for us in our right-hand-drive—a big welcoming party greeted us. Iranian reporters and a TV crew were filming, and some of the Peykan drivers were still there, clearly the heroes of the day. Volunteers gave us cold sodas and a huge packet of food: enough boxes of crackers and cookies for several families, cold bottled water, pistachio nuts, dates and other sweets. They also gave us bumper stickers and a map of the country. This rally was clearly a very big deal in Iran.

Zahedan was eighty-nine kilometers away, but the road was so awesomely beautiful we practically wept. For the first time in what seemed like weeks we had white lines, two lanes each direction, real railings on the edges, and actual shoulders; narrow in places, but graveled and graded like real shoulders should be. Prince Borghese and crew had the same ecstatic reaction to their first stretch of properly-paved road when they left Nijni-Novgorod on the Moskowskaja or Moscow road. They expected the city's pavement to turn into the same "wretched path" they had traveled across Siberia, but instead, Barzini wrote, "the straight solid road went stretching on evenly before us, and it never left us again. We had come to *the road, the real road! . . .* It seemed to us to mark the beginning of civilisation."

Strangely, here in anti-Western Iran, the road signs were in both Farsi and English; that would make navigating much easier. Our beautiful new highway held practically no traffic, only an occasional white Peykan or oil tanker. If the tanker was slow, it was a simple matter to pass it; no more teeth-grinding chicken-game like we'd been playing in Pakistan.

It felt more like flying than driving. The gorgeous multi-colored mountains with tortured folds lay on one side, a horizonless expanse of wavering, iridescent desert on the other, with mirages in the distance: floating, glowing spots that shimmered like oil on water. Distant sandstorms turned the sky a dark beige-gray, and whirlwinds danced in the near distance. Even in the false darkness of the blowing sand, the landscape seemed beautiful for its simple starkness.

Occasionally, in the middle of nowhere, we'd see a man walking a long distance from the road. Where could he be going? It reminded me of those lone prowlers in Pakistan, but these men were even farther away from the road, far from anything visible. Where could they possibly come from? Was that a machine gun in his arm, or just a shepherd's crook? Did Iranians hide villages as thoroughly as Tibetans, tucking rock-colored dwellings deep into the distant hills? They were too far away to be threatening, almost too far away to be real; the men seemed insubstantial, like projections on a distant screen in some huge desert amphitheater.

It was extraordinary desolation, made pleasing by the sheer smoothness of the asphalt. The miles spun away. Today would be longer by one hundred kilometers than the day before, the longest day of the rally yet. The only dissonant note was the hysterical percussion of our failing windshield tape. The heat over the last few days had robbed the glue of its stickiness. The edges were disintegrating into shreds, and anywhere that air could get in and lift it up it had, and it sang in seventeen-part syncopated disharmony. We flew with the wind whipping our tape, our scarves fluttering against our hair—remarkably cool in our coverings, it turned out. The Peykans, our brethren, multiplied, now in orange and white and occasionally avocado (oh! the variety!) and then the buildings and the murals began: ardent portraits of gun-toting freedom fighters, the stern Rasputinesque gaze of Khomeini and the mellower face of Rafsanjani. We reached downtown Zahedan around four-thirty in the afternoon.

Lonely Planet's *West Asia* sums up this city, where we would spend our sixth rest day, in one line: "Zahedan is not inspiring in any way." *Dangerous Places* warns only that southeast Iran, where Zahedan perspires in the intense heat, is the "major weapons and drug smuggling route from Pakistan and Afghanistan. Drug and arms smuggling convoys may include columns with tanks, armored personnel carriers and heavily armed soldiers. 'Miami Vice' doesn't have a prayer against these guys."

But something strange and wonderful had happened the moment we crossed the border. For the first time on the rally, our Hillman was the center of attention. No one had ever given it a second glance before. I have one great photo that captures the typical reaction to our passing: in India, two fellows on an ox cart swivel their bodies completely away from us, so they can watch the gorgeous 1927 Mercedes 630K. By the time our Hillman passed, they were already busy looking at the Rolls Royce behind us. Now, in Iran, the locals stared, taken aback; it only took them a moment to realize that under our black vinyl top, fancy Hillman trim, and Peking-Paris stickers, there was really a Peykan just like theirs! It was as if their little sister had gone off to Paris and come back decked out in the finest *haute couture*. But of course this analogy fails miserably in Zahedan, where the women are not only covered but shrouded head-to-toe in black.

We now expected our gender to be a big issue. Amongst the other ralliers it was inconsequential, beyond the habit of comparing us to the Gulls. During the first couple of weeks of the rally, we'd figured out pretty much who rooted for Francesca and Jennifer, and who rooted for us, in the "battle" for the Women's Cup. Those on our side grumbled about the Gulls getting an unfair slice of the mechanics' valuable time with their troublesome car. That argument pretty much ended with our accident. More suspension problems and the slow going had saddled the Gulls with an extra three hours and forty-eight minutes on the Quetta day. Their penalties now totaled nine hours, fifty-eight minutes. Now, even though we'd lost time ourselves, we were still four hours and four minutes ahead of them.

As to gender, there'd been no discussion of it among the competitors since the pushing-male-crowd problem in India. The Pakistanis, fundamentalist though they may be, were remarkably impassive. No doubt their experience with Benazir Bhutto had prepared them.

But here in anti-American, anti-woman fundamentalist Iran, with our car suddenly the center of attention, we were steeled for some negative reaction—vocal or physical disapproval (spitting? throwing things? I couldn't believe anyone would seriously consider kidnapping, despite my father's paranoid e-mails). Perhaps it would just be a quiet sort of shunning. What we got, instead, was the red carpet.

We were treated as guests of honor, honorary members of the National Peykan Team, and our sex was never mentioned. We were offered first dibs at the repair facilities, free service, and access to all the Peykan parts we desired. The deal about free service applied to everyone, thanks to the Automobile Federation, as did free gas for the full seven days of our Iran crossing. (In fact, it only amounted to about twelve cents a gallon.)

Our special-guest treatment ended once we separated from our car, however. Then we were just more difficult Western women, needing to be corralled by the black-clad female volunteers from the travel company called Pasargad Tours. Under their full-length chadors, these women were smart, no-nonsense, and oddly powerful. The volunteer men from the Automobile Federation almost cowered in their presence, especially in the presence of one older woman, who seemed to be in charge.

These women informed Linda and me, in the expansive, air-conditioned lobby of the Tourist Hotel, that we were once again designated to go to the secondary hotel. So we shuffled onto a bus for the ride to the Hotel Amin. We were greeted outside this humble inn by a handsome young soldier, in uniform with his machine gun at the ready. Inside, the lobby contained two small couches and fifteen full ashtrays.

Linda and I crowded onto the nicotine-stained couches beside Monica and George Tinzl, our Italo-Austrian compatriots from the Nainatal hotel, plus an assortment of Germans and Australians, most of whom immediately lit cigarettes in aggressive defense against the room's rank tobacco smell. At the smoky table, there was some discussion of our role as "second-stringers;" we were beginning to feel like exiles, always banished from the rally headquarters hotel. The rooms were first-come-first-served based on the date the fees were paid. Those of us in the "late-paying" group seemed to think a fairer method would've been to rotate everyone. So far, it had only been a minor inconvenience, as it was a bit harder to stay informed of rally news, with the official rally board always at the HQ hotel.

Our room at the Amin had stark, water-stained gray walls, high-ceilings, and one tiny window that opened onto an airshaft. We had our own plumbing: a hole in the floor. A clean hole, at least. Except for that bathroom, it reminded me of some of the funkier digs I'd settled for on my earliest budget trips to Italy.

Meals were served in a pleasant basement dining room. Dinner was good: a very salty barley soup, followed by saffron rice with dried pomegranate seeds and chelo kebab (skewered chicken or lamb). Breakfast consisted of nice sweet melon, thick creamy yogurt, big piles of buttery flat bread, and good coffee.

CHAPTER

⟋⟍30⟋⟍

*The local inhabitants, in order to defend themselves, swathe their heads in long black
veils which cover their chests and their shoulders. ... It gives the sinister impression of
some sign of mourning worn by a whole people.*

ZAHEDAN

[WEDNESDAY, OCTOBER 1]

As soon as we'd eaten breakfast, Linda and I went back to the Tourist hotel,
both of us decked out in our finest Nepali/Pakistani outfits. Linda went
off to the Peugeot dealership with the Hillman, and spent this rest day
presiding over our long list of repairs. I settled into one of the lobby's 1970s-era
armchairs with my notebook. Eventually, almost every other co-driver joined me;
the lobby chairs filled with men and women reading books, old magazines, or the
month-old copy of the *International Herald* that was making the rounds. Rich
Newman sat reading *Sarum,* Edward Rutherford's bestseller about ancient
England. I wondered if he were having an out-of-body experience, reading about
that faraway green isle in this distant, arid place.

This forced immobility was relaxing, at first, despite the back-killing angle of
the uncomfortable chairs. Before long, though, our collective boredom grew audible. Some talked about going out for a walk, and then I heard a woman say "they
won't let us out. They say the town is too dangerous." One of the British women
said "It's as if we're all under house arrest!"

Luigi Barzini had a similar feeling in Verkhne-Udinsk, the Russian army's military center for the Trans-Baikalia region. "Patrols passed along the streets shoul-
dering their rifles, and there was a clanking of swords and spurs over the wooden
pavements. Numerous sentries came on duty at the doors of banks and public
buildings. Even the telegraph-office was occupied by the military. . . . I felt as if I
was writing my telegrams in the ante-room of a prison."

Ninety years later, I felt as if I were wearing the prison. *Only in Iran for eighteen
hours, and I already resent the clothing restrictions,* I wrote in my journal. It wasn't so
much that it was uncomfortable, it was just irritating. The stupid scarf kept slip-
ping off my head, and I kept having to yank it back up. I looked up then at some

movement—several men rose, and walked over to consult two of the black-shrouded women volunteers. The youngest one scurried into a back office of the hotel, looking worried.

An official-looking man emerged then, walked over to where we all stood or sat waiting, and said, "You are all free to go where you like."

Within minutes, all the men disappeared. We women sat still, looking at each other. One of the Pasargad Tour women, the older, authoritative one, rushed over. "We are organizing a tour for you," she said in her excellent English, "to a hand-icraft shop and a museum. This town is not safe—we do not think it is a good idea for you ladies to go about on your own. We will have a bus ready to take you all on this tour in an hour."

Unsafe? I wondered. Were these women concerned that we might be kid-napped or mistaken for drug smugglers? I doubted it. More likely they feared that one of us—intentionally for political purposes or unintentionally out of touristic stupidity—would violate Islamic laws requiring us to stay completely covered.

We had all devised cover-ups, though not all in Asian style. Some just wore pants, long sleeves and headscarves (which was what I'd intended to do, if that helpful Nepali hadn't produced my special-extra-long outfit). Others made do with Western women's wear. The British woman from "Maurice" the Morris, for example, had given up her habitually skintight, revealing aerobic-exercise togs, and wore instead what looked like an evening gown (still a bit clingy, I thought). She had a large shawl covering her hair, but where the shawl came down and crossed below her chin, it was fairly loose; some neck and collarbone skin was visible. I heard later that she'd boldly left our de facto harem at the Tourist Hotel, and walked nonchalantly down the streets of Zahedan alone, in search of a bank to change British pounds into Iranian rials. Apparently, the good Muslims in the bank rushed her right back to the hotel, and severely impressed the Pasargad Tour women with the importance of keeping these Western women reined-in.

When I got a chance, I asked our Pasargad ladies about the restrictions. "The chador brings us closer to God," one said loudly. Later, another woman, speaking in a just audible whisper, told me, "This area is much more traditional than the North. In Tehran, where we are from, we wear loose overcoats, and a scarf of almost any color. We do not have to wear the chador." It became clear that these women looked down their sophisticated, urbane noses on this old-fashioned backwater of Zahedan. They honestly considered it a dangerous place; they didn't seem to want to leave the hotel themselves.

But they did, leading our small group of nine women onto a hot tour bus (no air conditioning; earlier, I'd heard someone say the temperature was expected to reach 120 degrees F). Jolijn Rietbergen from Holland (she and her husband Bart were in Kermit, the bright green 1965 Volvo #75) was almost as tall as me and needed something long and loose. Pat Dalrymple from the big Caddy, Sheila Morris, the friendly Welsh woman in Mr. Blobby, Monica Tinzl, Angela Riley and her mother, Helen McGugan, and Paula Broderick joined me and a new

Canadian woman named Jasmine Lovric. "New" because she'd only joined the rally at Kathmandu, replacing Canadian John O'Neill's Cypriot co-driver (he'd been unable to get a visa for Greece).

Our first stop, the handicraft shop, was a dud. There were some interesting blown glass vases, primitively painted leather, and hand-embroidered pillow slips and table cloths—all nice enough, but astonishingly normal-looking. The few items that incorporated traditional Persian patterns were still quite familiar; the design world has so thoroughly mished and mashed Asian/Middle Eastern/European influences that those napkins, once on my table at home, would look like I bought them at Target, not in Zahedan. I tried to look at everything with the kids in mind (for this long a trip, they were expecting killer presents), but there was nothing even remotely appropriate.

We all agreed when we got back on the bus that we wanted to skip the museum and go straight to the bazaar. Our two hostesses directed the bus driver in Farsi, once again using that no-nonsense, powerful voice reserved for ordering men around.

Zahedan's bazaar is no architectural wonder—plain brick from the outside, a simple enclosed mall on the inside—but we were able to solve some practical concerns: with seven more days of total cover-up required, none of us had adequate wardrobes. I think it was Jolijn's idea to try the men's *salwar kameez*: big cotton shirts with matching huge-waisted (but short) drawstring pants. We all ended up buying at least one set. Our last stop was at a shawl vendor's. The vendor was one of those amazingly wrinkled old men, wizened and white-haired, thoroughly middle-eastern. I tried to take a picture of him, but a handful of pre-teen boys made it impossible; they were trying to sell me something, and wanted me to take their pictures instead. What handsome people the Iranians are—even these little punks! They were as obnoxious as pre-teens are everywhere, but clean and healthy looking, and in general, the people, especially the children, are incredibly beautiful. They're blessed with gorgeous dark eyes, clear creamy mocha-colored skin, glowing smiles, and thick lustrous hair.

So much more the shame, I thought, that all those beautiful women have to spend their lives covered up.

We rode in our sweltering bus back to the Tourist. Even our guides complained about the heat: "This is much hotter than normal for this time of the year," one said, fanning her shrouded face. Once back, I had to wait for a second bus, since we second-class citizens weren't allowed to eat at the HQ hotel. After another plate of chelo kebabs in the Amin's dining room, I waited for yet another bus back to the Tourist; from there I wanted to go to the garage to help Linda. The Amin's lobby was filled with a half dozen chain-smoking businessmen, so I stood outside, examining the billboard-size mural across the street. The lovable Khomeini exhorted something in Farsi script, while a young machine-gun-toting soldier aimed at an invisible enemy. Our handsome young guard, who kept eyeing me as I stood there, looked alot like the soldier in the painting—all of seventeen, maybe. He was way too well armed for a hotel doorman. He spoke no English, and I no Farsi, so we just amiably pretended to ignore each other. When the bus finally arrived, the driver blocked my effort to get on, locked up the bus and went off to eat his lunch.

I was pissed. I went back into the hotel and spoke to the concierge about walking. "How far is it to the Tourist?"

"Oh no, you must not walk. You must wait for the bus." He ran away, shutting himself into a back office. I fumed quietly for a few moments, then spotted the phone. Maybe I could just give the Tourist Hotel a call, find out the phone number for the Peugeot dealer, and call Linda from here.

The phone was dead; I followed the cord and saw that it was unplugged. Now I was really pissed, and suffocating, standing amid those smokers. As I was getting ready to knock on the concierge's closed door, a young man wearing the Iranian Automobile Federation Peking-Paris T-shirt walked in.

"Can you get me a taxi?" I asked him.

Before long, a white Peykan pulled up in front of the Hotel Amin. I had the right amount of rials (I'd changed some rupees at the Tourist's front desk) and the address of the Tourist Hotel written in Farsi. I was there in five minutes, and though it would have been an easy walk, I was glad I didn't do it. I would have been a sweaty mess under my layers of cotton swathing; I can't even imagine how many times I would have had to readjust my headscarf.

I asked at the Tourist's front desk if someone could take me to the garage, and was met with a confused stare. People were coming *back* from the garages now, not going to them. I asked one of the Brits who'd just gotten back if he had seen Linda, and he asked, "Are you getting a whole new transmission? Your Hillman's spread out all over the place." Our list had included fixing our chattering clutch (that had been getting worse ever since Linda smoked it back in the Tibetan mud; in Kathmandu Paul had said it could wait until Iran), the new windshield, headlights, and a brake inspection to make sure that the gravel that had lodged in our wheel back in Nepal hadn't done any serious damage.

Fifty of the eighty rally cars (we'd come up again from seventy-five as the missing returned and the damaged were repaired) had gone off to one repair shop or another. Team Retro went to the Peykan factory. After repairing the suspension on John's car, Vic and Andy helped the American Bentley boys, Bill and Ned, with some fender repairs. Dick Taylor and the Arizona boys were with Linda at the Peugeot dealer, fixing a leaky fuel tank and replacing the windows shattered by that Pakistani truck. Carl and Don spent the day fixing their brakes.

I still wanted to find Linda and give her a chance to trade places with me. No one at the hotel had the phone number for the Peugeot dealer. Then Philip Young walked in and told me he'd just left her. "Can you call the garage for me?" I asked him, and within minutes I was handed the receiver.

"Linda? How's it going?"

"What? Who's this?"

"It's Genny. Do you want me to come out there?"

"What? Why? Is something wrong?"

"I thought you might like a break. Should I—"

"What? I can't hear you."

"Did you ever get any lunch? Do you want me to bring you something?"

"I'm okay. They brought me something. It's just really hot. See you later."

Philip was still nearby, so I asked him what was up. The tranny was out in order to get to the clutch (we weren't getting a whole new transmission). New brake pads and a new master cylinder had been installed, and a new windshield had been obtained but not yet installed. Linda would have to pay for the parts, but all the labor was free, thanks to the Iranian Automobile Federation. Philip said they'd also discovered that our rear axle had come loose and was wearing out the rear tire sidewalls. That and our intermittent ignition switch problem would have to wait until Esfahan.

I read, wrote and relaxed at the Tourist until Linda got back after five, then we bused to the Amin for dinner. The hotel may have been second-string, but the Amin did have fine food, and Zam Zam and Pipi to drink—cola and orange soda (Khomeini had kicked out the Great Satan corporations Coca-Cola and Pepsi). We retired to our room, and I spent until far into the night sewing a six-inch strip that I cut from the scarf of my "SHE" dress onto the bottom of its matching pants. Linda raised an eyebrow at my domestic preoccupation, and I did feel a little odd, sitting in our stinky room in Zahedan hand-sewing pants for myself, so my ankles wouldn't show.

Instead, I should have spent the time double-checking the math on our penalties back to Kathmandu. I only realized that much later, when it was too late.

We wished we could at least see a tree: a tree is sometimes a companion, a giant friend,
offering hospitality and refreshment in the shelter of his open arms.

ZAHEDAN TO KERMAN
[THURSDAY, OCTOBER 2]

The party scene that had welcomed us at the border was replayed at the morning's start line in Zahedan. Video crews, journalists, volunteers and locals crowded our exit. As we collected our first stamp, one of the volunteers handed us two brown paper bags marked "Iran Air." Inside were two airplane lunches: a sandwich, honey-drenched pastry, nuts or dates, and a juice bag.

Iran has less than half the population of neighboring Pakistan (59 million to 126 million), and almost half of the cars in the country are registered in Tehran. These facts became immediately obvious as we set off from Zahedan; we had practically no traffic. We drove directly northwest toward the first of Iran's two major deserts, the Dasht-e-Lut or Sand Desert. The road was still beautifully-paved, our only challenge the blowing sands. At one point, it was blowing so thickly we could barely tell the air from the ground. In the middle of this, a long line of buildings, houses or perhaps a military fort, appeared alongside the road. People were out walking, angled against the wind, their long striped robes blowing. It was completely surreal. How could anyone stand or walk in that air? How could they live in these stark conditions? The ground and the sky never stood still; it was impossible to tell one from the other; a universe of sand.

We reached our midday checkpoint, a place called Desert Cafe, a full hour early. We weren't alone. Rally cars filled the parking lot, a graveled expanse of nothingness in the middle of miles and miles of more nothingness. Desert fans always like to argue that deserts are far from nothingness, but since we'd left that last encampment, this one really seemed devoid of any life forms whatsoever—just sand, dirt, rock and a view of jagged mountains in the overheated distance.

There was one building here, though: a large square thing, with painted-out windows. If this was the "Cafe," it had been closed a long time. It did feature a

wide, arched veranda, the only source of shade, so we gathered there and sat on the cement, leaning against the building or one of its columns, waiting for our time to roll around so we could get our stamps.

Now, obviously, the required average speeds were much lower than conditions allowed. This first stretch required keeping an average of only 45 mph (75 kph) and we actually averaged closer to 75 mph (120 kph). We weren't breaking the local speed laws, as far as we could tell. The few local cars we met flew along just as fast or faster, and the ubiquitous oil tanker trucks cruised at about 60 mph. Every one of the local cars we met flashed their headlights in greeting. One heavily loaded Peykan—two women and two kids in back, two men in front—played a little game with us. It arrived suddenly on our bumper, tailgated tightly for awhile, then sped up and passed us—everyone in the car waving—then drove away at high speed.

So we relaxed at the "Desert Cafe" in the Dasht-e-Lut, eating raw pistachios offered by Robin and Ben, Ray Carr's video crew—they'd stopped at an orchard and picked their own—and drinking fruit juice provided by another Federation volunteer (excellent cherry juice, not ruined by excess added sugar as it usually is in the US). We caught up on rally gossip—who was out, who was in. We found out that Maurice the Morris had "packed up with a holed piston." The drivers had spent their time in Zahedan (after the woman's bank errand was cut short) trying to order in a shipment of pistons from England, only to discover that no fast freight service would deliver to Iran because of trade sanctions. So they ordered the pistons shipped to Istanbul, and were still back in Zahedan now, having someone weld up the hole.

As we sat, Lisa Klokgeiters-Lankes' Bumblebee MG appeared, loaded on the back of an Iranian truck; its motor had blown, too. The big black Buick, unseen since Pakistan, reportedly had lost its rear main seal completely. Another lower end was out on one of the Railtons. There were two of these classy 1930s British cars in the event, one driven by a Dutch Baron, the other by a young British couple. It was the British one that was hurting. Two of the three James-Bondesque Aston Martins (two1964 DB5s and one '66 DB6) had suffered damage: one had snapped a halfshaft (drive axle) back in China, and the other, one of the DB5s, was now a few days behind with some kind of major steering problem.

The Gulls had put a lot of work into their still-troublesome Volvo; this time it had been a broken rear suspension spring. The other Volvos seemed to be holding up well; there were five altogether, three driven by British and two by Dutch teams. The Italians in the Lancia had gone missing, apparently with gearbox failure, but the two other Italian crews, a humble green 1948 Fiat 1100 driven by a jovial Sicilian named Francesco Ciriminna, and the bright-yellow hopped-up Citroën 2CV, were doing fine.

Some problems were interpersonal rather than mechanical. Rich Newman had been complaining quietly to Linda and me about his co-driver Burt Richmond ever since Lanzhou, and it had now gotten to the point where Rich refused to speak to Burt at all. At one point he told me, "Only one of us will make it to Istanbul."

I laughed. "Hey, be careful what you say. Don't forget I write murder mysteries!"

"Ah," he said, "I see you understand perfectly."

Don Jones mentioned a pair of British men with a thirty-year friendship that was now on the rocks after the stresses of driving together for four weeks. The potential for a *Murder on the Peking to Paris* was all too clear to my overactive imagination. There were more potential murderers and victims here than in all of Cabot Cove.

We discovered the reason for the Cortina's fall from first place: broken rear shock absorbers. Father and son Catt had fixed them in Zahedan. The lead was now held by Phil Surtees and John Bayliss, two experienced British rally drivers, in the #97 Willys Jeep. The two men at first gave us the cold shoulder, rarely bothering to speak to Linda or me. It didn't seem personal; more the general disdain of "pros" toward amateurs like us.

Ted and Vic, in the #23 Ford, were now second overall, and John and Andy, in #24, were fifth. All three Iranian Peykans were still in the top ten; local heroes made good, so far. In sixth place was the Holden (an Australian GM) driven by my down-under buddies Gerry Crown and John Bryson. Gerry told me they'd lost twelve minutes on the Fort Munro mountain climb and nineteen minutes on the section coming into Quetta, arriving at the hotel before the Feits had their fatal accident. Their worst day had been the same day as our accident back in Tibet; their fan had quit, so the car kept overheating, and on one of the water crossings Gerry'd hung the car up on a rock. Luckily, that cooled the engine off long enough to get them up the day's long grade. They'd fixed the fan since then, of course, and the car was now running trouble-free through the hot desert.

And it was incredibly hot. We'd been warned to carry at least four liters of water each; we had a case of plastic liter bottles in the back, and we each kept one beside us in front. In the morning my bottle was cool to the touch. By Desert Cafe, the plastic was so hot, I had to use my scarf to unscrew the lid. I fished some tea bags out of our food bin. "Constant Comment or Liptons?" I asked Linda. I shoved two tea bags in each bottle, and set them back down on the floor of the car. Within ten minutes, we both had strong boiling-hot tea; it tasted better than plastic-flavored hot water.

Later that day, Don told me that the thermometer inside the '54 Packard had hit 140 degrees F that afternoon. It was probably about the same in our Hillman; the heat generated by the engine radiated up from the gearshifter boot, between the two bucket seats. Reaching for the gearshifter felt like putting your hand into a furnace. We occasionally doused our scarves and our feet with the non-tea water; once I used a water bottle that had been sitting in the sun (my tea-water bottle, I shoved under my seat), and literally burned the top of my feet when I doused them. The evaporation that followed—all too quickly—felt wonderful, though. I refused to wear socks, even though we'd been warned that even our feet should be covered. Linda declared that the socks stayed wet longer, helping to keep her driving feet cool.

The original Peking-Paris raiders dealt with this kind of heat in the Gobi, and in the uncovered Itala, their punishment was much more severe. "Our skin was parched as with fever," Barzini wrote, "and the sun beat so hotly on our hands and faces that it was as if there was centred upon us the most powerful light of an immeasurable lens. We had been conscious of the same feeling the day before; indeed it was upon that road that there first came to our minds the simile of a lens … but we had not then guessed that in the real desert the power of the lens would increase by so many degrees. We now understood why caravans never travelled during the day. But as for ourselves, by this time we neither would nor could stop. The only relief we could get we got by speed."

About 160 kilometers from Desert Cafe, we began to rise out of the Dasht-e-Lut into the Kuhha-ye Kuhpaye Mountains that form the desert's western border. The landscape was still bleak, until we suddenly arrived in a lovely oasis town named Bam. There were date palms and citrus trees and, directly across the street from the TC, a huge, ancient mud-and-wattle fortress—Arg-e-Bam, a restored seventeenth-century walled city (though the settlement reportedly dates back to the twelfth century). We were so taken with the sight we forgot about our scarves. One of the Iranian Federation volunteers rushed up to us, running alongside our slowly-moving car, crying out, "Please! Cover your hair!"

We obliged him, and then found a place to park. We had more than forty-five minutes before we'd have to check in, so I grabbed the time-card book (so I wouldn't have to run back to the car) and we set off on foot to explore this amazing place.

Just inside the main entrance to the ancient walled city, we ran into the three Jeepsters, looking happy and carefree in their golf hats and polo shirts. Like us, they'd gotten high on the smooth asphalt. "Our jeep purred along comfortably at fifty-five mph," Dick reported, "the fastest speed we've seen on the entire trip." With the Jeepsters, we walked the entire length of the surprisingly cool castle, some four to five hundred yards.

Except for the fact that we kept checking our watches to make sure our time wasn't up, we felt remarkably like normal tourists. After we'd come upon a concession stall and bought small cups of chocolate ice cream, I wandered off on my own a bit, and in the quiet coolness of those restored homes, shops and mosques, I had a strange feeling of an ancient human presence, like I was neither alone nor grounded in my own time. This ruined city was so recognizable and complete, the walls seemed to breathe with its inhabitants' memory, as if they'd been here just yesterday. It's the same kind of feeling I think most people have visiting the ruins of Pompeii.

On the way back to the car, I came upon Michael Kunz and almost mistook him for a soldier: he was wearing a *salwar kameez* in military green. The Jeep guys had looked—and would always look—thoroughly American, but some of the other male ralliers, perhaps in sympathy for their female comrades, had adopted aspects of the local dress. Phil Surtees of the leading Jeep, for example, had tied a white turban round his head, and he looked very old-world colonial.

About 160 kilometers after Bam (over 500 kilometers or 300 miles into the day), Linda offered me the wheel, and I accepted. Unlike some of the other crews, our testiness had abated. We drove companionably now for hours at a time, often in total silence now that our windshield was fixed and we had no more flapping duct tape. Even our raucous engine seemed quiet. Some of my small talk—it still popped out now and then of its own accord—was accepted and responded to in a friendly fashion.

In Kerman, we were once again sent to the secondary hotel, the Akhavan. Though our room was fine, there were grumbles from others about the plumbing. One of the Federation volunteers patiently explained that Islamic Law requires that a certain percentage of hotel rooms must keep the old fashioned hole-in-the-floor toilets, since it would be discrimination against simple people to require them to use those complicated newfangled things.

The Akhavan did have room for us to park right in front, which was a nice change from busing back and forth. Since we'd arrived before four o'clock, we had time to fettle the cars, which in our Hillman's case just meant a little cleanup. Someone had already provided a water hose, and by the time Linda and I pulled in between the Binnie Bentley and Phil Bowen and Rosie Thomas' Volvo, Phil and Bill were both busily washing their cars.

Phil Bowen was an attractive young Brit, not gorgeous like Dimples but handsome in a blond, rugged way. He was a motorcyclist and trekker who led tours through Nepal for a living. That was how he had come to be on the Peking to Paris; he'd heard about it from Mick O'Malley and had written to Rosie Thomas, the British writer whom he'd met the year before when he led her on a mountain trek. Would Rosie like to do the Peking to Paris? She would, and she paid for Phil to go as her co-driver/mechanic. It ended up being a much bigger job than he originally envisioned—physically and psychologically. But he handled it well; he was a realist and a joker, sometimes with a sarcastic edge. He seemed to have unlimited energy; if he wasn't working on the Volvo, he was jumping about, playing Frisbee or soccer with Dimples and Adam.

Those young British Bentley boys weren't at the Akhavan, but the older, American Bentley boys were. Bill Binnie was a joker, too. He and Phil got into a water fight, and though Binnie escaped into the hotel, Phil soon discovered that Bill's room was the first big window, right above the parking lot. Phil aimed the hose and Linda and I ducked as he squirted water everywhere.

Bill Binnie's sense of humor also had a bite to it. He'd had his first clash with Islamic culture in Zahedan, when he'd asked the hotel man for a room with a bathroom.

"That's not an unreasonable request, is it?" he'd asked.

The Iranian answered that it was indeed, and then scolded Bill for wearing short pants. "It is very disrespectful and is not allowed and you must change immediately!"

Bill answered "Sure! I'll change immediately. I'll take off all my clothes right here in the lobby and walk buck naked to the bathroom! I mean if I'm going to have to walk down the corridor to go to the bathroom . . ." Bill made motions as if he really meant to take his clothes off right there, and within minutes the Iranian miraculously found him a room with plumbing. Bill kept his clothes on.

We laughed at his telling, even though we all knew this was a dangerous subject to joke about. Luckily, there hadn't been any Mullahs, or secret police, hanging about.

Linda then took our nice clean Hillman out for gas. What should have been a quick errand turned into a strange interlude. First, it took her a great deal of effort to get out of the hotel; the concierge/guards wouldn't open the gates. Finally, after persuasion from John Matheson of the Queen's Rolls, who also needed gas, a guard let them both out. The two found their way through Kerman's confusing streets to a gas station, but were startled by the huge line of Iranians patiently waiting to fill up. "It was like the '74 gas crisis in the States," Linda said, "but here there's plenty of gas, and it costs practically nothing. Why do all these people have to wait?" We never found out.

Once I'd cleaned up, I decided that I wasn't going to spend the evening under house arrest in the lobby. Directly after a dinner almost identical to the previous night's fare—pomegranate rice and chelo kebab—I joined Michael Kunz and Richard Curtis for a trip to the bazaar. Richard was co-driver of Humpty Dumpty, the 1932 Ford Model B owned by Prince Idris Shah of Malaysia. Richard, though he looked English and spoke with a very proper British accent, had been raised in Kuala Lumpur and had grown up with the Prince (Idris for short). He'd been to Kerman years before, prior to the '79 Islamic Revolution, and was curious to see how it had changed.

Kerman is known for its pistachios, dates, cumin, and of course, carpets. The bazaar was full of them, but I was amazed at the many stalls full of luxury fabrics, like embroidered velvet, and elaborate, sequined cocktail dresses. It is part of the fascinating contradiction of Iran that women wear these extravagant dresses and then hide them under their *Hejab* (modest dress) or *chador* (veil).

The veil in Iran is different from the *Purdah* of other Islamic countries. It has its own history that reveals a great deal about the roles of both women and men in Iranian politics and culture. Its roots go all the way back to pre-Islamic times, and no doubt arose for practical reasons: protection from the harsh climate. Islam's great holy book, the Koran *(Qor'an)*, requires modest covering, but only in general terms, allowing great disparities in the definition of what is "acceptable" covering. Still, there is no argument about the function of the veil. Iranian author Farzaneh Milani explains in her excellent book *Veils and Words: The Emerging Voices of Iranian Women Writers,* that the veil "is a deliberate, obsessive attempt to keep that which symbolizes the private realm—that is, woman and anything associated with her—hidden. In fact, the veil can readily be compared to a portable wall, a strategic mobile segregation."

The first Iranian woman recorded to have unveiled herself as part of a public protest was the poet Tahereh Qorratol'Ayn. Her action, at an anti-Islam rally in

1848 (a revolutionary year the world over), was eventually punished by death. Half a century later, while Prince Borghese barreled across Siberia, Iranian women, like Suffragettes in England and America, rallied together to fight "traditionalism on political, social, and literary levels." A "constitutional revolution" had begun in 1905, and while women were actively involved, only a few of their goals were realized when the revolution was won: the 1907 constitution codified compulsory education for girls, but left out the franchise (women couldn't vote in Iran until 1963), and left the veil compulsory. When Reza Shah Pahlavi took power in 1921, he latched on to veiling as a symbol of the "obscurantism" and "black reactionary nature" of the mosque. In 1936, he ordered the mass unveiling of all Iranian women. A totalitarian ruler, he brooked no opposition: no veiled woman was allowed on the streets of Tehran or any provincial city.

This attempt to legislate women's emancipation was, in many ways, too much, too soon; it ignored the fact that the veil disguised more than women's bodies. It protected deeply entrenched traditions and divisions in Iranian society. When Reza Shah abdicated in 1941, passing power to his son Mohammed Reza Shah, the ban was rescinded. Still, the ban had propelled forces that would not easily be stopped: women, whether voluntarily or forcibly unveiled, were now admitted to Tehran University; literacy among women improved dramatically; they entered governmental and professional careers that had always been the exclusive domain of men. The new generation of women (equivalent to our Baby Boomers) grew up believing the veil, whether worn or not, would not inhibit their ambitions or desires.

In the 1970s, though, the tide began to turn back. As Mohammed Reza Shah's government grew more corrupt and repressive, many educated women adopted the veil voluntarily, as a sign of protest against predatory capitalism and Western cultural imperialism. Though these women contributed to the fall of the Shah, they were not ready to go back to compulsory veiling. When, only a month after taking power in February 1979, the Ayatollah Khomeini proclaimed that all working women should wear *Hejab,* a massive wave of demonstrations prevented legislation. The Prime Minister "emphatically assured women that there would be no compulsory veiling and that . . . the ayatollah believed in guiding rather than forcing women." The Prime Minister was proved wrong a year later, when the veil became compulsory for government and public offices. Reaction to this pronouncement was disorganized and dispersed; the regime took that as a sign of encouragement. Three years later, in April 1983, veiling was made compulsory for all women, including non-Muslims, foreigners and tourists.

Towering over both of them beneath my tourist veil, I walked with Michael and Richard through the Kerman bazaar. No quantity of fabric could disguise my foreignness, and I found it oddly contradictory that the veil broadcast my femininity (with my height, thin build and androgynous features, I can easily pass for a man). Two young Iranian men approached us and asked us in very good English where we were from. They identified themselves as university students and directed us to the Ganj-Ali-Khan part of the bazaar. The hamam (bathhouse) there is now a museum, full of mosaic and stuccowork from the early nineteenth century. The hamam had just closed, but we were able to slip into the similarly appointed tea house next door. Intricate turquoise mosaics and delicate paintings covered the walls and trimmed the lovely vaulted ceiling, and worn but wonderful carpets were spread over the split-level floor. A group of Australian and English tourists were just finishing up their tea (it was closing time, so we didn't attempt to order any) and we spoke with them about how warm our reception had been by the Iranians, even as Americans.

Don Jones described it well: The local people "seem to have the attitude that the only problem between Iran and the United States involves the capital cities and not the people of the two countries. Americans are looked on with great favor as being happy carefree people who are welcomed as visitors here in Iran." Our students once again stressed how much they and all their friends liked Americans, and wished us good luck on our journey before they departed.

Richard joked and talked nonstop as we walked from the bazaar, smiling and waving at everyone, Iranian and tourist alike. Once we'd flagged a taxi (yet another Peykan) to take us back to the hotel, he spun an elaborate tale for the taxi driver and his wife—she sat crammed into the corner of the backseat beside me, with Michael on my other side and Richard up front. "She's our wife," Richard told them, "We're her husbands. She has many other husbands. We were married in China.. .." He went on in this fashion, while Michael laughed and I tried to pull my hand back from the woman, who had taken a liking to my wedding ring, a simple gold band with no stones. "You," she would say, pointing at me, then at my ring; then, "Me?" Up front, the driver seemed to be buying Richard's elaborate tale of my reverse harem, while I showed this young woman beside me my pictures of Chris and the kids. It didn't distract her from the ring at all, but it became inordinately important for me to make her understand I was married to the man in the picture, not the crazy man ranting in the front seat, nor the one laughing beside me.

"Mine!" I said, stabbing at the photos. "Mine!"

CHAPTER

∽ 32 ∽

The desert became personified in our mind; that terrible adversary of man, that destroyer of caravans, that feared divinity of death. ... We thought of it as of an undaunted mighty power. The very word desert inspired us with awe.

KERMAN TO ESFAHAN
[FRIDAY, OCTOBER 3]

Once again we skirted desert, first along the western edge of the Dasht-e-Lut, then along the southern edge of the Dasht-e-Kevir, or Salt Desert. As we drove ever closer to the population center of Tehran (twelve million), more towns and traffic cropped up. We passed through the town that had recently been renamed after the last president of the Republic, Ali Akbar Hashemi Rafsanjani. Rafsanjan was crowded with boys and men out looking for us, most cheering and applauding as we passed, a few looking less pleased. The crowds were nowhere near as thick as in Nepal or China, but still created a definite driving hazard, especially when the young boys darted in front of us. It happened so often, we came to expect it; we were ready to slam the brakes or swerve at a moment's notice.

I was driving, and we were back on full rally schedule with checkpoints. It was easy to go fast between towns. At 75 mph the car was tremendously loud, even with the noisy duct tape gone. I spent long hours humming to myself, sometimes singing aloud if I thought the wind noise would cover my wobbly voice.

Most of the traffic was trucks, but passenger cars picked up, too, usually Peykans, or sometimes old French Citroëns or Renaults, or old American models like Chevy Novas. The cars usually held three or four people, and the drivers all wanted to play. The driver would pull up close and ride on our bumper for a while, then pass us with great bravado, often at a dangerous spot, like on a blind curve. Then he'd slow down to 50 mph or less, forcing us to tailgate or fall back.

In my competitive mindset (incited by the rally clock), these local boy-racer wannabes irritated me. Should I pass them and start the game all over? Or slow down and cruise on their bumper? Or pass them and speed way up and try to leave them behind? I thought about the last one often, but never did it, partly

211

because I thought Linda might have screamed, and partly because the car would have protested even more loudly. I wasn't sure our motor would survive 90 mph.

Eventually, I tried to think differently about these local drivers. What they were doing was a kind of communication; they were talking to us with their cars, their message essentially friendly.

About noon we neared the town of Yazd, perched at the intersection of the two great deserts. Marco Polo stopped here on his way to China, along the ancient Silk Road caravan route, in the thirteenth century (in fact, our route from Kerman northwest would follow Marco Polo's all the way to Sivas, Turkey). He called it "a considerable city on the border of Persia, where there is much traffic." Though Islam invaded all Persia in the seventh century, Yazd had long been (and remains) the center of Iran's ancient Zoroastrian religion. The prophet Zoroaster (or Zarathustra) lived sometime between 628 and 551 BC, and his theology influenced Greek, later Jewish, Christian and Muslim thought. In Zoroastrianism, the sole creator and lord of the world, Ahura Mazda, fights an eternal battle with evil spirits, but Ahura Mazda will eventually triumph, and the old world will be destroyed by fire. That central, cleansing role of fire is celebrated in Zoroastrian temples, some of which remain in Yazd. Just outside of town, we passed ruins of a "Tower of Silence," a crumbling adobe structure that dates back to the seventeenth century. Zoroastrians took their dead to these circular, unroofed towers and left them for the vultures.

In one of our many discussions about Islam, one Federation volunteer had claimed to be Zoroastrian, and several others said they weren't Muslim. (One mentioned that his family makes excellent wine.) My guidebook says that Iran is 95 percent Shi'ite Moslem and 4 percent Sunni Moslem, leaving only 1 percent to cover all the Christians, Jews, Bhuddists, Baha'i, agnostics/atheists (if that's legal) and Zoroastrians. Most of the latter fled Persia back in the tenth century, settling near Bombay in India (today these Indian Zoroasters are known as Parsis). Still, one of the women from Pasargad Tours was insistent that we Westerners be careful when we characterize Iran: "We are not an Arab country," she insisted. "We are Persians. Our origins go back to Zoroaster. Just because we are predominantly Muslim does not mean we are Arabs!"

After Yazd we came to Na'in, the town in the exact geographical center of Iran. Here's where we turned westward toward Esfahan, instead of following the highway that led straight northwest to Tehran. For some unfathomable reason, the TC here had been changed to a PC (passage control). After getting our stamp, we decided to change places, so I settled into the navigator's seat for the last 142 kilometers into Esfahan.

Strangely, since we were now headed away from the two big deserts, between Na'in and Esfahan the sky darkened into an odd brownish-gray. It looked like a fire had filled the air with smoke way in the distance, but there was no plume or sign of anything burning. It continued to darken until visibility, at times, was reduced to less than twenty-five feet. It was a sandstorm, and I was worried. I'd never driven in one and I wondered if all that sand might damage the engine.

Linda felt more comfortable, having weathered a few in Australia. The air was dark and thick, as if we were driving through heavy fog at sunset; it had texture, with visible swirls and eddies.

Prince Borghese and his crew drove into a sandstorm on their last day in Mongolia. "A sinister darkness surrounded us," Barzini wrote. "We were now witnessing a phenomenon frequent enough in these provinces—a sand-storm. We were in the centre of a vortex; our car was shaken by it. We all crouched down low on the machine. The sand travelled along the ground like some fluid matter, forming yellow streams, heaping itself here and there and rising in whirlpools."

Ten of our modern ralliers were driving topless automobiles like Borghese's Itala. These intrepid crews had weathered rain in China, snow in Tibet, incessant sun ever since and wind always, and now a sandstorm. My admiration for their endurance grew daily.

We had slowed our speed due to the limited visibility, but we still made Esfahan well within our due time, clocking in before six o'clock. We had climbed some in elevation, and the air now was fresh and cool.

This city, called "the Paris of Persia" and "half the world," is Iran's third largest (population 1.2 million), and has always been the number one tourist draw. The locals were out in force to greet us, and there was a contagious feeling of gaiety in the air. Our hotel for the next two nights—we were to stop a day for rest and repairs—was probably the finest anywhere in Iran, and turned out to be one of the best of our whole journey. The Abbasi Hotel was built in the seventeenth century by the mother of Shah Sultan Hossein, the last Safavid ruler (the Safavid Era lasted from 1501-1736), as a caravanserai. Restored before the Islamic Revolution, the complex includes a large central garden featuring a long rectangular reflecting pool ringed by fountains. Ranged round the garden are 225 luxury rooms, and inside the main building, every square inch of surface is covered with elaborate decoration: "authentic Persian miniatures, paintings and tiles, gilt ornaments, mirror, inlaid and plaster works," as the Pasargad brochure boasted. Particularly stunning is the main dining room, now the Chehelsotun Restaurant. Crystal chandeliers hang down from the gilt-rimmed mezzanine; down below, the walls are painted with figures and fables, fancifully rounded sixteenth-century style Persian warriors and princesses on colorful horses. We were banqueted here on our first night, with an exotic meal of many courses. The main dish seemed like polenta or cornbread, but was actually a saffron-rice confection, with lamb and savory vegetables.

The hotel was important in recent history, too. One of the earliest skirmishes of the Islamic revolution took place here. Richard Clark, of the black Buick, had witnessed it first hand, nineteen years before. In August 1978, Richard had stayed at the Abbasi on holiday. His job was with a bank in Bahrain, and he and his wife and two daughters had come down to see the Pearl of Persia. It was the epitome of luxury then—not showing twenty years' wear, as the post-revolution version does today—and was therefore a sign of all that was wrong with the Shah and the Iranian government, specifically Western decadence, and the concentration of great wealth in the hands of the very few. In the evening that August day, a mob broke down the glass front doors, beat and shot the hotel guards, and then rushed downstairs and set the elaborate dining room on fire. Once the mob had cleared and the fire was put out, all the guests, including the Clark family, were moved to rooms near the front. As they tried to sleep, they were awakened at 2:00 A.M. by the sound of breaking glass. They thought it was another mob attack, but it turned out to be repairmen fixing the glass facade. That was enough for the Clarks, though. They got a taxi and fled to the airport, taking a 5:00 A.M. flight back to Bahrain.

Richard and Ken had finally caught up with the rest of the rally, arriving in Esfahan that morning at five o'clock. Both men had polished British accents and healthy-looking tans, seemed to be in their fifties, and were great storytellers. Richard was a bit smaller and clean-shaven, while Ken was larger and mustachioed. Ken told me the story of their hectic ride into Esfahan.

The Buick had been leaking oil ever since China, so it was no great surprise when the main seal blew, causing the engine to throw a rod on the way into Kerman. They immediately tried to arrange for a truck (the closest repair facilities were in Esfahan), but the first volunteer's vehicle was too narrow for the car to fit. They'd just about given up finding a large-enough truck when, by pure luck, a trucker appeared looking for a load to carry to Esfahan. Getting it on board was no mean feat; the Buick must have weighed three tons. The Iranians wanted to lift it by sliding a log through the windows, and then using a crane to lift the log. Ken and Richard were able to convince them this method wouldn't work—it would have sheered the car's top right off! With a lot of manual labor and long boards for ramps, they finally got the Buick loaded by 1:30 P.M.

They hit the road and drove north without stopping for any meals. By about 11:00 P.M., the truck driver started falling asleep. Ken had to nudge him several times before they all decided it'd be best to stop. The driver pulled into a small house where the carpeted front room was already full of sleeping truckers. They lay down right there, and after a fitful few hours, awoke at 3:00 A.M. As they prepared to get back on the road, the proprietor insisted they have some breakfast. "Come," he said, "have some hot goat stew." He motioned for them to look into the pot.

"There was a complete goat head, eyeballs intact, staring up at me," Ken said. "It was the most ghastly thing I've ever seen in my life!"

They declined the proprietor's offer and got back on the road, finally arriving at the Abbasi two hours later. The Buick was delivered to the Peykan garage, where by the time I spoke with Ken and Richard, they'd already heard that some machine work on the #3 piston would soon get them back on the road. They didn't expect to be able to leave with the rest of us, but hoped to catch up with us by Tabriz.

CHAPTER

❦ 33 ❦

It is a sparkling of gold domes over a white, diaphanous expanse of buildings; an amazing
apparition, like a dream.

ESFAHAN
[SATURDAY, OCTOBER 4]

A notice had been posted on the official rally board that Philip Young, John Vipond, and Martin Clark, the Clerks of the Course, would be available from 9:30 A.M. to 11:00 in a meeting room at the Abbasi for "One–on–One Questions." Hostility toward Philip, and by extension the marshals and clerks of the rally, had grown to a fever pitch since the deaths of the Feits. Most of the ralliers seemed as if they couldn't wait to tell Philip what they thought of him. Along with the feeling that he was too cheap to produce enough gold medals, there were accusations that the upcoming day of our ferry crossing, from Patras, Greece, to Ancona, Italy, was designed to eliminate anyone who hadn't already been pushed out of the gold-medal ranks by the terrible Quetta day.

This last accusation was supported by a story that had supposedly come from Theo Voukidis, the jovial Greek doctor who was piloting a black-and-white Chevy Bel Air. Theo knew the roads in question, and in his new Mercedes Benz (not his old, slower Chevy), it took him more than eight hours to drive the six hundred or so kilometers that we were expected to negotiate before 6:00 P.M. (in order to catch the 7:00 P.M. ferry). How could the slow antique cars—like the lit-tle Aston Martin International—possibly make it in so little time? Many figured that competitors were therefore being forced to decide whether to go for it, and risk missing the ferry, or forfeit their chance at a gold medal by taking the quicker highway. Missing the ferry would mean arranging alternate crossing, only possible the next day, or departing from a different port.

I decided I wanted to take advantage of the meetings, so I didn't join Linda on the morning's sightseeing tour of Esfahan. I found the designated room promptly at 9:30, expecting a long line of competitors waiting their turns. Team Retro was already inside, and one other British couple stood at the door, but no one else showed up. I couldn't believe the low turnout, and neither could Philip and his marshals.

I went in with only four questions, and almost immediately after I left the room I thought of twenty others. First, I wanted to understand how they had determined the required average speeds. I still couldn't believe they'd expected us to average 50 mph through that horrible stretch of Pakistan.

The original recce drive, a year before, had determined the speed, they told me. Philip kept relatively quiet at first, letting his clerks, both very experienced ralliers, do the talking. "Then why did you decide to shorten them," I asked. "Because the authorities allowed it," they said, using Iran as an example, where the speed limit is much higher.

"You weren't trying to thin the leader board?" I pressed. "Is there a limit on the number of gold and silver medals that will be awarded?"

This was the question they'd been waiting for. All three men lunged forward, and speaking over each other, swore that the only limit on medals would be the number of competitors who qualified. Philip immediately personalized my questions: "What are you worried about? All you've got to do now is kick back and cruise into Paris!"

"It's not about me and Linda," I answered, now on the defensive myself. "There are a lot of accusations floating around . . ."

"Exactly what are they saying?" Philip asked, but before I could answer John Vipond jumped in.

"I can't believe the things people are saying," he said. "We're running this thing professionally, no different from any other motor sport competition. I'm offended, *highly* offended that they think I'm capable of—"

"And they none of them have the balls to come here and say it to our faces!" Martin cut in. All three men were now at table-banging volume. When the air cleared, they all looked at me.

"Well, for example," I said, "they're saying the run to the ferry has been designed to prevent—"

"Alternative routes will be posted tomorrow," Philip snapped. "No one will be left behind. And if by some piece of bad luck they really can't make it, they'll have a whole list of other ferries they can take."

"You know," Martin put in, "half of these—" I think he was about to say *buggers,* then stopped himself. "Half of these people complain that the times are too tough, we're forcing them to drive too fast. The other half complain that there's no competition, that we've made it far too easy. It's not a rally but a joyride. We just can't please all the people all the time."

I admitted to them then my surprise that so many of the competitors were first-time ralliers, rather than the experienced drivers and navigators I'd expected. Why hadn't the event attracted more experienced people? I asked.

"Well, it's the money, ain't it?" Martin answered.

"And the time." John put in. "Seven weeks is too long for a serious racer. Messes up the rest of the season."

Once they'd all calmed down, I asked if the rally had gone as they'd expected, and what had been their biggest surprise or disappointment so far.

"The biggest surprise is everyone's tenacity," John answered, and Philip and Martin both nodded in agreement. "Philip expected no more than twenty-eight to finish. I thought maybe as many as sixty, but now it looks like there may be more than seventy."

Containers, ready to ship up to forty cars, had been ready at Kathmandu, and had left that city empty. "The way the cars drop out—instead of being shipped off home, they get fixed and come back—it's unlike any other rally I've seen. These people are out of the competition, but they don't care, they want to finish with the rest of them, driving into Paris."

"And is that upsetting?" I asked.

"No, it's fabulous!" Martin answered, "But it does make for a bit of a headache, keeping track of everyone. But overall, no, we're very pleased at the tenacity of everyone on this event."

On my way out I met Paula Broderick, who was ready for her turn. "I feel like I'm going to the headmaster," she said, blanching.

"Have at 'em," I said, "Hardly anyone else is!"

"Yes," she said, "It's the one-on-one that's scaring them away. Well, here goes!" And she went in, looking far less confident than she normally did.

I found out later that most people who went in used the time to protest particular penalties. I still hadn't taken the time to go over our time-card book and double-check the math against the rankings posted nightly. When I finally did, long after the rally was over, I found several discrepancies (including the inclusion of penalties for canceled stages) that would have moved us up a couple of places.

There in Esfahan, with the Feits' deaths still fresh in my mind, our relative ranking didn't seem worth getting worked up about. In fact, just a couple of doors down from the one-on-one meeting room, a special memorial book had been set out. We were all invited to write our condolences to Mrs. Feit and her family in the book. A long line snaked away from the door; clearly, more people felt a note to Mrs. Feit was a better use of time than wrangling with Philip and the marshals. As I walked by, one of the Germans, a man with whom I'd never spoken but whom I'd seen aboard one of the old Mercedes, emerged from the room in tears.

I had dried my own tears earlier that morning, after my telephone call with Chris and the kids. My homesickness had reached the point where I felt physically sick while I talked to them; even though I was terribly happy to hear their voices, my stomach was in knots. When I'm far away and I know as I hang up I won't be seeing them anytime soon, I cry.

After lunch, I checked the rally notice board in the lobby and discovered that Dutch Lisa in the Bumblebee MG had been charged with "reckless driving." The note said the marshals would consider the charge and render a judgment by Istanbul. I asked the other ralliers reading the board if they knew what that was about; apparently, Lisa had driven into a TC too fast and careened into the organizer's Vauxhall, sending the timekeeper scrambling up onto the car's hood. The man (Mick

O'Malley, someone said) escaped injury, but the Vauxhall had been dented.

Next, Linda joined me and Dick Taylor for a walk to the center of town. There was no longer any hint from our Iranian hosts and hostesses of limited access or warnings of exterior dangers. It was a gorgeous sunny day, and the walk was not far—past the yellow and turquoise dome of the Madrassah Chahar Bagh (Theological School) right next to the hotel, through a lovely park that contained the Hasht Behesht, or "Eight Paradise" Palace built in 1669, and finally coming to the Maidan-e-Naghsh-e-Jahan, the huge central square. Though the original settlement here dates back 2,700 years to a small Jewish colony known as Yahuddiyeh, the glory days of Esfahan were in the period of the Safavid kings, especially Shah Abbas the Great. He came to power in 1587, and once he drove out the Mongols and Ottoman Turks and reunited Persia, he set out to turn Esfahan into the "jewel of Islam." The extraordinary square at its center is one of the largest in the world and holds Shah Abbas's greatest architectural efforts.

At the southern end of the square, defined by a continuous wall of blind arches, sits the Masjid-e-Imam or Imam Mosque. This impressive edifice, which *Lonely Planet* names "one of the most stunning buildings in the world," is remarkable for its strange slant: to keep the mosaic-bedecked entrance square with the plaza, and still have the Mosque properly oriented toward Mecca, the builders cleverly constructed a false front that connects through a turning hallway to the principal Mosque.

On the east flank sits the lovely, though humble, Masjid-e-Sheikh Lotfollah, named after an evangelical Sheikh of the time. This minaret-less family or "Ladies Mosque" features tiny, intricate mosaic works that capture and transform the sunlight as it hits the dome, turning it from cream to pink as the day wanes. The mosaics inside are just as intricate; the blue and yellow tiles on every wall mimic the patterns of Persian rugs. Across the square on the west side sits the Ali Qapu Palace and the Chehal-Sotun, or "Forty-Column" Palace. This wooden complex is architecturally reminiscent of the Italian Renaissance. From the Ali Qapu, royal spectators could watch the polo games that used to take place in the center of the plaza. Behind, in the Chehal-Sotun, they could relax under the twenty columns, and gaze down at twenty more in the reflecting pool. This is one explanation of the name "Forty-Columns"; the other is the fact that Persians use the number forty synonymously with "many."

The northern edge of the plaza is filled with the immense Qaisarrieh Bazaar— over five kilometers of shops with examples of Iran's finest rugs, tin, copper and wood work. Linda and I were both fascinated with the "millefiori"—intricate patterned veneers created by bundling thin strips of multicolored woods together and slicing them at the ends into sheer layers. Linda found a little jewelry box of this material for her daughter.

A little further south, spanning the Zayandeh River, were Esfahan's lovely bridges, including the glorious Sio-Se-Pol or Bridge of Thirty-three Arches, which dates back to 1596. I saw these later, when I joined Eric Christiansen, Rich Newman, Michael Veys and Michael Kunz for a dinner outing.

We'd heard of a good restaurant nearby called Scheherazade. When we still hadn't found it after walking a few short blocks, stubborn Eric refused to walk any further. He insisted we all return to the Abbasi and get a second recommendation. A taxi driver met us before we even regained the lobby, and heartily recommended the Espanada, a "lovely" restaurant right on the river. Imagining a nice waterfront patio, we agreed, and after loading into his and another taxi, we arrived at what turned out to be the restaurant of a humble businessman's hotel, probably owned by our taxi driver's family.

I was the only woman with my four men friends, and walking into that restaurant was the first time in Iran I'd felt the full heat of hostile stares. I had on Western wear—my loose cargo jeans and a loose cotton shirt—and of course, a headwrap. But the restaurant was devoid of any females, and these diners clearly weren't pleased to see me. We ignored them, of course, and settled down to a boring meal (more chelo kebab) and an interesting conversation.

Eric, who called himself the "meanest old cus on the rally," had decided after the Quetta day to voluntarily drop from the competitive class into Touring. Since then, Eric had been choosing his own routes and ignoring all the start and stop times. Michael wasn't pleased about it; they now often traveled outside the reach of any assistance from the rally staff, and also missed out on some of the camaraderie.

After we ordered, Eric regaled us with his opinion on the quality of steaks worldwide. "Bolivia," he said, "is the best place for beef. There you can choose the Brazilian beef or the Argentine beef. One has more flavor but is tough, the other has less flavor but is tender. Now in the Bahamas, we have no good meats, so I must fly my jet over to Fort Lauderdale. The prices at the Costco there are wonderful. I buy all my meat there."

He went on to talk about his favorite restaurants around the world—in Dallas, Paris, Brussels. Then, leaning back in his chair, he said, "But of course, I hate to travel."

We all looked at him, our jaws hanging open. They snapped shut one by one, and we all tried to contain our laughter. Rich bravely said, "Now Eric, the question all of us here at this table would like to put to you right now is," he paused for effect, "why are you here?"

Eric grinned slyly: "Insanity runs in my family."

We all shared some of Eric's insanity, both in our travel habits and our classic car mania. Eric had more than just the '65 Rolls Royce Silver Cloud. He had several Rolls and Bentleys parked at his various homes. Rich Newman owned a collection of classic motorcycles; I had my Fiats; and Michael Kunz nursed a weakness for two British marques, Lotus and Mini Coopers. Though Michael was born in New York, he moved to London once he had his law degree, then to Hong Kong, where he's lived for six or seven years. He competes in classic car races with the Hong Kong club, which gathers on tracks in Southern China and Macao.

Michael, like Rich Newman, was at serious odds with his co-driver, John Thomason. Michael and Rich commiserated, two frustrated navigators—but Michael had a distinct advantage, as John let him drive occasionally.

Back at the Abbasi, I ran into David Drew, who'd returned to the rally. Though still in a bit of pain, he'd convinced his doctor that he could manage completing the rally. He was back at work already; Jonathan Lux's Rover needed work on its differential.

The Jeepsters arrived late, disheveled and hungry. They had worked all day trying to solve a generator or voltage regulator problem, but they weren't successful. "The locals said—after several hours of trying—that they can't help us. They're sure that the next town will have the parts we need, so we'll just have to run off the battery until then."

It was almost midnight when I got back to the room, and when I unwrapped my hair from its elaborate coverup, I felt as if I'd lifted a huge weight off my shoulders. I'd been trying hard not to get angry about it—what's a few feet of cotton fabric? When I travel, I always try to be sensitive to local traditions. I have no problem covering up before entering a Catholic church in Italy, for example. I kept thinking about nuns—the chador is superficially similar to a habit—and now, having fiddled with this get-up for four days, I could see how the daily process of covering up would be a valuable, conscious, reminder of one's decision to devote one's life to God.

That's fine for religious women, who make that decision *voluntarily*. But I am not a devout Muslim, nor are any of the other women on this rally, nor are many Iranian women. Only about 30 percent of Iranian women consider wearing the veil a religious act, according to one of the Pasargad Tour women I spoke with; the rest only do it because it is required by law.

Linda spent that evening with Don Jones, as his special guest on his satellite phone broadcast. Don told Linda that earlier that day, he had witnessed two women being picked up by the *Pasdaran,* or Revolutionary Guard, the special branch of law enforcement that enforces the clothing strictures. On the first offense, the women are taken to the police station. On the second, they're taken to court. If there's a third time, Don said, "they face very severe and very real punishment."

Don asked Linda to talk about her experience, and she said, "We're not used to being told how to dress, and we have no choice in the matter here. Everybody is sort of a policeman in reminding you that your scarf has fallen or that your hair is showing. We're all looking forward to it ending. It's a shame because the people themselves are quite wonderful. I've noticed when we drive away from the hotels on the rally, we often get groups of women giving us a little more of a cheer than some of the others. It seems to me as if they're saying, 'Well, somebody is out there doing things that we all know we can do, but unfortunately aren't allowed to.' Even though we've brought outfits or purchased them along the way to conform to and respect the Iranian culture, our clothing still sets us aside because we have all decided to wear bright colors, floral prints from India, Nepal or Pakistan, and it turns out that Iranian women are usually dressed in black from head to toe. So as much as we are trying to go along with the code, we still stand out. I can tell from the way women look at us and the shock in their faces that this is most unusual and they're having a hard time getting used to it, seeing a bunch of us walking around. So we're looking forward to getting across the border and taking our scarves off for the last time."

The Pasargad Tour woman told me that "Iranian women suffer no discrimination—not in education, property, marriage, divorce, anything!" Her feelings were supported by an e-mail we received at our webpage:

> I am an Iranian living in Switzerland, I do not wear an Islamic scarf and consider myself a very liberal woman. However, I do not understand why the traditional way women dress in Iran should be considered repressive. This is the way women have dressed for centuries and wearing western style clothes will not in any way 'liberate' them.

Iranian author Farzaneh Milani disagrees: "The veil, in its traditional sense, not only polarizes but delineates boundaries. It consigns 'power,' 'control,' 'visibility,' and 'mobility' to one social category at the expense of the other. It not only separates the world of men and women not related to each other by marriage or blood but also creates hierarchies across this divide. The indoors, the domestic, the 'private,' the 'personal,' the world of women is trivialized. And the out-of-doors, the 'public,' the world of masculine politics and money is affirmed, elevated."

Even the men on the rally felt it. Dick Taylor wrote to the Arizona *Republic* that the chador makes women "look like they are in mourning. Wearing such a black garment in the hot sun must be very trying. . . . On the other hand, most of the men dress in western style clothes, markedly underscoring the submissive role to be played by women, at least in public."

Don Jones encountered another aspect of the divide when he met the Iranian rally drivers' families. Their wives, kids, and parents had come down from Tehran to spend the rest day.

> I got to meet the families of the six Iranian drivers. . . . After being introduced to the children of the family and extending hands and greeting them, I was introduced to the spouses of some of the drivers. I extended my hand only to have the lady step away. I was politely told in a matter of fact way that under Islamic practices a lady was not allowed to touch another person, or specifically another man.

In this cultural milieu, women are the private possessions of their husbands (or fathers or brothers), and as such are off limits to any other man, even if that man merely offers an innocent greeting. Don also reported that "We've learned in talking to the local people, that the relationship between men and women here is described as 'ugly.'" This is supported in Milani's book: "A society that veils its women is a veiled society. In other words, women are not the only ones veiled. Men are veiled, too. . . . Escaping a physical veil, Iranian men carry a mental veil. They are indeed prisoners in jails of their own making. To begin with, although women are the secluded ones, the degree of man/woman access remains curtailed for both sexes. The restriction is thus not on women alone; it is against heterosexual interactions in general."

After living the ritual for four days, I knew firsthand that what I had hoped would be a minor matter—the dress code—in fact serves as a powerful method for reminding the world of the restricted status of Iranian women. One only needs to think of the horrifying situation in Afghanistan, where the Taliban have completely dehumanized all women, to realize the dangerous direction these kinds of restrictions can take.

Thankfully, that is not likely to happen in Iran. "A real revolution is, in fact, shaking the foundations of Iranian society, a revolution with women at its very center," Milani wrote in 1992. "Veiled or unveiled, Iranian women are reappraising traditional spaces, boundaries, and limits. They are renegotiating old sanctions and sanctuaries. They are challenging male allocations of power, space, and resources. Exercising increasing control over how reality is defined, they are redefining their own status."

CHAPTER

$\backsim$ 34 $\backsim$

*Alas, we met no longer with the same good-natured friendliness ... these men received
us with a certain hostile astonishment, as if we represented the arrival of some unknown
enemy.*

ESFAHAN TO HAMADAN
[SUNDAY, OCTOBER 5]

At breakfast back in Kerman, Don Jones had mentioned that he'd heard
over the satellite phone that the Iranians had flown into Iraqi airspace,
and that there was a possibility President Clinton might order the
Nimitz into the Persian Gulf. He hadn't been able to confirm it; there were no
English newspapers or TV news available. Then, the morning we were preparing
to leave Esfahan, we heard that Clinton was threatening to bomb Iran. It made no
sense. Why would Clinton do Sadam Hussein's retaliation for him? It turned out
to be the original rumor, told and re-told and twisted around, the bloated result
of a rumor passed among two hundred news-starved Westerners.

Military thoughts crowded our day in any case. Every town had its own set of
murals featuring Khomeini or Rafsanjani (I wondered how long it would take to
produce giant images of the new president Khatami). Dick wrote in his Jeepster
report: "We are constantly reminded of the military's role in Iran by encountering
military or police checkpoints every five to ten miles, some even equipped with
vehicle-mounted heavy machine guns. Everywhere we find huge military camps,
and billboards glorifying the military and the holiness of war. It's a very frightening atmosphere."

The day's drive, with Linda at the wheel, took us into much more varied terrain. The climate was still desert-like, but now we climbed over several grades that
offered expansive views of the green-tinted valleys and high peaks of the two large
mountain ranges that paralleled our northwestern path: the Zagros Mountains to
the west and the Qohrud Mountains to the east. The towns were more closely
spaced than they had been the day before. We could tell when we approached one,
as a "dual-carriageway" appeared just before the town limits, then disappeared
immediately after. Banners proclaiming "Welcome Peking Paris Athletes" and

223

"Dear Friends We Are Glad to Have You in Our City" greeted us everywhere, especially at gas stations and cafes near the TCs. As before, the streets in every town were lined with men and boys, waving and shouting and throwing things. The boys were hyper; they stood in the median strip and ripped the heads off the flowers, then tossed them at us. Occasionally they grabbed the whole plant, roots, clumps of dirt and all, and hurled the mass.

Once I got a pile of marigolds, roots and all, in my lap. It made me so angry I grabbed the scratchy mass and hurled it right back, and then realized that I'd tossed my pencil out along with the vegetation. That annoyed me further, as our supply of writing utensils had been depleted by the sheer mass of mileage.

In the town of Khomein, birthplace of the Ayatollah Khomeini, the boys were joined by hostile men, and stones joined the plant material that came flying at our car. By now we'd gotten into the habit of rolling up the windows, despite the heat, so though there were a couple of nasty-sounding pings and bangs, we drove through unscathed.

It was much harder, of course, for people in open cars. One of the British Bentleys suffered a broken windshield, many cars suffered rock chips, and when a boy threw a stone at Ned Thompson and hit him in the shoulder, Ned stopped the car, jumped out, and chased the boy down the street! The boy escaped—I imagine he ran a bit faster than middle-aged Ned—so Ned gave up and regained the Bentley.

Our collective euphoria at Iran's friendly reception was deflated some that day. We'd all known there would eventually be some manifestation of twenty years of anti-Western propaganda. It's only too appropriate that the message would be delivered most vehemently by the residents of Khomein.

For Prince Borghese, the cold shoulder came just after crossing the provincial border between Siberia and Perm. They weren't in Europe yet; European Russia did not begin until the Ural Mountains, a day or two further west. In the province of Perm, though, the Mujiks had neither the amazement of the Chinese and Mongolians, nor the welcoming spirit of the more urban dwellers in Moscow. For these rural Russians, the motor-car was a symbol of unwelcome changes. "A few of the men fled," Barzini wrote, "the others looked at us sullenly, and stood in an attitude of defence. Some women went through a strange ceremony of protection against evil, spitting in our direction."

Near the town of Arak, we drove by the biggest oil refinery complex I have ever seen. Our road book mentioned that the complex had been one of the main targets during the Iran-Iraq war, but the bustling, modern refinery now shows no signs of damage. It did remind us of our proximity to the Iraqi border, and those belligerent rumors we'd been hearing for several days. The river bridge beside our second TC looked as if it might have been a casualty of that horribly bloody conflict: what our road book called a "very old bridge" looked as if it had been bombed. We arrived very early, and relaxed in the sun; it wasn't too hot now, as we were continuing to climb. On either side of the narrow river, brushy green tamarisks grew, but otherwise the vegetation was still sparse. We sat near the car and ate our airplane lunches. The sandwich today featured a green sponge-like substance—possibly pressed spinach? A slice of green carpeting, according to Pat from the '49 Caddy. Whatever. It didn't taste bad, and the honey-soaked pistachio pastry more than made up for it.

In contrast to the people of Khomein, the denizens of Hamadan, about one hundred miles further on, welcomed us with high ceremony. We were stopped at what looked like a police checkpoint, but instead of interrogating us they showered us with gifts: grape juice (the harvest was underway, and the fresh table grapes were wonderful), a big map, a tourist brochure (in English and Farsi) and a stack of postcards. A banner high above the street said pleasantly, *We hoddarrive cars of match Paris Peking!*

The little brochure stated that Hamadan had been designated "one of the five cultural cities of Iran," and described its many historical delights. The city was an important center all the way back in Median (700 BC) and Achaemenian (549-330 BC) times, and was known by the ancient Greeks as Ekbatana. Hamadan's archeological sights include the Ganj-Nameh or Treasure Book, ancient Persian inscriptions about the exploits of Achaemenians Darius I and Xerxes I on two stone panels; the Sang-e-Shir Stone Lion from Parthian times (330-300 BC); and two major tombs: that of Esther and Mordecai, which explains Hamadan's large Jewish community; and the twelfth-century Alavyan Tomb Tower, a large square brick building with lacey relief work decorating the arch over its church-like front door.

Our hotel was on the edge of the sprawling town. Hamadan was spread out on a 5,850-foot plain under the shadow of 11,616-foot-high Mount Alvand. Linda and I spent some of the afternoon relaxing in our room, and as we sat and lay around talking, she opened up more than she had since Oxfordshire. It started out innocently enough with Linda describing her home in Melbourne. But soon the subject turned to Geoff and his troubled health.

"Those damn psychologists in Australia . . ." she said, shaking her head sadly. "They weren't getting anywhere. It was scary, I mean, he was getting so despondent! I had to do something, even though we weren't living together anymore. So I took him to San Francisco. The psychiatrist there recommended this new drug therapy. It sounded like it could really make a difference. But now the damn doctors in Australia won't follow through. It makes me so angry. ...."

What should have been a simple matter of filling a prescription had become a battle between differing medical ideologies. The faxes from Geoff, and his phone calls, had been uneven; sometimes he was so low she had to talk him up. I recognized the dynamic; one of my three brothers had a schizophrenic break at sixteen, and now, at thirty-three, is considered "bi-polar" (he still needs assisted-living). I'd been in Linda's position, on the phone with someone I love when he's in one of those blacker-than-black moods. If you've been there, you know there are times when the impulse to take care of that person and make everything right, is replaced by the equally urgent desire to be at the opposite end of the globe.

I headed down to the lobby at about five-thirty to find that all the ralliers at our hotel had gathered in the "bar" for Zam Zam, Pipi, coffee or tea. We were all counting the minutes to Turkey—the men for their long-missed beer, the women for the glorious day when we could dump our depressing scarves. Our new mantra was: Border, Beer and Bonfire (Death to the Scarves!). Despite the absence of alcohol, in this strange forced sobriety, we were now much more comfortable with each other. There was still a sense of being under house arrest, but by now we knew it was mostly self-imposed.

That evening, we were all bused to a park on the edge of town, where we were treated to a table full of fresh fruit, cookies, honey-soaked tea cakes, and soda. It was an odd replay of the Lahore Governor's Tea, but in full dark in this odd park that featured a sad zoo—cages full of birds, rabbits and other small creatures—and what seemed like a military cordon ringing the outer fence. The highlight was watching the video of the Iranian news broadcast featuring coverage of the Peking-Paris on a TV that had been rolled out to this strange outdoor setting.

Later, back at the hotel, Linda, Rich Newman, Bud Risser and I had dinner together. When we asked Rich if he and Burt were getting along any better, Rich's answer was a resounding no.

"Back in China, when we had dinner with the Italians in the yellow 2CV, " Rich said, "Burt was holding forth on something or other, and one of the Italians said, 'Ah, the man who knows everything.' That sums it up exactly."

Rich felt that Burt was unwilling to consider any input from him whatsoever, so he had simply stopped talking.

"Not even a navigational direction?" I asked.

"Oh no, I still navigate. I'm just not talking."

He was even considering, that night, riding the rest of the way to Istanbul with Bud in the Chevy. Bud's co-driver for this stretch was his old college roommate, Grant, who'd joined the rally in Kathmandu. But Grant had to leave at Esfahan due to prior commitments. So Bud now carried an ever-changing crew: sometimes a Discovery journalist, or one of the British video crew, or Casper Noz (who, like Lord Montagu, continued to ride along with the rally however he could).

Such a move would disqualify Burt and Rich both from the competition, though, as any crew change meant dropping into the non-competitive Touring category. I wondered if Rich was really angry enough to go through with it.

Even the fatigue we felt was not sufficient to make us rest soundly. Every hour of halt seemed to us a wasted hour. We longed to be running all the time, not exactly in order to make a record, but because we wanted to go far and fast, and to be soon again amid our own friends and back to the life on our native soil. It was just a month to the day that we had started.

HAMADAN TO TABRIZ
[MONDAY, OCTOBER 6]

We left Hamadan and immediately turned off the major road, heading directly north. For about a hundred miles we drove along the western edge of Hamadan's plain, passing through only a few villages, until we arrived at the Kurdish town of Cesame Bigar. Here, in the northern reaches of the Zagros Mountains, Linda and I were thrilled to see a group of women dressed in multi-colored scarves and full, colorful skirts and dresses—no more black chador! We were now in the Kurdistan province, and these women were members of one of the sartorially obstinate Kurdish tribes. Kurds in Iran number five to seven million, in Turkey twelve to fifteen million, and in Iraq, despite Saddam Hussein's genocidal efforts, four million Kurds survive.

So far, there were no visible signs of the PKK, the violent Kurdish Workers Party. In *Dangerous Places,* I'd read that "the Kurds as a people do not necessarily condone or even care about the terrorist group's actions. The actions of the PKK do little to help the Kurds gain political and financial clout. The possibility of creating a new country carved out of Iran, Iraq, Turkey and Syria is as likely as Saddam taking a military planning job at the Pentagon."

Even our Pasargad tourist brochure said "A strongly tradition conscious people, the Kurds are fierce fighters and have bravely guarded Iran's western borders throughout its long history." For me and Linda, the simple fact that these women stubbornly resisted the Mullahs' clothing dictates was reason enough to rejoice. Only one more night in Iran, and we'd finally be free of scarf imprisonment.

We followed our small but fast road to the TC at Sharif Abad, where a very old bridge traversed a trickling river. The town itself was behind an ancient wall, still adobe and desert-like in its construction, though the terrain now supported a few pines. We climbed from there to Maiinbolagh (Miyandoab on the map), a

hundred kilometers further north, and at 7,475 feet, our highest point in Iran. Here, still in Kurdish territory, our second TC was inside a small, pleasant tea house that served chunks of fresh honeycomb. From here, we continued on down a twisty mountain road that grew busier and busier as we neared Tabriz. On the map the large salt lake of Orumieh (Orumiye) seemed just on our left, but I only caught a glimpse once as we drove by.

Just past Miyandoab we left Kurdistan for East Azerbaijan. The historic region of Azerbaijan is now split between Iran's two provinces (East and West) and the Republic of Azerbaijan to the north (formerly part of Russia); the natives speak Azeri, a Turkish dialect. East Azerbaijan's capital, Tabriz, was our stop for the night. The city has been traded back and forth between conquerors for centuries. The Mongols were in charge when Marco Polo passed through in the thirteenth century. Polo wrote that Tabriz "is a large and noble city belonging to the province of Iraq, which contains many other cities and fortified places; but this is the most eminent and populous. It is so advantageously situated for trade that merchants from India, from Baudas [Baghdad], as well as from different parts of Europe, come there to purchase and to sell a number of articles. Precious stones and pearls in abundance may also be procured here." After the Mongols came the Moghuls; Emperor Jahan-Shah built the beautifully tiled Blue Mosque here in 1465. Shah Abbas the Great (from Esfahan) brought Tabriz into Persia in 1618. Then the Turks came back in 1721-30; the Russians held the city in 1827-28 and then again in 1945-46. The area is an active earthquake zone, so the city has been rebuilt many times. Today, it looks like a fairly modern middle-class town, with distinct Russian overtones. The population is the second largest in Iran.

The day's 580 kilometers had flown by quickly; we arrived well before 3:28 P.M., our due time. We were so early, in fact, we were able to park in one of the six parking spots directly in front of our hotel. From the balcony in our room high up on the tenth floor, we had a bird's-eye-view of the city as well as of the roof of our Hillman.

Once again I joined the gathering in the hotel lobby. As I sat sipping hot tea, I was approached by an Iranian college student. I'd watched him making the rounds, interviewing various ralliers with a serious batch of questions. He asked me politely if he could interview me, and I agreed.

"Do you think the American government understands the people of Iran?" he asked. I told him I had no idea. "Your government does not understand us," he went on. "We young people are not the same as our fathers."

I told him that we had been pleased by the welcome we'd received from the Iranian people, then changed the subject. "So what do you think about the chador?" I asked him. "And what is the significance of black?"

"It is traditional," he said. "I do not like it either, but it is changing. You will see." I hope so, I thought, but was disappointed at his vague answer. Later, Bill Binnie told me the student had been carefully "de-interviewed" by a man who had been watching him from a corner of the lobby.

At about six-thirty, Bud Risser asked if anyone wanted to go for a walk. Michael

Kunz and I jumped at the opportunity and the three of us set off toward a neon-lit shopping street. Even though the women were dressed more colorfully here—brown and camel-colored chadors joined the black—the stares I received at every step were far more shocked than any I'd experienced since Zahedan. Perhaps Esfahan's still-active international tourist industry has allowed its citizens to grow more accustomed to the sight of a six-foot-three-inch Western woman dressed in half-assed Asian garb.

The three of us were drawn into a pastry shop by the irresistible smell of fresh baked breads and sweets. Elegant glass display cases ringed the large, belle époque store, filled to capacity with every manner of Viennese, French, and Iranian pastries. We purchased a selection of these, then bought more humble loaves of bread from a free-standing kiosk. I ate mine as we walked (perhaps violating yet another Islamic stricture?) ripping pieces from the fragrant, soft white center of my loaf. While I munched, Michael examined an array of belts spread along the sidewalk by a street vendor. We'd all lost weight, but Michael, who'd begun the journey quite heavy, had lost so much that none of his belts would do. He found a bargain (the exchange rate of the Iranian rial with the dollar or pound made everything incredibly cheap), and we headed back to the hotel for another chelo kebab dinner.

Bill Binnie and Burt Richmond joined us this time. First we caught up on rally gossip. Rumor had it that the Dutchman in the beautiful white 1927 Mercedes 630K roadster had rammed Peter Nobles's Bentley in the rear, because he was watching a "skirt." I found it hard to believe there'd been any skirts to chase since India. (Is there such a thing as a chador-chaser?) Another rumor put the Bentley's damage down to a run-in with a "dog the size of a donkey." Until we found the perpetrators or victims we'd never know the truth of the matter.

The conversation inevitably turned to the status of women. Bill Binnie said "send any man to Iran and you'll make him a feminist." In response, Burt launched into a little lecture on the origins of feminism, claiming it started in the United States during World War II, when women like Rosie the Riveter went to work in factories. He hadn't gotten much further before both Linda and I jumped in. "It's a little more complicated than that," I started, and Linda said something more blunt, along the lines of "You don't know what you're talking about, Burt." She said it without rancor; she and Burt were good friends, and he never seemed to take offense at her direct approach. Our little verbal tussle amused Bill, who said "Burt, next time you have a thought like that, will you please keep it to yourself?"

As we were leaving, the Jeepsters walked in. They'd had a tough two days, driving with the constant awareness that their battery was not recharging. In Hamadan, they worked on it most of the night at a local garage. At one point, "when nothing seemed to be happening," Dick told me, "we inquired, and they told us 'we are wasting time.' They meant they had to wait for something, but the simple translation seemed more appropriate to us."

They thought the problem had been fixed, but a short while after leaving Hamadan, it recurred. To make matters worse, they had to stop on the roadside to replace the carburetor, then later, the ignition system went out. Here in Tabriz, they'd gone to a shop first thing, but the needed parts were still unavailable. Dick and the crew were very discouraged.

Team Retro had better luck. They had been greeted at the Tabriz hotel by an Iranian who had lived in the States for seven years. He owned an auto shop, and had come looking especially for Americans. After helping both Team Retro and Don and Carl in the Packard with their repairs, he invited the Americans to join him for some taboo Scotch—behind closed doors, of course. The man was very nostalgic for the US, and he fondly dreamed of returning some day.

CHAPTER

∾ 36 ∾

By these military works we feel the approach of the frontier-line. They stand almost like sentinels, watching the movements of the stranger.

TABRIZ, IRAN TO PALANDÖKEN, TURKEY
[TUESDAY, OCTOBER 7]

We were up before dawn again for an early 6:00 A.M. start, necessary because today's trek would be a long 593 kilometers, with a potentially difficult border crossing in the middle.

Outside Tabriz, we passed through a town that seemed to be filled exclusively with girls and women. They lined the streets, in what looked like school uniforms, all black except the short white chador. They seemed overjoyed to see the ralliers, especially Linda and me, when they realized we were two women in our own car. Their smiles and waves stayed with us for the rest of the day. The only odd note was the question of why they were all concentrated in one area. Are all the girls' schools isolated in this one northwestern town? Or had the girls in other, more conservative towns not been allowed out to watch us pass?

We wouldn't enter Europe until Istanbul, but for us, the border between Turkey and Iran marked the end of the East and the beginning of the West. For Iran, the West was no ally, and the military presence grew even more visible as we neared the border. Now instead of villages, there were military encampments. The locals were no less welcoming, though. At our last gas stop, a bright yellow banner hung from the station's fence. In bright green letters it read *Pioneers who bring the message of friendship of nations are welcome.*

As if compensating for the bleak military atmosphere, the gorgeous snow-covered peak of Mount Ararat, or Agri Dagi, the mountain where Noah's ark is said to have come to rest, rose into the sky as we neared the border. This 16,689-foot volcano, the highest point in Europe, dominates the low treeless plain so singularly, it's as impressive (some said more so) as Everest.

We reached the border complex at about 10:00 A.M. Despite its formidable appearance—military men and materiel stretched for several kilometers on both

sides of the frontier—we cruised through the formalities with no trouble, clocking out on the Turkish side only one hour later. A huge truck parking area testified to the great deal of trade that travels between the two countries, punitive sanctions notwithstanding. The only surprise was that between the fresh paving on either side, one deeply rutted dirt lane served as the only access to Turkey. Apparently, this stretch is deliberately left in disrepair to break the axles of anyone unwisely attempting to crash the border.

We were welcomed by representatives of Turkey's Dedeman Hotel chain. They'd prepared an information packet for us, including a map with our route traced in green, and phone numbers for English-speaking assistants in all the regional cápitals. Back on the road, we instantly observed stark differences. I'd noticed facial features changing ever since Tabriz, from the round-eyed Persian to the more etched and angular Mediterranean look. Now everything else changed too: the cars (no more Peykans); houses were no longer low adobe buildings, but were now multistoried stucco, reminiscent of Italy and Greece; school kids wore Western ties and jackets; and the women still covered their hair but now with colorful scarves, and their clothing varied from traditional skirts to almost modern Western wear.

We had changed money at the border. I traded 334,000 Iranian rials for 1,300,000 Turkish lira. "I'm a millionaire!" I laughed, but the three-way math to figure out what all those zeros amounted to in US dollars escaped me. We purchased forty liters of gasoline for 5,400,000—all mine plus some of Linda's "frugals" from her stash. Later, I purchased 168,000 lira for one US dollar. Every note featured a portrait of Atatürk, the father of modern Turkey, but my favorite was the 5,000,000-lira note. There's nothing quite like knowing you have five million in your pocket. I tucked one of these away to bring home to the kids.

The landscape was still largely brown and ochre, with touches of pale green—possibly wheat—on the distant plain. As we cruised through the small town of Dogubeyazit, thirty-five kilometers from the border, the jagged volcanic mountains flanked us on one side, while the wide open plain spread out on the other. Just to the north was Ararat, rising almost 13,000 feet above the plain. (The plain itself is 3,689 feet above sea level.) There at its base, Carl and Don had a fright. They were blissfully riding along in the '54 Packard under the shadow of the mountain when smoke suddenly poured from the dashboard. They stopped and grabbed their fire extinguisher, but the smoke soon subsided; some of the wiring under the dash had overheated, melting their tachometer and disabling several instruments including, sadly, their CD player.

Linda drove all day and I navigated. Though we'd lost the handy English translations provided by the Iranians—and the Turkish language, with all its cedillas, umlauts and accents, was unlike anything I'd ever seen—navigation wasn't too difficult. The high plateau of Eastern Anatolia supports more sheep than people, partly because it is often buried in snow in the winter. Still, archeological finds go all the way back to the eighth millennium BC, making this one of the oldest areas of human settlement on earth. In the town of Pasinler, we could see the high Hasankale Fortress, built by Emir Hassan in the fourteenth century. The three-walled stone construction hugged a cliff overlooking the town.

Thirty-eight kilometers later, we came to the town of Erzurum, the largest city in Eastern Anatolia. Like Tabriz, the town has been on the major east-west thoroughfare since long before Marco Polo; the ancient Greeks called it Theodosiopolis. The road in was crowded with military materiel—we saw a row of slowly moving tanks—running exercises out of the Turkish Third Army's base (one of NATO's most important frontline units) stationed in Erzurum. Unlike in Iran, however, here there were no townspeople to greet us, no men or boys beside the road. Our cars caused the occasional head to turn, but we were no longer a strange phenomenon.

That is perhaps the biggest single difference between our rally and the original Peking to Paris. In 1907, even if the people weren't always astonished by a motor-car, the horses certainly were. On the day Prince Borghese and crew drove out of the busy town of Perm, the Itala caused pandemonium. A long line of lightweight Russian carriages called *telegas,* led by nervous horses, were converging on the town for the market. "The first horse in the line of *telegas* began to shy. We slackened the speed of our car to a walking-pace, but this was a useless precaution, the horse jerked to one side, and its *telega* was upset. The *telega* was carrying milk and eggs: little white and yellow streamlets coursed all about the road. We were just about to try and make up to the man for our involuntary misdeed when, like a flash, this panic fear spread to the other horses one by one. The second *telega* was upset, then the third; there is nothing more contagious than bad example. In a moment all the *telegas* were overturned, milk was flowing everywhere, and the peasants, encouraged by their wives, were throwing themselves in our direction. What was to be done? What can you do when you are on a 40 hp motor-car, and threatened by a crowd of Mujiks anxious and able to fall upon you? The matter becomes simple: regretfully, but firmly, we put down the speed lever, and our machine took to its heels, and was soon far out of reach of the peasants' sticks."

That was bad enough, but the same scene repeated itself within a half-mile. "*Tableau!*" Barzini wrote, "Milk and eggs on the road, sticks up in the air, and our car racing off at top speed."

Speed turned out to be the solution: if the Itala roared past the traffic without a pause, the horses "had scarcely time to see the passing of our monster before the monster had disappeared, and they went on their way completely reassured." As an added benefit, instead of reaching for their sticks in anger, the peasants cheered, "smiling surprised at the sight of that lightning speed."

Our night's destination was a ski resort named Palandöken. A gravel road led us up a very steep incline to the Dedeman hotel complex. We arrived before 2:00 P.M. All together on the otherwise empty mountain, featuring a twelve-thousand-meter downhill ski run touted as Europe's longest, we celebrated the three Bs: Border, Beer and since we'd neglected to build a bonfire, more Beer. The scarves were off and shoved into plastic bags, ready for the garbage can. Linda would have tossed ours at any rate, but my conservationist nature prevented her: I couldn't bring myself to throw away good fabric, even if I do resent the suppression those swaths represent. I crammed both hers and mine into a corner of my duffle bag, and rejoined the party at the bar, drinking my first few pints with Team Retro. Part of the Discovery crew, Robert and Drew, were working on stronger stuff, and when Linda joined us she went straight to her favorite, the first passable martini she'd had since the rally began. We were joined by Casper Noz, the Dutch-Californian who'd been hitchhiking ever since his Ford A Pickup died in Beijing.

Outside, the Jeepsters ended their difficult day ignominiously, on a tow-truck's hook. Just before the last two hundred yards up to the resort, the Jeep's exhaust pipe had broken and slipped down next to the gas line; the heat on the line caused fuel starvation. They couldn't stay to party; they set off for Erzurum to get the pipe welded.

The Jeepsters weren't the only ones towed up that hill. I watched the Morris Minor being pulled up (apparently the hole had reappeared in Maurice's welded piston), and later the old Fiat, #19, arrived on the bar with the indefatigable Signor Ciriminna. His car had broken a half-shaft on the way to Tabriz; either the repairs had been insufficient or some other trouble bedeviled the little Italian sedan. Burt's and Rich's 2CV had trouble pulling up the steep road in second gear; Burt blamed it on the extra weight of the gas the little car carried in its just-filled reserve tank.

For others, like the Gulls, things were now running smoothly. The Iranian rebuild of Richard and Ken's big black Buick seemed to have done the trick, as they were now keeping up with the rally; the Dutch Citroën station wagon that had dropped behind for several days due to gearbox failure was back, as was the similarly-afflicted Italian Lancia Flavia. Even Lisa Klokgieters-Lankes' Bumblebee MG, which had needed a crankshaft regrind and Toyota bearings to rebuild it, was back on the road with a sign on the back window reading "Please Overtake—Running In Engine" (British for "breaking in"; engines have to be driven carefully at variable speeds when they're newly rebuilt). The Aston Martin DB6 had succeeded in repairing their *second* half-shaft, but now the newest car in the event, a '74 Austin 1800 Landcrab, had broken a piston ring; the car's unusual mechanical configuration, with the transmission and engine as one unit, would make repairs a lengthy prospect. The Austin's British drivers planned to catch up by heading straight to Istanbul with no stops.

We'd been running now for four weeks and almost twelve thousand kilometers. Everyone—and the cars—had taken thirty-two days of relentless punishment. The top ten were unchanged, but we'd dropped a few more down into Touring; the total number now in the competitive classes was seventy. Intellectually, I understood why some cars had to struggle to climb up to eight-thousand-foot

Palandöken. But as I gazed out over the Erzurum valley from my perch on the deck of this lovely resort, happily inebriated in the cool evening air—we'd been warned it might freeze that night—it seemed ironic that this measly little hill had got the best of vehicles that had so recently conquered the Himalayas.

∽ 37 ∽

So long as we travelled, we were kept up by the nervous tension of continual vigilance: driving so fast was feverish kind of work, even if no accident occurred. But when we stopped, we were suddenly overcome by an inexpressible prostration.

PALANDÖKEN TO NEVSEHIR
[WEDNESDAY, OCTOBER 8]

The Dedeman representative, Iskender Aruoba, had written a long letter to accompany the packet we received at the border. Iskender planned to drive the route with us, and he gave us phone numbers for shops and the Klasïk Otomobïl Klübü, the Classic Automobile Club of Turkey. He ended the letter with this advice: "PLEASE DRIVE EXTRA CAREFULLY, OVERTAKE IF 100% SURE, because unfortunately Turks are very good people but very lousy drivers. (There are some which are good !!)"

The inexorable logic of alternating gave me the wheel on this, the highest mileage day of the rally. It seemed only fair, after Linda had been saddled with the Tibet/Nepal border, the river-crossings, and most of the Quetta day. We'd been warned that the roads in Turkey were not as good as those in Iran, but in fact all 739.2 kilometers (459 miles) turned out to be perfectly fine, as well paved as any in California (of course, if you've driven in California, you know the roads are littered with potholes). Still, the driving was uneventful, and we averaged 75 mph, easily staying with or passing the locals, coming in early to all our checkpoints.

We slipped down Mount Palandöken and regained the high central Anatolia plateau. Ancient wind-cut volcanoes folded by seismic ridges lined our route; Turkey is one of the world's most active earthquake zones, as the Arabian, African, Eurasian Aegean, and Turkish plates all converge here. Sivas, near our midday TC, was called Sebastia by the Romans and Byzantines, and then came under the rule of the Turkish Seljuks in 1055. From their capital in Baghdad, the Islamic Seljuks ruled Central Asia until they were defeated by the invading Mongols. Despite constant earthquake activity, several Seljuk buildings from the sultanate of Konya or Rum, which lasted until 1243, remain in Sivas. Unfortunately, our route directed us onto a new bypass around the city and into a suburb named Tastan.

Don Jones described our trek through Turkey as "moving through different centuries." Southern Turkey is "seventeenth or eighteenth century in its architecture and its customs. The eighteenth and nineteenth century we passed through today.. . . The twentieth and twenty-first century are about to appear as we proceed to a more cosmopolitan and urban part of Turkey." The gas stations were certainly equal to those found along any US Interstate: new complexes with minimarts and snack bars and recognizable brand names. Our TC was in one of these, though the restaurant nearby was a step up from typical US-highway fast-food joints. Thanks to our high average speed, we were able to linger a little over a pleasant lunch on a nice sunny patio.

While Prince Borghese had many pleasant meals, often served with great ceremony by the local officials, he rarely had the chance to enjoy the sun. Either it was too hot and withering, as in the Gobi, or it had disappeared altogether behind the impenetrable rainclouds that blanketed Siberia that entire summer.

It was on one of these terrible wet days that the Itala suffered its most distressing blow since the fall through the Baikal bridge. The Itala's wooden wheels had been damaged in the unending war with the Siberian mud: to gain some traction, the Prince invented tire-chains, lashing the wide wooden drive wheels with chains. The stress from those chains damaged the rims where the spokes attached; the left driving-wheel had suffered the most. As they neared Perm, tiny cracks were visible at the end of each spoke, but these cracks disappeared when the wood was swollen by the rain. Every added mile, though, expanded the cracks, until the driving-wheel's creaking grew so loud they had to stop the car. The cracks had broadened to the point that the spokes were moving in their sockets. Ettore the mechanic took strong string and wound it round the spokes and then pushed it into the cracks. Thus bound, the wheel carried the trio into Perm.

There, they decided to restring the wheel with fresh, strong rope, and to soak the mass in water to force the string to swell and fill in the cracks. The only tubs large enough for the soaking were in a public bathhouse. "Thus it came about that a sick wheel of a motor-car was sent to a hydro to take the waters."

The next morning, the wheel was back on the Itala by 4:00 A.M., and the crew was convinced it was cured. That was the day of the scrambled eggs and milk. Once they'd escaped those *telegas,* Borghese and crew were inundated by a violent storm. The rain was so intense they barely covered twenty-five miles over the next four hours. When the sun finally came out and the road began to dry, they got up to speed. But now the wheel was drying too. The creak became a groan, the groan grew to a shriek. A few yards more, and the Itala crashed to a stop. Prince Borghese jumped down, looked at the wheel, and said, "We're done for. We can't move another foot."

The Itala's wheel had splintered to pieces.

Our Hillman's tires were shredding with each rotation of the wheel, but we fig-ured we had enough rubber to make it safely to our next rest day in Istanbul. Traffic was light as I drove from the Sivas ring road southwest on a small country road. The countryside had mellowed into rolling hills—green, with red, orange and yellow fall leaves; whole gorges glowed red and golden. As the miles ticked away, I sang to myself. I completed my entire repertoire of memorized Joni Mitchell songs, then reached into the depths of my early childhood for Judy Collins and other folk classics. With not a single song lyric left in my head, I lis-tened to the air. The car was noisy still, but now that fall weather had finally arrived, we could ride with the windows up. Conversation might actually be pos-sible. I ventured a question to Linda.

"What would you do," I asked her, "if you had to get a job?"

"Oh, I dunno," she said, then thought for awhile. "Maybe get back into the bike tour business. Or run an art gallery—that might be fun."

"What do you—" Let me see, I thought, how do I put this? "You know," I started over, "most people spend their lives striving for wealth. You don't have to do that. Would you say there's something like that, something overriding that you consciously strive for?"

"Hmmm," she said. A few miles clicked by before she answered. "Truth."

"Truth?" I asked. After all that thought, I'd expected more than a one-word answer.

"Yes. Truth in relationships. It's very hard, you know, people always lie to pro-tect each other. Even family. It happens with my mother and my sister . . . and Geoff, he gets so defensive sometimes he's simply unable to hear the truth. But if you're not true to yourself and others, it just makes everything harder. I decided a long time ago that there are three things that will always get you into trouble: assumptions, expectations, and taking things personally. So I always keep those three things in mind, and I've found it really helps."

I thought about this as a few more miles unfolded. She was right—just about everything that had upset me on this journey so far could be attributed to an incorrect assumption, a dashed expectation, or taking an off-hand comment or action too personally.

"Do you think this rally will change your life?" I asked.

"Ask me a month after I get back home."

I told her I would.

"Do you want to know what really *did* change my life?" she offered.

"Motorcycling?" I guessed.

"Sort of—it was that trip I did across Australia. I'd only been separated for about six months, and my relationship with Geoff was still new. I'd gone back to San Francisco after that first tour and we had a mad, two-month love affair over the fax machine. As soon as I could, I flew back to Oz—took off on Christmas Eve and lost Christmas on the dateline. Geoff and I did another tour he called the Boomerang that was supposed to last eight days, but took twelve. After that he was tied up for two weeks, so I took off across Australia by myself on the bike. It took me eleven days to get to Perth and back, and then I joined him on his next tour.

"That solo trip felt to me like a walkabout. It was as if I had closed the door on the only life I knew up until then. That was the bridge I needed to my new life. Without that Perth trip, I wouldn't have even known about, much less considered, this Peking to Paris thing.

"There's something special about a solo journey," she said. "It's the only way to find out what you're really capable of."

We were now smack in the center of the country, in a region called Cappadocia (Kapadokya in Turkish), famous for amazing tufa and sandstone rock formations and caves. A tenth-century history called the residents here "troglodytes," because "they go under the ground in holes, clefts, and labyrinths, like dens, and burrows." In 1907, while Prince Borghese partied in Moscow, a French Jesuit riding through Cappadocia on horseback wrote "Our eyes were astounded. I remember those valleys in the searingly brilliant light, running through the most fantastic of all landscapes." From the car we could see some eroded spires, and entrances to a few cliff dwellings. Some three thousand rock churches fill the area between Kayseri, which we passed through at about 4:30 P.M., and the Ihlara Valley west of our night stop in Nevsehir. Only eight kilometers from our hotel was Göreme, a place *Lonely Planet* calls one of the most amazing sights in Turkey. Bright painted frescoes, protected from the aging effects of sunlight, cover the walls of these underground churches that date back to the eighth century. The soft rock hid these early Christians from the conquering Muslims.

Dick and the Jeepsters negotiated this territory with difficulty. The Jeep never had much power, but thanks to the exhaust problems, it would only go 15 to 20 mph climbing up even moderate slopes. At dusk, only about fifty kilometers from the night's stop in Nevsehir, they finally spotted a sign that said "otoeletrik." That's Turkish for auto-electrics, and the proprietor immediately understood their generator problem. With translation provided by a Turk who had lived in Australia, the proprietor agreed to provide a rebuilt alternator to replace the Jeep's failed generator, and his friend, in a shop across the street, fixed the exhaust system. "We placed our Jeep in their hands," Dick said, "explaining that we had to leave in two hours, or we were out of the competition. Miraculously the work was done very quickly and professionally."

At Nevsehir, after Linda handed in our time-card book at the TC, she discovered that, once again, we had to move on down the road to the secondary Kavas Hotel. With the exception of Golmud, the secondary hotels hadn't been all that bad; they were just inconvenient. This time, the difference was drastic. The huge, high-rise Dedeman was truly a first-class hotel, with over four hundred rooms (which made it seem all the more unlikely that there were no rooms for us). The down-at-heel Kavas reminded me of the tattered beach motels that post hourly rates in places like Venice, California, and Ocean City, New Jersey.

As we schlepped our bags up the moldy stairs to our room, we were met by Sylvia Esch, who with her father was piloting a '52 Mercedes Benz 300B. Sylvia spoke very little English (they were from Luxembourg and spoke German) but somehow the three of us talked about the hotel—how disgusting the rooms were (ours stank of cigarettes, and the brown carpet looked like the expectorations of a tobacco chewer) and how unfair it was that night after night, the same group of us always got shunted to the dumps. Sylvia said we should all complain to the organizers together.

Linda's emotions can seldom be read on her face, but behind her exterior calm, her anger seemed to have reached a critical mass. We set off—her much shorter legs stretched to the point where Sylvia and I had to trot to keep up— upon the half-mile or so that separated the two hotels. She started at the TC desk, accosting the marshals, and they fobbed her off onto the hotel concierge, who called to Sarah, Philip Young's overworked young assistant, to deal with these irate rally women. I was angry too, which felt very strange indeed, as I've overnighted voluntarily in much shabbier circumstances than those offered by the Kavas. Still, I got into the argument with Sarah about the unfairness of rewarding early payers. Philip, when he showed up, immediately personalized Linda's complaints. "Your room is unacceptable? We'll get you another one," he said, ignoring the fact that Sylvia Esch, the Tinzls, Dick Taylor and many other "late-payers," felt the same way.

"Look," I argued, "you've had all the money, even from us latest payers, more than six months before the rally started. That should've been plenty of time to book a sufficient number of rooms. Why weren't they all booked at once?"

Before Sarah could answer, Iskender, the Dedeman representative who'd been following us through the country, volunteered his own room in exchange for ours. While Sylvia continued the conversation with Sarah, Linda agreed to take Iskender's room. Before long, we'd reloaded our overnight bags into the Hillman, driven the half-mile back to the Dedeman, and installed ourselves into much more comfortable quarters—the general manager's room.

Over dinner, the discussion continued. As we ate and talked there in the banquet hall of a hotel that could easily accommodate more than twice our number, we decided that the real cause of the problem must be that Philip and company had assumed most of us would drop out sooner. If we'd been reduced from ninety-six cars to twenty-eight by Kathmandu, as Philip had expected, he'd have been stuck with a lot of empty hotel rooms. So he probably never booked them in the first place. When it became clear that there would be so many survivors (only a few weeks ago) it was too late to book more rooms in the classier hotels. If that were truly the case, it would have been much fairer to rotate us all through the available rooms. We were all equally guilty of surviving the Peking to Paris Motor Challenge.

After dinner, we'd all been invited to witness the Whirling Dervishes. I was aware this practice had to do with Sufi beliefs, but I knew little else about it, and I was curious. After having to pass by so many interesting sites along the route, I refused to miss this display, even though the gin and tonic I drank after the argument ended, combined with dinner, had made me very sleepy.

I sat with Don and Carl in the discotheque, an odd half-circular room with tables along the outer arc, and waited. It was after ten when seven men entered wearing long white dresses: chef-style shirts above full pleated skirts. On their heads were tall conical caps, which resembled elongated fezes. They sat still on their haunches in a row at the edge of the wooden floor. The music started— slow, traditional, distinctly middle-eastern. The men sat, and sat, and sat, doing nothing.

Oh! I suddenly realized, they were meditating. This is serious stuff, not quick-cut pop entertainment. But it made keeping my eyes open that much tougher; the slow music and motionless dervishes were soporific. I sat up, blinked my eyes, and vowed to stay until someone whirled.

They finally rose, and taking slow deliberate steps, began to turn. Not whirl, just turn, with a curious lilt to their toes, a practiced rhythm in their steps. Some stopped then and sat, others kept turning, rotating around the dance floor. The music, a monotonal drone overlaid with a subtle melody, grew a bit more insistent, and they finally began to whirl. Not the men—the skirts. The men were still just turning, but their voluminous cotton skirts fanned out into flowing cones of luminous white cloth. The men were in a trance, eyes closed or unfocused, their arms swinging out and around, hands perfectly relaxed, feet moving of their own accord. The heads moved too, at a different pace, the practiced once-around sweep of a ballet dancer, never seeming disturbed or unbalanced.

Every whirl worked like the swing of a hypnotist's watch, or a dose of some narcotic; I simply couldn't stay awake any longer. I snuck out of the dark disco while they were still in mid-whirl.

We had often talked of the moment when we should pass from one continent to the other, that fleeting and yet significant and memorable instant when we would end our journey over Asiatic soil. That instant was bringing to its close our journey across the whole of Asia, from its most distant point on the Pacific Ocean. ... A royal road of conquest and ideas, of religion and riches, of legends and trade, of armies and of gold.

NEVSEHIR TO ISTANBUL
[THURSDAY, OCTOBER 9]

I awoke still thinking about those mysterious dervishes. What did it all mean? There had been no introduction, no spoken words in English or Turkish. I found some explanation in a brochure that I picked up as we left the hotel. It made interesting reading on the 734-kilometer route between Nevsehir and Istanbul, with good roads and decent signage (which meant my job, navigation, was easy).

The dervishes date to 1207, when Mevlana Jelaleddin Rumi was born. He came to the Seljuk capital of Konya (southwest of Nevsehir) at the age of twenty-two, already a scholar of Arabic, Turkish, Greek, Hebrew and Persian, the official language of the Seljuk kings. "It was only at the age of thirty-seven," the brochure explained,

that Jelaleddin Rumi discovered the inner secrets of transcendental love. He took up poetry and immersed himself in passionate whirlings as he cited his ecstatic poems. During his lifetime Mevlana created a huge amount of poetry and prose which were collected in his Mesnevi (consisting of some 26,000 couplets) . . . above all, Mevlana was a champion of universal peace, of understanding and of divine and humanly love which he perceived as a single ideal:
> *Come, come again, whoever,*
> *Whatever you may be, come*
> *Heathen, fire-worshipper,*
> *sinner of idolatry, come*
> *Come even if you broke*
> *your penitence a hundred times,*
> *Ours is not the portal of despair*
> *or misery, come . . .*

The whirling ritual (Sema) is a very aesthetic ceremony, carrying to ecstasy and mesmerizing its spectators. The ethernal [sic] Mevlevi music is an inseparable part of this rite, which has influenced not only secular Turkish music, but other musical traditions, including jazz.

The attires of the whirling dervishes (Semazens), their gestures and motions all have symbolic significance. Their cloaks symbolize Mevlana's coffin, the white attires, his shroud and conical hats, his tombstone. But don't be misled by these macabre connotations. The whole Mevlevi philosophy as well as its serene and passionately beautiful rituals are full of joy from the heart and the mind.

After reading this, I wondered why we didn't have Whirling Dervishes in Santa Cruz, California. My hometown is known worldwide for attracting practitioners of alternative lifestyles, translated variously by the unsympathetic as kooks, cults, hippies, yogis, deadheads, trolls, witches, warlocks, freaks and other New Age denizens. Rumi would have been welcome.

I was homesick. Driving's intensity helps one to stay focused on the here, and forget the everywhere-else. There in the navigator's seat, though, all I could think about was my hometown, my husband, my daughter and my son. I missed them.

We had come south to Cappadocia, so now we turned north again, toward the capital city of Ankara. Our first TC sat in a petrol station on the modern high-speed ring road just south of the capital at Golbasi. From there we had almost five hundred kilometers of brand-new motorway, heading westward through the fall-colored hills and woods toward Istanbul. The highway was almost empty because the tolls made it too expensive for the locals. With only our fellow ralliers and big trucks for company, Linda kept up an average of 70 to 80 mph while we talked about the difference between driving cars and motorcycles.

"On the bike," she said, "it's so much more sensual—you're right out there, in the world, you can smell everything, and there's no frame like a windshield to close you in. The down side is obvious—it's not as safe in most cases. I say *most* because there have been situations—in Spain and in India—when being on the motorcycle *saved* my life. Those were places where there was no way a car could have squirmed through.

"But the very best part" she said, "is that I've never been on a bike trip when I haven't been approached by hundreds of people. This was especially true when I was on my own, when I went across Australia. Every time I stopped the bike someone came over to talk to me. They wanted to know where I'd come from, where I was going. In a car, you're isolated—from the world, from other people. No one talks to you. We've been getting a lot of attention on this rally, but that's because we're such a spectacle, especially back in those Third World countries. Notice how it's all died down now that we're back in civilization."

She was right; back when my husband and I had been doing long-distance bicycle rides, I'd experienced the same things; both the open-air sensuality of the ride, and the more open friendliness of people along the way. On a bicycle there's also the physical dimensions of time and geography; the world passes by so much more slowly, and with so much more effort, as you struggle up every grade. Still, I argued, a classic car—unlike a modern car—preserves much of the sensuality of the journey. Riding in an open roadster feels very much like riding a motorcycle, and even the 1960s cars don't really separate you from the world the way modern cars do.

"Maybe that's just because there's no air conditioning," Linda said.

"No, it's not just that," I answered. The stranger, more exotic or lovelier the classic car, the more likely people are to talk to you once you stop. I told her what happens when Chris and I and the kids drive around in our three-wheeled Messerschmitt, or in our little bubble-shaped Fiat 500. "People stare, with huge, surprised grins when we pass, then run over when we stop and assail us with questions: 'What is it?' 'How fast does it go?' 'My dad had one of these when I was a kid,' and 'I saw one of these in Italy,' or 'I saw one of these when I was stationed in Germany after the war. ...' A classic car can bring back some of that connection with people."

"That's not gonna happen with a Hillman Hunter," Linda said, and we both laughed.

The highway abruptly ended. We had come to Bolu Mountain, an area famous in Turkey for its cooking; in fact, our road book said the restaurant at Boludegi that served as our TC had excellent food. That was little consolation for what turned out to be the slowest-moving traffic jam of the rally so far. The many trucks that had been easily passed on the motorway now crept slowly down the steep mountain, with our rally cars sandwiched between them. Signs of construction made it clear that a tunnel would someday bypass this steep route, but for now we had no choice but to creep and crawl our way down the mountain.

From Dusce, where we regained the motorway, I could see on the map that Kara Deniz (the Black Sea) was only thirty-six kilometers north. The sight of the sea had become something I craved; not just for its symbolic significance as the beginning of the end of our journey, but as an evocation of home; I had lived on the California coast since I was nine. My homesickness had become a constant now, on this thirty-fourth day on the road.

Back in 1907, the Italian ralliers were thrilled when they caught their first glimpse of the sea. They had left Konigsberg in the German Empire, and were driving on good European roads. "We pass little villages, as graceful as if they had been made for some artist purposely to put in pictures," Barzini wrote, "with little lakes, ponds which reflect the green of the woods, and canals full of boats. Suddenly we give a cry of astonishment; down there on the horizon is the blue line of the sea! It is Frische Lagoon, an iridescent lake like a great shell. Far off, beyond it, is the Gulf of Danzig [Gdansk]. We joyfully greet this sea, whose waters come from the Atlantic. We cry to it: 'Welcome, old sea of our land! The Pacific

Ocean sends you his greetings!'"

I wanted to offer a similar greeting to the Sea of Marmara, but what should have been our first glimpse of blue was a gray streak largely obscured by smog and smokestacks. The authorities of the port city of Izmit apparently made no effort (or their efforts failed) to staunch the flow of thick black effluent from the many factories, trucks and tanker ships. What must once have been an awe-inspiring sight—the sea after so long a landlocked journey over the ancient Silk Road—was a depressing reminder of the terrible curse of modern industry.

It was fitting preparation for the road into Istanbul, "the center of this part of the world" as our Dedeman host Iskender had written, with a population estimated at fourteen million. We had been warned that Istanbul's traffic is "horrendous," and indeed, the cars and trucks on the famous Bosphorus Bridge (a modern construction built by Japanese and reminiscent of the other grand Japanese bridge we'd crossed in the middle of Nepal), were stopped dead. Through the smog, lighter here than in Izmit (the passenger cars were mostly small, fuel-efficient Fiat-based econoboxes), we could see quite a distance. Nearby I spotted Canadian Captain O'Neill's VW Cabrio, his daughter and her husband's Peugeot, and several other rally cars, sprinkled over the many lanes like classic car confetti. Way ahead, where I couldn't yet see, was another competitor, Bud Risser, in his red-and-white '55 Chevy. His passenger that day was Christina from Discovery, and her webpage article faithfully described the moment:

> We arrive at the Bosphorus bridge at rush hour. The Bel Air jolts and heaves with heat fatigue. Halfway across, the car stalls. Smoke begins to billow from under the hood. "Fire!" Bud yells and scampers out to raise the hood. I follow with the fire extinguisher. Cars honk, commuters gesture with exasperation. Standing on the cusp of Europe and Asia, we watch flames engulf the air filter, before we put out the fire with a squirt of powdered foam.

Fuel vaporizing around loose wires caused the fire, and though the wiring was now a mess, Bud got the car going again without much delay. Linda and I successfully navigated the crowded maze of Istanbul by following the Peugeot, which followed the VW, which followed a taxi driver paid to drive to the Dedeman hotel. Serious ralliers might consider it cheating, but this method of third-party navigation was legal for this competition; it was even recommended in the road book.

We clocked in at 6:12 P.M., handing our second time-card book to the marshal. I zipped our second road book into the Hillman's navigator pocket, permanently. The rally was now officially two-thirds over. Only four thousand kilometers to go.

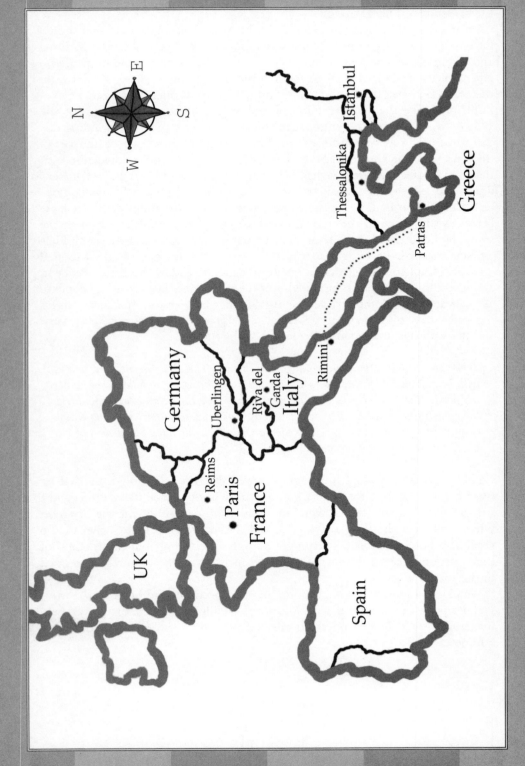

ISTANBUL
TO
PARIS

CHAPTER

～ 39 ～

It is a city both Western and Eastern at the same time, and in which matters of business are up-to-date and the fashions are old.

ISTANBUL

[FRIDAY, OCTOBER 10]

From the Dedeman we were promptly directed to a second hotel, but before either Linda or I could utter a word, we were told—quietly so our Dedeman sponsors wouldn't hear—that the Plaza Cevahir Hotel was actually nicer. It was also more convenient to the car park, which was in a locked "Gendarmerie" barracks, right across the street.

We got up early on the morning of our final rest day to meet with "Tipsy," (his business card said Ahmet Ziyalar, General Manager of Ar Otomotiv). Tipsy had volunteered to direct the cars to appropriate repair shops. He gave us directions to a nearby tire shop, and we set off for the barracks. Our needs were minimal, we thought: two new tires. We were now wearing out fronts and backs; the Pakistani alignment had lessened the front tire wear but not eliminated it, and our loose rear axle was now shaving the rears.

The damp night air had deposited heavy dew all over the Hillman's windshield. I flipped on the wipers to clean it, and nothing happened. The wipers were dead. Time for a new wiper motor? Or was this just another manifestation of the demon Lucas? We'd have to find out if we wanted to see in the rain.

I realized then how lucky we'd been weather-wise. A freak ten-minute rainstorm in Nepal, and one or two wet days in China. For an autumnal journey across Asia, the odds of there being as many dry days as we'd experienced seemed improbably high.

We had the car at the tire shop by 8:30 A.M. The place was tucked underneath a highway overpass and beside the busy boulevard, so traffic noise was amplified two or threefold. Speech was impossible—even if we spoke the same language, we wouldn't have been able to hear. Through sign language, we made the shop owner understand what we needed. Then we waited, but we had nowhere to go to

escape from that audio torture chamber. Though the men worked diligently, balancing our two new "Toyos," mounting them and aligning the car by 9:45, we both had massive headaches when we left.

Now there was just the matter of the windshield wipers. We had no idea where to go, but on the way back to the hotel, we spotted a Mercedes Benz dealer. We pulled in, thinking such an upscale dealership would have an English-speaking salesperson, with knowledge of repair facilities nearby. We found a woman who spoke very limited English. She recommended we go to "Modern Oto." How do we get there? She drew a map with a long straight line that turned left. She labeled the straight line "Atatürk Sanesi Stesi," marked "Petrol Ufisi" to signify the gas station we should pass, then wrote "Modern Oto" at the top.

We were on Atatürk Sanesi, we thought, so it seemed easy enough—one block up and left. We decided to hire a taxi to follow, just in case. The taxi stepped on it, and we followed him. Next thing we knew, we'd gone more than ten kilometers, out to a suburb called Maslak. This wasn't just any suburb; it was a whole town of auto-related shops. We couldn't tell the scale of it at first, but found out from Carl Schneider later that there were 128 acres with over two thousand different auto shops, including new and used car dealers, specialty brake and electrical shops—a gigantic auto-mall.

Modern Oto turned out to be a Mercedes specialist, and sure enough, two of the rally Mercedes, the '27 630K and the black '65 220A (the same one that had hit the Tibetan) were already there. This was a sophisticated, bilingual shop, but the second language wasn't English, it was German. We had to ask one of the Germans to translate for us.

"Oh, electrics?" The man in charge shook his head. We were told to go down around the corner. We found Kaya Elektronik Ltd. easily enough, but no one there knew any English. I tried my French and Italian, but only German or Turkish would do. We telephoned Modern Oto, and once they'd located our German compatriot, had him explain to Mr. Kaya that we needed both wipers and headlights repaired.

The shop was very busy, so between other customers and the language difficulties, it wasn't until around noon that we learned a new wiper motor had been ordered, but wouldn't be delivered for several hours. With much frustration we figured out that they'd need to keep the car at least until 4:00 P.M. So we got in a taxi and went back to the hotel, both of us holding our aching heads.

After medication (aspirin) and lunch in the hotel's restaurant, we took a taxi downtown to check out the major sights: Sancta Sophia, the Blue Mosque, and maybe the Topkapi Palace.

"It's Istanbul not Constantinople . . ." I'd had that novelty song in my head ever since the Bosphorus Bridge. I knew the basic history one learns in Western Civ: the ancient capital city of Byzantium turned into Constantinople when the Roman Emperor Constantine moved there in about 300 AD. Two hundred years later the Emperor Justinian started construction of the greatest cathedral in all Christendom: the Ayasofya (translated variously as Hagia Sophia or Sancta

Sophia). Today this church is the fourth largest in the world, after St. Peter's in Rome, St. Paul's in London, and the Duomo in Milan. Or it would be if it were still a church. Back in 1453, it was converted to a mosque, and then in 1930 Atatürk turned it into a museum.

The many-domed pink exterior is impressive, but faded. The interior, now hollow and somewhat dingy, shows evidence of a glorious past. From the level of the vast floor, the green-speckled marble columns and gold-filigreed pulpit impresses first. From the gallery, the huge hanging medallions bearing gilt inscriptions dominate the view. Many of the walls and interior domes have suffered serious water damage; all are in need of restoration. We walked around eyeing the ancient Christian mosaics, eventually wandering back outside. We crossed the plaza toward the Blue Mosque.

A carpet salesman latched onto us. I'd been warned that this is the signature tourist experience of Turkey. These charming gentlemen, some of them dashingly handsome, first offer to be your guide through whatever sights you'd like to see. They work the tourist circuit with you and then take you to the carpet "factory" or the carpet "museum." Ours was young and good-looking and had excellent English, but we brushed him off immediately. "We're not buying anything," Linda said, before he'd gotten very far into his spiel.

The Blue Mosque (or Sultanahmet) was, as the predominantly Muslim Turks no doubt intended, much more impressive than its faded neighbor. The silver-white building bulged with many more domes, and its six thin minarets jabbed rocket-like into the sky. We tucked our shoes into a plastic bag and went inside; delicate tile work covered every surface—white with intricate floral designs in bright greens, blues, purples and reds—and bands of gold-inscribed blue edged every panel. More gold-encrusted, intertwined inscriptions climbed like banners around and up into the high central dome. The only less-aesthetic note was the metal frame holding the low-hanging electric lights. Knowing that this was a working mosque and that those lights were needed for worship somehow made up for the intrusion, and gave the place a holy feel that was definitely lacking at Ayasofya.

We emerged and unbagged our shoes in bright sunshine, and decided we had time for a little walk. Accosted by many of the young urchins who sold postcards ("One dollar! One dollar!"), I finally succumbed, and was glad. I bought one twelve-card set of the Ayasofya and another set of the Sultanahmet. All of Sophia's mosaics and the Sultan's tiles were now in my pocket, and I'd made the kid rich (two US dollar bills equaled 336,000 lira. Of course, with the current inflation rate, he'd be poor again in a week).

On the turistico map I'd brought from the hotel, the Topkapi Palace seemed nearby. We headed into Gülhane Park and walked for a while before we found the palace's exterior wall. We seemed to be directly behind the entrance. Which way around would bring us there quicker? We picked a direction, and walked, and walked. We found the Gülhane's lover's lane (where a lot of groping was going on under scarves and big coats) but not the entrance to the palace. The wall ended at the top of a bluff overlooking the Bosphorus and the Golden Horn, reward enough for our long walk. I later learned that the Topkapi was not just a palace, but a huge complex containing the palace, a church, mosque, and three museums surrounded by gardens. Originally built by Ottoman Sultan Mehmet in the fifteenth century, the complex was elaborated on by every Sultan that followed over the five-hundred-year Ottoman history.

It was time to catch a taxi back to Maslak and our Hillman. Once we arrived, we could see they had our new wiper motor, but it had not yet been installed. The proprietor offered us tea in those characteristic Turkish tulip glasses, and we sat listening to the shop radio blare Turkish pop music—it had a fast, jazzy beat that I liked—for another hour and a half.

When the Itala's wheel broke, it left Prince Borghese and crew stranded some four miles from the nearest village, at about eleven o'clock in the morning. The car could not be moved—not even pulled by horses—and so Borghese cobbled a temporary fix by splicing small bits of wood, like extra spokes, into the sundered wheel, and wrapping the whole thing in string. Before this laborious process was completed, an old Mujik came by and informed the trio that the best cartwright in the region lived only three miles away. Borghese's wheel creaked and groaned terribly as the Itala crept to the carriage-builder's small white house. There, the cartwright and his assistant fashioned an exact duplicate out of aged pinewood, using nothing more than their expert hatchets. "The hatchet becomes in the hands of the Russian peasant a wonderfully exact tool," Barzini wrote in admiration. The cartwright fashioned the metal rim in his forge, put in the screws and tightened the nuts. "In less than it takes to say so, Ettore put the wheel back in its place on the machine; it was seven P.M. when we got on our way again."

The Jeepsters had to devote their entire rest day in Istanbul to repairs. Coming into the city, the Jeep had quit running entirely just after the final TC, and had to be towed to the parking lot. In his report to the *Republic,* Dick wrote:

> Yet another rest day without rest or any opportunity for sightseeing in this historic city bridging Asia and Europe. We spend the day finding auto parts and working on the Jeep. This time, however, we make real progress, solving our remaining exhaust, ignition and fuel system problems with some assistance from other competitors. The spirit of cooperation among everyone is marvelous, as we all understand that we are competing to overcome the adversities of twelve thousand kilometers in many foreign countries, and it pulls us together.

That night, Dedeman and the Klasïk Otomobïl Klübü sponsored a big reception for us, with special awards and a floorshow. The ballroom was filled to capacity with ralliers, Turkish press and TV crews, the Governor and who's-who of Istanbul. Linda and I arrived a little late, and as we walked past the table containing the crew of Mr. Sparkle—the pink Rolls Royce sponsored by Coopers-Lybrand and the *Financial Times*—I thought I heard someone say something like "Not good enough for you, are we?"

Surprised, I said something like "Are you talking to me?" John Stuttard (I think) said, "You're welcome to join us," and waved at the empty seat beside me. Linda continued on, joining the Jeepsters about two tables away. How could I refuse an offer from such a cultured gentleman? Both John and his co-driver Gordon Barrass had impressed me as true British gentlemen, not in terms of class, but in terms of courtesy, erudition, sophistication and humor (the latter evidenced more by the sparkly pink paint than anything else). Roy O'Sullivan, their mechanic, always seemed to be assisting another rallier. I sat opposite a man I'd never seen before, and he turned out to be a new crew member named David Colvin. He'd flown in from Brussels, where he's a diplomat in Her Majesty's Belgian Embassy.

The speeches began, first from the President of the Dedeman Group (who introduced the founder, his ninety-two-year-old father), then the Governor and Mayor of Istanbul. Some spoke only in Turkish; others alternated between Turkish and heavily-accented English.

Then came the prizes, sponsored by the Klasïk Otomobïl Klübü. The first prize went to the first car into Istanbul, Surtees and Bayliss, the two British gents in the Willys Jeep. Next was called "Gentleman of the Rally," and was given to Kjeld Jessen, a Dane driving one of the open Bentleys. What was that about, I wondered. Linda and I had only spoken with Jessen twice, and both times he'd been barely civil. I thought any of the men at my table would've been more deserving.

Then I realized that Mr. Jessen must have done something—perhaps many things—that I didn't know about. Journalist or no, I couldn't keep track of eighty-five cars and two hundred people from twenty-two countries over all forty-three days (well, thirty-five so far). Then, naturally, Francesca Sternberg won the "Lady of the Rally" prize, to balance out that Gentleman's prize, no doubt, though once again I wondered at the criteria. How did these Turkish car club guys decide on who won what? Perhaps I was a little jealous, but I wasn't surprised. Besides, I thought (thinking of our three-and-a-half hour lead), at least this way the Gulls would win something.

Another award went to Don and Carl for "Overcoming Adversity." Now this one I understood: with two days, fourteen hours, fifty minutes of penalties and a Packard that people teasingly called a road plow (it still sat low on its beleaguered suspension), Carl and Don definitely deserved this one. Don gave an entertaining thank-you speech, singing a bar from "I Left My Heart in San Francisco" and holding out his belt to show how many new notches he'd had to cut into it.

The final "official" prize went to Gerry Acher and Bruce Young, who'd struggled all twelve thousand kilometers in their tiny 1932 Aston Martin International. It was for "Overcoming Adversity" in the Vintage class, similar to Don and Carl's award for the Classic class. Philip then announced that the Vintage Class One—under 4.1 liter engine capacity—was being split into two categories. This redressed a terrible imbalance: before, the 1500cc 1932 "baby" Aston Martin, the 607cc Citroën 2CV and the 4000cc Team Retro Fords had all been in the same class! There'd been some resentment against the Fords anyway, and not just because of their larger displacement: thanks to the devastation of World War II, European automotive technology in 1950 was far behind American.

The support crew, Jingers and Tony and the rest, then awarded their own special prize. They called it the "Richard Head" (i.e., Dickhead) award and it went to David Arrigo's Allard, the car that had damaged our door that long-ago day in Tianjin. The Allard had been the support crew's bane, apparently, as it had broken down just about every day of the event.

Then, the stage went dark and a spotlight came on, illuminating a spinning, four-foot-high world globe! I almost laughed out loud, despite the serious tone of the music; all I could think of was "As the Worm Turns," the old Carol Burnett soap-opera parody I'd watched as a kid. A man in a skintight "black-tie" leotard and a woman in a shiny silver body suit danced out, rushing to each other in an overwrought pas-de-deux. If Prince Borghese witnessed any such "Dance of the Ralliests," Barzini has kindly drawn a veil.

CHAPTER

40

"We were eager to pass the Russian frontier; I do not know why; we had the impression that on the other side the difficulties of our journey would be ended; we harboured, in fact, the glad illusion that our progress beyond that spot would be reduced to a long series of promenades."

ISTANBUL, TURKEY TO THESSALONIKI, GREECE
[SATURDAY, OCTOBER 11]

We clocked out of Istanbul at 6:49 A.M. In the dim early light, we discovered that our headlights were still inoperable, in spite of all those hours at electrics shops. The rising sun allowed us to put aside our headlight worries as we traveled the 260 kilometers of motorway into Greece, our entry into the European Union. Why does every border, after so many crossed, still cause a visceral thrill? Turkey's land was beautiful, its history fascinating and its people welcoming and pleasant, but we still couldn't wait to cross that line.

At the border, the Turkish volunteers, including our good buddy Iskender, gave us a grand *Güle Güle*—translated as "go with a smile." On the other side, a lovely Greek woman handed us a bundle through the window: two "Elva" petroleum company duffel bags (evidently our sponsors in Greece), T-shirts, two pens, and a box of cookies. We waited for someone to ask for our passports, but we were waved on through, past a couple of gun-toting guards looking bored as they leaned against a bridge railing. A low cement-bottomed water splash served the purpose of the rutted lane between Iran and Turkey. Nine kilometers later a sign said *Welcome to the Country of Gods, Heros* [sic] *and Civilization*.

This border crossing was the slickest yet, bureaucratically speaking, but I struggled at the low speeds required to roll through: the gearshifter balked going into first and second. It took a good shove, and, I learned, a pump or two on the clutch. Third and fourth, and our handy overdrive, were unaffected. So as long as we could cruise at speed, the gear problem was easily forgotten.

To celebrate yet another border crossed, I stopped the car just outside the next town, Alexandropouli. Since we'd left Marco Polo and the Silk Road behind, we'd picked up—in reverse—the route Alexander the Great took when he set out to conquer the East. Alexander, born in Macedonia in 356 BC, flashed across the

known world like a meteor. Taught by Aristotle and a big fan of Homer's heroic epics, the young conqueror took Anatolia and Persia, was crowned Pharaoh of Egypt, founded Alexandria there, and even invaded the Punjab before retreating to Ekbatana (Hamadan) and trying to establish a new race of Greek-Iranians to people his empire. When he died suddenly at the age of thirty-three, he had been deified, but he had left his empire's government in a shambles. Still, the Greek culture he brought left an indelible stamp on Central Asia.

We both needed a pitstop, so I parked the Hillman next to a small Pizzeria. Across the street and behind a thin row of trees lay the Aegean Sea. Not land-locked lakes and rivers like the "seas" around Istanbul; this was a true sea, and it reminded me all too much of home. I ordered Cokes while Linda walked off to find the restroom.

I had stopped to celebrate, but instead I was overtaken with sadness. I had never felt so alone. I sat at the little outdoor table with our drinks, watching the occasional rally car drive by, on the verge of tears. Linda reappeared. She'd found a little market next to the cafe and bought a couple of bars of Cadbury's chocolate. She opened one, and I laughed about the healing powers of that marvelous sweet, but inside I felt beyond healing.

The ever-present worry of arriving late at the next checkpoint was part of it, but the feeling was a fundamental kind of loneliness, the kind reserved for the lack of the ones you love most. Perhaps, too, it was the realization that Linda and I had forged a friendship that would only go so far. Besides the rally, what did we have in common? In my depression, it seemed there might not be much.

Back on the road, the route, and navigation, grew trickier. The signs were almost all in those mathematical Greek letters, and there were now many little roads to choose from. Linda worked assiduously at the constant math required to adjust for our trip-meter's error, and only once did we head down the wrong road, but we soon realized our error and turned around. The Aegean shimmered in the sun-light on one side, the mountains of Thrace loomed on the other. When we turned inland toward Komotini, we wound through rustic villages nestled between olive groves and cotton fields. From Xanthi we turned south again, heading back to the coast and the city of Kavala. The crenelated gray walls of its thirteenth-century Byzantine citadel dominated the city, and across the water we could see the island of Thassos.

Then we headed inland again, but before we lost sight of the sea, we spotted Mount Athos rising in the blue distance. We regained the Gulf of Strimon (Strimonikos) fifty kilometers later, and turned westward to skim the northern shores of Lake Volvi and Lake Koronia. These roads had once hosted super-fast stages of the Acropolis Rally; professional drivers took sedans like our Hillman over these roads at speeds up to 100 mph. It was motorsports' toughest event in the 1960s, and is part of the pro-rally circuit to this day.

From Langadas the road became a major tourist route that funneled us quickly into Thessaloniki (Salonica). We were due at 6:01, but we arrived almost a full hour early. We parked right on the strand, between the roadway and the water, and the curving bay offered a lovely view of the old port town. The afternoon had brought a warm haze that hovered over the water; on a clearer day, we would have been able to see Mount Olympus in the south.

Those balking gears needed attention, so I requested help from the volunteer Greek mechanics. Alas, they were overworked; too many of us needed help. While I waited my turn, I consulted other competitors for diagnoses. Maybe we'd sprung a leak, and lost all our transmission fluid (or it had gunked up or something). Checking it meant putting the car up in the air and climbing under. We jacked up one end, and with the Iranians' help, discovered the fluid was fine. Next I consulted Vic and Andy. Their theory was that the clutch slave cylinder needed bleeding, since air bubbles in the hydraulic system could cause the clutch to hang up. These two southern gentlemen did the work for us (one pumped the clutch while the other carefully opened the bleeder valve and refilled the clutch fluid reservoir). We ordered manual transmission lube from the Greek mechanic; if the problem were internal to the transmission, we hoped the lube would ease up the shifting.

The Makedonia Palace Hotel had a broad veranda bar, where everyone who wasn't working on his car gathered. Once the Hillman was squared away, we joined Vic, Andy and Ted Thomas. Ted, Phil Surtees and John Bayliss had already had a beer or two; Ted wore a comical hat that looked like a Hawaiian shirt tied in knots. The men were all laughing, but the discussion had a serious edge—Phil and John had tossed two-week-old rotten eggs out the window of their leading Jeep back toward the Ford. They claimed they'd discovered their eggs had gone bad and were merely disposing of them, but Ted and Vic knew better. "I could smell those things from 200 feet behind," Ted said. "You may have mobility, but we've got power. If that fails, we still have a few tricks up our sleeves."

Linda and I hadn't socialized much with Phil or John. Phil always seemed to be on edge—he took the competition very seriously. He was a serious rallier in any case; he'd lost two fingertips in a rally accident not long before the start of the Peking to Paris. And only a few months after we were due in Paris, Phil planned to drive the grueling LEJOG, a British rally that runs from the southwestern tip of England at Land's End to the northeastern tip of Scotland at John O'Groats. That event requires twenty-four-hour driving stints in nasty winter weather.

As the current leader of the rally, Phil had every right to worry. He knew his four-minute lead over Ted and Vic's Ford was vulnerable. "All I need is a puncture and I've lost," he said. "I'm praying over those Michelins."

He was on the defensive, too, about his Jeep. Rumors had erupted back before Istanbul that the '42 Willys was technically illegal. Dick Taylor, for one, wondered how a Jeep twenty years older than his had so much more power, especially up the hills. The answer was a 1950s-era overhead cam conversion that Phil had put on his earlier motor. Was it legal? That question had to be decided by FIVA, the *Fédération International des Véhicules Anciennes*, the rally-oversight organization. Several FIVA stewards had visited the rally in different cities; Linda and I had shared a pleasant dinner with Henk Bruers, a Belgian FIVA rep. Now, faxes on this question were supposedly flying back and forth between FIVA headquarters and the rally office.

There was also a residue of resentment toward all the four-wheel-drive vehicles, which had focused on Phil and John as the leaders. Now, with modern roads, the advantage the Jeep had back on those terrible roads of China and Pakistan should disappear. In reality, the time allowances in the Vintage class were so generous, the Jeep's slower speed, which wasn't so slow thanks to their upgraded engine, turned out to be plenty fast enough.

Clearly, for those in the top ten, these were hot issues. Further down the line, many once-competitive drivers no longer worried about time penalties. That afternoon, for example, Thomas and Maria Noor, in their grand Mercedes with the backseat cooler, celebrated their arrival in Greece with a forty-nine-minute lobster lunch on the waterfront at Kavala. It dropped them from fifteenth place to nineteenth, and they didn't care—this was Greece!

Though Linda and I both professed not to care, I checked our progress against the Gulls every night. I couldn't help it. We still held our three-hour-thirty-seven-minute lead.

Our numbers had miraculously swollen since Istanbul. Crew changes were expected—Fran Risser flew in from Florida to join her husband Bud in the Chevy Bel Air, and several sons traded places with daughters to join their fathers—but less expected was the return of three cars and crews we'd lost long before. Lord Montagu, who'd been renting modern transport ever since the Nepal border in order to keep up, had a Blower Bentley delivered from his home (the National Motor Museum in England). David and Adele Cohen, South Africaners-turned-Canadians, were back in a rare eight-liter Bentley (they'd had the Stutz in China), and finally, the flamboyant Hermann Layher was back, meeting the rally at the Greece-Turkey border. The sound of that 1907 La France "Funkenblitzen" ka-chunking down the road was unmistakable. And Hermann the German, though outspoken as ever, had the look of one recently chastened. "Back in China," he told Robert of the Discovery crew, "I remember hearing the voice of my mama: Do you have a pullover for the Himalayas?" This time he was prepared; when the La France chugged into Thessaloniki, Hermann was well bundled in a sheep-skin-lined leather overcoat.

That night, I joined Bud and Fran Risser and Michael Kunz as they set out to explore the town and find dinner. Thessaloniki, named after Alexander the Great's sister, is the capital of Macedonia province and the second largest city in Greece. It was the second largest in Byzantium, too, but suffered a succession of conquests that beleaguered it through the centuries. There's still a Turkish feel, left over from the Ottoman rule that didn't end until 1912; a beautiful white-stone tower built by sixteenth-century Turks dominates the waterfront. We walked past that tower, through a sea of parked tour buses, into narrow, boutique-filled streets. An earthquake in 1978 caused substantial damage, so the rebuilt streets have a modern feel.

At first we seemed to have the town to ourselves. We settled at a nearly empty restaurant with a large outdoor patio. By the time our food was served, though, the streets had come to life, and the tables around us had filled. Everyone came out to walk: families with little kids, old folks, and thousands of teenagers. So many of the latter, I wondered if Thessaloniki was a college town. The scene reminded me of Italy's nightly *passegiata,* when the whole town, in cities large and small, gathers on the main *piazza* to walk, talk, see and be seen.

The wine was an excellent Macedonika red, and my meal was a wonderful oven-baked dish called Hanoumaki—veal baked in a tomato, potato and egg-plant stew, all covered with melted cheese. It was a beautiful night, with a radi-ant moon, and very pleasant company. My mid-morning depression, for the moment, was forgotten.

That speed inebriated and dazed us. Not so much for the physical sensation of its swift-
ness, not so much for the mad joy of flight which is the essence of the passion of the
motor-car, but rather through a deep, full, and inexpressible intellectual satisfaction, that
came from being there.

THESSALONIKI TO KAMENA VOURLA
[SUNDAY, OCTOBER 12]

The stage from Thessaloniki to Kamena Vourla provided, perhaps, the best driving roads of the whole event. Turkey's geography had been as varied and beautiful, but we'd been routed across the country in such a hurry we'd had to keep to straight, fast roads. The mountains of Greece now gave us steep curvy roads with hairpins and surprising views; most had new paving. Our road book said many of these roads were gravel in the 1960s when the Acropolis Rally ran through. Now, stretches of gravel were scarce. This was the kind of driving classic ralliers dream about.

We circled Thessaloniki's bay down to Katerini, heading straight toward Mount Olympus. Distant heavy clouds threatened rain, but the sunlight that managed to slice through cut rays so majestic one immediately thought of Zeus and Apollo, piercing the clouds for sport. We cut westward on the mountain's northern edge, then circled around on a small road, past the spot where the local Olympic games were held in the fifth century, through the tiny village of Aghios Dimitrios and back down onto the plain and the village of Elasson. On the map, these roads are so skinny you need a magnifying glass to see them.

A forty-four kilometer special stage had been set up before Kalambaka with a time allowance of fifty-three minutes. These tiny roads, some of them still gravel, with frequent turns to Greek-only-labeled hamlets, were a challenge for both navigator and driver. We didn't get lost, and Linda easily kept the pace at the required average of 30 mph, giving her arms a great workout. We came quickly around one of the last turns and almost missed the TC out of simple inertia; the organizer's Vauxhall was parked in a narrow turnout, with hardly any room to stop before it. Linda pulled us off in time, we got our stamp, and immediately set off again. Only a few hundred yards on, we were stunned by the sight of an ancient

building perched high on the top of an eroded rock pillar.

It was one of the Metéora monasteries. We stopped the car as soon as we could, on the next pullout. Now we could see many more, on top of every promontory in sight. There were twenty-four altogether, built between the fourteenth and sixteenth centuries, though now only four are working monasteries. The geology of the area is amazing on its own: the black-and-red rock pillars are thought to be large salt deposits left over from a primordial sea. With these immense man-made structures on top, the sight was breathtaking.

How could they have been built? Before suspension bridges were added in the twentieth century, the only way up was on an extremely long rope ladder, or in a rope basket pulled up by the monks. Each brick and plank had to be lifted in the same fashion. Once these ropes were pulled up, the monasteries were virtually inaccessible. That was the point, of course; they were built in a time when Christians sought refuge from persecutors and foreign invaders. As in Cappadocia, Turkey, the Christians first went underground; ninth-century hermits built a church below the rocks called Stous Ayious. A monk named Athanasios the Meteorite was the first to build his monastery in the air in 1356. His successors followed in his lofty footsteps, seeking security in mid-air.

The rocks looked familiar, and for a moment I wondered if I'd seen them on some TV travel show. Then I remembered the image of a rope-dangling hero, dodging machine gun bullets: Roger Moore hung out here, as James Bond, in *For Your Eyes Only*. That 1981 movie helped to make the nearby towns of Kastraki and Kalambaka popular tourist destinations.

We couldn't pause to explore any of the interiors, of course (some of the monasteries have well-preserved frescoes). Instead we drove down into Kalambaka, where a buffet lunch had been arranged for us. I sat with the Peugeot 404 (#76) crew. These were the two men who'd passed us in Tibet, their dust blinding us. British Paul Grogan and French Paul Minassian (the only Frenchman on the rally) drove so aggressively that Linda and I weren't alone in thinking them reckless. Before now, I'd hardly said hello, on purpose. After our accident, I'd heard that they'd left their time-card book behind at Lanzhou—an automatic six-hour penalty. Instead of slowing them down, the error seemed to make them even crazier, as if driving faster would make up for that big chunk of time they'd lost.

I thought all this but said nothing about it during lunch. That accident was old news now; my resentment had mostly faded away. I asked them how they were doing, and we talked amiably about the rally. "This isn't a real rally," Grogan complained. "It's a joyride. The times are ridiculously generous."

"Perhaps that's because there are so few experienced ralliers here," I said.

"Maybe so," Grogan answered. He didn't say it in so many words, but it was clear he was disappointed to be competing against so many rank amateurs.

Back in the Hillman, we set off down onto the Thessalian plain and then climbed back up into the next range of mountains, where more Acropolis rally roads gave Linda another chance to work her biceps. I looked out the window and imagined flying along these same roads, in a similar (or newer) car, with Chris sitting beside me.

About mid-afternoon, it began to drizzle. The road immediately grew slick, so Linda slowed up. As we came down around a corner, we saw two cars, Howard Bellm's Camaro and a Dutch-crewed Volvo, stopped in the middle of a bridge. Getting onto the bridge required a hard right turn, and it looked as though the two cars had crashed.

We stopped and asked if they needed our assistance, and they waved us on. It turned out only the Volvo had crashed—they'd spun in the slick and bashed their fender against the bridge. Howard had only stopped to help.

While we zipped around pretending to be 1960s rally drivers, Dick Taylor piloted his underpowered, overly heavy Jeep up the steep, curvy roads. "The only vehicles we could pass were tractors pulling heavily-laden trailers or parked cars," Dick told me. "Buses, heavy trucks and even mopeds zipped by us with ease. With visions of Stirling Moss-like four-wheel power slides cornering on these mountain gravel roads dancing in our heads, we endured ten miles-an-hour crawling up the hills."

Linda didn't complain about driving all those twisty roads, but she didn't seem to be too happy about it, either. The local auto club greeted us when we pulled into Kamena Vourla's Hotel Astin Galini, with their fancy cars (mostly sports cars, like Fiat Spiders, MGs, and Austin Healeys). They handed each of us a big bronze medal, a Greek flag, and an oversized club calendar. As we unloaded our bags for the night, Linda grumbled that she was "tired of the whole thing." Sheila Morris, unloading Mr. Blobby nearby, asked: "When did the worm turn?"

"Oh," Linda answered, "about a week ago. This thing is about two weeks too long."

CHAPTER

∽ 42 ∼

The burning desert, the wild prairies, where the camels and antelopes live, seemed now things of a dream or a nightmare. The change had been violently sudden; all was altered—landscape, people, climate. We felt as if we had been transported out of Asia by some magic power.... The change enraptured us. We found ourselves suddenly in surroundings like those of our native land.

KAMENA VOURLA, GREECE TO SUPERFAST FERRY
[MONDAY, OCTOBER 13]

Greece, with a population of ten million, hosts eleven million tourists each year. The people extend a spontaneously friendly welcome everywhere in the country. At one of our first gas stops in Greece, still far in the north away from the crowded coast, as we fiddled with our drachma trying to gather the right amount to pay, the gas station proprietor waved all the money away. I thought he meant I'd offered the wrong bills, but he said, "No, no, for rally, petrol is free! Please!"

That morning as we prepared to leave the fishing-village turned health-spa resort of Kamena Vourla, a battered commode sat on the hood of the support crews' white Vauxhall Frontera. A note taped to it read "Please don't forget my throne, Prince Idris. Passing people say this is the best car to carry it as it has the most bullshit of any."

I hadn't spent any time with Prince Idris Shah or his co-driver Richard Curtis since that night in Kerman. There seemed to be a practical joke war heating up between the support crew and the Bentley boys (Dimples and Adam) and, apparently, the Prince. Now that the good-quality roads and familiar cultural conditions had eased the "challenge," there was more energy and time to goof off.

The day was originally to have contained over six hundred kilometers of tiny mountain roads, heading first around Mount Parnassos, then the long way around the Peloponnese. Thanks to the controversy that had swirled around the possibility of some ralliers missing the ferry, the marshals had slashed the route by two hundred kilometers. We were now supposed to stick to the coastal motorway straight from Corinth to Patras.

It was my turn to drive, and normally I prefer the longer, twistier routes. But today, those Olympian clouds that had teased us with a few sprinkles the day

260

before, let loose. In the rain, I am a far less aggressive driver. The only accident I've ever had in my many years of driving was caused by a rain-slick road (I spun my little Fiat 600 around two or three times, bashing it into both guardrails on a free-way cloverleaf. Luckily, no other cars were near).

At first the rain didn't matter. We were on modern highway up to Thermopylai, where a monument commemorates the spot where King Leonides and his three hundred Spartans sacrificed themselves to the Persians in 480 BC. From there, we turned south, across the Kalidromo plain, toward Delphi and Mount Parnassos. The rain slowed me down as we ascended, then descended, the tight wet turns of the 28.5-kilometer "speed stage." The required average speed to come in "clean" was 33 mph. I was one minute late at the TC, which means I averaged 32 mph. That felt plenty fast enough for me on those rain-slick hairpins, but I still felt bad; it was our first penalty since Quetta.

Up at the head of the pack, this special stage created a little excitement. The "blue book" Vintageants, which included both the leading Jeep and Ted and Vic in the second-place Ford, had thirty-eight minutes. The Ford cruised up and down the wet road and arrived with eight minutes to spare. The leading Jeep barely made it; the rain and a balking clutch delayed them. "We slipped all the way down the hill and made the time check with twenty seconds to spare," Surtees told the Discovery crew.

That stretch illustrated the advantages of taking turns: while I was busy driving, Linda wrote in the road book "Rainbows!" I missed them. Eight-and-a-half kilometers later, though, I stopped the car where Linda told me the road book said "Fantastic view of Vale of Delphi and sea to RIGHT." Though the rain clouds obscured the ancient oracle's valley, the view of the mist-shrouded mountains was ample reward for the difficult drive up.

The next section took us down towards Thebes and Eleusis, and we avoided Athens and the busy ports of Piraeus by turning westward onto the national motorway. Then we flew across the four-mile-wide isthmus that ties the Peloponnese to the rest of Greece; the shadowy form of the island of Salamis was just visible in the rainy sky on our left. About fifty kilometers later we crossed the narrow Corinthian Canal almost without noticing it—the twenty-six-foot drop to the water below was cut into the white rock in the 1880s—before we pulled off the highway to our TC at a McDonalds restaurant.

This taste of home marked the end of the road book for the day; the instructions that would have led us to the town of Olympia, site of the first Olympic games in 776 BC, were now all crossed out. Instead, we clung to the coast of the Gulf of Corinth on the national highway. The Corinthians, with ports on both sides of the narrow isthmus, threw their weight from Athens to Sparta and back in ancient times, eventually supporting the Spartans in the Peloponnesian War. Athens lost that conquest 2,400 years ago, but won the longevity war: today, with a population of more than three million, Athens rules modern Greece. Patras, which had sided with Athens in that long-ago conflict, was founded 3,100 years ago, and today is a sleepy port town, serving tourists by funneling them out through its Gulf onto the Ionian sea.

As we sped over that highway to Patras, I thought about Charles Godard, the con-man-turned-motorist of the original Peking-Paris. Five days after Borghese's Itala broke its wheel, Godard finally regained his disabled Spyker. His journey thus far had been grueling: stalled by lack of petrol in the Gobi for several days, Godard had raced from Udde to Urga in Mongolia, a stretch of 617 kilometers in twenty-three hours, to catch up. His co-driver du Taillis telegraphed that fact back to Paris, where it was logged into the record books as 385 miles in twenty-four hours, an open-road record that stood until the advent of the "24 Hours of Le Mans" in 1923. Despite exhaustion and bleeding hands, Godard drove on, only to have the Spyker's magneto fail the day he and du Taillis left Irkutsk. The De Dion-Bouton men tried to fix it, but soon gave up; Godard encouraged them to continue without him. Faced with no source of parts or assistance until Tomsk (about 850 miles closer to Paris), Godard decided to transport the Spyker there by train, have it repaired, then transport it back to Irkutsk and resume driving where he'd left off. Du Taillis continued on with the De Dion-Boutons, but not before advancing Godard two thousand francs, through *Le Matin*'s account, to cover the Spyker's train fare. From Irkutsk, Godard telegraphed to Spyker to deliver parts and a mechanic to Tomsk; once in that Russian city, he posed in front of the scrubbed Spyker to make a set of picture-postcards. He posted one (rather than telegraphing, since that would have revealed the accurate date) to Jacobus Spijker with the note, "Your car is the only one that has not needed any repairs since leaving Peking." The excursion cost him eighteen days; on the day Godard loaded the repaired Spyker onto the eastbound train, Borghese crossed from Asia into Europe. By the time Godard regained Irkutsk and set off again, Borghese was nearing Moscow.

Alone and with little money for food or lodgings, Godard drove for eighteen-hour stretches, from 3:00 A.M. until 11:00 P.M., finally driving all through the day and night until the early morning hours of July 30. He stopped in a small village seeking refreshment, and found the young mechanic with his box of spare parts, sent by Spijker. Bundling the man into his car, he set off immediately for Omsk, arriving at 8:00 A.M. that same day. In twenty-nine hours of nonstop driving, Godard had completed a cross-country journey later calculated to cover 865 kilometers. That drive far exceeded his own established record, but because the end points had not been documented by telegrams, Godard's fantastic flight across Siberia could not be counted in any record books.

Linda and I set our own record for early arrivals that day in Patras; we arrived at the TC a full three hours before our ferry was due. The road book directed us into the ferry's dock, but the early hour and our numbers so overcrowded the area that we were stuck in a line at the port's entrance. Our Hillman, in fact, ended up right under the arched gate, definitely an awkward place. The car was hemmed-in by other ralliers, so we couldn't move it. We hung out for a while drinking sodas and leaning on our cars. Linda went down and talked to Burt in the Citroën, then came back and said, "We're going to check out a museum with a special motorcycle exhibit. Bye."Then Rich came by and asked me if I wanted to go for a walk to check out the town.

I did, but I had the only door key for the Hillman. "The ferry's not due till seven, right?" I asked. Rich said the ferry would be even later; he'd heard that someone had thrown themselves overboard on the way in, and there'd be some delay as the authorities conducted an investigation. I didn't like leaving the car in such a bad spot, but I couldn't move it. I couldn't leave it unlocked, because Linda's money bag, with several thousand frugals of all shapes and sizes, rested under the front seat. So I walked over to one of the organizers' Vauxhalls, and found Chris Bruce and Mick O'Malley lounging inside it. (Chris was in charge of the scoring; he spent every night loading the times from all our time cards into his laptop computer).

"Do you think our Hillman will be okay if I leave it there locked up?" I asked them. They looked at each other and shrugged.

"How long do you think I have? One hour, two?"

"I dunno. Don't think we're goin' anywhere until six at least," Chris answered.

"I'll be back at six sharp," I told them, and Rich and I set off. It was easy to find our way around Patras on foot. Once we'd gone a few blocks inland, we could see a huge white stone ruin high on a hill directly in front of us. The street ran straight up to it.

We walked the length of this street and stopped at the base of an immense staircase. I've never seen one like it; it looked like an illustration for the stairs leading to St. Peter's gate in heaven. Except for the graffiti, which was artfully stretched over several stairs and read S-E-X.

Rich was in fine form. We'd been talking and laughing the whole way, and now he had fresh inspiration from these extraordinary stairs and the long, continuous bannisters coming down each side.

"Can you imagine the kind of souvenir shop we could set up here?" he started. "We could sell teflon pants, and all different grades of oil—olive, 20/50—or maybe bannister wax, like ski wax. ..." We climbed the stairs, laughing between gasps for breath.

The ruin turned out to be a thirteenth-century Venetian *kastro* or fortress, built on the ruins of a sixth-century Byzantine structure that had, in its turn, topped an ancient Greek acropolis. White square stones and marble column drums littered the grassy hilltop, some stacked loosely, others rebuilt into recognizable walls and ramparts, some, with Corinthian scrolls and other inscribed hints, arranged like puzzle pieces not quite fitting together on the ground. One large part of the complex had been rebuilt, but its wooden door was padlocked. Short remnants of spiral staircases fascinated me. How much higher could the building have climbed, from this starting point already far above the town? Along the edge of the hill the crenelated battlements made a great place to sit and enjoy the view. The city's streets were laid out with rectangular precision; the town had been rebuilt in a neo-classical style after the Turks destroyed it during the Greek War of Independence.

We walked back by a slightly different route, and still with plenty of time to spare, we stopped for iced cappuccino at one of the busy sidewalk cafes. We talked about Rich's business, being run in his absence by his son, and our significant others; Rich had long been divorced, and I talked about Chris, saying out loud what I'd been thinking for days: how much more I'd enjoy the trip with Chris at my side. Rich spoke with longing of someday doing a similar rally with a significant other of his own. It sounded like he currently had few likely candidates.

Rich lingered to look at paperback books (we found a stand of English bestsellers near the waterfront) but I kept going so I'd arrive before six. As I neared our car, I passed Drew Fellman, the Discovery photographer. He said, "Man, are you in trouble!"

"I am?"

"Yeah, Linda's really pissed."

I hurried on. The car wasn't where I'd left it. When I found it, off to the side near where the Vauxhall with Mick and Chris had been, Linda was sitting nonchalantly on the hood.

"The police had a fit," she said evenly, clearly angry, but not nearly as angry as I was.

"They told me six o'clock," I said defensively as I unlocked the car. "I had no idea how long you were going to be—"

"I've been back for an hour," she said, then made it clear the conversation was over. "Let's go. They want us to move the car down by the ferry."

I started up the car and drove in anger. Our destination was only a few hundred yards away, around the first building. The Superfast ship was in, but we obviously had another long wait in front of us. Linda got out of the car and went over to talk to the Iranian Peykan crew, leaving me to fume and wonder alone. How did they move the car without unlocking it? Had I parked it in gear? (I usually do.) Or put on the emergency brake? (I usually don't.) Perhaps the police had a tow truck. So stupid not to have a second key.

The boat which carried us was different from the bridges or boats or rafts by which we had travelled across the other rivers. This was a regular steamer, and seemed to us as grand as a transatlantic passenger-liner.

IONIAN SEA TO RIMINI, ITALY
[TUESDAY, OCTOBER 14]

We didn't board the ferry until something like nine o'clock. At about seven-thirty I had a beer and ham-and-cheese pie from a nearby vendor; it turned out to be the only food I'd have that night. I had plenty of wine once we were on board—the worst Greek wine I've ever tasted—while everyone else tried to get a meal in the ferry's restaurant. At midnight, the folks who'd ordered first were still waiting to be served. I retreated to our cabin, where Superfast T-shirts, pads and pens had been set out for us. The boat was brand new and, judging from the name, fast; yet we were told our crossing to Ancona, Italy, would take twenty hours, which didn't sound particularly fast to me.

In planning the rally, Philip and crew had to choose between this watery route through the Ionian Sea up to the Adriatic, or an overland path through the Balkans. The political circumstances in Albania, Serbia, Croatia, and Bosnia-Hercegovina made the latter choice too dangerous; it also would have added several more driving days. So we were pleased to sit back and relax on the ferry. But for someone who has been driving from morning till night for six weeks, twenty hours did indeed feel like a long, long time. For some, it must have felt even longer; we found out later that Albanian refugees had stowed away; they had clung to the underside of some semi-trucks as they were loaded on the ferry. They were arrested as they disembarked in Italy. One of the Discovery photographers caught the arrest on film, only to have an Italian policeman grab his camera.

We all slept late in the morning, since there was no time card to stamp or road book to follow. Breakfast was leisurely, and I spent the rest of the long morning writing. After awhile I was joined by Adele Cohen. She wanted to know all about the stretch she'd missed since her Stutz had failed—basically from Lanzhou to Istanbul, the bulk of the rally. We talked amiably for several hours.

I wandered around the boat. I lost track of Linda, then heard she'd gone for a tour of the bridge. Eventually I settled down near the Discovery crew; they were interviewing Philip Young. He'd been invisible since Cappadocia; he hit the road hours before us each day, so that he could arrive at the night's halt early. The only thing he revealed I hadn't known before was his fear, back in China, that the Chinese would throw a last-minute wrench in the works. Their demands, over four years of negotiations, were varied and expensive. Originally, he said, he'd offered the Chinese four different possible routes: the one we took over the Himalayas, a shorter southern route more faithful to the old Silk Road, or a northern route to Siberia and Russia more closely following Prince Borghese's. The Chinese chose the Himalayan route—despite their sensitivity about Tibet—because it was the longest. Philip had agreed to pay a per-diem, so he figured they chose the longest route because it would make them the most money. The figure he quoted to Discovery was around one million US dollars.

Here on the ferry, we had him cornered. I knew many people were still very angry with him, and wondered if they'd take this chance to chew him out. Instead, it seemed as if everyone treated him as a hero. In one sense he really was. Without him, none of us could have made this journey. On the other hand, there was universal agreement that his personality made him difficult to work with. One of the support crew said "If Philip were in the US, he would be in therapy. In the UK, he runs rallies." Don Jones put it even better: "Philip has one of those multiple personality situations, like eccentrics in horse racing circles. They tend to be roguish, flamboyant, anti-social. They also tend to be visionaries, dreamers and schemers. They tap into a unique urge that people have in their lives."

Later, Lord Montagu joined the little group. In his characteristic upper crust mumble, he explained to us why he'd supported the Peking to Paris. "We humans are herd animals," he said. "These are places we wouldn't go to without having all these other humans with us."

I left the herd behind to have lunch alone. I was still having spells of that same deep loneliness I'd felt when we first drove into Greece. I sat outside on the stern deck. There was an awning, but cold wind and occasional blasts of wind-blown rain chilled me to the bone. Eventually, the winds grew to gale force and the boat began a queasy pitching and yawing; sitting or walking on the deck became impossible. I went in to warm up and stow my notebook in our cabin, and found Linda there fast asleep.

We'd been resting all day, but most of us walked like spaced-out zombies down to our cars in the big boat's belly when the time finally came to disembark; the rough seas had made many of us ill. The sun had set long before the boat docked in Ancona, so it was an odd reversal of our many pre-dawn starts to gather around our cars in the dark of true night. As we rolled off the ramps and assembled around the Vauxhall that would be our "Out" TC, Linda fiddled with our double headlight switches. At first neither worked. She flicked them aggressively; she would be driving the 108 kilometers to the hotel. Finally, just as I got our stamp at 7:18 P.M., the lights clicked on.

As we drove north on the *autostrada* on a flat expanse that I knew to be Italy's Marches (a province, just like Umbria and Tuscany, this one ranging from the Appenines to the Adriatic coast), about halfway to Rimini, one of our compatriots pulled up alongside us. He motioned frantically behind. I rolled down the window and he yelled "You have no taillights!"

Linda and I just laughed. We still hadn't exorcized the Prince of Darkness!

The Hotel Intercontinental on Rimini's waterfront looked like a yellow and white wedding cake, even at night. The minute we walked in, my mouth began to water; the smell of Italian food coming from the dining room almost made me swoon. The restaurant was about to close. We'd clocked in at 9:42, and after depositing our bags in our room and returning to the lobby it had to be after ten. But someone from the rally had convinced the kitchen to stay open. We dined with the Jeepsters, and I got to play travel guide as I explained to them how here in Italy (it felt almost as if I were home), one orders *il primo* (the first, usually pasta or soup) and then *il secondo* (the meat or main course). The food was as good as any I've had in Italy: creamy *crespelle* followed by mixed seafood on a skewer, and a good local wine.

44

You know this only, that you must arrive, that you will arrive—and from this idea comes the only strength remaining to you: the great power called Patience. You gather your patience, and so, On!

RIMINI TO GARDONE RIVIERA
[WEDNESDAY, OCTOBER 15]

I was happy to be back behind the wheel the next morning, even with the lower gears acting up. I was on familiar roads, heading to a place I'd visited only months before—lovely San Marino, the world's oldest independent republic. Italy's *Mille Miglia* (Thousand Mile) classic car rally sends over three hundred classic racers over San Marino's famous *Rocca* every May. The Peking to Paris took us teasingly up the mountain, following the signs to the town's *Centro Storico* (historic center), but then Linda, reading the road book, sent us right back down. It didn't make sense to me, to take us so close and not let us see the town. So I said something like "Are you sure? That can't be right."

Something broke in Linda; she'd had enough of navigation. As we climbed up the curvy side of Monte Maggiore—the mountain opposite San Marino, with a great view of the city from afar—Linda and I shouted at each other. I asked her if she was carsick or wanted to drive; she said she wouldn't like driving either. When I asked her about the numbers in the road book, she said, "I can't do it. I hate math. I'm no good at it."

I didn't think she was as bad at it as she thought she was. She didn't seem to trust herself; she looked down at the books and calculator and stressed out over the numbers instead of looking up at the road and watching for signs. I told her to forget the math and just give me signposts.

This was a different side of Linda; I'd never seen her admit to anything less than complete competence. I told her that if she just gave me the names of the next towns, we wouldn't get lost—I've found my way around some very obscure places in Italy. Then, probably to her great distress, I kept talking. I tried a few little uplifting speeches. "The journey's the thing," I started, a handy old platitude. "It doesn't matter where we're going, on these kinds of roads, the point is just driving." She

answered my clichés with silence. Finally I said, "You know, I'm just trying to cheer you up."

That didn't work either. The worm had definitely turned: she was totally burnt out.

Others were too. Andy Vann had reached a showdown with John Jung, in the #24 Ford, on the long stretch of motorway leading to the ferry in Greece. "Navigation was real simple," Andy said. "We were going down the toll road with no real navigating to do, and John decided he wanted to know exactly where we were. I said 'John, just follow the car in front of us.' But John wanted to know exactly how far. I said, 'John, it doesn't matter. We have a full tank of gas and we'll get there in plenty of time.'"

John lost his temper, launching into a tirade that included one particular obscenity that really got to Andy. "I lost my temper and hit him," Andy said. "He immediately slowed down, pulled off the road and told me to get out. I got out, got my stuff, slammed the door and he left. Luckily, I was right by a blackberry patch. Greece has great blackberries. Different rally people stopped and asked what the problem was. I told them John and I had a fight and he threw me out. They didn't have room to give me a lift, so I sent them on and told them some-one would be by. As I waited and ate blackberries, I saw John backing back down the highway, on the shoulder."

John stopped the Ford every now and then, working his way slowly back to where Andy stood; it took him about thirty minutes. "We had about a fifteen minute talk," Andy said. "I told him if he ever called me that again, I was going to hit him more than once. He apologized, and I apologized, and put my stuff back in the car. From then on, we got along fine."

After our brush with San Marino, we wound our way up through Emilia-Romagna, Italy's exotic-car-producing region (Lamborghini, Ferrari and Maserati are all situated between Modena and Bologna). Centuries before it became famous for its automobiles, this area started out Etruscan (600-400 BC), then, of course, became Roman. The Roman-built Via Emilia connects the dots of the region's major cities. The land is flat and agricultural—Italy's bread-basket—though grapes and sugar beets grow beside the grains.

In Maranello, where Ferrari was celebrating its fiftieth anniversary, we were wel-comed at the Galleria Ferrari, a museum of automobiles and artifacts from the life of Enzo Ferrari. Our lunch took place on the patio in back; the food was solid Italian deli fare, but there was one oddity: no tables or chairs! We crouched on the cement or in the damp grass, picnicking with no blankets in the warm sunshine of Italy's famous Indian Summer.

Here I found half of another antagonistic pair. Michael Veys was beside himself with anger at Eric Christiansen. Eric had gone off in the Rolls Royce and left

Michael behind. Michael was ready to pack it in and continue to Paris on his own, but first, he joined me and Michael Kunz for a cappuccino. As we walked down the street to a little café, we could hear the distant whine of a powerful race engine: Formula One champion Michael Schumacher was testing a Ferrari at the nearby Fiorano test-track.

The idyll ended, as always, with the call of the clock. Michael Kunz and I left Michael Veys, looking bereaved, at the café, and walked back to the Galleria's parking lot. Dimples and Adam had somewhere come up with a very battered mannequin's head. They were playing ventriloquist with the fright-wigged thing, shaking it on Big Don's shoulders, then finally tried to mount it over the Bentley's radiator cap. It wouldn't stay, but someone came up with a broom handle, and the head ended up riding between the Bentley boys as we all set off toward Lake Garda.

We circled around the busy city of Modena and about fifty kilometers later crossed the Po, Italy's longest river, just before the Passage Control at Ostiglia. The high banks built to prevent that river from flooding were visible from the *autostrada,* down which we cruised at high speed until we reached the base of Lake Garda at Peschiera. The only trick was catching the right exit (the *autostrade* or toll-highways have very few exits, some as much as fifty kilometers apart). The Jeepsters missed it and didn't have any Italian between them to translate the signs. They found their way back all right, only picking up a few penalty points; they had added thirteen minutes since getting off the ferry in Ancona.

The rally ranks were swelling yet again, though not with competitors; we were still at sixty-six Vintage and Classic plus sixteen in Touring. Now, family, friends and hangers-on in cars (rented or otherwise) met us en route and followed along with us as we traversed Italy. All the Italian crews had family with them now, as had Theo the Greek doctor back in Greece. Someone had delivered an Irish Setter to the Noors, so their brown convertible Mercedes now sported a panting dog as well as a full cooler. Two couples from the States had joined up with Team Retro: one in Rimini, the other in Maranello. We had always made our own traffic; now we made our own traffic jam. Add in the car-crazy local Italians, and it made a huge traffic jam all the way up the length of Lake Garda. From the busy town of Desenzano, we crawled northward along the lake's eastern shoreline. The lake is so wide and deep, it keeps the climate moderate year round, despite its location at the base of the Dolomite Mountains. Olive groves, cypress, and vineyards gave way to lemon trees and evergreens as we drove north. Before our night's halt at Gardone Riviera, we rode for many kilometers behind the Cohen's 8-liter Bentley. Though it's truly a beautiful car (far more elegant than the more utilitarian 4 1/2-liter Bentleys), riding behind it for any length of time makes one a great fan of catalytic converters.

Gardone Riviera, though named for the lake, seemed as if it should've been named after its almost-homonym, the English word *garden*: so much luxuriant greenery lined both sides of the road in this lovely resort town. The Grand Hotel, our home for the night, was also appropriately named. It seemed as long as the lake, stretching up the coast as far as the eye could see; that way, most rooms have a balcony and lake view. Wavy, antique glass paneled the many French doors, lovely *belle époque* decorations adorned every piece of furniture and interior trim, and our bathroom was the size of half my house in Santa Cruz.

We found our rooms with Fred Multon and Tim Laughton, two British men in a blue Austin A90 that'd been trailing us for weeks. In fact, we'd been bracketed by two almost identical Austins since the Quetta day; Fred and Tim's #55 and David and Sheila Morris's Mr. Blobby #57. We were beginning to think our Hillman wanted a marque-change operation.

As Tim opened the door to his room just down from ours, he said, "What a romantic place to stay! Too bad I'm sleeping with Fred."

I laughed and said "Yes, that's my problem too."

He laughed but he knew. All of us with missing significant others knew what we would've given to have our lovers beside us now. I walked out onto the balcony to watch the moon rise. The first full moon had been at Everest; now here on Lake Garda, one of Italy's most romantic spots, another full moon shimmered down on the lake, streaking the rippling surface with its liquid silver light. Its luminous beauty both eased and aggravated the chronic ache of my homesickness.

In the bar I found the two Michaels; Eric had finally come back to retrieve his co-driver in Maranello, having only gone off to a restaurant for a long lunch. Everyone, even almost-abandoned Michael Veys, seemed to be in a great mood, and the gaiety was contagious; it took the edge off my loneliness. We were in the home stretch.

A group of us wandered out onto the esplanade together, in search of a restaurant. Rich Newman had joined us, as had Peter Cordrey and his co-driver Gordon Phillips, and Gerry Acher and his co-driver Bruce from the "baby" '32 Aston Martin. We settled on one of the first restaurants we came to, where a beautiful blonde woman named Angela waited on us.

Peter instantly fell in love with Angela, even before the wine arrived. What is it about Italian restaurants? I had seen this happen in Rome, when a girlfriend fell for a handsome waiter (by the time we had *tiramisu* the waiter and my girlfriend—who spoke fluent Italian—were discussing their wedding date). Peter spoke little or no Italian but Angela spoke good English, and the romance played out against the tragicomedy of Peter's outbursts. He was always laughing, but sometimes in a demented way. "Perhaps it's senile dementia," Gerry joked. Peter seemed seriously upset (when Angela wasn't around) that this trip hadn't revealed the meaning of life to him. We talked about the life-changing aspects of the Peking–Paris, if any.

For Gerry Acher, still active at KMPG, the trip was simply a much-needed vacation: "I never thought about work once." Gordon's work is psychiatry, so before long we were talking about mental health, including Peter's dementia; Gordon threatened to have him "sectioned," (British for committed). Rich Newman vowed that this trip had, indeed, changed his life. And he didn't just mean that it ended his friendship with Burt (they still weren't communicating). It was the fact that he'd been able to leave his business in Chicago in his son's hands, and his son was handling it fine. "The torch has passed," he said triumphantly.

We commiserated over the Land Rover accident ("very lucky chaps") and, though everyone thought about the Feits, no one said a word. We all felt it a kind of duty, I think, to maintain the frivolity. We drank several bottles of an excellent Montalcino red, and though no negatives were spoken aloud, there was a slight sense of sadness already in the air. The end was indeed near.

C H A P T E R

45

We passed from one place to the other with that continuous illusion which never seems to fail to comfort man, that the place where he does not find himself at any given moment must always be better than the one where he is. Envy is a fault which probably arises from this illusion.

GARDONE RIVIERA, ITALY TO UBERLINGEN, GERMANY
[THURSDAY, OCTOBER 16]

Everyone was talking about the weather as we prepared to leave Lake Garda. Reports said several feet of snow had already fallen on Austria's Alps, and more was due today.

The drive through Italy's Alto Adige toward Merano with Linda at the wheel made my homesickness worse. Chris and I have spent many romantic evenings nearby—he likens this area to Yosemite Valley—in a friend's condo outside of Dro. When Chris read the route so many months ago, and realized we'd drive through here, he gave me specific instructions to stop and pick up a bottle of Polli Grappa, the best we'd found anywhere in Italy, from a minuscule grapperia near Lake Toblino. Now we skirted the lake and the lovely castle that gave the lake its name, climbing through long stretches of vineyards and apple orchards below the snow-capped Dolomite Mountains, but we couldn't stop. We had four hours and forty-nine minutes to go 240 kilometers to Resia, an easy average of 31 mph (this was apparently the European legal limit), but you never knew what might happen: a flat tire, traffic jam, catastrophic gear failure. Linda kept driving.

Thanks to the European Union, the border between Austria and Italy at the Resia pass in the Alps was marked only by signs. We now had several Alpine passes to climb, and "secret" Passage Controls—PCs not mentioned in the road book. Now that the required speeds had to be so slow, the only way to create any competition was by testing the navigators. Those who took short cuts or missed turns would miss their PC stamp, dropping them from gold to silver medal status.

We found our way with ease, despite the fact that the blustery cold became a blizzard by the time we climbed up the pass to St. Anton. Visibility between there and the Arlsberg Pass—where modern downhill skiing started in the 1940s—was extremely limited in the foggy, blowing snow. The TC in the Arlsberg Hospiz

Hotel gave us a chance to warm up inside a warm ski lodge. A young woman there gave each of us a black ribbon to tie onto our cars. Later on, we'd be driving near the Feits' hometown in Germany, and our ribbons were to show our solidarity with the grieving family in case any of them came out to watch us pass.

The first secret PC turned out to be just past an almost invisible turn signposted Lech, not far from the summit of Flexenpass (5,762 feet). Linda negotiated the tight turns of this little road up to the Hochtannberg, our last Alpine pass. Our road book called this 5,444-foot peak "a mere pimple compared to what you have already crossed." Here, the support crew lay in ambush with snowballs, which they heartily lobbed at us—Jingers was still in his shorts, his legs as pale as the snow— plastering our windows with snowy slush. The open roadsters, once again, suffered worse punishment.

As we drove toward Bregenz the snow turned to rain. The road's engineering amazed me: whole sections built into the side of the mountain, or elevated on skyscraping girders in long sweeping curves over deep mountain valleys; snowy ramps in the sky. Then we began the long descent toward Germany.

After his wild ride across Siberia, Godard finally caught up with his compatriots in the De Dion-Boutons on August 8, two days before Borghese arrived in Paris. The three cars stuck together from then on, crossing the German Empire's border more than two weeks after Prince Borghese had left. As soon as they crossed the frontier, Godard was forcibly removed from the Spyker.

News reports at the time claimed that Jacobus Spijker threw him from the car in disgust over the many debts he'd incurred in the company's name. In fact, the automaker by now recognized the publicity value of Godard's great drive, and had reconciled himself to writing off the debt. The actual culprit was *Le Matin*. Godard's advance for the Spyker's trainfare had been the last in a series of "loans" taken on the newspaper's account stretching all the way back to China. But it wasn't just the money that had the paper's management steaming. It was the possibility that Godard's Dutch motor-car might arrive in Paris before the French cars. The whole point of the race had been—besides increasing *Le Matin*'s circulation—to promote the French automobile industry. To have an Italian take first and a Dutch car take second would be unacceptable. Godard's unpaid expenses gave *Le Matin* a handy excuse; the newspaper arranged for the German Imperial police to arrest Godard on a charge of False Pretences.

Jacobus Spijker had heard of *Le Matin*'s plans, so he came to the German border with a test-driver to take Godard's place. Jean du Taillis, the *Matin* reporter who had ridden by Godard's side, protested, but there was nothing he could do. Godard was taken away as the three cars set off for Paris.

PRINCE BORGHESE'S TRAIL

In our Hillman Hunter, we didn't even notice the border into Germany; with no language change to signal it, it was virtually invisible. We now descended toward Lake Constance, which the Germans call the Bodensee, and the only difference was the traffic—a soggy, slow-moving mass of Audis, Opels, VWs, Mercedes and BMWs. So slow moving, in fact, that I gave up all hope of clearing this section—we were in for some serious penalties. The only consolation was that we wouldn't be the only ones.

Up ahead of us, a bad instruction in the road book caused trouble for Vic and Ted in the #23 Ford. The instruction said "Turn left—SP Reisenberg," but once they turned, the sign to that town pointed to the right. The Retro boys decided to follow the Reisenberg sign, and immediately ended up on the *autobahn*. They couldn't turn around, and were heading completely the wrong way. Vic pulled out his maps and plotted a new course. They rocketed across the German countryside and came into Reisenberg from the wrong direction, but well ahead of the rest of us. They had just made what Vic called "a particularly hairy pass on a bus" when they were flagged into one of the secret passage controls. The marshal there told Vic that because of the heavy traffic, there would be no late penalties. They had twenty kilometers to go in twenty-seven minutes; they would have made it when none of the rest of us could.

I'd despaired of the book at that Reisenberg instruction, too. I'd used maps to get us back on track, but I wasn't certain we'd chosen the right route until we saw other rally cars, stuck like we were in the molasses traffic. By the time we hit the PC, we only had fifteen minutes left, and knew we couldn't make it. It was a great relief to hear they'd canceled the stage.

Two other teams had a tough time that day. David Bull's Rover lost the rear axle, sending a wheel flying off the road. The break cost them thirteen hours of penalties, sending them from twenty-fourth to forty-sixth place. Angela ran around the hotel in a tizzy, trying to find a replacement axle that could be delivered immediately. The leading Iranian Peykan also had a serious failure: their half-shaft broke. I felt badly when they asked if we had any spares they could borrow. I'd lost track of how many spares we'd been given by them back in Tibet and Nepal, and now we had nothing to offer. Of course, we'd left Beijing with practically no spares in the first place.

The big black Buick, though, was running smooth now after its full rebuild. I dined with Ken Hughes and Michael Kunz at the hotel. Ken regaled us with tales from the Buick's off-route journey. After that tempting offer of goat's-head stew in Iran, they'd had some fun in Turkey. Two English teachers in Erzincan took them out to a folk music club, for a night of traditional Turkish music and dance. They drank beer disguised in coffee mugs, which seemed sufficient to avoid offending the fundamentalists in the crowd.

CHAPTER

❧ 46 ❧

The last few hours seem everlasting. They are hours of joy, but also of anguish—of a sudden, vague, inexpressible anguish, which makes us silent and gives us all the appearance of disappointed men.

UBERLINGEN, GERMANY TO REIMS, FRANCE
[FRIDAY, OCTOBER 17]

We had 556 kilometers to cover to Reims, so we set out early, at ten-to-eight. As we cruised on the *autobahn* toward Stuttgart, the still-visible, almost-full moon hovered in the pink clouds over the mountain, resting on a sea of fog; the Black Forest below was a mass of autumnal reds and yellows, spreading in patches over smooth green rolling hills.

In the old scheme of things, it would've been my day to drive. This morning, though, we spoke in unison: "Why don't you drive?" I said as Linda asked "Would you mind if I drive?" I think she was greatly relieved.

"You can drive from here on out," I said. "I'm happy to navigate."

We turned west into the Black Forest, toward the great Danube River near its source in Donauschingen. Lovely mountain roads took us up to the Kandelpasshohe, covered in snow but, unlike yesterday, under clear skies. Some couldn't resist the photo-op offered by the nice flat snow-covered field across from the TC at the Berghotel Kandel. Three Volvos drove out onto it: Phil Bowen's #82, the Gulls #62 and a young dimpled British gent named Dan Orteu (he was one of the proletariat like me, having mortgaged his home to pay the entry fee) in #69. The Gulls had their picture taken and regained the pavement, but Phil and Dan got into a spinning contest that ended up burying Dan's rear wheels in the snow. It took a lot of laughing competitors to push the heavy Volvo free; Dan was lucky not to accumulate any penalties.

From the top of the Kandelpasse we could see all the way across the Rhine Valley to France's Vosges Mountains. Our cars followed our line of sight almost as the crow flies, and before long we were crossing the Rhine into France at a peculiarly un-scenic spot; big industrial complexes lined both banks. We celebrated the border crossing vicariously by following the only Frenchman in the rally, Paul

Minassian in the #76 Peugeot. Paul howled the French equivalent of *yahoo!*, stuck his fist out the window and screamed "*Vive la France!*" We honked our air horn in agreement.

The 1907 Raiders had performed a more thorough tour of Germany; they were feted by every branch of the German Imperial Automobile Club. Near the Rhine, the club greeted them with a racing car that served as a guide, though it went with "the most bewildering speed at something like sixty miles an hour and dragged us on, in a most furious and desperate race." After the Prince was persuaded to make a speech in Cologne (Barzini wrote that "in order to win a motor-race from Peking to Paris, you must be not only a motorist, but an orator as well") the racer intended to lead the Itala to Aix-la-Chapelle, but instead crashed straight into a house, entering "precipitately through its demolished outside wall!" Fortunately, there was no loss of life.

Just as our entrance into France went unnoticed by the locals in their Renaults and VWs, Prince Borghese's crossing into Belgium attracted little attention. "For once the telegraph has not announced our arrival," Barzini wrote. "To those who meet us we are simply three very odd-looking creatures upon a most extraordinary motor-car." Instead of a cry of welcome, they were greeted by an oft-repeated epithet: "*Oh, les laids!*" (Oh, the uglies!)—their black and dusty faces over ragged clothes made them appear "exceedingly grotesque." In one village, an old peasant woman hollered down from her window, "I know you, *canaille!* It was you who ran over my hen last Thursday. Pay up!" Later, a policeman stopped the suspicious-looking crew, and demanded to know their identities. Prince Borghese, at the wheel, answered, "I am Prince Scipione Borghese." The policeman thundered in response: "A prince—You? You are a Belgian chauffeur—I know you! I will immediately summon you for an excess of speed. You know the regulations: eight miles an hour." The policeman pulled out his paper and pencil and demanded the Prince's address. When Borghese responded with "Palace Borghese, Rome," the policeman shouted in frustration, "Enough with your pleasantries. Show me your papers!" Even the papers didn't convince the man: "Why pretend to be a prince? *Chacun gagne son pain comme il peut.*" (Everyone earns his bread as he can.) Only when he asked from whence they came, and heard the word "Peking," did the light begin to dawn.

"Peking . . . Borghese . . . Ah!" Suddenly full of regret, the policeman stood aside and saluted obsequiously, "*Passez, monseigneur, bon voyage.*"

In this part of France, Alsace-Lorraine, everything looks German. Of course, it was, several times. In the twentieth century alone, the area was German until 1918, then French from 1919 to 1940, German from 1940 to 1945, then finally French ever since.

The town of Riquewhir, which hosted our TC, reminded me of Rothenbergab-der-Tauber, a restored walled village in southern Germany. Riquewhir had opened its normally closed-to-autos center, so we drove slowly right under the medieval entry arch, got our TC stamp in front of a lovely old hotel, and drove right out the back arch. We had time for lunch, so we parked in a special lot where a welcome tent offered us shot-glasses of the wonderful local wine. We walked back down into town, and decided to buy a baguette and some chèvre (goat cheese) and apples for lunch. We crouched along the wall on the narrow lane, and ate our picnic right there, watching the rally cars cruise up to the TC.

The next stage went straight up the Col du Bonhomme (Gentleman's Hill), a regular part of the Monte Carlo rally and the last climb on the route; from here it really would be downhill all the way to Paris. This tiny one-lane road was full of hairpin turns, and was lined on both sides with deep forest in the gorgeous colors of fall. We were the only traffic, and I wondered if this time the organizers had actually succeeded in closing the road. We cruised behind Don and Carl's Packard and the yellow Italian 2CV. There was no room to even think about passing, and anyway, Linda wasn't interested. The timing was generous enough that our comfortable cruise didn't earn us any penalties.

The next TC was in the town of Wassy, where the Mayor, an old car fan, made a big production of our welcome. Several antique French cars, including several De Dion-Boutons like those driven by Borghese's rivals in the first Peking-Paris, were on display. A lot of local kids had come out to see us and to volunteer at the Mayor's welcome stand; they handed us orange drink, cookies, and a rose bud.

We only had 77 miles (124 km) left until Reims, and we raced there on the *autoroute* (the French toll highway), with chardonnay, pinot noir and pinot meunier vineyards—all grapes used in the area's famous champagne—rolling along beside us in a blur. Once near the city, the road book's instructions grew confusing. All the rights turned out to be lefts and vice versa, and since the town's old center is mostly one-way streets, we almost all were forced to loop crazily around the town several times. It must've been on purpose—a last-ditch effort to rearrange the leader board.

Linda was very tired now. The gears had gotten incredibly hard to shift (they had been easier for a couple of days after Vic and Andy bled the clutch slave, but then inexorably grew worse). Now, every gear change was a bicep-building struggle. My navigational failure at this last bit didn't help, so we were both in foul moods by the time we reached the hotel.

We decided some of Reim's famous *Veuve Cliquot* champagne would help. The bar was already crowded when we got there. Team Retro was surrounded by their families; every one of the team of four seemed to have a three- to four-person fan club there celebrating with them. Vic was reunited with his wife Sara, and Andy with his wife Mary Ann. Don and Carl's wives and grown children were all there, too. German and British family members were legion.

Once again we ventured out en masse, eleven of us, descending on a nearby Italian restaurant in our raucous good cheer. The place was noisy anyway—there was a soccer team at the long table behind us—and once the wine came, we didn't bother to hold back. Rich Newman sat opposite me, and he kept ordering bottles of Montalcino as fast as we all could drink it. Loud Peter (bereft of his Italian waitress Angela) and Gordon, Michael Veys and Michael Kunz, Linda, Fred and Tim from the Austin and several more ate, drank, yelled in several languages, then tried to pay the bill with seven or eight separate credit cards.

But Vic noted the fragile nature of our high spirits in his journal:

> *Everyone was festive but at the same time people seemed a little bewildered. A very intense part of our lives was winding down and people seemed to be having a hard time dealing with it. Tomorrow it will all be over—but what then?*

Prince Borghese and crew were met at the French border with champagne; then, accompanied by three Itala motor-cars similar to their own, they raced toward Paris by way of Reims. More champagne greeted them there, but they continued on, stopping for the night at Meaux, thirty miles from Paris. "We got no sleep during the last night of our pilgrimage across two continents," Barzini wrote. "It is precisely this nearness of Paris that disturbs us. We seem to *feel* that great city. We seem to hear in the stillness of the night the powerful pulsations of its life."

The last few days' flight over Europe had been almost too quick for the Italians. It had taken them twelve days to cover the first six hundred miles out of Peking, and only two-and-a-half days to cover the last six hundred miles before Paris. "We have not had time to get accustomed to the idea of arriving," Barzini wrote.

Six hundred miles was little more than a day's journey for the Second Peking to Paris Motor Challenge. Yet we, too, had been so busy driving, arriving seemed somehow impossible. Italy, Austria (a blink!), Germany, and France had passed by so quickly, our minds were still deciphering the alphas and omegas of Greece; picturing the cave-dwellings of Turkey; shrugging off the veils of Iran. The mud under our wheel wells still smelled of Tibet, and the shadow of death still shrouded our memories of Pakistan. Indian- and Chinese-accented "hellos!" still rang in our ears, the tica of Nepal still colored our brows.

Yet tomorrow, sleep or no sleep: Paris.

CHAPTER

⤸ 47 ⤹

We have formed a habit by now of travelling continuously, and at the hour of departure we instinctively leap out of our beds. To keep going—always to keep going—has become the object of our existence.

REIMS TO PARIS
[SATURDAY, OCTOBER 18]

We were up before daybreak on the forty-third and last day of the Challenge. We left two at a time for our last long stretch, 150 kilometers to the outskirts of Paris. There, at the La Villette sports complex, we were supposed to regroup in finishing order and parade the last eleven kilometers into the Place de la Concorde. The rankings had been posted at the HQ hotel in Reims; the only way to get any additional penalties would be to suffer a major mechanical failure. The Bull-Riley Rover had miraculously reappeared; an axle had been found in Vienna, flown to Uberlingen, and David Bull had installed it and driven straight to Reims. His wife Angela and her mother Helen looked radiant as they prepared to leave Reims with the rally. The Iranians, too, had recovered, cobbling their half-shaft together and dropping only to eighth place from third. Our Hillman would finish thirty-second out of seventy-two (not counting the sixteen Tourists). We were to follow Bill Binnie and Ned Thompson in their Bentley, and Fred and Tim in their Austin A90 were right behind us. David and Sheila Morris in Mr. Blobby had been bumped up one, to thirtieth place, when Bill Binnie had dropped down. The Jeepsters would be pulling up in forty-first place, and Carl and Don would be two ahead of the Queen's Rolls in fifty-fifth place.

No one seemed to have any idea what was going on there at the sports complex beside the busy Périphérique (Paris's beltway); it was an odd replay of the disorder back at the start at the Great Wall. We waited for what seemed like hours: *Go! No, don't go! Get in order. No, don't worry about order. Just go.*

So we went.

Traffic was intense. I'd spent a summer in Paris, and this was far worse than anything I'd seen then. Perhaps it was the route along Canal St. Martin—a

swath of pretty greenery cutting through the working-class *dixième arrondisement*—because today was market day. We crawled. The gears had gotten so bad, Linda had to turn off the car to get into first gear. She did that often, as we also had to stop several times because of Bill Binnie's Bentley. It kept overheating—Ned jumped out, ran to a fountain, filled a bucket of water and ran back to the steaming old automobile. Then Linda would turn the key, start 'er up, rev, jerk forward, stop, click, shift, jerk forward.

Finally, we got past the market. The Bentley revved up and roared away. We roared after, but lost them in the thick traffic. Along the Seine now, I spotted Notre-Dame, and as our bridge neared I said "follow the signs to Concorde," but I missed the small print under the second-to-last instruction: "keep left of Underpass." We were in the right lane—down we went, under the bridge we were supposed to cross!

"Turn around, first chance you get!" I yelled. We immediately reversed our error, but we pulled up now, approaching the finish line, right behind Lisa Klokgieter-Lanke's Bumblebee MG.

Did it matter? It shouldn't have. But as we crawled slowly forward, impeded now by the crowds gathered to welcome us, we couldn't help but think about how Lisa had blown an engine; how she'd been trucked for at least part of the route; and last but not least, how she'd been censured for reckless driving! (Though we never did find out what, if anything, the penalty amounted to.) Her ranking at Reims had been fortieth; it seemed ignoble to come in behind her. On the other hand, it was silly to fret over this since not a single soul there at the finish line, except perhaps a few other competitors, knew or cared about our relative placement. The ones who cared were way up ahead of us: in their '42 Jeep, Phil Surtees and John Bayliss were showered with champagne when they drove up to the finish line first-overall. Right behind them were Vic and Ted in the #23 Ford. Father and son Catt in their Cortina pulled in third, with John and Andy in Team Retro's #24 behind them. All three Iranian Peykans were not far behind, finishing in the top ten.

Sitting on Lisa's bumper, watching her Bumblebee assaulted by Dutch fans, I caught a glimpse of a strangely familiar face. Neither Linda nor I expected anyone to be there to greet us; Linda's daughter Maida had opted to stay home, and though I'd wanted Chris and the kids to come, Chris and I had argued, finally deciding we simply couldn't afford the tickets to Paris (and I couldn't ask Linda for any more money). Then a shout came from that familiar face: "Linda! Genny!" It was Paul Jackson, the man who'd built our Hillman. It was as if a long lost brother had come to greet us.

At the finish line we got our final stamp and a handshake from Philip Young and David Steel, the MP who, if not for politics, would've been our Hillman teammate. We were handed certificates declaring us Gold Medal Winners, and a plastic cup half-full of champagne. When Robin, Ray Carr's videographer, aimed his camera into our cockpit, I said incredulously "We made it!"

Linda shouted much more dramatically. "Hooray! California! USA!" and shoved her fist into the air.

"Paris is twenty miles off—now fifteen—now eight," Barzini wrote. "There is everywhere around us cheering, applause, the waving of handkerchiefs; Prince Borghese smiles no longer with his habitual enigmatical, ceremonious smile, but with spontaneity now. His admirably steady control of himself is not sufficient to repress the joy which is in him, and which opens itself a way in that smile."

Borghese's car was so battered, though, that it was the shiny new Itala behind it, carrying the French journalists, that received the adulation of the crowds. The rain began to fall, but the crowds did not falter. Instead, hundreds of cyclists gathered and circled the car; an omnibus decorated with French and Italian flags, holding trumpeters and trombonists, pulled in front of the crawling Itala. Amidst the cheering, Barzini could hear the cries of the street-vendors selling souvenir postcards: *"Le Prince Borghèse, quatre sous! Quatre sous, le Prince Borghèse!"*

It took the horse-mounted Republican Guard to clear a space in the crowds before the banner-bedecked offices of *Le Matin,* the finish line. Prince Borghese released the clutch and put on the brake. The car stopped. "The race is ended," Barzini wrote, "The ovations of the crowd are loud and full. We remain seated in our places, confused, stunned."

Linda parked the Hillman on the edge of the Place de la Concorde. We stood, stretched, and watched the rest of the ralliers drive through this final gauntlet. Lord Montagu arrived, decked out in period goggles, behind the wheel of his Blower Bentley, then Hermann the German ka-chugged in atop the La France. The crowd and the media went wild; not a soul among them could know that these two media-friendly gents had driven less than a third of the route. I caught the sidelong glances of other ralliers watching this show; there were some unhappy looks. Several cars, I now noticed, carried new protestations: Mr. Wong's MGA and Mr. Ciriminna's Fiat both wore signs that said *Never trucked once!* Malayasian Mr. Wong had in fact driven *more* than the entire route: somehow he had missed the instructions to bypass Olympia in Greece; he'd driven the entire 608-kilometer tour of the Peloponnese, and still made it to Patras in time for the ferry.

Linda climbed atop the Hillman's roof and sat Indian-style, surveying the crowd, while a French TV crew approached and asked for an interview. When I admitted to speaking French I embarrassed myself by using it on camera. An Australian auto writer/videographer and Hillman fan interviewed us, then hung around for a while. A nice American couple who'd stumbled on our finish line with no idea anything like this was happening were thrilled to hear we'd made it. A couple of jogging French women stopped and asked in French "Are you really going to drive from Paris to Peking?" No, I answered, we just did it, the other way round. "Ooh, la la," they said, and jogged away.

Huge groups of Dutch and Germans had come to welcome their teams; the Dutch 2CV's driver Johan Van der Laan was a school teacher, and 135 elementary-school-age children swarmed him with flowers. The Noors, who owned a hygienic paper company (like Baby Wipes) seemed to be welcomed by half their employees. American and British kids were running all over the place—Bill Binnie had four, climbing all over him and his Bentley. Both Dimples (Jonathan) and Adam had looked too young to have kids, but Adam now cradled a small boy in in his arms. Even adult children clung to their parents. Several of the women co-drivers, clutching their daughters and sons, had tears in their eyes.

"This whole rally has been about people, so it only seems natural that the finish would be so personal," John Bryson told Discovery's Robert Thomas, as he sat clutching his wife and son who'd flown in from Sydney. "We don't need another official party," Burt Richmond said, "It's enough to watch people reunited with their family and friends." I hadn't realized how much the joy of the finish would depend on seeing loved ones; I never would have guessed. I was jealous, and worse—distraught. For me, I realized with sudden, heavy regret, the Challenge wouldn't be over until late Monday, when I'd finally see my family. Linda, as usual, betrayed little emotion beyond the relief of the finish. If she craved the company of her daughter or Geoff the way I craved Chris and the kids, she wasn't saying.

We still had a lot to do before the night's big banquet. Burt may not have cared, but we didn't want to miss it. We took a larger load than usual (since we knew tomorrow we had to unpack the car completely) and went off to find a taxi. We discovered then the reason for the terrible traffic: it was the week that the new fall fashions are introduced, and the entire world of *haute couture* had converged in Paris. Thirty people stood at the single taxi stand, desperate for a ride. I offered to lead us through the Metro and even walked Linda across the street to the Metro's entrance, then balked: we were lugging too much, I didn't have the right change, I didn't have a Metro map, and had no idea which stop would be close to our hotel. We went back across the street and kept walking until we finally flagged down an unoccupied taxi.

At the Hotel Royal Monceau, we tried to claim our boxes. I'd asked Chris to ship my thirty-year-old black velvet cocktail dress (a hand-me-down from my mother) to the hotel so I'd have it for the banquet. Chris wrapped it up with shoes and hose, insured it for fifty bucks, and shipped it. It was there waiting for me; the bellhop said it would be delivered to our room. Linda had asked her personal assistant to do the same, only Linda's box was insured for an amount so high, customs red-flagged it, and refused to release it to anyone other than Linda.

"Fine, where's the Customs office?" Linda asked.

"They are closed until Monday, Madame," our concierge replied.

"What am I going to do?" Linda screeched. "The banquet's in three hours!"

"No problem," I told her. "We'll shop. Call a taxi," I ordered the concierge. We left our luggage right there and walked back out to the street. The taxi, when it came, crawled through the traffic, and came to dead stop near l'Opéra. "I think we can walk from here," I said, and conferred with the taxi driver. We jumped out and almost jogged toward Boulevard Haussman until Linda said, "Wait, let's check out this boutique." Gold and silver lamé bodysuits in the window tempted her. Linda spotted one she liked, but decided to wait.

A few moments later, we entered one of the world's swankiest department stores, Galleries Lafayette. I hadn't known the place was such a tourist attraction during fall fashion week; shoppers were body to body. Luckily, the top floor, which featured designer-wear, wasn't as crowded. Linda found a black Kenzo jacket she liked, and the sales clerk helped her find a matching skirt. Then she bought shoes and hose while I rewarded myself with a gold necklace dangling a single pearl (similar to one Linda wore, which I'd admired) and matching earrings. We went back to the little boutique and Linda bought the gold leotard. All told, I'd spent about eighty dollars; Linda's bill was in the high three figures US. I was quietly aghast, but I knew she didn't care; she didn't need to.

When we got back to the hotel, it was after five, and the banquet started at six at a different hotel. We picked up our keys at the desk, and the bellhop jumped up, pulling our luggage from a corner where he'd stashed it. It seemed odd to me that they hadn't delivered it to our room, as they'd promised. We soon found out why.

When we opened the door to our room, a woman in a bathrobe appeared.

"This is our room," we said.

"No, it isn't," she said, in heavily accented English, and shut the door.

We turned to the bellhop. Hopefully, his understanding of English expletives was limited. He rushed down the stairs, promising to return with a different set of room keys.

We sat at a small table at the top of the grand staircase, our luggage parked beside us on a rolling rack, and waited. The bellhop finally reappeared a good fifteen minutes later, and led us to an empty room. It was nice, but very small, and worth far less than the eight hundred dollars a night US I'd heard the hotel would normally have charged us.

Linda was in the shower when I opened my box from home. I wasn't pre-pared for what I found. Sitting on top of my black dress were two folded pieces of paper. The first said "From Molly To Mommy 10/11" and featured Molly's drawing of Pocahantas, a blue-ink line-drawing with Magic-Marker lips so red they bled through the paper. The next page said "From Jesse To Mom 10/11. Dear Mommy, How are you doing? I am doing god." followed by two hearts and his name signed in his brand-new cursive. His picture was of a rock musician playing the guitar, a drummer behind him, and the heads of the audience in the foreground.

I sat on the bed and cried.

By the time Linda emerged, I was dressed and stoic. It was already six o'clock. I brushed my hair, slapped on some lipstick and eyeshadow, and we dashed down to the lobby. We were relieved to see we weren't the only ones running late. The tour bus that was to transport us to the Hotel Intercontinental had long gone, so we were all now dependent on the scarce taxis. At least the hotel kept a steady stream of them coming.

When it was finally our turn, we joined two other women, relatives of another competitor. They'd followed some of our progress—and the Gulls—on the Internet, and were impressed that we'd made it, and their respect and excitement were contagious; my homesickness abated. We arrived at the Intercontinental to find the party well underway. The men were all in black tie (we'd grown used to seeing each other in grubbies and exhausted, with bags under our eyes) and the women wore fabulous get-ups. Miriam El Accad, who together with her husband Jonathan Prior had driven (and trucked) a 1936 Railton that had undergone three separate low-end rebuilds, wore a full-length, blue velvet gown embroidered with the Peking-Paris route twisting from her low neck-line, around her sensuous curves, down to her hem.

Linda and I barely had time to look at the photos mounted around the ball-room—the British photographer's eight-by-tens were for sale, including a cou-ple of good shots of our Hillman—before the award presentation began. We were all standing, shoulder to shoulder in the crowded room, some eight hun-dred people: two hundred competitors plus friends and family.

Philip Young restrained his anti-social tendencies and handled the evening's introduction well, starting with fifteen seconds of silence for Josef and René Feit. Then he introduced Lord David Steel, who became the master of ceremonies. Steel was well spoken and funny, even joking about Philip's difficult personality. Then the awards began; the wall behind the speakers was obscured by hundreds of silver trophy plates and cups. Two "concourse" awards for the prettiest cars were given each category: in Vintage, it was the 1932 Packard 903 convert-ible, a car driven by an American named Don Saunders. He'd suffered mechan-ical problems early and often, ending up in the Touring class in last place overall. The prettiest Classic was the Austrian Dichtl's 1950 Rolls Royce Silver Dawn. Next up were the winners of that newly-created "smallest, oldest" (under 1500 cc) class, Dutch Johan and Willem in their 2CV.

The Coupe des Dames (Women's Cup) was announced next, and Linda and I went up on stage for our moment of glory. I thought there was only one silver cup, so I was very surprised to be handed one of my own. As we were leaving the stage, a blonde woman I'd never seen before yelled from the audience, "What about Jennifer and Pogs?" I put thumbs up and said, "They were great!" as I walked off the stage. The woman glared at us with pure hatred.

It bothered me all night. I wanted to know who she was, and what she thought we were supposed to do—give our cups to Francesca and Jennifer? Perhaps she just wanted David Steel or Philip to say something about them. We had thought we might be given the opportunity to make a thank-you speech, but we weren't let near the microphone.

Then came the class awards, and with trophies awarded for first through third in eight different classes, it took awhile to get to first overall. No surprise there; Phil Surtees and John Bayliss in the Jeep still had their four-minute lead over Ted and Vic in the Ford.

Surtees was the only one allowed a speech. He said some thank-yous— especially to the support crews, which drew a standing ovation—and then talked ominously about someone of us ralliers—"I know who you are"—who had threatened to sabotage his jeep the night before in Reims. He'd been forced, he said, to hide the vehicle. He didn't suspect Team Retro, though. He told how on the way into Paris, Ted and Vic had helped him fix a clutch problem rather than let him fall behind. Surtees made no secret of his disdain for Philip Young, and it began to seem as if he were trying to wrest control of the evening away from Young; he began to announce awards for the support crew, when Young cut him off and shuffled him off the stage, then announced that there'd be a short film followed by dinner.

The film, put together by the British "World Action Sports" crew, was only a minute or two long, but it raised a great hue and cry and swelled us all with pride. It's one thing to remember crossing a few rivers; it's quite another to see the water splashing out from wheels you know are yours. We were all happy and abuzz when we went in to dinner.

There'd been a sign-up sheet for table assignments days before, and Dick Taylor had invited us to join the Jeepsters and their wives. Rich Newman joined our all-American table; he stuck to his vow of silence, but never did abandon Burt, and the two had won a trophy for second in the under-1.5-liter class. After the six-course dinner that featured a main course of *Selle d'Agneau en Croûte Dorée,* I left the table and made an utter nuisance of myself visiting every other table with my pen and my notebook. For me this was a work night: I wanted these people's addresses for possible future car articles. Perhaps it was predatory, but with many of them it was also genuine affection; I didn't want to go home and never talk to either Michael again, or Fran and Bud Risser, who now felt like fast friends. Rich Newman, of course—we'd had several conversations that seemed to contain words worth more than those wasted on mere acquaintances. The Alabama guys and John Jung, of course; Vic and Dick Taylor and Don and Carl all agreed to share their reports with me that night.

I hoped to keep in touch with Michael Kunz, and Ken and Richard from the Buick, in case I ever got to Hong Kong or Singapore. Gerry Crown and the other Australians—maybe someday I could combine a visit to Linda in Melbourne with a visit to them in Sydney. Bart and Jolijn from Kermit the Volvo offered to show me the auto museums of Holland; one Briton, who'd been the riding mechanic for a Dutchman, hinted that he might be able to get me access to Formula One-boss Bernie Ecclestone's multi-million-dollar car collection. I didn't count on it, of course, but I took his phone number and gave him my card. There were many, many more—David Drew of course, and the Iranians, though they're more likely to get to the States than I am to get back to Iran. It seemed as if I had a fond memory of almost everyone, or a work reason to want to see them again.

Then I got to the Gulls' table. "It's a shame we didn't spend more time together," I said, truthfully. The woman who'd yelled at us from the audience was there, and somehow I gathered she was Jennifer's sister. She clearly didn't like me (and she made no effort to hide her feelings), but Jennifer showed no resentment. Francesca, looking radiant, sat beside her American husband. They were celebrating more than just the finish line: she'd been delighted to discover during the last leg of the trip that she was pregnant!

CHAPTER

~48~

An American comes up to offer us champagne even while we are cleaning up. ... He gives us his congratulations and good wishes, but adds sincerely that he cannot understand what pleasure there can be in doing such a journey without making anything from it.

PARIS

[SUNDAY AND MONDAY, OCTOBER 19 AND 20]

After dinner, we all went back into the ballroom for more speeches, and those awards for the support crew. John Dick, an American expatriate, spoke with a marvelously deep voice. He started his speech by acknowledging Philip Young's unique personality—"Did I hear Arrogant Bastard?"—but ended by declaring Philip's glory: This one man had done what so many others had tried to do and failed. He'd persevered, and we all owed him a debt of gratitude. The speech ended to grand, foot-stomping applause, and for most of us, Philip was forgiven.

But not for all. I spoke to Phil Surtees a couple of months later, and he was still angry about several things, including the way Philip had shunted him off the stage. According to Surtees, this was more proof of Young's miserliness: he supposedly had to get us all out before midnight, or some sort of fee would apply and Philip would be out thousands of francs, paying waiters and busboys overtime to clean up after us.

As it turned out, Linda and I did head back to our hotel about midnight. Linda had her new shoes in her hands (her feet were killing her) as we walked down the street looking for a taxi. Back in our room, Linda called Maida, then Geoff. It was the toughest phone call of the trip; Geoff was so depressed, he didn't even seem to register that Linda had made it to Paris. He was disgusted with his Australian doctor, who'd put him off yet again, and was threatening to drive out to the Bush and never come back. Linda begged him to wait until she got back to San Francisco and had a chance to talk to that doctor who'd helped him there.

By the time that call was over, I was too exhausted to make my own call home. I didn't call in the morning either; by then I knew it was the middle of the night in California. Linda had gone to breakfast before me (I'd slept in), so I rushed off,

grabbed some food, and then we headed to the car to clean it up.

We separated everything we wanted to keep, leaving a good deal of car stuff to go back to England with the car. Linda had decided to exercise her option, offered in the original purchase agreement, to sell the Hillman back to Tom Coulthard at the end. We knew the car would end up back at Paul Jackson's garage, but from there, we had no idea. Sarah Catt had volunteered to drive it to Oxfordshire, and that morning we met with her and warned her about the terrible first and second gear. She'd be convoying with her father and brother (John and Simon) in their Cortina, so she wasn't worried about the gears.

I kept far more stuff than Linda did; she figured she'd have no use for it. We lugged it all back to the hotel, and I thought about calling home again, but instead, seeing that it was after 2:00 P.M., I decided I'd better go. I'd promised an old friend (we went all the way back to elementary school) that I'd visit her; she had moved to Paris twenty years before but we'd kept in touch.

It was a very strange afternoon. My friend was struggling through one of those horrific divorces that drags on for years, messing up the kids (she had two, a little older than my own) and parents alike. As usual with newly divorced women, her finances were suddenly precarious; she could no longer afford her minuscule Paris apartment. She was worried about her boys, her legal status, her financial status, and needed someone to vent to in English.

This hit me like a slap in the face; a reminder that real life was not a drive around the world. I did not belong to that group of devil-may-care, globe-trotting millionaires I'd left behind in one of Paris' most expensive hotels. This was my true milieu: financially strapped thirty-something women to whom things like the Peking to Paris are so foreign they're truly incomprehensible. She did ask me once about my adventure. I told her the route and she said, "Wow, you drove the whole way? Did I tell you about what that asshole did to me last week?"

I'd promised Linda and Team Retro I'd meet them for dinner at six. I got back on the Metro after five, my head swimming—who am I really? The struggling writer my friend knows, who barely makes enough to pay for a trip to Europe once a year; or the well-heeled (by inference) journalist my Peking-Paris cohorts took me for? What would I be when I got home: richer by contagion? Or poorer and burdened by this strange new debt? And my kids: would they ever forgive me for leaving them for so long? Would my husband?

I had ten minutes to wash my face, brush my hair and meet Team Retro in the lobby. Once again there was no time to call home. There were no messages for me, though, so I assumed the fax service from the Rally Office had at least let everyone know that we'd finished.

I drank a much-needed gin and tonic while Team Retro and their large extended family decided what to do for dinner. The Alabama crew chose a restaurant that only had room for eight, so Linda and I joined John Jung, his dear friend Richard, and Richard's mother, who was waiting for us in her hotel around the corner from the Arch de Triomphe.

I'd already met John's friend Richard in Istanbul. He was an actor from Dallas, but often visited San Francisco with John. He was charming, and his mother reminded me of an older version of my own mother, who is such an intimate part of my family that I missed her almost as much as I missed my kids. We had a pleasant dinner and got back very late.

I don't know why I didn't call home right then. I still had received no messages. By now, I think, my homesickness was so intense, I knew I'd cry as soon as I heard Chris's voice. And I didn't want Linda to hear me cry.

After all, we were supposed to be celebrating our triumphant arrival.

"It all seems absurd and impossible; I cannot convince myself that we have come to the end, that we have really arrived." Barzini sat on the Itala's step, and had to dismount before either the Prince or his mechanic could move, but the Prince, too, sat still. It took a great cry of *Venez!* and the hands of a porter from *Le Matin* to pull the men down to their welcome. Hugged, hands shaken, champagne poured, arms filled with roses, the trio was transported into the building, the Prince rushed up to the balcony, where he bowed repeatedly to the crowd cheering below.

Barzini escaped then. "I went off quietly, and had the happiness to mingle once again unknown among the crowd, leaving to the Prince alone the onerous burdens of popularity."

Twenty days later, on August 30, 1907, the three other crews—sans Godard—ate their last meal together in a shady glade near Enghien, eight kilometers from Paris. Godard had easily freed himself from police custody—the charges were legally insupportable—and at Enghien he caught up with his former cohorts just as they prepared to turn the starting levers. He pushed through the crowd to the Spyker and climbed into the driver's seat.

"*Ça va?* All right?" he called to du Taillis and the De Dion-Bouton drivers. They were surprised, but they smiled and answered their old companion in kind. Immediately, two of *Le Matin*'s henchmen approached, shouting, "Get out!" Godard tried to shift into first gear, but the men grabbed his arm. With much effort, they dragged the big Frenchman down from the high Dutch car, and wrestled him to the ground. The Spyker works driver jumped up and reclaimed the driver's seat, but du Taillis had climbed down to protest.

"Don't be a fool, du Taillis. This is not your business," one of the henchmen told him.

"Business!" he responded. "God wither business!" He made to walk away and leave them all behind, but instead stopped, turned back and spoke with Godard.

"One of us had better do it," du Taillis said. "If it can't be you it will have to be me. I'll take her in."

Linda and I hugged goodbye Monday morning. Since I couldn't let all the car paraphernalia go to waste, I ended up taking a ridiculous amount of luggage with me to the airport. During a layover in Saint Louis, I was finally able to phone Chris. The kids were in school. I found out, to my horror, that not calling had been a terrible mistake. The fax service from the Rally Office had ended cryptically, saying "yet to receive written confirmation from Paris . . . almost twenty-four hours after the finish." With no call, Chris and my father and mother had assumed the worst—that our Hillman had suffered some catastrophic failure, and we hadn't made it. Chris had called the Hotel Royal Monceau three times, leaving messages that never found me. (Perhaps that woman in the bathrobe got them?) Had I gotten one, I would've dropped everything and called. I apologized profusely and—as I'd anticipated—spent the whole conversation (and the rest of the layover) in tears.

Drying my tears on the last leg of the flight, I thought about all the contradictions this rally had forced me to face: rich versus poor; first world versus third; old cars versus pollution. Unlike many other competitors, comfortable with their wealth and their place among the world's corporate elite, I have always been a left-leaning liberal, with barely enough money to pay my mortgage and my travel bills. Now, for seven weeks, I'd been immersed in two contradictory worlds: the first-class-hotel, whatever-it-takes world of the wealthy, and—outside the windows of our Hillman—the hovels-in-the-dirt reality of desperate poverty. On the one hand I was a snob; if I couldn't be wealthy, I wanted to be with them, even emulate them. On the other hand, it pained me to know that the money it took to make a 1927 Rolls Royce roadworthy, much less to keep it running halfway round the world, could pay for a year's worth of medical care for an entire Nepali village. It reminded me of the dilemma of space exploration (I'd always been a big space buff, too): do we feed the poor with that money, or build a rocketship to explore Mars?

The answer, I think, is we must do both; we must do it all. Every one of us on this planet contributes something, each in our own, unpredictable way. Every action has an impact on someone, somewhere. Every reaction has both good and bad, but we cannot fixate on the bad.

The Peking to Paris Motor Challenge was a huge, flamboyant action, an ostentatious display of Western wealth, but also a loud exhaust-tinged call for international cooperation. Our long drive was an act of connection. Our cars connected the past to the present. Our route connected the capital of Beijing with the high muddy roads of Tibet, the crowded streets of Delhi to the barren sands of Baluchistan, the Orient to the Middle East to the West. We made it known—to any who would hear—that we brought those places with us as we traveled. If our less-than-harmonic symphony of engine sounds could have called out words, it would have shouted to all in their own languages: *You are connected to the rest of the world!*

Perhaps even more powerful than our coordinated act as a rally, were our individual actions along the road. We might have made a few enemies, but more often we created instant friends out of shopkeepers, mechanics, policemen, young boys and girls, everywhere we went. Perhaps our most simple acts were the most powerful: a smile and a wave, seen by a young Iranian woman, shy behind her veil—those smiles from two American women that communicated thoughts like *we are driving our own car, we are not vassals of some Great Satan, we are not the property of any man, we are free. One day, you will be too!*

Our actions after the event will have their impact, too. All of us who saw half the world through our windshields can no longer pretend ignorance of the global scale of issues like overpopulation, pollution, and poverty. Already there'd been talk of establishing funds for Nepali children, for Tibetan independence, for Indian clinics. Linda and I talked about what we could do to help Afghani women (a cause that neither of us had heard much about before we witnessed the heart-rending sight of those *burqah* with our own eyes).

At last, the plane touched down in San Francisco. I have no words to adequately describe how it felt to finally see my kids, hugging them for all they were worth, and my husband, and my mom, and my brother and his partner. I had never been so happy, nor so relieved, so exhausted, so . . . home.

I took the trophy out of my backpack and handed it to five-year-old Molly.

"You won! You won!" she yelled. Everyone around us in the airport looked over and smiled.

"Well, I didn't win the race. I won the Women's Cup. That's what this is."

"I know Mommy!" she said as she hefted the heavy cup; it was almost half her height. "I'm a woman, so I won, too!"

A few hours later, on the Boulevards, which had reverted to their normal appearance, the street-vendors were still selling the souvenir post-cards. But now their cry was: "Le Prince Borghèse—un sou!" No longer four sous, but one. What a solemn lesson lay in that fall of price! Our popularity had fallen seventy-five percent in two hours. Sic Transit Gloria. . . .

Dick Taylor ended his final report to the Arizona *Republic* with this:

When I embarked on this adventure I knew two questions would linger. First, was it worth the eight months of preparation, the seven weeks away from our normal lives, the anxiety and exhaustion of the trip itself, and the small fortune it cost? The answer is an emphatic yes! For each of us, novice ralliers, it was truly the experience of our lives. I think we all bring a greater appreciation of our own world back with us, and we have developed insight into the lives of people covering nearly half the world.

The second question to be answered is whether I would do this again. I certainly would, but I would take the knowledge learned from this challenge, and I would be better prepared next time.

Carl Schneider left Don Jones behind in Paris and rushed home to the States. Only a week later, he was behind the wheel of a 1951 Oldsmobile, driving in Mexico's Carrera Panamericana. Pat O'Dell, Carl's co-driver in that event, called him a lead-foot, but his technique paid off. They finished that two-thousand-mile, extremely competitive event in first place overall. John Jung took the #24 Ford (modified to fit the Carrera's rules) down to Mexico and finished the 1998 race first in class and eleventh overall.

Ted Thomas will race on in various venues; he's preparing an Oldsmobile for the next Carrera Panamericana, and he's planning to do the 2000 London to Sydney (Australia) with Bill Binnie. Dick Taylor and Rich Newman separately signed up for the London to Capetown (South Africa), and both are planning to do an event in 2000 called "Around the World in 80 Days." The Hillman Linda and I drove, now owned by a British couple, will be competing in that one too.

For these guys, a journey like the Peking to Paris Motor Challenge is a logical culmination of a lifetime love affair with automobiles and travel. For Linda, it was a little more complicated. After seven intense weeks, I still knew very little about this complicated woman. I knew why she'd decided to undertake the event in the first place: "because it was there and I could," she said, but then admitted that her break-up with Geoff and her father's recent death were two things she appreciated distraction from. That last call with Geoff put an end to whatever solace that distraction had offered, and her worry clouded her mood those last days in Paris. Then, two weeks after we got back to San Francisco, Linda called me, ecstatic. The Australian doctors finally agreed to prescribe the drug Linda's doctor had recommended for Geoff. After only two-and-a-half days of therapy, Linda said, "he's a changed man!" His depression had gone and he was finally on his way to recovery. She sounded as happy as she'd been back on that finish line.

But did the Peking to Paris Motor Challenge change her life? I asked her that a couple of months later, as I'd promised, and this is what she wrote back:

> *If I hadn't done the trip across Australia by myself in 1990, I think I would have had profound changes. . . . This is not to say the Peking-Paris wasn't a huge thing. Goddess, it was! Call it another plus in the confidence column. Call it being able to be very proud of an accomplishment that only a few other people can call their own. And just think of all the friends we did make, and all the problems we did solve . . . and all those incredible sights we saw. We will never forget them. And last, but not least, our friendship. We were literally tossed together under the most unusual of circumstances and what a great team we were! Didn't we have an uncanny way of taking turns at being in a bad mood?*

In the preface of the original Italian edition of Barzini's book, Prince Borghese wrote to Luigi Barzini: "I will preserve a lively admiration of you and a deep feeling of friendship which will resist time."

Barzini and Borghese never met again in their lives.

On the plane flying home, I wondered if Linda and I would follow in their footsteps. In those last few weeks, after the worm had turned, she swore several times she'd never do another classic car rally. She'd be back on her motorcycles, and I'd be back with my family, our cars, my magazines, and my dreams of publishing novels.

It didn't turn out that way. We kept in touch, and then, a year almost to the day after we crossed that finish line in Paris, Linda went out and bought a classic car, a gorgeous '63 Jaguar E-type. She and Geoff plan to drive it in a rally across North America.

As for me, I was flying high when I first got home. My husband and kids quickly forgave my long absence, and I proudly told the world all about my exploits. But the excitement died down, and within a month or so of my return, my love of driving had disappeared. I hated driving anywhere. The local roads seemed clogged by an execrable series of standstills. My kids' school had been invaded by SUVs, ostentatious displays of environmental ignorance—how could the politically-correct denizens of Santa Cruz not know that these gas guzzling behemoths did not benefit from any pollution control devices? As they sat with their SUVs idling in the school parking lot, waiting to pick up their one-point-five children, I could taste the smog of India.

But it wasn't just SUVs. Even my relatively clean-burning old Fiat seemed a decrepit piece of junk; the new cars I drove for journalistic purposes felt like isolation tanks, divorcing me from the world, from other humans, from any sensations whatsoever. Even a fast ride in a beautiful classic Ferrari left me feeling strangely numb. I jokingly called it Post-Peking-Paris-Stress-Disorder.

Then in mid-summer, Chris and both kids and I crammed onto the bench seat of our 1975 Chevy car hauler (with our Fiat on its back) and set off across the country. We were heading for my father's place in Maryland, by way of a big Fiat club event in North Carolina's Smokey Mountains; then we'd have to drive all the way back home. I had been dreading the trip; all our friends predicted we'd want to kill the kids—or they'd kill us—before we hit the Mississippi.

The predictions were wrong. Driving our "big-rig" was a completely new experience that revealed its own charms (I started swaggerin' like a truck driver). When I wasn't driving, I relaxed with the kids glued to my sides (serving as their pillow), while we sang old folk songs like "She'll Be Comin' Round the Mountain," and "On top of old Smokey, all covered with cheese. . . ." We read stories to each other, and wrote or drew in our trip journals. We had a great visit with my father and stepmother—he'd recovered from his e-mail worries—and by the time we got home, six-thousand-some-odd miles later, my Post-Peking-Stress-Disorder was cured.

Now once again I drive, and navigate, with joy. The older the car, the better. New cars are okay too, though I still lose my temper at those road-hogging SUVs. I am ready and willing to conquer another long-distance rally. I can't afford it, but my attitude about money has changed, too: it's out there, lots of it. Just because I don't have any now doesn't mean I won't somehow find a way to afford an expensive journey. The trick for next time is to figure out how to bring along my husband, maybe even my kids. We'll head for one of those places on this incredible globe where geography, history, and humanity combine in awe-inspiring synergy.

A place like Greece.

We'll drive up a steep, narrow road. The tall, straight cypress and craggy, crooked olive trees will climb the hillside beside us. The warm air will smell of dust, oregano, and our own exhaust. When the road suddenly falls away as we crest the summit, we'll glimpse far below us an ancient abode of the gods: tumbled marble and tilted columns lying silent at the base of a high, volcanic mountain. A phosphorescent sea will ripple green and blue on the horizon, as we drive to the heart of the world.

APPENDIX A

GROUP 1: VINTAGEANTS (PRE-1950-TYPE)
• **CLASS 1:** UNDER 4.1 LITRES • **CLASS 2:** 4.1 LITRES AND OVER
• (A)DDED EN ROUTE: UNDER 1.5 LITRES

CAR	CREW	MOTORCAR	CLASS
1	Lord Montagu of Beaulieu/Doug Hill (GB)	1915 Vauxhall Prince Henry	1
2	Hermann Layher/John Dick (D)	1907 La France Hooper sports	2
3	Walter Rothlauf/Fritz Walter (D)	1928 Bugatti Type 40 tourer	1 (A)
4	Gerry Acher/Bruce Young (GB)	1932 Aston Martin International	1 (A)
5	Gerhard Weissenbach (D)/ Susanne Huslisti	1928 Rolls Royce Phantom I boat-tail roadster	2
6	David Cohen/Adele Cohen (CDN)	1930 Stutz M Lancefield coupé s/c	2
7	Etienne Veen (NL)/Robert Dean (GB)	1927 Mercedes 630K sports	2
8	Kjeld Jessen/Hans-Henrik Jessen (DK)	1929 Bentley 4-1/2-litre VdP LeMans	2
9	Prince Idris Shah (MAL)/Richard Curtis (GB)	1932 Ford Model B saloon	1
10	Brian Ashby/Duncan Ashby (GB)	1930 Delage D8 drophead coupé	1
11	Charles Kleptz/Arlene Kleptz (USA)	1919 Marmon 34 Touring 4 Person	2
12	Chris Dunkley/Janine Dunkley (GB)	1935 Bentley 3-1/2-litre open tourer	1
14	Baron Willem Bentinck van Schoonheten(NL)/ Werner Hastedt (D)/Pieter Le Febvre (NL)	1935 Railton Straight 8 Fairmile	2
15	Don Saunders (USA)/Roger Coote (GB)	1932 Packard 903 convertible	2
16	Jonathan Prior (GB)/Mariam El Accad (D)	1936 Railton Cobham saloon	2
17	William Binnie/Edward Thompson (USA)	1928 Bentley 4-1/2-litre HM	2
18	Francis Noz/Casper Noz (USA)	1928 Ford Model A roadster	1
19	Francesco Ciriminna/Michele Ingoglia(I)	1948 Fiat 1100 Cabriolet	1 (A)
20	Raymond Carr (USA)/Mike Wyka (POL)	1939 Ford V-8 convertible	1
21	Adam Hartley/Jonathan Turner (GB)	1929 Bentley 4-1/2-litre VdP Le Mans	2
22	Pat Brooks/Mary Brooks (USA)	1949 Buick 59 Straight 8 Woody	1
23	Ted Thomas/Vic Zannis (USA)	1950 Ford Club Coupe	1
24	John Jung/Andy Vann (USA)	1950 Ford Club Coupe	1
25	Richard Clark/Ken Hughes (GB)	1948 Buick 8 Special Sedanet	1
26	David Dalrymple/Patricia Dalrymple (GB)	1949 Cadillac Series 62 coupé	2
27	David Arrigo/William Caruana (Malta)	1948 Allard M-type drophead coupé	1
28	Kurt Dichtl/Roswitha Dichtl (A)	1950 Rolls Royce Silver Dawn	2
29	Roby Hellers/Nicholas Thill (L)	1951 Sunbeam Talbot 90 dhc	1

CAR	CREW	MOTORCAR	CLASS
41	Burt Richmond/Richard Newman (USA)	1953 Citroën 2CV	1 (A)
42	John Matheson/Jeanne Eve (AUS)	1967 Rolls Royce Phantom V	2
43	Johan Van der Laan/Willem Graal (NL)	1958 Citroën 2CV	1 (A)
46	John O'Neill/Susan O'Neill-Tsicrycas (CDN)	1960 Volkswagen Cabriolet	1
49	Lisa Klokgieters-Lankes (NL)/James Wheildon(GB)	1951 MG YB saloon	1

GROUP 2: CLASSICS (PRE-1968-TYPE)

• CLASS 3: UNDER 2.1 LITRES **• CLASS 4:** 2.1 LITRES AND OVER
• CLASS 5: 3.1 LITRES AND OVER

CAR	CREW	MOTORCAR	CLASS
44	Richard Sackelariou/Andrew Snelling/ Susan O'Neill (AUS)	1966 Wolseley 24/80	4
45	Jennie Dorey/Geoffrey Dorey	1960 Morris Minor	3
47	John Thomason (GB)/Mike Kunz (USA)	1963 Triumph Vitesse	3
48	George Tinzl/Monica Tinzl (I)	1963 Peugeot 404	3
50	John Catt/Simon Catt (GB)	1965 Ford Cortina Mk I	3
51	Linda Dodwell/Genevieve Obert (USA)	1968 Hillman Hunter	3
52	Nigel Broderick/Paula Broderick (GB)	1967 Ford Anglia Estate	3
53	Maurizio Selci/Andrea Campagnoli (I)	1965 Citroën 2CV	3
54	Werner Esch/Sylvia Esch (L)	1952 Mercedes Benz 300 Adenauer	4
55	Fred Multon/Tim Laughton (GB)	1955 Austin A90 Westminster	4
56	Peter Cordrey/Gordon Phillips (GB)	1961 Rover 100 P4	4
57	David Morris/Sheila Morris (GB)	1956 Austin A90 Westminster	4
58	Dr Theodore Voukidis/Stelios Vartholomaios (GR)	1955 Chevrolet Bel Air	5
59	David Bull/Angela Riley/Helen McGugan (GB)	1965 Rover 3-litre P5 coupé	4
61	Peter Noble/Susan Noble (GB)	1955 Bentley Continental Mulliner	5
62	The Honourable Francesca Sternberg/ Jennifer Gillies (GB)	1964 Volvo 122S Amazon	3
63	Erik Christiansen (Bahamas)/Michael Veys (GB)	1965 Rolls Royce Silver Cloud	5
64	Derek Radcliffe/Nigel Webb (GB)	1953 Jaguar Mark VII saloon	5
65	Carl Schneider/Don Jones (USA)	1954 Packard Straight 8 convertible	5
66	Renger Guliker/Gerda Guliker	1956 Chevrolet pick-up	5
67	Roberto Chiodi/Fabio Longo (I)	1964 Lancia Flavia coupé	3
68	Melissa Ong/Colin Syn (Singapore)	1963 Porsche 356 SC coupé	3
69	Daniel Orteu/Jonathan Davies (GB)	1962 Volvo P122S Amazon	3
70	Peter Janssen/Gunter Klarholz/Wolfgang Meier (D)	1965 Mercedes Benz 220A	4
71	Antonius De Witt/Herman Haukes (NL)	1964 Volvo 122 Amazon	3
72	Josef Feit/René Feit (D)	1967 Volkswagen Cabriolet	4
73	Klaus Koppel/Peter Kuhn (D)	1968 Triumph TR6	4

CAR	CREW	MOTORCAR	CLASS
74	Dr Friedrich Flick (D)/Felix Mumenthaler (SW)	1964 Mercedes 220 SB	4
75	Bart Rietbergen/Jolijn van Overbeehe-Rietbergen (NL)	1965 Volvo PV 544	4
76	Paul Minassian (F)/Paul Grogan (GB)	1962 Peugeot 404 sedan	3
77	David Hardman/Philip Dean (GB)	1964 Aston Martin DB5	5
78	Murray Kayll/Amanda Kayll (GB)	1967 Mercedes Benz 250 SE	4
79	Anthony Buckingham/Simon Mann (GB)	1964 Aston Martin DB5	5
80	Thomas Noor (D)/Maria Bouvier-Noor (F)	1966 Mercedes Benz 250SEC	4
81	John Goldsmith/Murdoch Laing (GB)	1966 Aston Martin DB6	5
82	Jane King/Phil Bowen (GB)	1968 Volvo 122 Amazon	3
83	David Wilks/Andrew Bedingham (GB)	1974 Austin 1800 saloon	3
84	Ivar Moe/Tom Granli (N)	1969 Morgan Plus 8 sports	5
85	Seyed Amir Ali Javed/Homayoun Kamal Hedayat (Iran)	1970 Peykan Hunter	3
86	Vahid Kazerani/Roozben Razzaghi (Iran)	1970 Peykan Hunter	3
87	Mohsen Eijadi/Ramin Khadem (Iran)	1970 Peykan Hunter	3
88	Gerald Crown/John Bryson (AUS)	1964 Holden EH saloon	5
89	Anton Aan de Stegge/Willemien Aan de Stegge (NL)	1966 Citroën ID 21	4
90	Richard Dangerfield/Jill Dangerfield (GB)	1965 Holden HR saloon	5
91	Howard Bellm/Christopher Taylor (GB)	1968 Chevrolet Camaro	5
92	Rolf Meyer/Gerrit Geiser (D)	1968 Mercedes Benz 280SE	4
93	Jonathan Lux/David Drew (GB)	1972 Rover 3.5 P5B coupé	5

• CLASS 6: CLASSIC 4-WHEEL DRIVE

CAR	CREW	MOTORCAR	CLASS
96	Nigel Challis/Anthony Jefferis (GB)	1955 Land Rover Series I	6
97	John Bayliss/Phil Surtees (GB)	1942 Ford Willys Jeep MB	6
98	Carolyn Ward/David Tremain (GB)	1961 Land Rover Series IIA	6
99	Richard Taylor/Larry Davis/David Pierce (USA)	1962 Willys Jeep Station Wagon	6

• CLASS 7: TOURING CATEGORY

CAR	CREW	MOTORCAR	CLASS
31	John Stuttard/Roy O'Sullivan/Simon Anderson/ Gordon Barrass/David Colvin (GB)	1934 Rolls Royce 20/25 saloon	7
32	Herbert Handlbauer/Elfi Handlbauer/ Lisbeth Handlbauer (A)	1938 BMW 328 sports tourer	7
33	Joao Netto/Jose Costa Simoes/Jose Machado/ Jose Netto (P)	1932 Ford Model B saloon	7
34	Bill Ainscough/William Ainscough/ Barry Attwood/Andrew Walker (GB)	1929 Chrysler 77 open sports	7

CAR	CREW	MOTORCAR	CLASS
35	Arnold Schulze/Jutta Breuer/Nora Schulze (D)	1950 Bentley Donnington special	7
36	Jeff Fortune/Joan Fortune/Bud Risser (USA)	1955 Chevrolet Bel Air wagon	7
37	Peng Yew Wong/Win Win Wong/ Suet Lyn Wong/May Lyn Wong (MAL)	1954 MGA sports	7
38	Eustache Tsicrycas (GR)/Christoforos Karaolis (CY)/ Jasmine Lovric (CDN)	1955 Peugeot 403 sedan	7
39	David Brister/Brian Miller/Keith Barton (GB)	1963 Rover 110 P4	7
40	Mark Klabin (I)/John Dick II (USA)/ Jorg Holzwarth (D)	1964 Land Rover Series IIA 109	7

APPENDIX B

#	CREW	CAR	PENALTY	POS. O/A	POS. CLS
TOP TEN:					
97	Surtees/Bayliss	Ford Willys Jeep MB	43d 0h17	1	1
23	Thomas/Zannis	Ford Club Coupe	43d 0h21	2	1
50	Catt/Catt	Ford Cortina Mk I	43d 0h44	3	1
24	Jung/Vann	Ford Club Coupe	43d 0h53	4	2
88	Crown/Bryson	Holden EH saloon	43d 0h55	5	1
52	Broderick/Broderick	Ford Anglia Estate	43d 0h59	6	2
85	Javid/Hedayat	Peykan Hunter	43d 1h42	7	3
87	Eijadi/Khadem	Peykan Hunter	43d 2h08	8	4
28	Dichtl/Dichtl	Rolls Royce Silver Dawn	43d 2h12	9	1
86	Kazerani/Razzaghi	Peykan Hunter	43d 2h15	10	5
THE REST:					
77	Hardman/Dean	Aston Martin DB5	43d 2h18	11	2
78	Kayll/Kayll	Mercedes Benz 250 SE	43d 2h19	12	1
90	Dangerfield/Dangerfield	Holden HR saloon	43d 2h30	13	3
98	Ward/Tremain	Land Rover Series IIA	43d 2h56	14	2
48	Tinzl/Tinzl	Peugeot 404	43d 3h26	15	
21	Hartley/Turner	Bentley 4-1/2-litre VdP LeM	43d 3h30	16	2
44	Sackelariou/Snelling/O'Neill	Wolseley 24/80	43d 3h44	17	2
47	Thomason/Kunz	Triumph Vitesse	43d 3h59	18	
80	Noor/Bouvier-Noor	Mercedes Benz 250SEC	43d 4h7	19	3
82	King/Bowen	Volvo 122 Amazon	43d 4h18	20	
43	Van der Laan/Graal	Citroën 2CV	43d 4h29	21	1
92	Meyer/Geiser	Mercedes Benz 280SE	43d 4h30	22	
41	Richmond/Newman	Citroën 2CV	43d 4h42	23	2
74	Flick/Mumenthaler	Mercedes 220 SB	43d 5h17	24	
69	Orteu/Davies	Volvo P122S Amazon	43d 5h27	25	
26	Dalrymple/Dalrymple	Cadillac Series 62 coupé	43d 5h39	26	3
58	Voukidis/Vartholomaios	Chevrolet Bel Air	43d 5h55	27	
71	De Witt/Haukes	Volvo 122 Amazon	43d 5h58	28	
53	Selci/Campagnoli	Citroën 2CV	43d 6h16	29	

#	CREW	CAR	PENALTY	POS. O/A	POS. CLS
57	Morris/Morris	Austin A90 Westminster	43d 6h35	30	
17	Binnie/Thompson	Bentley 4-1/2-litre HM	43d 6h55	31	
51	Dodwell/Obert	Hillman Hunter	43d 6h57	32	
55	Multon/Laughton	Austin A90 Westminster	43d 7h43	33	
76	Minassian/Grogan	Peugeot 404 sedan	43d 8h17	34	
20	Carr/Wyka	Ford V-8 convertible	43d 9h3	35	3
19	Ciriminna/Ingoglia	Fiat 1100 Cabriolet	43d 10h18	36	3
91	Bellm/Taylor	Chevrolet Camaro	43d 10h22	37	
73	Koppel/Kuhn	Triumph TR6	43d 10h24	38	
62	Sternberg/Gillies	Volvo 122S Amazon	43d 10h35	39	
49	Klokgieters-Lankes/Wheildon	MG YB saloon	43d 12h20	40	
99	Taylor/Davis/Pierce	Willys Jeep Station Wagon	43d 13h30	41	3
75	Rietbergen/Overbeehe-Rietbergen	Volvo PV 544	43d 15h53	42	
54	Esch/Esch	Mercedes Benz 300 Adenauer	43d 15h55	43	
68	Ong/Syn	Porsche 356 SC coupé	43d 15h59	44	
10	Ashby/Ashby	Delage D8 drophead coupé	43d 20h36	45	
9	Shah/Curtis	Ford Model B saloon	43d 21h7	46	
12	Dunkley/Dunkley	Bentley 3-1/2-litre tourer	44d 2h2	47	
59	Bull/Riley/McGugan	Rover 3-litre P5 coupé	44d 3h16	48	
8	Jessen/Jessen	Bentley 4-1/2-litre VdP LM	44d 4h14	49	
14	Schoonheten/Hastedt/Le Febvre	Railton Straight 8 Fairmile	44d 5h13	50	
4	Acher/Young	Aston Martin International	44d 12h7	51	
67	Chiodi/Longo	Lancia Flavia coupé	45d 4h19	52	
83	Wilks/Bedingham	Austin 1800 saloon	45d 5h8	53	
89	Aan de Stegge/Aan de Stegge	Citroën ID 21	45d 6h52	54	
65	Schneider/Jones	Packard Straight 8 conv	45d 17h23	55	
39	Brister/Miller/Barton	Rover 110 P4	45d 17h55	56	
42	Matheson/Eve	Rolls Royce Phantom V	48d 16h15	57	
7	Veen/Dean	Mercedes 630K sports	49d 2h38	58	
81	Goldsmith/Laing	Aston Martin DB6	49d 17h15	59	
27	Arrigo/Caruana	Allard M-type dhc	50d 8h53	60	
64	Radcliffe/Webb	Jaguar Mark VII saloon	50d 11h34	67	
70	Janssen/Klarholz/Meier	Mercedes Benz 220A	50d 13h45	68	
16	Prior/El Accad	Railton Cobham saloon	51d 13h51	69	
56	Cordrey/Phillips	Rover 100 P4	52d 9h15	70	
25	Clark/Hughes	Buick 8 Special Sedanet	54d 12h6	71	
79	Buckingham/Mann	Aston Martin DB5	55d 10h58	72	

TOURING:

#	CREW	CAR	PENALTY	POS. O/A	POS. CLS
93	Lux/Drew	Rover 3.5 P5B coupé	43d 0h1		

#	CREW	CAR	PENALTY	POS. O/A	POS. CLS
36	Fortune/Fortune/Risser	Chevrolet Bel Air wagon	43d 1h50		
37	Wong/Wong/Wong /Wong	MGA sports	43d 2h8		
35	Schulze/Breuer/Schulze	Bentley Donnington	43d 18h1		
40	Klabin/Dick II /Holzwarth	Land Rover Series IIA	44d 0h42		
46	O'Neill/O'Neill-Tsicrycas	Volkswagen Cabriolet	45d 8h33		
3	Rothlauf/Walter	Bugatti Type 40 tourer	46d 9h58		
38	Tsicrycas/Karaolis/Lovric	Peugeot 403 sedan	48d 4h40		
31	Stuttard/O'Sullivan/Anderson / Barrass/Colvin	Rolls Royce 20/25 saloon	48d 23h14		
29	Hellers/Thill	Sunbeam Talbot 90 dhc	49d 10h48		
45	Dorey/Dorey	Morris Minor	51d 2h26		
32	Handlbauer/Handlbauer/ Handlbauer	BMW 328 sports tourer	53d 2h30		
63	Christiansen/Veys	Rolls Royce Silver Cloud	54d 0h52		
34	Ainscough/Ainscough/Attwood/ Walker	Chrysler 77 open sports	55d 0h1		
61	Noble/Noble	Bentley Continental Mulliner	62d 23h0		
15	Saunders/Coote	Packard 903 convertible	64d 7h45		

ACKNOWLEDGMENTS

This book would not have been possible without generous contributions from many of the participants in the Peking to Paris Motor Challenge. Linda Dodwell was, of course, the *sine qua non;* Vic Zannis volunteered the full text of his personal journal; Don Jones and Carl Schneider offered me their entire web diary; Richard Taylor sent every article he submitted to the Arizona *Republic*. Many others answered questions during and after the event clarifying events along the way that I was unable to witness directly, especially Andy Vann, Nigel Challis, Ferri Salamat, and the crew of Discovery Online's Peking-Paris webpage. The Classic Rally Association and its director, Philip Young, deserve special thanks for their amazing organizational achievement.

Along with the two great accounts of the original 1907 Peking-Paris (Allen Andrews's *The Mad Motorists: The Great Peking-Paris Race of '07,* J. P. Lippincott Co., New York, 1965, and Luigi Barzini's *Peking to Paris: Prince Borghese's Journey Across Two Continents in 1907,* The Library Press, New York, 1973), several other books were invaluable. Barbara Erickson's *Tibet, Abode of the Gods, Pearl of the Motherland* (Pacific View Press, 1997) and His Holiness the Fourteenth Dalai Lama of Tibet's *My Tibet,* (photos & introduction by Galen Rowell, University of CA Press, 1990) helped me understand that amazing and mysterious place. Farzaneh Milani's wonderful *Veils and Words: The Emerging Voices of Iranian Women Writers* (Syracuse University Press, New York, 1992) elucidated Iran's complex gender politics in a way my short stay never could have. Fielding's *The World's Most Dangerous Places* (Robert Young Pelton, Coskun Aral, & Wink Dulles, Fielding Worldwide Inc, 1997) and Tony Wheeler's Lonely Planet Publications were indispensable, and for history I consulted *The Travels of Marco Polo* (Milton Rugoff, ed., The New American Library, New York, 1961) and George Schuster's *The Longest Auto Race: New York to Paris, 1908,* (with Tom Maloney, J. Day Co., New York, 1966). Perspective on automobiles and the modern age was gleaned from Virginia Scharff's *Taking the Wheel: Women and the*

Coming of the Motor Age (University of New Mexico Press, Albuquerque, NM, 1992) and K.T. Berger's *Where the Road and the Sky Collide: America Through the Eyes of its Drivers* (Henry Holt & Co., New York, 1993).

There are several anecdotes included in this book that I could not substantiate. I tried to identify all of these clearly, and they are included as humorous examples of the role gossip and rumor play in an event of this nature, and are not meant to be put forth as true fact. I apologize in advance if any of the two-hundred-plus people involved with our great adventure are distressed by any of the descriptions, nicknames, or opinions I have repeated herein.

Finally, thanks are due to Kevin Bentley, Melissa Lilly and Shannon Willis for their hard work putting the book together, and to Lea, for being at the right place at the right time. Extra special thanks to Chris, Molly, Jesse, Ann, Brian, Jeff, John, Paul, Mike, and Roxanne: You all know how much you mean to me, and how none of this would ever have come about if not for your steadfast assistance, patience, and love.